PF 9/88

Library of
Davidson College

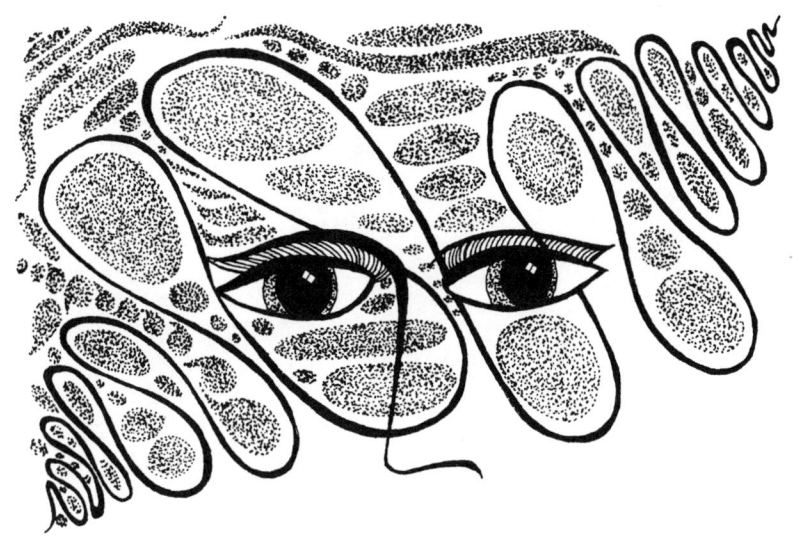

Psychology and Literature
in the
Eighteenth Century

AMS Studies in the Eighteenth Century, No. 8

ISSN: 0196-6561

Other titles in this series:

1. Modern Language Association of America. *Proceedings of the 1967–68 Neoclassicism Conferences.* Edited and with a Selected Bibliography, 1920–68, by Paul J. Korshin. 1970.
2. Francesco Cordasco. *Tobias George Smollet: A Bibliographical Guide.* 1978.
3. Paula R. Backscheider, ed. *Probability, Time, and Space in Eighteenth-Century Literature.* 1979.
4. Ruth Perry. *Women, Letters, and the Novel.* 1980.
5. Paul J. Korshin, ed. *The American Revolution and Eighteenth-Century Culture.* 1986.
6. G. S. Rousseau, ed. *The Letters and Papers of Sir John Hill.* 1982.
7. Paula R. Backscheider. *A Being More Intense: A Study of the Prose Works of Bunyan, Swift, and Defoe.* 1984.
9. John F. Sena. *The Best-Natured Man: Sir Samuel Garth, Physician and Poet.* 1986.
10. Robert A. Erickson. *Mother Midnight: Birth, Sex, and Fate in Eighteenth-Century Fiction (Defoe, Richardson, and Sterne).* 1986.

Psychology and Literature
in the
Eighteenth Century

Edited and with an Introduction by
Christopher Fox

With Illustrations by
Michael DePorte

AMS PRESS
NEW YORK

Library of Congress Cataloging-in-Publication Data
Psychology and literature in the eighteenth century.

  (AMS studies in the eighteenth century, ISSN 0196-6561; no. 8)
  Bibliography: p.
  Includes index.
  1. English literature—18th century—History and criticism. 2. English literature—18th century—Psychological aspects. 3. Psychology and literature. 4. Psychology in literature. I. Fox, Christopher II. Series.
PR448.P75P79 1987   820'.9'005   85-48001
ISBN 0-404-61474-4

Copyright © 1987 by AMS Press, Inc.
All rights reserved

Manufactured in the United States of America

CONTENTS

Acknowledgments	vii
Notes on Contributors	ix
Introduction. Defining Eighteenth-Century Psychology: Some Problems and Perspectives CHRISTOPHER FOX	1
Towards a Profile of the Word *Conscious* in Eighteenth-Century Literature JEAN H. HAGSTRUM	23
Psychology and Politics in William Godwin's *Caleb Williams*: Double Bond or Double Bind? MELINDA ALLIKER RABB	51
Vehicles of Delusion: Swift, Locke, and the Madhouse Poems of James Carkesse MICHAEL DEPORTE	69
The Storied World: The Alloy of Imagination in Otway's *Venice Preserved* JOHN DAVID WALKER	87
Association, Madness, and the Measures of Probability in Locke and Hume JOHN P. WRIGHT	103
Belinda's Hysteria: The Medical Context of *The Rape of the Lock* JOHN F. SENA	129
Addison and Hutcheson: Literary Theory and the Psychology of the Audience ROBERT L. MONTGOMERY	149

Accounting for Dreams in *Clarissa*: The Clash of Probabilities
    JANET E. AIKINS   167

Coalescence: David Hartley's "Great *Apparatus*"
    STEPHEN H. FORD   199

Eighteenth-Century Spleen
    WILLIAM B. OBER, M.D.   225

Yorick and the "Eternal Fountain of our Feelings"
    JOHN A. DUSSINGER   259

The New Rhetoricians: Psychology, Semiotics, and Critical Theory
    JAMES ENGELL   277

Selected Bibliography of Primary Materials
    DAVID G. SCHAPPERT   303

Index   347

ACKNOWLEDGMENTS

For help at various stages of this project, I would like to thank Paula Backscheider, P.-G. Boucé, John A. Dussinger, James Engell, John Irwin Fischer, Vincent Freimarck, Donald Greene, Stanley Gutin, Jean H. Hagstrum, Mario Klarer, Nancy Kozemko, Elizabeth Mazzullo, William Ober, Irwin Primer, Philip Rizzo, Phillips Salman, Yvette Simmons, John David Walker, and Ian Watt. Frederick M. Keener, John F. Sena, Jill P. Whitehead, George Wolak, John P. Wright, and John W. Yolton have given continual encouragement and advice. Melinda Alliker Rabb offered generous help with the bibliography, as did Julia E. Miller, who spent hours searching the ECSTC data base. Barbara White, the Rare Book Librarian at the University of New Hampshire, made a valuable volume available to us at a key point in our work. I also express my indebtedness to the National Endowment For The Humanities for a summer at Oxford, during which this work was conceived. Finally, I would like to mention those who have helped with this project, almost on a daily basis, over a period of two years: James G. Buickerood, Michael J. Conlon, Michael DePorte, Thomas Kaska, and David and Catherine Schappert. To them: great thanks.

John Dussinger's and John Sena's essays have appeared, in altered form, in *Ariel* and *Eighteenth-Century Life*. I thank both journals for the right to reprint. The editor and contributors also wish to thank Dr. William Long and Robert Harris of AMS Press for their valuable assistance with this project, from beginning to end. Timely help was also given by Dean Nathan Hatch and the Notre Dame Institute for Scholarship in the Liberal Arts; and by Paul William Child, who is responsible for the index.

Notes on Contributors

JANET E. AIKINS is Associate Professor of English at the University of New Hampshire. She is currently working on a study of serious drama from 1670 to 1720 as it bears on the development of the novel.

MICHAEL DEPORTE, Professor and Director of Graduate Studies in English at the University of New Hampshire, is the author of *Nightmares and Hobbyhorses: Swift, Sterne, and Augustan Ideas of Madness* (1974). His recent publications include an essay, "The Consolations of Fiction: Mystery in *Caleb Williams*," which appeared in *Papers on Language and Literature*, and an introduction to the AMS reprint edition of Marius D'Assigny's *The Art of Memory*. He has also worked as a book illustrator and is responsible for the line drawings in this volume.

JOHN DUSSINGER, Associate Professor of English, has been on the faculty at the University of Illinois since 1965 and has taught periodically in England and Scandinavia. Author of *The Discourse of the Mind in Eighteenth-Century Fiction* (1974) and of numerous articles and reviews on various eighteenth- and early nineteenth-century authors and subjects, he is presently finishing a book on Jane Austen and the language of emotion.

JAMES ENGELL, Professor of English at Harvard University, is the author of *The Creative Imagination: Enlightenment to Romanticism* (1981) and the co-editor of Coleridge's *Biographia Literaria* (1983). More recently, he has edited and contributed to *Johnson and His Age* (1984).

STEPHEN H. FORD enjoys several amusements and occupations, which include collecting illustrated editions of *The Rime of the Ancient Mariner*, and teaching philosophy only part of the time at York University in Toronto. He is currently completing a long-term study of the imagination in Descartes.

CHRISTOPHER FOX, the editor of this volume, is Associate Professor of English at the University of Notre Dame and author of a forthcoming book on identity and consciousness in early eighteenth-century Britain. His recent publications include "The Myth of Narcissus in Swift's *Travels*" which appeared in the Fall 1986–87 issue of *Eighteenth-Century Studies*. An earlier article ("Locke and The Scriblerians") in the same journal received an Honorable Mention for the James L. Clifford Prize.

JEAN H. HAGSTRUM, the John C. Schaffer Professor Emeritus of English and the Humanities at Northwestern University, has written on Johnson, Blake, the relation of the arts, and other eighteenth-century and Romantic topics. His latest books are *The Romantic Body: Love and Sexuality in Keats, Wordsworth, and Blake* (1985) and *Sex and Sensibility: Ideal and Erotic Love from Milton to Mozart* (1980). He has been lecturing for Phi Beta Kappa as a visiting Scholar, and serving as a Mellon Senior Fellow at the National Humanities Center.

ROBERT L. MONTGOMERY is Professor of English at the University of California, Irvine. His book on faculty psychology and Renaissance literary theory, *The Reader's Eye*, appeared in 1979. More recently, he has done a translation of Giacopo Mazzoni's introduction to *On the Defense of the Comedy of Dante* (1983).

WILLIAM B. OBER, M. D. is Director Emeritus of Pathology at Hackensack Hospital, Clinical Professor of Pathology at New Jersey Medical College, and an Assistant Medical Examiner in Bergen County. Previously, he was a pathologist at hospitals in New York City and held professorships at New York Medical College and the Mt. Sinai School of Medicine. The author of over one hundred and sixty articles in medical journals, he has also written *Boswell's Clap and Other Essays: Medical Analyses of Literary Men's Afflictions* (1979) and *Bottoms Up! A Pathologist's Essays on Medicine and the Humanities* (forthcoming).

MELINDA ALLIKER RABB is Assistant Professor of English at Brown University. She is the author of articles on Pope, Fielding, Sterne, Richardson, Berkeley, and others.

DAVID G. SCHAPPERT is the Director of The Keystone Library in Pennsylvania. In addition to his interest in eighteenth-century culture, he is engaged in a study of American literary naturalism.

JOHN F. SENA, Associate Professor of English at Ohio State University, is the author of *A Bibliography of Melancholy* (1970) and *The Best-Natured Man*, a biography of Samuel Garth. He has published numerous articles on the relationship between medicine and literature and is a member of the editorial board of a new journal titled *Medical Heritage*.

JOHN DAVID WALKER, Associate Professor of English at SUNY-Binghamton, has published poems in a number of journals, including *Poetry Now*, *MSS*, and *Choice*. He has also written articles on Homer, Pope, Herbert, and contemporary American poetry.

JOHN P. WRIGHT, Associate Professor of Philosophy at the University of Windsor, is the author of *The Sceptical Realism of David Hume* (1983). He is presently engaged in an extended study tentatively titled "Mechanical Man: Mind and Medicine during the 17th and 18th Centuries," and serving as a member of The Institute for Advanced Study, Princeton, New Jersey.

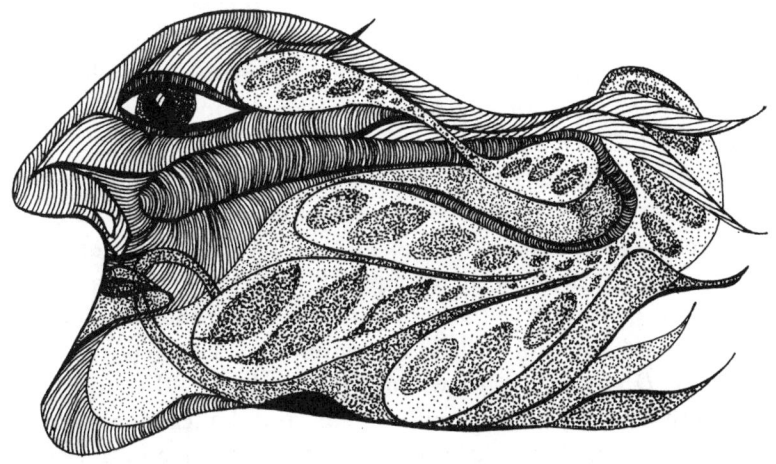

INTRODUCTION

Defining Eighteenth-Century Psychology: Some Problems and Perspectives

CHRISTOPHER FOX

In the *Preface to Shakespeare,* Johnson points to a phenomenon that separates Shakespeare's age from his own. In Shakespeare's day, we are told, "speculation had not yet attempted to analyze the mind, to trace the passions to their sources, to unfold the seminal principles of vice or virtue, or sound the depths of the heart for the motives of action." These and other inquiries, then "unattempted," were the products of a later era, when "human nature became the fashionable study. . . ."[1] That era, we can reasonably assume, is the latter part of Shakespeare's century and Johnson's own.

Johnson helps define the direction of the present volume in at least two ways. First, he locates its time period, the late seventeenth and the eighteenth centuries, and its topic, the emergence of "human nature" as a "fashionable study." Second, his comments come in a work that asks readers to see Shakespeare in his own age and on his own terms—in this case, without imposing their assumptions about human nature, drawn from later inquiries, on him. This volume has a similar aim. It attempts to approach some late seventeenth- and eighteenth-century writers *not* from any modern psychological perspective, but from that of the psychology available to them in their own time.

This approach is more difficult than it might seem. In the twentieth century, most of us assume we know (or have at least a vague idea of) what psychology is. After all, it is enshrined in the universities with the venerable status of an academic discipline, entrenched in the professions, and consulted in the courtrooms, despite the occasional embarrassment of contradictory expert testimony. Though not defined in Johnson's *Dictionary,* the word "psychology" did appear in seventeenth- and eighteenth-century texts, as did questions about legal pleas of insanity and the like, if we judge by works like John Brydall's *Non Compos Mentis* (1700) or Locke's chapter on personal identity in *An Essay concerning Human Understanding* (second edition, 1694). So we have the appearance of similar issues and the existence of the same term, psychology. Why not take the next step and simply assume that nominal identity implies conceptual identity, that psychology meant the same thing to eighteenth-century writers it does to us?

That would be easy, but quite possibly wrong. I say "quite possibly" because, at this point at least, we simply do not know. For one thing, the eighteenth century was not our age of specialization. Historians of early modern science have long recognized that establishing boundaries between the sciences is a risky task. What then do we do with this so-called "social science"—the latter term itself largely a nineteenth-century invention?[2] Though closely related to other disciplines, psychology was not officially in the eighteenth-century British curriculum. Nor is there, to my knowledge, any detailed study of how or where it was taught. There have been some attempts to track down the term. It might help to mention a few of them here, if only to suggest problems we face in tackling this topic.

In his "Origin and Evolution of the Term 'Psychology'" (1970), Francois Lapointe tells us that though the word was "widely used" in eighteenth-century France and Germany, the "first employment of the term psychology in Great Britain . . . would seem to have been among a group of Aberdeen philosophers toward the end of the eighteenth century." In attributing the word specifically to George Campbell of Aberdeen, Lapointe is right. Campbell did use "psychology" in his *Philosophy of Rhetoric* (1776) and was, as James Engell here demonstrates, interested in what we would call psychological issues. However, that Campbell also identified "psychology" as one of "the branches of physiology" is not discussed by Lapointe; here and elsewhere in Lapointe's survey, there is little attempt to analyze terms or isolate different historical uses of the same word. We moderns might feel momentary comfort, for example, in seeing psychology classed under another word we recognize, *physiology*, until we learn that "physiology" for Campbell includes "astronomy, geography, mechanics, optics, hydrostatics, meteorology, medicine, chymistry" along with "natural theology," or the study of "the Supreme Being."[3] What do we make of that? Can we continue to say that psychology is, after all, psychology, just as physiology is—well—physiology?

A much earlier survey of the word psychology may help us here. In his *Lectures on Metaphysics and Logic* (published 1859, though delivered in 1836), Sir William Hamilton connects Campbell's classification with the old Aristotelianism: "Aristotle's treatise *On the Soul* being, (along with his lesser treatises on *Memory and Reminiscence*, on *Sense and its Objects*, etc.,) included in the *Parva Naturalia*, and, he having declared that the consideration of the soul was part of the philosophy of nature, the science of Mind was always treated along with Physics." Adam Smith invokes this category when he claims that since "the human mind" and "the Deity" are "parts of the great system of the universe," the Greeks made them a "part of the system of physics." And Paul Pownall argues in 1795 that insofar as "intellectual phenomena" are "equally natural as material phenomena," what we call psychology should be called "intellectual physics." Thus, Campbell, who claims to be using "physiology" in its "largest acceptation," can see psychology as a branch of what would also be called natural philosophy or physics. In its survey of the word psychology, the *Oxford English Dictionary* says that David Hartley in 1749 is the first writer in English to use the word in a "modern sense." Yet Hartley similarly classes "Psychology, or the Theory of the Human Mind" under "Natural Philosophy," the parts of which include "Mechanics, Hydrostatics, Pneumatics, Optics, Astronomy, Chemistry, the Theories of the several manual Arts and Trades," and "Medicine."[4] How Hartley's use is "modern" perhaps needs more explanation than the *OED* provides.

More than one scholar has suggested that psychology itself is an accident—an offshoot of developments in seventeenth-century science, a discipline defined negatively as the study of what the new physics left out.[5] If we consider psychology and physics more broadly, there are key historical connections between the two. David Hume argued that a redefinition of the cosmos called for a corresponding redefinition of man in the cosmos. In the preceding century, Descartes's followers suggested that Augustine and the Fathers lacked an adequate definition of mind because they lacked an adequate definition of matter. We know that the definition of matter, which changes dramatically in the eighteenth century, radically alters the definition of mind.[6] Can we then see eighteenth-century psychology as a branch of natural philosophy or physics?

Not exactly. Dugald Stewart, for one, criticized this classification, as did Hamilton, who tells us that "professors of Natural Philosophy have ... long abandoned the philosophy of mind, and this branch" has been "more appropriately" taught by "Professors of Moral Philosophy ... Logic and Metaphysics."[7] Hamilton does not tell us *when* this happened, but his comments suggest other contexts. The word psychology itself is a relatively modern compound of two Greek words: *psyche*, meaning "soul," and *logos*, "discourse." As a discourse of the soul, it is not strange to see psychology classed under metaphysics. A computer search of the *Eighteenth-Century Short Title Catalogue* produces only two works between 1700 and 1800 with the word psychology (or a derivative) in a main title, John Broughton's *Psychologia; Or, An Account of the Nature of the Rational Soul* (London, 1703) and Charles Crawford's *Dissertation On The Phaedon of Plato ... To which is annexed, A Psychology: or, An Abstract Investigation of the Nature of the Soul* (London, 1773). Both works are largely exercises in metaphysics, investigations of the human soul and previous speculation about it, with references to writings like Locke's *Essay* and, in Crawford's case, not only Plato and Locke but *Tristram Shandy*.[8] We also may not be surprised by Hamilton's reference to "Moral Philosophy," especially when we consider theorists like Francis Hutcheson, Adam Smith, and Thomas Reid. What about logic, however? In a recent book, John Yolton noted the rise in the late seventeenth century of a new kind of logic, which "concentrated more upon the nature and operation of the faculties than upon arguments and valid inference forms."⁹

One late work which brings logic, moral philosophy, and metaphysics together is James Beattie's *Elements of Moral Science* (1790-93). Beattie titles the first part of his book "Psychology," defined as a "science" which "explains the nature of the several powers or faculties of the human mind." This sounds more modern than Campbell's earlier classification—until we recall that for Beattie, "Psychology" along with "Natural Theology" is part of a larger science called "Pneumatology." In his *Dictionary*, Johnson defines the last term as "2. In the schools, the doctrine of spiritual substances, as God, angels, and the souls of men." Psychology, in this scheme, appears to be one division of a three-fold science that includes the spiritual substance of God (*Theologia Naturalis*), of angels and devils (*Angelographia, Daemonologia*), and of men and sometimes brutes (*Psychologia*).¹⁰ A work with "pneumatology" in its title, Philip Doddridge's *Course of Lectures on the Principal Subjects in Pneumatology, Ethics, and Divinity* (London, 1763), includes a forty-two page section on "the Powers and Faculties of the HUMAN MIND." Here, we find definitions of the understanding, memory, passions, will, and "the power of moving some parts of the body." We also find references to a wide range of writers: Henry More and Humphrey Ditton on the soul; John Balguy and Joseph Butler on moral philosophy; William Duncan, Issac Watts, and John Locke on logic; Locke and Berkeley on the faculties; Hutcheson and Descartes on the passions; Descartes, Malebranche, and Rohault on physiology; Cheyne on nervous function; Keill's *Anatomy*, along with the *Spectator* and Pope. As his title indicates, Doddridge places his study in a broad theological and moral context. This suggests a point sometimes ignored by historians of science. Many attempts in the age to understand the mind were not done for the purposes of psychology itself, but to gain some certainty in religious and ethical matters. (In his "Epistle to the Reader" Locke, for example, relates the program of his *Essay* to the need to solve difficulties in "*Morality and Divinity, those parts of Knowledge, that Men are most concern'd to be clear in.*")¹¹ In any case, given works like Beattie's and Doddridge's, can we then see psychology in the eighteenth century largely within the context of metaphysics, logic, moral philosophy, or pneumatology?

Not completely. Doddridge, for instance, suggests at least two other frames of reference. The first returns us to physiology (in a more modern sense). The *OED* tells us that the word psychology made its first appearance in the language long before George Campbell, in a translation of Blancard's medical dictionary in 1693. That date may need to be revised. Ten years before Blancard, in Pordage's 1683 translation of *Two Discourses concerning the Soul of Brutes*, Thomas Willis terms his study of corporeal souls (to us, of comparative anatomy and physiology) a "Psychelogie or Doctrine of the Soul." Three decades before that, an anonymous "Doctor of Physick" called the opening section of his *Anthropologie Abstracted* (London, 1655) "*Psychologie*, the nature of the Rationall Soule discoursed." I cite these not to multiply examples, for other pre-*OED* uses can be found.[12] Important is the context which, here, is medical and physiological in scope.

One scholar has suggested that the first real psychologists were not philosophers but physiologists.[13] In approaching that age, such disciplinary designations may be dubious. Nevertheless, one writer who certainly brings "philosophy" and "physiology" (and many of the earlier mentioned disciplines) together is Descartes. If his consideration of that *res cogitans* (only known by reflection) influenced subsequent psychological thought, so did his analysis of that other half of the human composite, the body. "The greater part of our motions," Descartes claimed at one point, "do not depend upon the mind at all." A good deal of his physiological thought is devoted to demonstrating how much the body can do on its own. His *Treatise of Man*, for example, posits a hypothetical "machine" which can "be moved in all the ways that our body can, solely by the force of the animal spirits which flow from the brain to the nerves. . . ." Here and elsewhere, he often gives mechanical explanations for what we would call psychological events. Long before Locke noted the impact of childhood associations upon later life, Descartes had much to say on the subject. In *The Passions of the Soul*, for instance, we learn about a cat frightening a child in the cradle and leaving a lasting "imprint"—a lifelong aversion to cats.[14] In a letter to Chanut in 1647, Descartes considers his own case—a long-term passion for cross-eyed women which he himself had never been able to understand. Finally, he recalled that one of his first childhood flames was a girl with that condition. After he remembered this, he was cured. How modern, we might think. However, as John Wright shows in his "Mechanical Man" (1980), such "associational links" for Descartes are not attributed to the mind but to the *body alone*. Freud would call them "reasons," Descartes "causes" (though some details in his account remain to be worked out).[15]

Though much of Descartes's own physiology was derivative,[16] his influence here—either directly or indirectly, through writers like Malebranche and Boerhaave—was enormous. We see it in the debates over mechanism which raged all the way through the eighteenth century. (As John Dussinger asks, to what extent is Yorick an automatical man?) We sense it in the pervasive metaphor of the body-as-machine, a metaphor Arbuthnot burlesques brilliantly in the *Memoirs of Scriblerus* yet uses himself in *An Essay On the Nature of Aliments* (London, 1731). In the *Enquiries*, Hume also speaks of the "human body" as "a very complicated machine," and even in his and Locke's analyses, which ostensibly avoid such matters, the bodily mechanism is never far from mind.[17] Descartes's physiological speculation may have also encouraged at least two other developments. The first is a tendency among later writers to find physical causes for mental disorders—a point that may help us understand why "eighteenth-century physiologists," in Rather's words, "were apt to concern themselves with problems that would today be assigned to . . . psychologists."[18] The second is a tendency to "translate mental events into nervous structures." Both strains can be found in Willis's "Psychelogie" in *Two Discourses concerning the Soul of Brutes*. When we experience insomnia, it is not because of care or worry (Willis tells us) but because our "animal spirits" refuse to "lye down and be quieted." Willis's work with what he calls the "Nervous stock" signals the growing interest in the nervous system. Marcello Malphigi (1628-94), who first described the fiber tracts of that system, cooked sections of human brains to examine them microscopically. Vieussens (1641-1716) refined this method by "frying brain sections in oil for better study of the white matter." Both saw the nervous system as a center of sensation and perception. Boerhaave's later view of the human being as a *machina nervosa* (a "moving nervous machine"), Jerome Gaub's "neural man," the debates between Whytt and Haller over "sensibility" and "irritability"[19]—all might suggest how being "nervous" becomes almost an eighteenth-century pastime.[20] Such writings also support Rather's claim about the physiological interest in psychological matters, and suggest why we might find references to doctors and physiologists in a book like Doddridge's *Pneumatology*.

Doddridge's references to the *Spectator* and Pope suggest a further

ANTHROPOLOGIE
ABSTRACTED:
OR THE
Idea of Humane Nature
Reflected in briefe
Philosophicall, *and Anatomicall*
COLLECTIONS.

Ὦ πηγὴ σοφίας! ὦ τεῦχος ἀειπρεπές! ὄντως
Ἦν ἄρα τοῦτο σοφὸν, ΓΝΩΘΙ ΣΕΑΥΤΟΝ ἔπος!

*Isaac· Casaubon. in Elogio suo Audr. Laurentij
Anatom.*

LONDON,
Printed for *Henry Herringman*, at the
Anchor in the lower walke in the New
Exchange. 1655.

OF THE NATURE
OF THE
HVMAN SOVL.

CHAP. I.

*A*NTHROPOLOGIE, or the History of Human Nature, is, in the Vulgar (yet just) impression, distinguished into two Volumes; The first entituled *Pfychologie*, the nature of the Rationall Soule discoursed: the other *Anatomie*, the Fabrick or structure of the body of man revealed in dissection. This we shall visit only *in transcursu*, and draw a transitory Landschip of so much only, as may present the method of the Soules *Oeconomy*, and her manner of dispensing orders to each distinct organ of the body: of the former, we shall in a distracted rehersall, deliver our Collections.

B   The

context in which eighteenth-century psychology may be viewed. In his paper on "Hysteria" and the *Rape of the Lock*, John Sena shows Pope drawing upon medical writers to answer a question put elsewhere by Mandeville: "What is it that so much consumes the Spirits in Girls of eighteen? . . ."[21] Important here is Sena's revelation that not only did Pope draw on physicians, but that later physicians *drew on Pope*. From Blackmore's talk of delusional "Goose-Pye[s]" in 1725 to Dr. Nicholas Robinson's "Tea Pots, Glasses, and Goose Pyes" in 1729, or Dr. William Battie's mention in 1758 of splenetic states in which "Men prove with child," or Dr. Thomas Arnold's comments in 1782-86 on those imagining themselves to be "vessels, pipkins, jars, teapots, etc.," or Dr. Alexander Crichton's *Inquiry Into the Nature and Origin of Mental Derangement* (1798), which quotes "Arnold's" passage verbatim—the imagery of Pope's poem pervades eighteenth-century discussions of "hysteria" and related disorders.[22] In a recent review article on "Literature and Medicine," G. S. Rousseau points out that literary scholars tend to see the flow of ideas in "one direction": in this case, "*from* medicine *to* literature."[23] As Pope's example indicates, the flow can also move the other way, especially in an age when many doctors (as William Ober reminds us) wrote for popular audiences and considered themselves men of letters, or when "literary" authors like Samuel Johnson wrote articles for Dr. James's *Medicinal Dictionary* (1743). In 1768, J. F. Zückert, physician and physiologist, notes that Richardson provides a textbook case in *Clarissa* of the morbid effects of "heartbreak"—"slow consumption," gradual wasting away of the limbs, and death.[24]

The literary impact on other fields does not stop at physiology and medicine—or, in Doddridge's case, at pneumatology, for that matter. In his *Principles of Moral Philosophy* (London, 1740), George Turnbull thanks six authors "from whom I have received the greatest assistances in this work": Shaftesbury, Hutcheson, Berkeley, Butler, John Clark, and Alexander Pope. The last author has "*shewn us, that the seemingly most abstruse matters in philosophy, may be rendered, instead of dry and tedious, exceeding pleasing and agreeable.*" Indeed, "*it is impossible for any one to express such profound abstract truths in prose, so shortly as he has done in verse.*" Turnbull shows his indebtedness to Pope by quoting him on the title page, and throughout the entire work. In the same year Turnbull's *Moral Philosophy* appeared, Hume published the last two volumes of *A*

Treatise of Human Nature (1739-40), a corrected copy of which was sent to Alexander Pope. Little has been done on Pope's influence on Hume, Though the connections are there, particularly in their mutual consideration of the passions. At one point in the *Treatise*, for instance, Hume speaks of how "a predominant passion swallows up an inferior, and converts it to it self." ("And hence one master Passion in the breast," Pope had written, "Like Aaron's serpent, swallows up the rest.") The Popean echoes in Hume may serve to remind us of something we sometimes forget: that on such subjects, poets also have ideas of their own. Hutcheson recognized this when he noted that, though "Philosophers have confusedly mentioned" complicated passions "under some general Names," the "*Poets* and *Criticks* have sufficiently shown, that they felt these Differences, however it did not concern them to explain them."[25] In his essay here on *Venice Preserved* (1682), David Walker shows Otway evolving a strikingly original interpretation of the role played by the imagination. In "Vehicles of Delusion," Michael DePorte shows Swift developing a critique of Locke which is unique. Elsewhere, Kathleen Grange points to the man who controls the weather, in *Rasselas*, as perhaps the first case study in English of what we call "schizophrenia," or to Johnson's new use of an old word "repress."[26]

In a list of "our British Psychologists" drawn up in 1798, Crichton gives six names: Locke, Hartley, Reid, Stewart, Kames, and Priestley. The last two "Psychologists" (Kames and Priestley) were also associated with a group James Engell calls the "New Rhetoricians." Another member of that group, George Campbell, claims that rhetoric is "the pleasantest way of arriving at the science of the human mind."[27] Here, as Engell and Robert L. Montgomery suggest, is a literary activity which not only produced new psychological insights but which was regarded by some as an exercise in psychology itself. The analysis of aesthetic and literary experience becomes an analysis of the mind, particularly when that study probes the problem of language and human communication. This problem was not simply confronted in criticism but also in fiction, as Melinda Rabb's essay on *Caleb Williams* demonstrates. Another novel central to that topic, *Tristram Shandy*, also evokes a related area of eighteenth-century inquiry: non-verbal communication. "It is certain there is a meaning in many acts and gestures," said William Wollaston in 1724. Diderot would later give us a "theoretical mute" who manages to get along quite well without words, Condillac would study the "*dance of gestures*" or "the mode of speaking by action," and Reid would posit a theory of "natural language," based on such phenomena as facial countenance and bodily posture.[28] A legitimate question to ask here would not simply be "How was *Tristram Shandy* influenced by such accounts?" but "In what ways did this book contribute to that discussion?" For literary writers were not only influenced by eighteenth-century psychology; they also helped shape the way that psychology was perceived.

If the discussion so far has still not told us what eighteenth-century psychology is, it at least suggests some problems in studying the subject. The first, the problem of contexts, is demonstrated in the wide range of contexts in which psychology has been shown to appear— physics and natural philosophy, metaphysics, moral philosophy, logic, pneumatology, physiology, medicine, literature, aesthetics, and criticism. This list, of course, is not complete, for other possible contexts exist. We have limited rhetoric, for example, largely to critical theory, though forensic thought might also be important here. Ever since Aristotle's analysis of the passions in the *Rhetoric*, books on public speaking have addressed the question of how to move a given audience. And if we consider works from, say, Marius D'Assigny's *Art of Memory* in 1697 to Gilbert Austin's *Chironomia; Or, a Treatise on Rhetorical Delivery* in 1805, forensic theory provides another possible context, as does eighteenth-century acting theory, in manuals such as Charles Lebrun's *A Method to Learn the Design of the Passions* (1698). Economic theory, as A. O. Hirschman's *The Passions and the Interests* (1977) suggests, certainly has a bearing on our subject, as does the political and social thought of writers like Montesquieu and Hobbes. Educational theory may offer another frame of reference. Think of Rousseau's plan, in *Emile*, for educating the emotions. Or of the earlier work of Locke. Along with his other interests, Locke also studied drugs, as did Robert Hooke, who reported on marijuana in 1689 and found no ill effects, aside from excessive laughter. Pharmacology, then, might be of help here. So might folk medicine, in works like John Wesley's *Primitive Physic* (1747).[29]

If smaller contexts might say something about psychology, so of course would larger ones. We know, for example, about the early efforts of Thomas Sydenham and others to treat disorders of the mind.

But how did the treatment of mental illness become the special province of the physicians? Such a question leads us into the history of the professions, of institutions, and of institutionalization, as M. Foucault reminds us. The recent work of Lawrence Stone, Jean H. Hagstrum and others suggests another context, contemporary attitudes toward the family, sex, and marriage. What could these tell us about our topic? A good deal, I suspect. If we look at eighteenth-century psychology solely from the perspective of one of these contexts, however, we might be left with only a partial picture. The numerous contexts may point to a need to go beyond our own specializations and look at the subject more broadly. For studying eighteenth-century psychology is an interdisciplinary endeavor, involving work in any number of fields.

The various attempts to trace the word psychology point to a second problem: terms. Eighteenth-century writers recognized this problem and complained about it. In his *Essay concerning Human Understanding*, Locke tells us about a revelation he experienced in "a Meeting of very learned and ingenious" persons: that is, "how doubtful and obscure those Words are in their Signification, which in ordinary use appeared very clear and determined." A Mandeville character would later exclaim: "You Gentlemen of Learning make use of very comprehensive Expressions; the Word *Hysterick* must be of a prodigious Latitude, to signify so many different Evils." To George Cheyne in 1733, the *"Spleen* or *Vapours,* as the Word is used in *England,* is of so general and loose a Signification, that it is a common Subterfuge for meer Ignorance." In the *Conduct of the Passions* (third edition, 1742), Hutcheson notes the "considerable Confusion in some of the Terms much used on these Subjects." Madness, William Battie observes in 1758, has "shared the fate common to many other distempers of not being precisely defined." In *Observations on those Disorders commonly called Nervous* (third edition, 1767), Robert Whytt asserts that "physicians have bestowed the character of *nervous* on all those disorders whose nature and causes they are ignorant of." At the end of the century, Crichton raises the issue of terms repeatedly. Consider "sensation," for example:

> The word sensation ought either to be made equivalent with nervous impression, or consciousness; and whenever employed by an author, it ought to be accurately stated which of the two it is intended to express.

Or "imagination":

> The word imagination has been indiscriminately applied to many phenomena, and operations of the mind, which, although they resemble each other in their general character, are very different in their real nature.

No wonder Philippe Pinel, at the beginning of the next century, claimed that one of his greatest difficulties in writing was finding precise and "proper terms," a problem he tried to solve by consulting "modern pneumatologists."[30]

To understand eighteenth-century writers on their own terms, we need to understand the terms. The above catalogue should induce caution rather than despair. If eighteenth-century writers had difficulty with their own terms, we should be doubly cautious in basing generalizations on those terms, before they have been examined. All of us might pause to ask about "pneumatologists." But what about a word that sounds familiar—"consciousness," for example? "Every Man feels and knows by Experience," said Samuel Clarke, "what Consciousness is, better than any Man can explain it." There were, nevertheless, many attempts to do so. In Cudworth's *True Intellectual System of the Universe* (1678), the second edition of Locke's *Essay* (1694), the anonymous *Essay On Consciousness* (1728), and later works, "consciousness" is an incredibly complex term, varying in different texts and, even in the same writer, within different contexts. Its history in the seventeenth and eighteenth centuries, yet to be written, will involve hard work with primary texts (the type of work done here by Jean Hagstrum on the related eighteenth-century term "conscious," and by Stephen Ford on "coalescence"). The eighteenth century abounded in terms we still use. Can we take them for granted? In his *First Lines of the Practice of Physic* (1777) and other works, William Cullen was "one of the first," we hear, "to use 'neurosis' as synonymous with nervous disease." Was it our "neurosis"? Possibly not.[31] "Hypochondria" did not mean "morbid preoccupation with one's physical health." "Nostalgia" was a serious disease that killed.[32]

We have enough trouble understanding eighteenth-century terms without imposing our own. We have tended for instance to talk about the "unconscious" in eighteenth-century writers before we even know what "consciousness" meant. There may be merit, as Jean Hagstrum shows, in asking whether the "unconscious" lurked in the eighteenth-century word "conscious." However, as Esther Fischer-Homberger reminds us, in "trying to validate modern ideas by their former existence, one should not forget that one's thoughts might be following a circle." Though we might find what *we* see as pre-Freudian passages—say, in Cambridge Platonists like John Smith and Henry More—we should proceed with caution, for we might be unconsciously (*i.e.*, unthinkingly) turning the tube. Leibniz, for example, is often hailed as the age's Freudian prophet. "The discovery of the unconscious," one historian of psychology assures us, is "still experienced by thinking men everywhere and this must have been so for Leibniz himself." Must it? This author points to Leibniz's *"petites perceptions"* and promptly—perhaps too promptly—renames them "the unconscious."[33] Could these perceptions instead simply be isolated masses of thought, confused (though *conscious*) perceptions which the mind hasn't ordered yet? Though we might find the latter view disappointing, it is quite possibly correct.

If petite perceptions won't work, perhaps "association" will: this term, we are told, leads to the very "threshold of the unconscious." With qualification, that might be true in the long run. But does this happen in the eighteenth century? When we listen to a physician, in 1765, telling other doctors about the "Art of breaking false associations of Ideas," we may begin to wonder.[34] As John Wright shows, however, we might again be disappointed—that is, if we wish to find association as an "unconscious" activity that is exclusively or almost exclusively "mental." In the seventeenth and eighteenth centuries, association may turn out to have more to do with "brain-traces" and the paths the animal spirits take and make than with anything completely and recognizably modern. To judge by Isaac Watts's account in 1733 of the role of animal spirits in dreaming, such physical entities also play a part in the eighteenth-century discussion of a realm we would certainly call "unconscious." Even here, however, that term needs qualification. In Watts's interpretation, for instance, "consciousness" is also at work in dreaming, for "THE SOUL NEVER SLEEPS." As Janet Aikins's paper on *Clarissa* and eighteenth-century dream theory demonstrates, there was a good deal of contemporary speculation on the subject. If we approach that speculation in hopes of discovering the unconscious, we might find the view we set out to find. But it may not be the eighteenth century's own.

There are other terms we may take too much for granted, terms that might clutter more than clarify our understanding of the subject. Take "rationalism" and "empiricism," for example. Christian Wolff of course wrote a book titled *Psychologia Empirica* (1732). And we sense that the growth of what Johnson called the "fashionable study of human nature" is closely tied to developments in early modern science. Can we then consider that study as largely "empirical" in scope? If so, what do we do with so-called "rationalists" like John Norris or William Wollaston or Samuel Clarke, who wrote on topics like the mental faculties, action theory, and consciousness? Or with Wolff's other book, *Psychologia Rationalis* (1734)? It has been convincingly shown that, in Hume's age at least, the status of "empirical science" was not all that clear. Nor have the terms "rationalism" and "empiricism" been defined with any consistency, either in Hume's day or our own.[36] In approaching eighteenth-century psychology, should we perhaps give these labels up—at least until the requisite work with primary texts is done? In talking about writers like Locke, we can always fall back on another word, "epistemology." Or can we? As mentioned above, John Yolton has noted the rise in that age of a new kind of logic. In this context, it is interesting that when Voltaire praised Locke for writing not "the Romance of the Soul" but its "History," he praised Locke specifically as a "Logician."[37] In a recent paper, James G. Buickerood has shown that Locke's *Essay* was largely conceived and later studied in the eighteenth century *not* as an epistemology but as a logic. There was in Locke's age, Buickerood tells us, "no recognized discipline or body of knowledge known as 'epistemology'"—a point suggested alone by the "complete absence of that term" in pre-nineteenth-century texts. In fact, the earliest known use of "epistemology" occurs in James Frederick Ferrier's *Institutes of Metaphysic* in 1854.[38] Though we may find this an unsettling question, it is not unreasonable to ask: What *was* an eighteenth-century epistemologist?

The problem of terms points to a third problem which can be briefly mentioned here: scholarship. In an important review article on the history of psychology and related fields, R. M. Young discovered in 1965 a "wholly inadequate corpus of scholarship." Nearly two decades later, G. S. Rousseau still largely supports that judgment and notes that a genuine history of eighteenth-century psychology remains to be written.[39] Literary scholars are particularly hampered when they come to this subject, for aside from some helpful books—DePorte's *Nightmares and Hobbyhorses* (1974), for example, or Keener's *Chain of Becoming* (1983)—there is very little work in this area with the concerns of literary study in mind. Whatever the field, however, the place to start is suggested in David Schappert's selected bibliography of eighteenth-century materials. The topic needs close study, directed to primary texts.

In exploring psychology in the eighteenth century, there is thus much to do. That will be the work of the following essays and, the contributors hope, of a good many more to come.

NOTES

1. *Johnson on Shakespeare*, ed. Arthur Sherbo, vols. VII and VIII of the Yale Edition of the Works (New Haven, Conn. and London: Yale University Press, 1968), VII, 88.
2. See Fred R. Shapiro, "A Note On The Origin Of The Term 'Social Science,'" *Journal of the History of the Behavioral Sciences*, 20 (January, 1984), 20-22.
3. See Francois Lapointe, "The Origin and Evolution of the Term 'Psychology,'" *American Psychologist*, 25 (July, 1970), 643; and George Campbell, *The Philosophy of Rhetoric* (London, 1776), I, 143.
4. See Sir William Hamilton, *Lectures On Metaphysics and Logic* (Boston, Mass.: Gould and Lincoln, 1859), I, 89-90; Adam Smith, *Wealth of Nations* (New York: Modern Library, 1937), p. 725; [Paul Pownall], *Intellectual Physics, An Essay Concerning the Nature of Being, And the Progression of Existence* (Bath, 1795), p. 6; Campbell, *Philosophy of Rhetoric*, I, 143; and David Hartley, *Observations On Man. In Two Parts* (London, 1749), Part I, p. 354.
5. On this point see, for example, E. A. Burtt's *The Metaphysical Foundations of Modern Physical Science* (New York: Anchor Books, 1954), p. 320; and Albert G. A. Balz, who notes in *Cartesian Studies* (New York: Columbia University Press, 1951), pp. 195-196: "Psychology, as that term is understood in the history of modern thought, is really a by-product, a somewhat unexpected incident in a much larger story. It is a by-product of metaphysical, theological, and methodological interests in the science of physical nature."
6. For Hume's comments, see *The Treatise of Human Nature*, ed. L. A. Selby-Bigge, rev. P. H. Nidditch, 2nd ed. (Oxford: Clarendon Press, 1978), pp. xvi-xvii and 282. On Descartes's followers and the Fathers, see Balz, p. 198. For the changing concept of matter, see Arnold E. Thackray, *Atoms and Powers: An Essay on Newtonian Matter-Theory and the Development of Chemistry* (Cambridge, Mass.: Harvard Monographs in the History of Science, 1970); and Robert E. Schofield, *Mechanism and Materialism*

(Princeton, N.J.: Princeton University Press, 1970). For the connection of matter and mind, see John W. Yolton, *Thinking Matter: Materialism in Eighteenth-Century Britain* (Minneapolis: University of Minnesota Press, 1983). Some other helpful studies pertinent to this point are: Stanley W. Jackson, "Force and Kindred Notions In Eighteenth-Century Neurophysiology And Medical Psychology," *Bulletin of the History of Medicine,* 44 (1970), 397-410; Aram Vartanian, *La Mettrie's L'Homme Machine: A Study In The Origins Of An Idea* (Princeton, N.J.: Princeton University Press, 1960); and Theodore M. Brown, "From Mechanism to Vitalism in Eighteenth-Century English Physiology," *Journal of the History of Biology,* 7 (1974), 179-216.

7. See Dugald Stewart, *Collected Works,* ed. Sir William Hamilton (Edinburgh, 1854), I, 17-18; and Hamilton, *Lectures,* I, 90.

8. Charles Crawford, *A Dissertation On The Phaedon of Plato . . . To which is annexed, A Psychology: Or, An Abstract Investigation of the Nature of the Soul* (London, 1773), p. 287.

9. See John W. Yolton, "Ideas in Logic and Psychology," in *Perceptual Acquaintance From Descartes to Reid* (Minneapolis: University of Minnesota Press, 1984), especially p. 105.

10. See James Beattie, *Elements of Moral Science* (Edinburgh, 1790-93), I, 1 and xiii-xiv; and Samuel Johnson, *Dictionary* (London, 1830), s.v. "Pneumatology," p. 891. On psychology as a division of pneumatology, see the *OED* (s.v. "Psychology") and Hamilton, *Lectures,* I, 94n.

11. See Philip Doddridge, *A Course of Lectures on the Principal Subjects in Pneumatology, Ethics, and Divinity* (London, 1763), Part I, pp. 1-42. (Doddridge died in 1751.) Also see John Locke, *An Essay concerning Human Understanding,* ed. P. H. Nidditch (Oxford: Clarendon Press, 1975), p. 11.

12. For pre-1693 uses of "psychology," see Thomas Willis, *Two Discourses concerning the Soul of Brutes,* trans. S. Pordage (London, 1683), p. 7; and *Anthropologie Abstracted: OR The Idea of Human Nature Reflected in briefe Philosophicall, and Anatomicall Collections* (London, 1655), p. 1. The 1655 occurrence may reflect earlier continental uses of the word by writers like Otto Casmann, who published *Psychologia Anthropologica* (1594). Like Casmann, the 1655 author sees *"Psychologie"* as one of the two branches of "Anthropology," the other being "Anatomy." In his *Lectures* (I, 95), Hamilton notes that this division had persisted in Germany. In Britain, however, this does not appear to be the case. In his *Cyclopædia* (London, 1728), Ephraim Chambers defines "PSYCHOLOGY, a Discourse concerning the *Soul"* as one of the two parts of *"Anthropology,* or the Science which considers Man"—the other being "Anatomy." He also notes a recent book by Drake which limits "Anthropology" to the "Anatomy of the Human Body"; it is this restricted use which Johnson would appeal to in his *Dictionary* when he defines "ANTHROPOLOGY" as "the doctrine of anatomy." (See Chambers, s.v. "Anthropology" and "Psychology"; and Johnson, s.v. "Anthropology.") For another use of "psychology" predating the *OED* citation, see Ralph Cudworth's *Treatise of Freewill,* ed. John Allen (London: Parker, 1838), pp. 19, 20, 21. Here, sometime before his death in 1688, Cudworth uses the word three times in attacking the "vulgar psychology" of modern writers, most certainly Hobbes. I thank James Buickerood for calling Cudworth to my attention.

13. See Barbara Carr Ross, "Psychological Thought Within The Context Of The

Scientific Revolution: 1665-1700" (Diss.: History of Psychology, University of New Hampshire, 1970), p. 106. This is a helpful study of psychological ideas in the *Philosophical Transactions of the Royal Society*.
14. See the following by René Descartes: *Reply to Objections IV*, in *The Philosophical Works*, trans. E. S. Haldane and G. R. T. Ross (Cambridge: Cambridge University Press, 1911), II, 103; *Treatise of Man*, French text with English trans. by T. S. Hall (Cambridge, Mass.: Harvard University Press, 1972), p. 29; and *The Passions of the Soul*, Part Second, Article CXXXVI, in Haldane and Ross, I, 391.
15. See Descartes, *Letter to Chanut*, 6 June 1647; and John P. Wright, "Hysteria and Mechanical Man," *Journal of the History of Ideas*, 41 (1980), 233-247 (esp. 244-246).
16. See T. S. Hall's introduction to the *Treatise of Man* (pp. xxxi-xxxiii) and his "Descartes' Physiological Method: Position, Principles, Examples," *Journal of the History of Biology*, 3 (1970), 53-79. Though much of his physiology (as Hall notes) owed something to predecessors, particularly Galen, Descartes did make a major discovery about the eye: that the lens changes shape rather than position. (See A. C. Crombie's excellent "Early Concepts Of The Senses and The Mind," *Scientific American*, 210 [1964], 108-116, esp. 112). For some helpful comments on Galenic ideas, many still prominent in eighteenth-century psychological concepts, see Stanley W. Jackson, "Galen—On Mental Disorders," *Journal of the History of the Behavioral Sciences*, 5 (1969), 365-384.
17. See the *Memoirs of the Extraordinary Life, Works, and Discoveries of Martinus Scriblerus*, ed. Charles Kerby-Miller (New Haven, Conn.: Yale University Press, 1950), p. 141; John Arbuthnot's appeal to "The Mechanism of Nature" (p. 8 and elsewhere) in *An Essay concerning the Nature of Aliments* (London, 1731); and David Hume, *Enquiries concerning Human Understanding*, ed. L. A. Selby-Bigge, rev. P. H. Nidditch, 3rd ed. (Oxford: Clarendon Press, 1975), p. 87. In his *Thinking Matter* (especially a chapter on "The Physiology of Thinking and Acting," pp. 153-189), John Yolton has discussed Locke's and Hume's mutual emphasis that "psychological and physiological states work together" (p. 176). In *The Sceptical Realism of David Hume* (Minneapolis: University of Minnesota Press, 1983), John Wright has discussed Hume's use of physiological concepts and his connections, here, to Descartes.
18. L. J. Rather, *Mind and Medicine in the Eighteenth Century: A Study based on Jerome Gaub's De Regemine Mentis* (Berkeley: University of California Press, 1965), p. 166n.
19. On translating "mental events" into "nervous structures," see Roger Smith, "The Background Of Physiological Psychology in Natural Philosophy," *History of Science*, 11 (1973), 87. For Willis, see *Two Discourses concerning the Soul of Brutes*, pp. 139, 87. On Malphigi and Vieussens, see K. D. Keele, *Anatomies of Pain* (Oxford: Blackwell Scientific Publications, 1964), pp. 86-87. For Boerhaave's *machina nervosa*, see B. P. M. Schulte, "Boerhaave On Psychic Function And Psychopathology," in *Boerhaave And His Time*, ed. G. A. Lindeboom (Leiden: E. J. Brill, 1970), pp. 96-100. For Gaub's "neural man," see Rather, *Mind and Medicine*, pp. 64-66. On Whytt and Haller, see esp. R. French, *Robert Whytt, The Soul, and Medicine* (London: Wellcome Institute of the History of Medicine, 1969). Some other helpful studies are: E. T. Carlson and M. M. Simpson, "Models of the Nervous System in Eighteenth-Century Psychiatry," *Bulletin of the History of Medicine*, 43 (1969), 101-115; Karl M. Figlio, "Theories of Perception and the Physiology of Mind in the Late Eighteenth Century," *History of Science*, 12 (1975), 177-212; Sergio Moravia, "From *Homme Machine* to *Homme Sensible:* Changing Eighteenth-Century Models of Man's Im-

age," *Journal of the History of Ideas,* 39 (1978), 45-60; Moravia's "The Enlightenment and the Sciences of Man," *History of Science,* 18 (1980), 247-268; and John Mullan, "Hypochondria and Hysteria: Sensibility and the Physician," *The Eighteenth Century: Theory and Interpretation* 25 (1984), 141-174.

20. In *Medical Cautions . . . for the Consideration Of Invalids* (Bath, 1786), James Adair notes that before the publication some "thirty years ago" of "a treatise of nervous diseases" by Dr. Whytt, "people of fashion had not the least idea that they had nerves; but a fashionable apothecary of my acquaintance . . . derived from thence an hint, by which he cut the gordian knot—'*Madam, you are nervous*'; the solution was quite satisfactory, the term became fashionable, and the spleen, vapours, and hyp, were forgotten." See this account in *Three Hundred Years of Psychiatry: 1535-1860,* ed. R. Hunter and I. Macalpine (London: Oxford University Press, 1963), pp. 489-490.

21. Bernard Mandeville, *A Treatise of The Hypochondriack And Hysteric Diseases,* 2nd ed. (London, 1730); rpt. in *Collected Works,* ed. Irwin Primer and B. Fabian (New York: George Olms, 1981), p. 239.

22. See Sir Richard Blackmore, *A Treatise of the Spleen and Vapours* (London, 1725), pp. 161-162; Nicholas Robinson, *A New System of the Spleen* (London, 1729), pp. 190, 230; and Sena, p. 137 below. See also: William Battie, *A Treatise of Madness* (London, 1758), p. 49; and Alexander Crichton, *An Inquiry Into The Nature And Origin Of Mental Derangement, Comprehending A Concise System of the Physiology And Pathology Of The Human Mind. And A History Of The Passions And Their Effects* (London, 1798), I, xxiv-xxv.

23. G. S. Rousseau, "Literature and Medicine: The State of the Field," *Isis,* 72 (1981), 409.

24. See J. F. Zückert, *Von den Leidenschaften* (Berlin, 1768), pp. 61-64; and Rather, *Mind and Medicine,* p. 227, n. 125.

25. See George Turnbull, *The Principles of Moral Philosophy* (London, 1740), I, vii, xi; Maynard Mack, "Pope's Books: A Biographical Survey With a Finding List," in *English Literature in the Age of Disguise,* ed. M. E. Novak (Berkeley: University of California Press, 1977), p. 214 and entry 97, p. 266; Hume, *Treatise,* p. 420; Pope, *Essay on Man* II, lines 131-132; and Francis Hutcheson, *An Essay On the Nature and Conduct of the Passions,* 3rd ed. (London, 1742), p. 78.

26. See Kathleen M. Grange, "Dr. Samuel Johnson's Account of a Schizophrenic Illness in *Rasselas* (1759)," *Medical History,* 6 (1962), 162-168; and "Samuel Johnson's Account of Certain Psychoanalytic Concepts," *Journal of Nervous and Mental Disease,* 135 (August, 1962), 93-98.

27. See Crichton, *Inquiry Into . . . Mental Derangement* (1798), I, xxvii; and Campbell, *Philosophy of Rhetoric,* I, 16.

28. See William Wollaston, *The Religion of Nature Delineated* (London, 1724), p. 8; Denis Diderot, *Letter On The Deaf and Dumb* (1751), in the *Early Philosophical Works,* trans. M. Jourdain (New York: Burt Franklin, 1916), esp. pp. 163-165; Etienne Bonnot De Condillac, *An Essay On The Origin Of Human Knowledge,* trans. T. Nugent, rpt. with an introduction by James H. Stam (New York: AMS Press, 1974), pp. 178, 174; and Thomas Reid, *Essays On The Intellectual Powers,* in *The Philosophical Works,* ed. Sir William Hamilton (1846; rpt. Hildesheim: Olms, 1967), I, 122.

29. Under the influence of this drug—which comes, Hooke tells us, from "Hemp"—a

person is "very merry, and laughs, and sings, and speaks Words without Coherence, not knowing what he saith or doth; yet he is not giddy, or drunk, but walks and dances, and sheweth many odd Tricks; after a little Time he falls asleep . . . and when he wakes, he finds himself . . . exceeding hungry." See *An Account of the Plant, called Banque, before the Royal Society, Dec. 18, 1689*, in *Philosophical Experiments and Observations of the late Eminent Dr. Hooke* (London, 1726), esp. pp. 210-212. Portions of Hooke's account are reprinted in *Three Hundred Years of Psychiatry*, pp. 219-220. On folk medicine, see, for instance, G. S. Rousseau, "John Wesley's *Primitive Physic* (1747)," *Harvard Library Bulletin*, 16 (1968), 242-256.

30. On terms, see: Locke, *Essay*, 3. 9. 15 (Nidditch, p. 484); Mandeville, *Hypochondriack and Hysteric Diseases*, p. 267; George Cheyne, *The English Malady* (London, 1733; rpt. Delmar, N.Y.: Scholars' Facsimiles, 1976), p. 134; Hutcheson, *Conduct of the Passions*, pp. xiii-xiv; William Battie, *A Treatise on Madness*, p. 3; Robert Whytt, *Observations On the Nature, Causes, and Cure of those disorders which have commonly been called Nervous*, 3rd ed. (Edinburgh, 1767), p. iii; Crichton, I, 300-301 and II, 1-2; and Philippe Pinel, *A Treatise Of Insanity*, trans. D. D. Davis (Sheffield, 1806), p. 135.

31. On "consciousness," see Samuel Clarke, *Works* (London, 1738), III, 790-791; David P. Behan's "Locke on Persons and Personal Identity," *Canadian Journal of Philosophy*, 9 (1979), 53-75; and my forthcoming study of identity and consciousness in early eighteenth-century Britain. On "neurosis," see Walther Riese, "The Pre-Freudian Origins of Psychoanalysis," in *Science and Psychoanalysis*, vol. I, ed. J. H. Masserman (New York and London: Grune and Stratton, 1958), p. 66; and Ilza Veith, *Hysteria: The History of A Disease* (Chicago, Illinois: University of Chicago Press, 1965), pp. 171-172. Veith notes that, in Cullen's scheme, neurosis "bore little relation to its modern connotation" (p.172). For some qualifications of this view, see Donald Greene's "From Accidie to Neurosis: *The Castle of Indolence* Revisited," in *English Literature in the Age of Disguise*, pp. 131-156 (esp. p. 142). Greene's fascinating essay links eighteenth-century literature with several other significant developments: the waning of the old humoral tradition and the metamorphoses of Deadly Sins into modern psychological disorders.

32. On "hypochondria," see Veith, p. 145. "Nostalgia," also called *Heimweh*, was coined by the physician Johannes Hofer in 1678. See George Rosen, "Nostalgia: A 'Forgotten' Psychological Disorder," *Psychological Medicine*, 5 (1975), 340-354.

33. See Esther Fischer-Homberger, "Hypochondriasis of the Eighteenth Century—Neurosis of the Present Century," *Bulletin of the History of Medicine*, 46 (1972), 401; and David Rapaport, *The History of the Concept of the Association of Ideas* (New York: International Universities Press, 1974), p. 90.

34. On "association," see Rapaport, p. 69; and John Gregory, M.D., *A Comparative View Of The State and Faculties Of Man with those of the Animal World* (London, 1765), pp. 186-188, rpt. in *Three Hundred Years of Psychiatry*, p. 440.

35. Isaac Watts, *Philosophical Essays On Various Subjects* (London, 1733) in *The Works*, ed. George Burder (London, 1810), V, 550-551.

36. For some important comments on "rationalism" and "empiricism," see John P. Wright, *The Sceptical Realism of David Hume*, esp. pp. 5 and 9, n. 22.

37. See Yolton, *Perceptual Acquaintance* (note 9, above) and François-Marie Arouet de Voltaire, *Letters concerning the English Nation* (London, 1733), pp. 98, 94.

38. See James G. Buickerood's excellent paper, "The Natural History of the Understanding: Locke and the Rise of Facultative Logic in the Eighteenth Century," in *History and Philosophy of Logic*, 6 (1985), 157-190, esp. 165, n.30.
39. See Robert M. Young, "Scholarship And The History Of The Behavioural Sciences," *History of Science*, 5 (1966), 1-51 and esp. 4; and G. S. Rousseau, "Psychology," in *The Ferment of Knowledge*, ed. Roy Porter and G. S. Rousseau (New York and London: Cambridge University Press, 1980), pp. 143-210.

Towards a Profile of the Word *Conscious* in Eighteenth-Century Literature

JEAN H. HAGSTRUM

From one view *conscious* appears to be an empty word, requiring a phrasal neighborhood to give it content. When we encounter it standing alone we are impelled to ask, "conscious of what?" or "conscious to what?" The dative complement is unfamiliar today, but the genitive is fully familiar—as familiar as a noun clause following the word as its object: "I am conscious that my subject today is complex." In such constructions as these the word reveals its dependence. But it does possess viability even when it is deponent (or cut off and truncated), and it can stand alone when it has uncoupled its phrasal or clausal followers. In modern speech we are all too familiar with such verbal detachments: we speak of people who are, *tout simplement*, committed, detached, disinterested, convinced; and we praise—vulgarly and sentimentally, I am afraid—the "aware, caring person" without inquiring too precisely what it is that he is aware of or cares about.

In eighteenth-century usage the word *conscious*, like the word *sensible* without its *of*, should give us pause when it remains an unattended adjective, modifying, to be sure, but itself unmodified. Do we know immediately or precisely what a conscious moon is, a conscious night, a conscious heart, or why in Wordsworth the Parcae are conscious?[1] We reach for meaning when in Dryden "the conscious Priest . . . / Stood ready," when Pope says that "secret Transports touch'd the conscious Swain," when in *Clarissa* Lovelace makes a "conscious girl," who had just been described as *"sensible all over,"* blush again, or when in *Northanger Abbey* Henry Tilney is introduced to Mrs. Morland by her "conscious daughter."[2] Such adjectives, especially when modifying a real person and not a personified entity, are teasing or striking, perhaps even a bit upsetting. Even more so is the independent predicate nominative used by William Cowper as he ruminates before a fire: "I am conscious, and confess, / Fearless, a soul that does not always think."[3]

The reason such passages produce at least a brief pause of wonder is not simply that the meanings have changed since the seventeenth and eighteenth centuries but that an essentially parasitical word has been removed from its vine and allowed to stand unsupported, with the result that we must supply content, meaning, value, association.

It is today a fashionable practice—but also a very sound instinct—that leads us to etymology, and in this case the Latin supplies meanings that are simple and literal but also complex and even paradoxical. Such range and richness of meaning will be best served if I summarize this linguistic heritage by using a series of contrasts. *Conscious* refers to joint knowledge with another person (the prefix *con* being of importance), but it also refers to solitary knowledge, to knowledge of and by itself. Both the shared and the individual knowledge can be guilty: a secret shared is often only a titillating delight but in other circumstances it may be criminal or conspiratorial; possessed alone, it can be self-accusatory but it can alternatively be innocent, self-fortifying, or capable of strengthening the bond of friendship. *Conscious* was not only used of human beings but of animals, plants, inanimate natural objects, and literary personifications; it also suggests complex relations within people, among people, between man and his environment, man and his intellectual products. Perhaps the deepest-lying, at once the most disturbing and fructifying of these contrasts, is the one between guilt and goodness—if not moral goodness, then at least some kind of good for the individual concerned.

This last contrast can be best illustrated from the *Aeneid*, the ancient literary work that most influenced the English use of *conscious*. In its fourth book Dido and Aeneas meet in a cave and consummate their love. Though divinely arranged and even divinely sanctioned, this event Virgil indubitably regarded as evil—as a cause of death and woe; and Dido was as seriously deluded to think that it was love-inspired as she was sinful to veil it with the sacred name of marriage. To this union, pregnant with future suffering and peril, there are uncomfortable and disquieting witnesses: "fulsere ignes" (lightnings flashed), "ululuarunt . . . Nymphae" (nymphs howled), and "*conscius* Aether / conubiis" (literally, the air was knowledgeable with the "bridal" couple), the air and the lovers sharing a mischievous secret.[4] The use of the term is brilliant: the *con-* extends the guilty *-scius* to the natural surroundings, making an erring woman and man form with nature itself an ominous and menacing trio.

Book XII brings to a tragic end the heroic life of the third great character of the epic, the raging, warlike, but essentially courageous and noble Turnus. Not long before his grim death at the hands of Aeneas, Virgil describes his divided, tortured, but heroic mind in a subjectively directed passage highly congenial to the term *conscius*:

> Stupid he sate, his eyes on earth declin'd,
> And various cares revolving in his mind:
> Rage, boiling from the bottom of his breast,
> And sorrow mix'd with shame, his soul oppress'd;
> And conscious worth lay lab'ring in his thought,
> And love by jealousy to madness wrought.[5]

Dryden's "conscious worth" is Virgil's famous and influential "conscia virtus," which could also be conscious valor, might, or moral goodness. In any case, the phrase personifies a human quality and transfers consciousness from the person to the personification, directing attention not to nature outside, as *Aether* does, but to the inner man.

Aeneas's decisive encounters with both Dido and Turnus have evoked the word *conscius*, the first to mean a guilty knowledge which the lovers share with nature and the other inner knowledge arising from a caldron of conflicting and agitated emotions to help nerve the hero's final foe to action. Both uses accompany eminently human conditions and are instinct with Virgil's legendary pathos. Together, the two constitute a paradox or a potential ambivalence. *Conscius* means guilty or innocent, referring either to a shared secret that chooses the dark over the light or to an inner awareness that drives outward from the recesses of the heart to daylight action and accomplishment, heroic though doomed.

I

I shall in this paper be much concerned with these polarities of guilt and innocence in the English word *conscious* and also with the possible meeting, or the mutual cancelling out, of these and other extremes. I do not of course wish to ignore what is less frequent and certainly less dramatic in English, the etymological meaning that the *Oxford English Dictionary* gives first: "Knowing, or sharing the knowledge of anything, together with another. . . ." That usage can be illustrated in Swift, who keeps it poetically secret whether Vanessa meets any success whatever in wooing Cadenus but who does give several alternative possibilities. These "Must never to Mankind be told, / Nor shall the conscious Muse unfold" (lines 826-827), where I take it that the Muse, quite without guilt or censure, though not without some coyness, "knows with" the couple, whose secret she keeps.

Such plain, untortured meaning our word might have had more frequently had not that powerful Christian word *conscience* (etymologically synonymous with *consciousness*) entered Western culture with a panoply of divine sanction. A "conscious" person who is also a believer will not only recall and so witness his own actions and secrets, shared or unshared; he will judge them. C. S. Lewis has neatly summarized the word's history: *conscience* "passed from the witness-box to the bench and even to the legislator's throne."[6] So deeply did self-examination become involved with self-evaluation, that the two cannot easily be separated—nor can reason and the emotions, which it would seem inevitably unite under the pressures and complexities of the Christian moral life. As a medieval scholar has said of the period of his specialization, "Logically, there is a transition from being witness to being judge but, psychologically, recall and judgement are often simultaneous."[7] That simultaneity continued long after the Middle Ages and well into the eighteenth century, as the example of the tender-conscienced Samuel Johnson abundantly proves. For him merely to recall in solitude his inner state, present or past, was inevitably to judge it. Conscience in our culture simply cannot be divorced from conscious.

Believing this as I do, and have, it should not have been necessary to remind me that *conscious* is inevitably implicated with guilt, and I take this occasion to thank Arthur Sherbo for having brought back to my own consciousness the dark side of *conscious*.[8] Certainly the pre-Johnson dictionaries from 1662 on bear him out, where the word primarily and regularly means "inwardly guilty," "culpable," "self-convicted."[9] Since the verbal inheritance from the Latin permitted *conscious* to refer equally to self-indictment or to self-exculpation, the prominence of guilt-meanings in modern times seems eloquent tribute to the continuing hold of Christian guilt-feelings. Surely the emphasis upon original and all-penetrating sin bears out Donald Greene's belief that Augustinianism remained powerful in the eighteenth century,[10] and explains, much more satisfactorily than the classical context of poetic diction that Sherbo brings forward, the persisting fact that an originally neutral word like "knowing with" should be so deeply drenched in mischief. Those marvellously revealing letters of the religious and scrupulous Clarissa display the Christian's dilemma: God is "the first gracious Planter," and so when the girl looks within she finds guiding principles already "implanted" which she should be able to follow. But at the same time God is "the all-gracious Inflicter," who must chasten us because we vaunt ourselves on our "good inclinations" and are strangely drawn to sinning even "in our best performances."[11] *Conscious* being an inward-tending term, Clarissa as the most subjectively oriented of the great heroines of English literature may be one of our best guides to its meanings and implications even when she does not use it.

Arthos's list of the vocabulary of stock diction shows that most of the poetic uses of *conscious* from the seventeenth century on make guilty meanings predominate, as do Sherbo's more extensive word-surveys.[12] From Milton to Jane Austen the word often evokes some degree of guilt, and I do not need now to multiply examples. But because previous scholars have tended to concentrate on *conscious* as an instance of Latinate poetic diction, which often smells a bit of the lamp, I do need to assert that English writers often used the term with solemn moral purpose in prose and poetry, in Latin and English. In Milton's *In Quintum Novembris* (line 150) the *tellus* is *conscia* because it is stained with crime and vengeance; in *Paradise Lost* (VI, line 521) Night is "conscious" because it witnesses and is privy to the secret and abominable manufacture of the first artillery. In Dryden's translations of Ovid's epistles, the nurse in "Canace to Macareus" (line 56) is "conscious" because she sees and collaborates in the crime of incest, and in "Helen to Paris" Helen has "fearful conscious eyes" (line 143) because of her sin.

Some of these examples point to a peculiarly close association between the word *conscious* and sexual sin—an association forged because sinful lovers inevitably come in pairs and share guilty secrets, making the prefix of association (*con*) as apposite as the suffix of knowledge. Milton is quite explicit about this: he encumbers the post-lapsarian dreams of the first pair "with conscious [that is, guilty] dreams" (*P.L.*, IX, line 1050). Pope's use of the term echoes Milton's brilliantly: he transfers to the night the guilt of Eloisa's and Abelard's love, enriching and deepening the term by associating it with several oxymorons like "unholy joy":

> All my loose soul unbounded springs to thee.
> O curst, dear horrors of all-conscious night!
> How glowing guilt exalts the keen delight!
> (lines 224, 228-230)

Pope's lines, though morally serious, are nevertheless witty and stylish as he ramifies Eloisa's pleasing guilt—Abelard's "fair frame" is "That cause of all my guilt, and all my joy" (lines 337-338)—and they can be used to make still another point: that though *conscious* often refers to deep guilt and its attendant sufferings, it can concurrently be used lightly and whimsically. The "conscious tail" of Gray's cat is sensitive and expresses joy, but there is also about this organ of pleasure more than a tinge of guilt in the adjective because it points to an imminent fall. Thus though guilt may lurk stealthily in Selima's undulating, serpentine tail, the imbuing of it with consciousness is primarily light and witty.[13] Cowper is often capable of using the term in contexts of guilt and suffering and also of large, optimistic religious meaning; but he too can use it whimsically, delicately, in a mood of playful self-censure. He sits before a domestic fire and reflects on minds that think and on those indisposed to any thought at all:

> Laugh ye, who boast your more mercurial powers,
> That never feel a stupor, know no pause,

> Nor need one; I am conscious, and confess,
> Fearless, a soul that does not always think.
> *(The Task*, IV, lines 282–285)

One scholar has found Cowper's use of the term in this passage "epochal," a "pre-Romantic discovery of consciousness" that makes the decade of the 1780s notable.[14] Even though before Cowper wrote there had been a long philosophical debate about whether the soul thinks continuously—a tradition to which I shall return at the close—I am not sure that his *conscious* here means much more than this when he says, "I am conscious": I plead guilty now and then to having a vacant mind when I sit before my fire. The immediately subsequent passage, with its praise of the free play of fancy, may indeed be important in cultural history; the use of *conscious* I have quoted is not. A most charming example of the "unballasting" of a word that had for many years carried a heavy freight of guilty moral meanings, it is neither unique nor pioneering.

II

Only an exhaustive word-count, in the manner of Josephine Miles, with a careful assessment of meanings would show whether as the century progressed there was a bleaching out of the guilty stains in *conscious*, though I certainly do not wish to suggest that moral meaning was eliminated or even weakened. C.S. Lewis has suggested that when Hamlet says that "conscience does make cowards of us all," it is the fear of hell that should give us pause.[15] Whether between that day and Cowper's use of the word to mean guiltless guilt the word reflects an important change in religious *mentalité*, I am unable to say. But it is noteworthy that later dictionaries than those I referred to above—specifically Johnson's and Sheridan's—though they recognize both guilt and innocence in the noun *consciousness*, keep from their definitions of the adjective all overt traces of sin or evil.[16] If such lexical elimination of seriously guilty meanings from the word *conscious* reveals a wide consensus, this fact would represent, I believe, not the creation of new meanings for the term but a movement from one of the ancient polar meanings to the other. For we must recall that the heritage from the

Latin also includes the personification *conscia virtus*, which Virgil had used more than once and which appeared with noteworthy frequency in poetic translations and works influenced by the Latin classics. In Latin *virtus* could mean almost any kind of power, from force to moral goodness, though one supposes that the idea of power prevailed. It seems to have been different in Christian England where the term *conscious virtue* and its cognates seem mostly, though by no means always to invoke goodness of character. As that moralization, if not Christianization, of the phrase took place, *conscious* came to be attached to so many ethical and psychological benefits that its guilt-associations seem to a somewhat less than systematic surveyor to have been, if not forgotten, at least strongly competed with. The personified virtues or values that wear the label *conscious* are impressive in number and dignity. The "conscious virtue" that the old Emperor in Dryden's *Aureng-Zebe* possesses even in his withered age (Act II, lines 395–397) may be the strength of a soldier rather than goodness—the aged hero may indeed be Virgil's good old wrestler Entellus *redivivus*. But when Dryden says in *The Hind and the Panther* that "conscious merit may be justly bold" (3:1381), when Pope finds that "conscious Honour is to feel no sin" (Bk. I, Ep. i, line 93 of Horace), when Johnson rejoices that the "conscious heart / With virtue's sacred ardour glows" (Horace, *Odes*, I, xxii; line 1), and perhaps even when Swift praises "conscious pride" ("Sir W——T——'s late Illness," line ll), we encounter only a fraction of the many ethical valorizations of *conscious*. Admittedly my examples come from contexts of poetic exaltation—even at times from fairly direct translations—and are not entirely free of neoclassical artificiality. But consider a fine passage in Hume's prose:

> Who is not struck with any signal instance of greatness of mind or dignity of character; with elevation of sentiment, disdain of slavery, and with that noble pride and spirit, which arises from conscious virtue?[17]

This noble association of a grand civic spirit with the Virgilian term shows that the innocent *conscious* no less than the guilty *conscious* is vastly more important than a recurring flicker of poetic ornament.

What did *conscious* mean for Steele? It is Hume's meanings, though with somewhat less civic and more individual *éclat*, which I believe to be primarily present in his famous dramatic title. The term is capacious and sturdy and can easily bear the weight of honorific language from *Spectator* 75, par. 4: "Humanity and good Nature, fortified by the Sense of Virtue." In fact, the word *Sense* may be a close equivalent of *consciousness*. Fortunately Steele obliges us by using our term directly and in ways that show a self-aware word-definer laboriously at his task. Will Honeycomb describes a woman in a nearby box as follows:

> Behold, you who dare, that charming Virgin. Behold the Beauty of her Person chastised by the Innocence of her Thoughts. Chastity, Good-Nature, and Affability are the Graces that play in her Countenance; she knows she is handsome, but she knows she is good. Conscious Beauty adorn'd with conscious Virte!
> (*Spectator* 4, par. 6)

The passage is highly revealing, to say the least. Steele lays heavy emphasis on the *science* (knowledge, of course, and a wide-eyed knowledge at that!) in consciousness. If Indiana and Bevil Junior in the play are conscious in this manner, they will inescapably know it. It is thus not sufficient to be honorable and chaste; you must be fully aware of your virtues and willing to discuss them at the proper time. Long before she can be sure of a happy resolution of her difficulties and while her maiden aunt continues to doubt Bevil Junior's sincerity, Indiana says of herself and her lover:

> I'll wrap myself up in the integrity of my own heart,
> nor dare to doubt of his.
> As conscious honor all his actions steers:
> So conscious innocence dispels my fears.
> (last lines of II.ii)

The psychological effects of this inner assurance on the behavior of the hero and heroine are very salutary, however much we today may wish to turn away from such self-approving joy. Because guilt had so insistently lurked in the word *conscious*, Steele's banishment of it in his bold assertion of the value of what is elsewhere called the "pure Consciousness of worthy Actions"[18] had a wide resonance. It must also have been supported by an alliance with a powerful tradition, for Steele was far from being great enough to have been a solitary pioneer in effecting intellectual or emotional change. The tradition I shall discuss in a moment.

The resonance I detect as far away as Blake, who uses the word *conscious* four times, not once with any implication of guilt. On one occasion Blake uses the word indubitably of himself: a friend who had been kind to him he hopes to repay "with the courage of conscious industry," evidence that as late as 1804 a Virgilian personification with *conscious* could be used quite naturally in a quotidian context.[19] In another place Blake identified himself with the prophets who gave us "the Sublime of the Bible," and who were "consciously & professedly Inspired Men," a fact that nerved them and their followers to action.[20] A third instance is Blake's definition of the "strong Man," related to his concept of the prophet and also to his own concept of himself: he "acts from conscious superiority, and marches on in fearless dependance on the divine decrees, raging with the inspirations of a prophetic mind."[21] Fourth, Blake applies the term to one of his poetic characters, who is ultimately ground down by an envious community to despairing self-distrust—to what Blake sees as the real terror of dull, spiritless, and uncreative humility. But she had begun her career as an embodiment of beauty, freedom, charm, and love:

> Mary moves in soft beauty & conscious delight
> To augment with sweet smiles all the joys of the Night,
> Nor once blushes to own to the rest of the Fair
> That sweet Love & Beauty are worthy our care.[22]

Before she falls into lonely despair and outward conformity, Blake's conscious lover is much less concerned with honor, chastity, or even conventional modesty than Steele's. But they are alike in rejecting from their consciousness guilt, shame, and depravity, each developing a version of Virgil's *conscia virtus*.

Such is the resonance of Steele's title. And now for a word about the tradition. Behind Blake's and Steele's consciousness there was of course the "conscious virtue" of many English writers who, in their attempts at one or another kind of poetic effect, at the very least kept the Virgilian phrase current. Behind Blake's "Strong-Man"-Prophet there stood, at least for a while, Milton's Satan, who when he spoke to his followers on the burning marl of hell spoke as a dignified rebel "with Monarchal pride / Conscious of highest worth" (*P.L.*, II, lines 428-429). Behind Blake's "conscious" Mary were the likes of Dryden's "conscious" Eleonora, who "Scarcely knew that she was great or fair" and yet paradoxically did:

> For to be conscious of what all admire,
> And not be vain, advances virtue high'r.

> For to be conscious of what all admire,
> And not be vain, advances virtue high'r.
>   (lines 100-101)

And behind Blake and perhaps also Steele was a version of Christian conscience powerful in Anglo-Saxon culture—not the inner judge and lawgiver I discussed earlier but "the blessed assurance," to use the dissenters' idiom, which was at once the consolation and inspiration of those believers who rested their spiritual awareness on Romans 8:16: "The Spirit itself beareth witness with our spirit, that we are the children of God." To be conscious of that witness—to "know with" that kind of inward energy—was considerably different from an awareness of an internal judge or lawgiver. And it may be an irony of history that so strongly a Christian concept should have driven the *virtus* of *conscia virtus* back to the more primary pagan meaning of power and strength. For in order to restore power to consciousness Blake was purposely and often blazingly irreverent and even immoral in his rhetoric. Few others were so bold and individualistic as he, but no consideration of *conscious* in Protestant England could possibly ignore a tradition that was often charismatic and antinomian. God the Holy Spirit had breathed on the concept of consciousness.

III

Do you *know* or do you *feel* power within? Obviously no sharp separation can be made, though it strikes me as natural to say that we *know* an inner law and *feel* an inner energy. In other words, the content of consciousness affects its nature. The change that we have been noticing—from law to energy, from virtue as legal goodness to virtue as power—is a change in content. I believe there is a comparable shift in the suffix of the adjective itself—from science meaning knowledge to science conceived of as emotion. The dynamics of *conscious* shifts from "knowing with" to "feeling with," and the word takes its place in the complex history of sensibility.

It would, once more, be a mistake to set up a rigid contrast: Aristotle and Samuel Johnson were by no means the only thinkers in Western culture to emphasize that pleasure (and other emotions, too) accompanies knowledge and that in the end the two cannot be separated. Yet there is a scale of values running from reason to the heart, and human attention can register responses all along that range. Shared knowledge, one supposes, can theoretically be neutral enough, but the very fact that a secret is kept and shared tends to make the mutual knowledge tremble with fear or glow with emotion. The secret can eat like the canker worm, hell itself being an inexorable alliance with one's own preferences. But the secret within can also titillate—do I need to appeal to childhood experience? Such emotional associations perhaps explain why a word with *science* at its root should have entered poetry in the first place. And this much can certainly be said for even some of the most conventional personifications of poetic diction—that they often imply that the world is a great sensorium. The groves in Denham's *Cooper's Hill* (line 277) are "conscious" because they are associated with love and triumph; in Dryden's *Astraea Redux* (line 245) the winds that blow the royal vessel are "conscious of their charge"; Pope's "conscious morn" is painted with blushes (from Ovid: *Sappho to Phaon*, line 98); Gray's "conscious truth" possesses "struggling pangs" (*Elegy*, line 69); and Cowper's Deity, conceived of as a "conscious cause," exerts ceaseless pressure on matter (*Task*, VI, line 220). In these examples *conscious* is a means of uniting animated nature and human life in bonds of sympathy.

In the relations of man to man and of man to God the person we find a similar conflation of consciousness and sensibility. In one of his typically exciting sentences, the Restoration preacher, Robert South, says that "To be a friend, and to be conscious, are terms equivalent." The context of the remark is not, as one might think, that of the traditional classical essay on friendship, in which the friend is another self with whom we share knowledge. South's meaning is that Christian man is a friend of God, from whom no secrets are hid, and that God is a friend of man, to whom divine secrets are totally revealed. For this sublime knowing-feeling together, even the noble word friendship is not strong enough, for South says, "Love is the greatest of human affections, and friendship is the noblest and most refined improvement of love."[23] An eighteenth-century writer might thus have quite naturally referred to the "conscious Enoch" or the "conscious Abraham," both of whom walked and talked with God.

Setting aside both religion and animated nature for the moment, we must consider how purely human intercourse provides an emotional consciousness that takes on a peculiarly eighteenth-century coloration, at least in the ensemble or pattern of association that formed around the *coeur sensible*. Thomson refers to "the conscious heart of Charity" (*Winter*, line 354); the author of *Spectator* 224 refers to the "pure Consciousness of worthy Actions" and assigns this heightened awareness to the "generous mind," for whom such consciousness is itself "an ample Reward" (par. 2). Let me show how, in translating a simple and moving scene in *The Odyssey*, the translator embroiders it with the language of sensibility. Nausicaa, led to believe that she is destined to remain a maid not much longer, asks her father to give her a wagon in which to carry her wedding garments. Modest about the "coming" event, she is of course vague about her true purpose, which she covers up by pretending to be concerned about washing her brothers' clothes. But her father knows everything (παντα νόει [*panta noei*]) and provides the royal wagon at once. One may of course prefer Homer's simple directness—the girl addresses her father as παππα φιλ' (*pappa phil*) and Homer calls him πατρὶ φίλῳ (*patri philo*)— finding these brief simple words sufficient to convey all the necessary feeling. The eighteenth-century elaboration, however, is an interesting example of the sentimental associations of consciousness:

> ... blushes ill-restrain'd betray
> Her thoughts intentive on the bridal day:
> The conscious sire the dawning blush survey'd.[24]

The sire would not have deserved the honorific *conscious* had he not immediately granted her request, for the adjective here means perceptive, loving, kindly, considerate of the girl's natural embarrassment.

The juxtaposition in the translation of Nausicaa's blush and the word *conscious* brings me to my own juxtaposition of sex and sensibility. In a revealing bit of Podsnappery, Mr. Podsnap regards his young daughter as "a certain institution" in his mind—by which phrase I take Dickens to mean the foolish father's tendency to abridge the girl's actuality so that he can respond, not to the real girl but to his own stereotype of her, which he keeps calling "the young person." It is that stereotype, not what Dickens intended Georgiana Podsnap really to be, that interests me now:

> The question about everything was, would it bring a blush into the cheek of the young person? And the inconvenience of the young person was that, according to Mr. Podsnap, she seemed always

liable to burst into blushes when there was no need at all. There appeared to be no line of demarcation between the young person's excessive innocence, and another person's guiltiest knowledge.[25]

Christopher Ricks, who finds Podsnap "a very nineteenth-century figure," finds also that "the young person" embodies a paradoxical mixture of innocence and guilt which he finds romantic: "a disconcerting mixed feeling very different from the old clarity of demarcation."[26] But eighteenth-century explorations of the frontiers between innocence and guilt reveal that it knew very well this "disconcerting mix" and had already challenged the "old clarity of demarcation." The heroines of Otway, Richardson, and Austen, Sterne's portrayal of My Uncle Toby and the Widow Wadman, several of the girls in Watteau, Greuze, and Mozart's librettos, and Blake's virgin Thel often tremble with mixed guilt and innocence on the edge of experience, a confusion of which the blush was of course not always the overt sign.[27] Even the seasoned goddess Juno, partly no doubt because of her desire to maintain matronly respectability, colors in the manner of Miss Podsnap when in the *Iliad* she decides to distract Jove's attention from the battlefield by using the aphrodisiac cestus she had borrowed from Venus. The sexually-aroused father of the gods suggests that he be allowed to gratify his desires on Mount Ida in his golden cloud. As Pope translates Homer,

> He spoke; the Goddess with the charming Eyes
> Glows with celestial Red and thus replies,
> Is this a Scene for Love? (XIV, lines 373-375)

Maynard Mack says, rightly, that "Pope remembers [Milton's] Raphael on angelic love";[28] to express her sense of delicate embarrassment a lesser, though typical, poet might have given to Juno "conscious" eyes and "conscious" cheeks.

On a much less exalted level but with the same psycho-sexual dynamics, Richardson actually uses the word to describe the emotions of the younger Sorlings girl, who permitted Lovelace to kiss her. She immediately became *"sensible all over."* When her elder sister "popped upon her," "the conscious girl blushed again."[29] Professor Sherbo would have us read guilty for conscious,[30] but Lovelace is closer than the scholar to the complex though humble and quotidian reality his creator is developing: he believes the girl is truly innocent but only "confounded," embarrassed, and still hungry for his continuing attention. I do not want us to forget what I said earlier, that *conscious* often referred to overt and fixed feelings of sexual guilt. But I want us now to confront a sensibility of the erotic, sometimes delicately colored with guilt, sometimes not, which I find to be an important eighteenth-century literary mode. Milton's "blushing" Eve is of course not guilty; she is clad in "Innocence and Virgin Modestie" (VIII, lines 501, 511), and she also possesses "conscience of her worth" (line 502). Paradoxically, that "conscience" is not entirely unlike the consciousness of highest worth that gives force to Satan's confident rhetoric; to Eve it gives the dignified assurance, despite her modest fears, that she has a full right to require of Adam a formal suit for her hand. And yet Eve's skin, like that of Raphael's, is susceptible to the rosy red of angelic amorousness presaging the delights of the Edenic bower of bliss. Blake, who tried to create a more aggressive Daughter of Albion, free of guilty inhibitions, was an enemy of the blush. Milton and the eighteenth century were not. For the delicately complex mixture of guilt and innocence, of raptures at once desired and feared, conveyed by the blush, there could hardly have been a more appropriate word than *conscious*.

For the sake of completeness I must turn, however briefly, to the robust Dryden, who certainly respected female modesty and who could also use our term to denote real guilt. Neither applies to the love which Aureng-Zebe feels for his beloved's body: "my conscious Limbs presage / Torrents of joy, which all their banks o'rflow!" (Act IV, lines 540-541). Here the adjective refers to sexual arousal that appears not to be condemned, where human limbs stand as a not very subtle substitute for a more sensitive member.

In these ways, then—sexually and socially, delicately and robustly, institutionally and naturally—*conscious* was associated with feeling, and it may not be irrelevant to note that the Latin prefix *con* and the Greek *sun*, besides meaning *with*, were also intensifiers, adding the notion of *altogether* or *completely*. We should not therefore be surprised to find that influential and normative philosopher, John Locke, defining being, or self, in terms of sensibility. "*Self* is that conscious thinking thing, . . . which is sensible, or conscious of Pleasure and Pain, capable of Happiness or Misery, and so is concern'd for it *self*, as far as that consciousness extends."[31] Similarly, though later, Abraham Rees, who duly discriminates the traditional ethical and theological meanings, nevertheless defines *conscience* in its self-reflective qualities, as "the source and cause of all that joy, or dejection of mind, of those internal sensations of pleasure or pain, which attend the practice of great virtues or great vices."[32] Clarissa may at times have wished that her heart did not so often misgive her; nevertheless, she felt that she had to trust it particularly when it gave powerful signals: "in so strong and involuntary a bias, the *heart* is, as I may say, *conscience*."[33] Thus once again conscience and conscious come into phase, and we see the profound moral seriousness within the conscious of sensibility that may underlie even its lighter manifestations.

IV

If you conceive of conscience as based solely or primarily on the reason, you can perhaps regard daylight, waking introspection as sufficient for understanding the inner life. But the heart beats on in darkness and in sleep, and sensibility may, willy–nilly, bring us to the frontiers of the unconscious. At the very least we are led by our discussion of the emotions to ask: does the unconscious lurk in the eighteenth-century word *conscious*? I have already tried to show that in its range of greatly varied meanings, it is a complex word. Does it also possess the *structure* of a complex word? That is, do the surprising contrasts that William Empson found in words affect or reflect the very structure of *conscious*? We remember that he paused before the phenomenon of a word like *sensibility*, which was "rightly used to describe and praise discriminating reactions" but at the same time was "twisted round to describe and praise excessive reactions."[34] Well, *conscious* did, as we have seen, contain within it meanings as diverse as guilt and innocence. Centuries of religious introspection and evaluation had inevitably produced both acquitting and condemnatory responses in the consciousness. Our word is in itself neutral, even vacant, as we saw at the outset, and welcomes being filled up from the psyche or from whatever guides or forms the inner man. By its very nature, then—by its structure, if you will—the word is open to the conflicting meanings that have in fact been its referents. But I press on. Is the word also a primal word, with a sense inevitably antithetical to its basic meaning? Is it like Freud's *heimlich* which refers to the home and the intimately familiar but which attracted to its orbit its very opposite, the *unheimlich*, the uncanny or the terrible?[35] If so, the *conscious*, already a complex word with greatly diverse and even contradictory meanings, would sooner or later become linked with the *unconscious*. Today we like to think in this way, and examples abound in contemporary criticism of our fascination with antithetical, even mutually annihilating words.[36] What is more natural than for us to think that conscious calls up the unconscious as host invokes the lurking enemy *hostis*, as host also calls up parasite, as constituting invites deconstituting, analysis paralysis, idealism skepticism—or, most commonly and basically, as rational logocentricity invokes linguistic deconstruction.

The reality in eighteenth-century thought regarding the unconscious seems to be at once simpler and profounder, if the hypothesis I shall now propose has validity. But first we must note that the Restoration and eighteenth century certainly knew of the realm of the unconscious. Early in his career Dryden described the primal condition of one of his dramatic efforts "long before it was a Play; When it was only a confus'd Mass of Thoughts, tumbling over one another in the Dark: When the Fancy was yet in its first Work, moving the Sleeping Images of things towards the Light, . . . "[37] The realm of the unconscious was that of "the Chaos dark and deep, / Where nameless somethings in their causes sleep."[38] Both Dryden and Pope locate the sleeping prefigurations of art within the mind of man. Even Johnson, who was uncomfortable about fog and darkness in the psyche, certainly recognized the unconscious, at least in external nature. Imlac says that "all the notices of sense and investigations of science concur to prove the unconsciousness of matter," and *unconscious* means that matter is "inert, senseless and lifeless." But he does give to it "form, density, bulk, motion, and direction of motion"—the last two being noteworthy here. Johnson the amateur scientist and lover of experiments applied such active and dynamic "philosophic words" as the following from matter to the operations of the intellect: coalesce, dissolve, exhale, impregnate; elastick, volatile; attraction, oscillation, paroxysm, velocity.[39] Matter might indeed be unconscious, but it was far from being inactive or unproductive, as any chemist would know.

Let us return to human consciousness. In trying to show how the unconscious might conceivably operate there, I must remind you of a debate among the philosophers and psychologists of the eighteenth century regarding the existence of the self. Locke asserted flatly that we perceive our own existence plainly and infallibly: "In every Act of Sensation, Reasoning, or Thinking, we are conscious to our selves of our own Being; and, in this Matter, come not short of the highest degree of Certainty" (*Essay*, 4, 9, 3). Hume's consciousness possessed no such certainty, though he used, with some modification, the method of observation and reflection characteristic of his predecessor. Hume could never "catch" *himself*, as he put it; he caught only fleeting, particular glimpses of the self, and he therefore was forced to conclude that the self was only "a bundle or collection of different perceptions, which succeed each other with an inconceivable rapidity, and are in a perpetual flux and movement." The "I" is not an invariable identity, but only a succession of parts or a network of relations seemingly held together by some principle of union like soul or substance which we feign, by some cohering principle which we only imagine. When we sleep or after we die we surely lose identity. Hume means to say that by rooting our existence in perception and thought about perception, Locke had proceeded precariously. There are too many vacancies in our perception to permit the conviction of a continuous, identical existence.[40] The empirical tradition tended to lose permanent, unchanging, uninterrupted identity by anchoring it in consciousness, which experience can easily show has gaping vacancies within it.

Coleridge, on the other hand, though he found man to exist to himself only in moments, postulated a class of infinite beings, "who tho' not conscious of the whole of their continuousness, are yet both conscious of *a* continuousness, & make that the object of reflex consciousness."[41] Coleridge's subjectively-derived "continuousness" of being (which man can shadow) had been prepared for by almost a century of philosophic and religious thought and polemics. Joseph Butler refused to believe that personal identity could be grounded in memory or consciousness: " . . . consciousness of personal identity presupposes, and therefore cannot constitute personal identity."[42] Later, Thomas Reid refused to identify consciousness with memory and preferred to separate the present conscious from all recollection of the past and even from simple present empirical perception.[43] Zachary Mayne, the putative author of an *Essay on Consciousness*, which proclaimed itself a pioneering work, elevated consciousness above dreaming, above imagination, above all sensation, and based it on "the Mind's intellectual

Nature and Essence,"[44] even though the conscious mind could be involved in the lesser functions. And Berkeley, in a clearly pre-Kantian passage, shifted from "me" (the object of consciousness) to "I," its subject, which he distinguished sharply from color, sound, shape—indeed from all "sensible things and inert ideas": ". . . I know or am conscious of my own being; and that I my self am not my ideas, but somewhat else, a thinking active principle that perceives, knows, wills, and operates about ideas. I know that . . . I am . . . one individual principle. . . . "[45] We are not far away from Kant's "unity of consciousness which precedes all data of intuitions," not far from that "pure original unchangeable consciousness" which he named "*transcendental apperception.*"[46]

What does all this have to do with the unconscious? Simply this: that the philosophy of idealism and transcendence implies it. By shifting from me to I, from object to subject, from the known to the knower, you must posit an entity that itself slumbers not nor sleeps, that structures reality, produces rational forms, and makes imaginative, intellectual, and linguistic linkages while the body is in sleep, trance, rapture, perhaps even in senility and states of forgetfulness. Ultimately it is God who will have to sanction what Coleridge was so passionately desirous of having—continuousness of being. But on the purely human level, if he wants continuous identity, man must place the soul outside memory, outside daylight perception, outside empirical consciousness. It is not an exaggeration to say that without this postulation of identity in the unconscious the whole fabric of religion and the whole notion of human integrity would collapse. It is thus that the conscious implies the unconscious. Indeed, the demand of idealistic philosophy for the assumption of continuous, coherent identity, of Being itself, calls into dialectical existence the realm of the unconscious. Such is the Great Implication of philosophy. It prepared the way for a remarkable extension of the idea of the unconscious in the Romantic period, an enrichment and sophistication we cannot discuss here.

Some post-Modernist theory seems to insist that language itself inevitably erects binary structures and that the unconscious would of course be implicated in the conscious by the very processes of thought and rhetoric. But such linguistic and epistemological fatalism is not, I believe, characteristic of the Great Implication of the unconscious that I see in Berkeley and Kant and the lesser writers I have mentioned. All these, as religious men who wanted to be free and responsible, were shocked by the gaps and vacancies in continuity left by the empiricists. Idealist-transcendental thought extended being into these interstices and so created a logical continuum. But it also vitalized and personalized that continuum, creating not so much a Great Chain of Being as what Pope called "the chain of Love" (*Essay on Man*, 3:7).

V

Does what I have called the Great Implication of the unconscious embrace Johnson and Jane Austen, neither one a professional philosopher but both authors who used the term *conscious* frequently, sensitively, and in ways highly relevant to their art and thought? Johnson's definition of *unconscious* is brief—almost dismissive, in a way that would be impossible in our own day or even in the Romantic period: the word for him means, *tout court*, "Having no mental perception." But the most recent student of the creative imagination, James Engell, has said that "Johnson probes the unconscious mind . . . with a brilliant, stubborn persistence unrivalled before Freud. He is aware that the door is always open between imagination and every impulse, instinct, and emotion, at every level from the rudimentary to the sophisticated."[47] There is much to be said for this view, which had earlier been stated by Walter Jackson Bate. I should prefer, however, to put matters a bit differently. Johnson was of course aware that psychological links were automatically forged in the dark—that one vice, for example, could be magnetically attracted to another, sometimes a virtue to a vice, sometimes an excess to a defect—all this because of the very structure of the psyche, without volition, without choice. But such processes might easily darken reason or abridge freedom. In Dryden the fancy moves the "sleeping Images of things towards the Light [and now I finish the quotation given only in part earlier] there to be Distinguish'd, and then either chosen or rejected by the Judgment" (see note 37). Whether the fancy in such an operation always works automatically, unconsciously, I do not know. But I do know that Johnson wanted all such activities brought into the light, by an act of rational volition. In noting that Swift believed men to be "grateful in the same degree as they are resentful," Johnson may in fact be confronting a link formed in the unconscious by the very nature and structure of desire. But he goes on: "This principle, with others of the same kind, supposes man to act from a brute impulse, and pursue a certain degree of inclination, without any choice of the object; for otherwise, though it should be allowed that gratitude and resentment arise from the same constitution of the passions, it follows not that they will be equally indulged when reason is consulted" (*Rambler* 4, par. 16). Thus there is an unconscious, but that unconscious is not fate. For Johnson, moreover, even the realm of the unconscious could be conceived of as partly self-created, a realm that is dark because the self-flattering eye chooses to make it so by willfully not observing it. "It seems generally believed, that, as the eye cannot see itself, the mind has no faculties by which it can contemplate its own state. . . ." That belief Johnson finds sophistical—and all too easy. It has "commodious consequences"—that is, it soothes the ego. "Self-love is often rather arrogant than blind; . . . We are secretly conscious of defects and vices which we hope to conceal from the publick eye, . . . " (*Rambler* 155, pars. 2, 3). Note well that Johnson does indeed explore the unconscious, but with a searchlight that exposes it for what it really is: not the unconscious, really, but the "secretly conscious," a vastly different kind of realm, created by the self escaping itself—a realm, however, which can be reclaimed by the ethical reason.

> He therefore that would govern his actions by the laws of virtue, . . . must keep guilt from the recesses of his heart, and remember that the pleasures of fancy, and the emotions of desire are more dangerous as they are more hidden, since they escape the awe of observation, . . .   (*Rambler* 8, last par.)

Johnson, as profoundly religious a thinker as the eighteenth century produced, surely realized, as Coleridge did later, that "the spiritual in man . . . lies on the other side of our natural consciousness," which is the realm of observed fact and of the combining, judging mind. This realm of "ulterior consciousness," truly "a land of darkness" to the average man, must be where the primary imagination of Coleridge does its eternal, ongoing work of translating the infinite into the finite—a realm very close to the unconscious I have postulated as necessarily present in all idealist philosophy. But both Coleridge and Johnson realized that human creation and action take place in a more illuminated place. For Coleridge artistic creation occurs in the secondary imagination, which is a power "co-existing with the conscious will."[48] And, as we have just seen, Johnson believes that the good life—and surely good art as well—are created by the very same conscious will, which operates under what he calls, in the thrilling phrase I have quoted, "the awe of observation."

I do not know that such large philosophical considerations as these apply to Johnson's disciple, Jane Austen, or that she knew or cared much about the idealist-transcendental implication of unconsciousness or even of synapses made in the unreflecting psychic depths. I find possible Freudian *double entendres* in her work to be so infrequent as to be negligible,[49] though I do believe that her pages are often alive with amorous, even sexual, excitement. One of the many instruments of rendering that excitement was Austen's use of the word *conscious*, which is varied enough to constitute a summary of the meanings we have explored and subtle enough to provide examples of the word's employment in high art. The etymological meaning, involving both syllables of the word, is present. Near the end of *Mansfield Park* Fanny Price, her younger sister Susan, and Mr. Henry Crawford, now in pursuit of Fanny but of course inhibited here by the presence of the sister, go on a picnic in Portsmouth. In this situation he must content himself "with the indulgence, now and then, of a look or hint for the better informed and conscious Fanny" (III, x). Here the word means that Fanny knows more than Susan knows and that she knows it *with* Henry —knows, that is, everything that has gone before, including her coolness and his heat. When at the beginning of *Emma*, the heroine experiences a "gentle sorrow," it comes "not at all in the shape of any disagreeable consciousness," where "guilt" can be substituted for "consciousness" without any violence whatever to the meaning (I, i). Exempted from that kind of consciousness at the beginning, Emma feels it in her relations with Harriet at the end, for the heroine's dangerous prevalence of imagination has led her to tamper with another's soul. Emma senses resentment in her protegé's letter now that Harriet has learned to whom Mr. Knightley's love is indeed directed: "It might be only her own [Emma's] consciousness [that is, a perception colored by a sense of guilt], but it seemed as if an angel only could have been quite without resentment under such a stroke" (III, xvi). Variants of Virgil's *conscia virtus* appear everywhere in Austen; for example, the

Fanny Price who has become beautiful might now be called the "conscious Fanny," as she is elsewhere, for, like Blake's Mary, the girl now "saw that she was approved; and the consciousness of looking well, made her look still better" (II, x).

Austen's considerable arsenal of effects includes as a favorite weapon *conscious* as sensibility, or heightened feeling, both with and without erotic coloration, but especially with. Toward the end of *Northanger Abbey* Catherine Morland introduces the man she loves and will marry to her mother: "With a look of much respect, he immediately rose, and being introduced to her by her conscious daughter as 'Mr. Henry Tilney,' with the embarrassment of real sensibility began to apologize for his appearance there" (see note 2). Such sensitive consciousness can be very strong indeed, as Fanny Price learns when, after dismaying her uncle with her determined refusal of her suitor, she "walk[s] off in agitating consciousness" and finds "herself, as she anticipated, in another minute alone with Mr. Crawford"—a scene in which the "conscious" Fanny's emotions are complex indeed (III, i).

It goes without saying that the *conscious* in Jane Austen includes the social and ethical awareness that Johnson made fundamental in his teaching. Early in *Mansfield Park* Sir Thomas wants to "preserve in the minds of my *daughters* the consciousness of what they are, without making them think too lowly of their cousin" (I, i). At the end Sir Thomas has learned by hard experience that the cousin, Fanny Price, along with her brother and sister, possessed "the advantages of early hardship and discipline, and the consciousness of being born to struggle and endure" (III, xvii). What good consciousness included for Jane Austen appears in her judgment of Fanny's politely reared cousin Julia, who lacks "that higher species of self-command, that just consideration of others, that knowledge of her own heart [note this phrase well!], that principle of right which had not formed any essential part of her education" (I, ix). Austen had absorbed the Johnsonian lessons and seems also to have heeded Steele's implicit demand that the consciousness needs governance.[50]

But the term is artistically useful to Austen for other than ethical reasons. To "know with" oneself, to "know with" another, to be aware delicately, sensitively, erotically, even nervously and vividly, if we remember that *con* is also an intensifier—these are the very traits that separate the artistically rounded character from the caricature. Great faults, even potentially self-destructive errors of perception, do not necessarily forfeit our sympathies if the character is "conscious" —witness the career of Marianne Dashwood in *Sense and Sensibility*. Opposed to such characters as these is that gallery of fools and knaves, of conventionally or pompously good characters, sometimes cruel, more often thoughtless. These are the unconscious ones. And the two hemispheres of conscious and unconscious are indispensable to one another, rounding out to an artistic globe.

I cannot say that these obverse realms in Jane Austen, though one requires the other, do indeed interpenetrate or "interinanimate" globally. But it is my claim that they do within the word *conscious* itself—in Jane Austen and earlier—particularly when it embodies sensibility. Then the very word becomes a vital and organic world, where guilt and innocence meet and are sometimes revealed by the ambiguous blush, where shared secrets can have ambivalent relations, where sexual excitement joins charity and benevolence, where even awareness itself requires or impinges on the realm of dark, nameless somethings sleeping in a state of psychological pre-existence, and even where gaps in the empirically guided consciousness imply the unconscious existence of continuous responsible being. *Conscious* then discloses the structures of human sensitivity, and to describe its complex interior dynamics we may find the language of Wordsworth about "the best feelings of our nature" to be suggestive:

> feelings which, though they seem opposite to each other, have another and a finer connection than that of contrast. It is a connection formed through the subtle progress by which, both in the natural and the moral world, qualities pass insensibly into their contraries, and things revolve upon each other.[51]

NOTES

I wish to thank Marshall Brown, Christopher Fox, Donald Greene, and Paul Hunter, who read this paper in an early draft and made valuable suggestions.

1. *Laodamia*, line 65.
2. Dryden, "Sigismonda and Guiscardo" (from Boccaccio), lines 151-152; Pope, *Windsor Forest*, line 90; Richardson, *Clarissa* (London: Everyman's Library, 1932), II, 22; Austen, *Northanger Abbey* (Oxford: World's Classics, 1976), p. 262.
3. William Cowper, *The Task*, IV, lines 284-285.
4. *Aeneid*, IV, lines 165-172.

5. Dryden's translation (XII, lines 967-972) of *Aeneid* XII, lines 665-668. Virgil's use of *conscia virtus* (line 668) should be compared with his use of precisely the same phrase to refer to an inner power that impels the aged Entellus to drive a younger man before him in rekindled strength and fury (V, line 455).
6. "Conscience and Conscious," chapter 8 of *Studies in Words* (Cambridge: Cambridge University Press, 1967), p. 191.
7. Timothy C. Potts, *Conscience in Medieval Philosophy* (Cambridge: Cambridge University Press, 1980), p. 4.
8. In his review of my *Sex and Sensibility* (Chicago, Ill.: University of Chicago Press, 1980) in *Modern Philology*, 79 (February, 1982), 323-326. Responding to his corrections and suggestions, I have in this article attempted a fuller treatment than was possible in my book (Index, s.v. "Conscious"), or indeed in Sherbo's review or in his own earlier study of the word as a term of poetic diction. See *English Poetic Diction from Chaucer to Wordsworth* (East Lansing: Michigan State University Press, 1975).
9. See E[dward] P[hillips], *The New World of English Words* (London, 1662, 1706); [Thomas Blount], *Glossographia* (London, 1670); *Glossographia Anglicana Nova* (London, 1707); Nathan Bailey, *Dictionarium Britannicum* (London, 1730); Thomas Dyche and William Pardon, *A New General English Dictionary* (London, 1744).
10. Donald Greene, *The Age of Exuberance: Backgrounds to Eighteenth-Century English Literature* (New York: Random House, 1970), pp. 92-100.
11. *Clarissa*, II, pp. 306, 378-79.
12. John Arthos, *The Language of Natural Description in Eighteenth-Century Poetry* (Ann Arbor: University of Michigan Press, 1949), pp. 122–123 and Sherbo, *English Poetic Diction*.
13. "Ode on the Death of a Favorite Cat . . .," line 7: "Her conscious tail her joy declar'd." Geoffrey Tillotson's comment is sensitive but perhaps endows the line with too much loftiness and somberness: "No better word than *conscious* could be applied to the stealthy expressiveness of a cat's tail, but the word was enriched for the reader of 1748 because of the status and colouring of *conscious* amid the poetic diction of a great deal of the world's poetry. Its status had been of the highest, and its colour of the darkest." *Augustan Studies* (London: Athlone Press, 1961), p. 77.
14. Marshall Brown, "The Pre-Romantic Discovery of Consciousness," *Studies in Romanticism*, 17 (Fall, 1978), 387–412, esp. 398–399.
15. *Studies in Words*, p. 207.
16. Johnson, *Dictionary*: "1. Endowed with the power of knowing one's own thoughts and actions. . . . 2. Knowing from memory; having the knowledge of any thing without any new information. . . . 3. Admitted to the knowledge of any thing; with *to*. 4. Bearing witness by conscience to any thing." Thomas Sheridan, *A Complete Dictionary of the English Language* (2nd ed., London, 1789): "Endowed with the power of knowing one's own thoughts and actions; knowing from memory; admitted to the knowledge of any thing."
17. David Hume, *An Enquiry concerning the Principles of Morals*, in the *Enquiries*, ed. L. A. Selby-Bigge, rev. P. H. Nidditch, 3rd ed. (Oxford: Clarendon Press, 1975), par. 204 in sec. vii, p. 252. Also see the longer discussion "Of Greatness of Mind" in *A*

Treatise of Human Nature, ed. L. A. Selby-Bigge, rev. P. H. Nidditch, 2nd ed. (Oxford: Clarendon Press, 1978), III, iii, sec. ii, pp. 592–602.

18. *Spectator* 224, par. 2. The Spectatorial comments on consciousness are close to those of Joseph Butler in his Sermon "Upon Self-Deceit" (Sermon X of *Fifteen Sermons*): "Truth, and real good sense, and thorough integrity, carry along with them a peculiar consciousness of their own genuineness: there is a feeling belonging to them, which does not accompany their counterfeits. . . . " I quote from W. E. Gladstone's edition of *The Works* (Oxford: Clarendon Press, 1896), II, p. 179.

19. Letter to William Hayley, 23 October 1804, in *Blake: Complete Writings*, ed. Geoffrey Keynes (Oxford: Clarendon Press, 1969), p. 851. The friend is one John Hawkins.

20. Preface to *Milton* in *Complete Writings*, p. 480. It might prove fruitful to investigate the use of *conscious* in the literature of dissent to see if there is a specific background to Blake's usage.

21. *A Descriptive Catalogue*, Number V, *Complete Writings*, p. 580.

22. "Mary," lines 9-12, from the Pickering MS, *Complete Writings*, p. 428.

23. *Sermons Preached upon Several Occasions* (Philadelphia, 1844), Sermon xiv in Vol. I, pp. 225, 233.

24. The Greek phrases come from *Odyssey* (VI, lines 51, 57). The translation, quoted from Pope's *Odyssey* (VI, lines 79–81), is apparently by William Broome. See George Sherburn, *The Early Career of Alexander Pope* (Oxford: Clarendon Press, 1934), p. 260.

25. *Our Mutual Friend*, Book I, chapter xi.

26. *Keats and Embarrassment* (Oxford: Clarendon Press, 1974), p. 4.

27. See Hagstrum, *Sex and Sensibility* (Chicago, Ill.: Chicago University Press, 1980), Index, s. v. "Innocence."

28. Pope's *Iliad*, ed. Maynard Mack *et al.* (London and New Haven, Conn.: Methuen and Yale University Press, 1967), Twickenham Edition, Vii, p. cxlvii, n. 3.

29. *Clarissa*, II, p. 22.

30. "Quite flatly, the meaning of 'conscious' in Lovelace's letter is 'guilty'": Sherbo, *Modern Philology*, 325.

31. *An Essay concerning Human Understanding*, ed. P. H. Nidditch (Oxford: Clarendon Press, 1975), p. 341. I believe it is valid to associate Locke's view of the mind with sensibility, but I recognize that this association rests on a more fundamental matter, Locke's use of consciousness as the criterion of personal identity. For a searching discussion of this belief, the background for it, and the reaction to it, see Christopher Fox, "Locke and the Scriblerians: The Discussion of Identity in Early Eighteenth–Century England," *Eighteenth-Century Studies*, 16 (Fall, 1982), 1–25. The Lockean definition of the self is not an easy idea to derive from his work. Observe in *Essay*, 2, 27, 24–25 how he wavers between identifying it with substance and saying it comes and goes with consciousness. See the useful article by David P. Behan, "Locke on Persons and Personal Identity" in the *Canadian Journal of Philosophy*, 9 (1979), 53–75.

32. *The Cyclopaedia: or Universal Dictionary of Arts, Sciences, and Literature* (Philadelphia, n. d.), Vol. X, n.p., under "Conscience." The first edition appeared in London in 1728.

33. *Clarissa*, I, p. 460. Clarissa, now a prisoner of Lovelace away from her home, is in mental anguish not only about what she should do next, but because Anna Howe has been making imputations of *"latent or unowned inclination"* in Clarissa (I, p. 455).
34. William Empson, *The Structure of Complex Words* (Totowa, N.J.: Rowman and Littlefield, 1979), p. 250.
35. See Freud's "The Antithetical Sense of Primal Words" and "The 'Uncanny'," both of which appear, translated, in *On Creativity and the Unconscious*, ed. Benjamin Nelson (New York: Harper, 1958), pp. 55–62, 122–161.
36. See, for example, J. Hillis Miller, "The Critic as Host," in *Deconstruction and Criticism*, ed. Harold Bloom *et al.* (New York: Seabury Press, 1979), pp. 217–253.
37. Dryden's dedication to Roger, Earl of Orrery in his Preface to *The Rival Ladies* (first sentence). See Lancelot Law Whyte, *The Unconscious before Freud* (New York: Basic Books, 1962), where the Dryden passage is quoted and where other examples are given, notably one by Ralph Cudworth in *The Intellectual System of the Universe* (1678), cited on pp. 95–96.
38. Pope, *Dunciad* (A), lines 53–54. In the Dryden and Pope passages we must leave open the possibility that the authors refer, though with vivid metaphors, merely to the inchoate or unformed.
39. The *Rasselas* quotations come from chapter 48. The examples of Johnson's scientific terminology I have drawn from the long list provided by W. K. Wimsatt in *Philosophic Words* (New Haven, Conn.: Yale University Press, 1948), appendix A.
40. The quotations from Hume all come from the section entitled "Of Personal Identity" in *Treatise of Human Nature*, I, iv, 6, pp. 251–263.
41. Letter to Thomas Clarkson, 13 October 1806, in the *Collected Letters*, ed. Earl Leslie Griggs (Oxford: Clarendon Press, 1956–), II, p. 1197.
42. "Of Personal Identity" in *The Whole Works of Joseph Butler* (London, 1852), p. 264. The essay I quote from is the first of two dissertations appended to *The Analogy of Religion*. Christopher Fox has pointed out to me that Butler, Reid, and others who had difficulty in accepting Locke's analysis of the self erroneously saw him as assimilating consciousness and memory, the latter being only a single mode of consciousness, which in its totality constituted the criterion of self-identity. For a criticism of the view that Locke equates consciousness and memory, see the article by Behan cited in note 31 above, 54–56.
43. Thomas Reid, *Essays on the Intellectual Powers of Man*, I, i, 7, in *Works*, ed. Sir William Hamilton (Edinburgh, 1863), I, pp. 222–223.
44. *Two Dissertations concerning Sense and the Imagination. With an Essay on Consciousness* (London, 1728), p. 147.
45. From the third of "Three Dialogues between Hylas and Philonous" in *The Works of George Berkeley*, ed. A. A. Luce and T. E. Jessop (London: Nelson, 1949), II, pp. 233–234. See also II, p. 231.
46. Immanuel Kant, *Critique of Pure Reason*, trans. Norman Kemp Smith (New York: St. Martin's Press, 1961), p. 136.
47. James Engell, *The Creative Imagination: Enlightenment to Romanticism* (Cambridge, Mass.: Harvard University Press, 1981), p. 61.
48. The Coleridge quotations all come from the *Biographia Literaria* (New York:

Dutton-Everyman, 1934), chapters 12 and 13, pp. 139, 140, 167.
49. See *Sex and Sensibility*, pp. 269–270.
50. In *Spectator* 38, par. 4, Steele describes the affectation that arises from "an ill govern'd Consciousness." We can avoid such folly "when our Consciousness turns upon the main Design of Life" (par. 5).
51. The first "Essay upon Epitaphs" in *The Prose Works of William Wordsworth*, ed. W. J. B. Owen and J. W. Smyser (Oxford: Clarendon Press, 1974), pp. 52–53.

Psychology and Politics in William Godwin's *Caleb Williams*: Double Bond or Double Bind?

MELINDA ALLIKER RABB

> He is like those twin-births, that have two heads, indeed, and four hands; but, if you attempt to detach them from each other, they are inevitably subjected to miserable and lingering destruction.[1]

"Disorders of intellect," Imlac says in *Rasselas*, "happen much more often than superficial observers will easily believe. . . . [I]f we speak with rigorous exactness, no human mind is in its right state." Godwin's *Caleb Williams or Things As They Are* shows "things" to be as Imlac proposes: most of its characters experience mental aberrations and behave in abnormal or peculiar ways. Lord Falkland "displays the marks of a furious insanity" (p. 105) because "his intellects [are] disordered": "The melancholy that had taken hold of his mind was invincible" (p. 123). Squire Tyrrel's overabundant "gall" has "stimulated him to a degree little short of madness" (p. 54). The Italian Count Malvesi is "stung even to madness," while his beloved Lady Lucretia undergoes "all the torments of frenzy" (p. 13). Emily Melville's "fits of delirium" and "suspended reason" eventually "gave birth to the wildest chimeras in her deluded imagination" (p. 42). Mr. Hawkins's thoughts are "mere madness," and the old hag in the den of thieves acts "with uncontrollable insanity" so that the "spectacle of her emotions was inconceivably frightful" (p. 231). Most important, the central character and narrator, Caleb himself, moves in and out of states of insanity with exhausting speed and, in the disjointed final paragraphs of the manuscript ending, concludes in raving incoherence.

If few minds in *Caleb Williams* are in their right state psychologically, fewer still are in their right state in the other meaning of the word: their political state. England, too, suffers disordered and diseased social institutions: legal and economic systems, class and family relationships, systems of education, or reward and punishment are all, like the characters, at least temporarily unhinged. At first, Godwin's dual subject matter—the constitution of the individual mind and the constitution of society—seems a superimposition, a double bond, as two meanings are bonded in the pun on "state." Other phrases from the novel encourage this sense of mutual reinforcement. Characters who wish to be "masters" of themselves may be enslaved by passion, as well as by powerful political authority (see, for example, pp. 54, 284, 313, 316: "I have a secret foreboding I shall never again be master of myself," says Caleb). Characters who idealize "self-possession," another frequent term, require freedom from irrationality, as well as liberty from coercive laws (pp. 5, 7, 31, 136). Yet, even as language seems to bond together psychology and politics in double meanings and a dual-purposed plot, the two modes of describing human experience chafe against each other; they are interconnected, but incompatible.

Caleb Williams, generally, builds upon doubles and doubling: it has two titles, two endings, two subjects, two narrators.[2] The protagonist finds versions of himself mirrored in others; the story of Emily Melville's love for Falkland, for example, parallels his own. (Godwin, elsewhere, suggests the further parallel to Bluebeard's wife.)[3] One minor character is paired with another: the two engines of revenge, Grimes and Gines; the two intellectuals, Clare and Brightwel; the two virtuous women, Emily and Laura, and so on. The central pair of antagonists, Caleb and Falkland, dominate the narrative in a kind of symbiotic interdependence: they are servant and master, pursuer and pursued; they embody guilt and innocence, power and vulnerability, partnership and enmity.[4] Their mutual dependence leads inevitably to paradox. They come to need each other for self-definition, yet all of their actions of loving/loathing are mutually destructive. (In this, they resemble that other psychologically interesting pair, Richardson's Lovelace and Clarissa.)[5] In Godwin's fictionalization of socio-economic realities, one aristocrat, who has almost everything, and one servant, who has almost nothing, join together to satisfy a shared need, in this case a need of language and books. Caleb begins his long career as a maker of texts by transcribing his master's letters, dictations, and literary compositions (p. 6). Caleb reinscribes and, eventually, authors Falkland. But by the end, both figures are utterly erased: Falkland dies, and Caleb has "now no character that I wish to vindicate" (p. 326).

As "things as they are" disintegrate around Caleb in volume three, he idealistically (and politically) claims that if he had told a "plain and unadulterated tale" to Falkland, "he could not have resisted my reasonable demand" (p. 323). So Godwin had linked reason and truth, the individual and the state, in *Political Justice*.[6] McCracken argues that the author's "rational vision of man's perfectibility through the power of truth suffused his imaginative portrayal of things as they are."[7] But does not the psychology of the novel discredit the existence of either truthtellers or rational listeners? When Caleb hears a tale told with "simplicity and accuracy," he describes the gradual triumph of irrational distortion:

> At first I was satisfied with thus considering every incident in its obvious sense. But the story I had heard was for ever in my thoughts, and I was peculiarly interested to comprehend its full import. I turned it a thousand ways, and examined it in every point of view. In the original communication it appeared sufficiently distinct and satisfactory; but, as I brooded over it, it gradually became mysterious. (p. 107)

Brooding, interpreting, transforming—this is the work of the imagination, a faculty, in the eighteenth-century view, ready to snuff out what Locke calls "that dim candle, our reason." In a novel in which telling and re-telling stories constitutes most of the action, problems of belief, certainty, and clarity recur incessantly. Language and its ambiguities, feeling and its shifts leave characters in perpetual flux between perception and doubt. "How knew I . . . ?" asks Caleb again and again.

Godwin offers explanations for "things as they are" in language that draws on earlier accounts of the human mind. Many of his sources are literary. Like Robert Burton's Democritus, Swift's narrator in *A Tale of a Tub*, or Sterne's Tristram Shandy, Caleb writes therapeutically in an attempt to preserve his mental health: "I am incited to the penning of these memoirs, only by a desire to divert my mind from the deplorableness of my situation" (p. 3). Both Caleb and Falkland have an "invincible attachment to books of narrative and romance." Like the prototypical literary madman Don Quixote, chivalry scrambles their brains. Caleb says of himself that heroic stories "took possession of my soul; and the effects they produced, were frequently discernible in my external appearance and my health" (p. 4). And of Falkland, he says, "thou imbibedst the poison of chivalry with thy earliest youth; and the base and low-minded envy that met thee on thy return to thy native seats, operated with this poison to hurry thee into madness" (p. 326). Also like Don Quixote, at the outset the characters must create adventure in dull, confined situations. If provincial Don Quixote can scan the flat and treeless horizon of La Mancha to find giants, a provincial servant can scrutinize an unopened (and for all we know, empty) trunk to find evidence of exciting murders. Fittingly, the first information that Collins delivers about Falkland could easily be an interpolated tale from the romance tradition. Like tragic counterparts of Don Quixote and Sancho, Caleb and his master learn about life from one another and gradually become more alike, although their trials, political and psychological, lead us far from the world of comedy. Also like Cervantes's madman, Caleb often explains intractable realities by saying that they are "enchanted."

Other passages echo scenes of madness in Shakespeare: Hamlet practicing madness in the Danish court ("Do you think I will be an instrument to be played upon your pleasure . . . ?"); Macbeth's mental breakdown and hallucination ("Didst thou believe me impotent, imbecil, and idiot-like. . . . I will tell a tale—!"); Lear on the stormy heath ("I was in the midst of a heath . . . I was ill-defended by the miserable covering I wore . . . I muttered imprecations and murmuring . . . I was full of loathing and abhorrence of life . . . My distempered thoughts confounded . . . I cursed the whole system of human existence"). The literary rhetoric of fictive insanity thus often underlies Godwin's efforts to show things as they really are.

Also woven through *Caleb Williams* like a network of codes are most of the terms available to the eighteenth century for describing psychological abnormality: enthusiasm, frenzy, possession, conjecture, distraction, melancholy, infatuation.[8] Ancient theories about the humors work their way into the narrative: too much blood, gall, choler, or spleen unbalance the minds of various characters and make them rave, brood, flare up, or have fits.[9] Too much gall makes Tyrrel and the "witch" "ready to burst with . . . indignation," like Swift's spider. Choler provokes Malvesi to reckless action. Spleen depresses Falkland into melancholy. Ruling passions, too, drive characters to madness and death: in accord with Pope's pronouncement in the *Epistle to Cobham* ("You shall feel your ruling passion strong in death"), Falkland's end remains true to his obsession.[10] He becomes a "corpse" devoid "almost of life," yet "Falkland in the most helpless state was still Falkland," craving revenge for his reputation. Even Hobbes offers precedent for this portrayal: "Excessive desire for revenge," he explains, "when it becomes habitual, hurteth the organs."[11] Excessive self-love, another conventional source of madness, makes its appearance in Falkland's criminal devotion to reputation and in Caleb's increasing preoccupation with his own: "Why should my reflections perpetually centre upon myself? self, an overweening regard to which has been the source of my errors!" (p. 325). "Suspended reason," "tortures of imagination," and "haunted fancy" typify Godwin's vocabulary.

Further, the narrative's intervals of madness include the trappings familiar to readers of Pope and Swift, that is, the eighteenth-century signs of psychological trouble: dirt, prisons, bestiality, fitful dreams, specious reasoning.[12] Characters with matted hair and wandering eyes strike their foreheads, knit their brows, and grind their teeth together. Clouded reason plunges almost everyone into darkness. Only the mentally healthy—Clare, Brightwel, and Raymond—are associated with clarity, brightness, and rays of rational light.

But of all the inherited means of accounting for the workings of the mind, Locke (and associationist psychology) and the *tabula rasa* most interestingly inform *Caleb Williams*.[13] As a boy, Caleb is an ardent young empiricist, "desirous of tracing the variety of effects which might be produced from given causes" (p. 4). As an adult, he says that "the strictness with which [he] endeavoured to remark what passed in the mind of one man" made him "adept in the different modes in which human intellect displays its secret workings" (p. 123). These modes are "observation and experience" in the world and "reflection," in Locke's meaning of the word, the mind's perceptions of its own operations. "These reflections led gradually to a new state of my mind," writes Caleb (p. 108). The association of ideas is his most important conscious means of comprehending experience. "In saying this I touched the spring that wakened madness in his mind" (p. 117), he explains, or "[t]his thought led me to another," or, "by this accident, the name of Mr. Falkland was connected in her mind, with the sentiments of unbounded esteem" (pp. 147, 294). The description of Caleb's mental stresses in prison, where he is "shut up . . . in total darkness without any external source" of stimulation, echoes Locke's discussion of enthusiasm in the *Essay Concerning Human Understanding* (4, 19). The "ungrounded conceit" of enthusiastic subjectivity "accepts its supposed illumination without search and proof."[14] Caleb withdraws entirely into "the stores of my own mind" until he becomes "insensible" to his surroundings and gives "full scope to the impulses of my mind": "I mused upon these ideas till I was totally absorbed in thought. I repeated them till my mind glowed with enthusiasm" (p. 185).

The abundance of explanatory terms and phrases, the allusions and precedents seem appropriate, yet still inadequate. They can only take us so far into *Caleb Williams*. The coincidence of Locke's metaphor for challenging the theory of innate ideas—the *tabula rasa*—as a textual metaphor opens up new possibilities for appreciating the psychological insights of the novel. Godwin portrays "rebellion" and "revolution" in the minds of his characters because he wishes to evoke the same states in the minds of his readers; he hopes to "write a tale, that shall constitute an epoch in the mind of the reader, that no one, after he has read it, shall ever be exactly the same man that he was before."[15] The author writes on the blank page. The reader inscribes on the blank spaces of the self. The characters make texts. Caleb, at last, loses his identity and exclaims "But it is all a BLANK!" In other words, the explicit language of Godwin's sources of psychology does much to convince us that language *is* the source of psychology, that psyche and logos, that texts and text-making are primary sources of human identity. "By words alone" man is distinguished from beast; this is one of the century's philosophical truisms. Beyond the text—beyond our ability to write, rewrite, read, and interpret it—the workings of the human mind remain, to use terms crucial to *Caleb Williams*, "secret" and "mysterious." By means of language, we sort through a welter of impressions. By organizing words and other signs into sequence and configuration, we rescue our personal histories from chaos. Within the novel, both meaning and sanity are verbal constructs: narrative structure, configurations of character, setting, and plot, indirectly express psychological issues. At the center is an obsession with reputation and personal identity as text—with the public version of oneself that the world has "read" and the private version of oneself that is inscribed within.

Both Caleb and Falkland are men of words: both read and write; both are profoundly influenced by—that is, are written upon by—the very same text of chivalric romance. Their lives begin to intertwine when Caleb takes up residence in Falkland's library, writing his master's words while reading every "line of his countenance" and every volume on his shelves, both seeming "to an inconceivable degree pregnant with meaning" (p. 5). Caleb's curiosity, his narrative skills, and his "talkativeness" develop as he listens to the story of Falkland's life. The words of one stimulate the words of the other. Or, conversely, when Caleb "endeavoured to answer, but [his] speech failed," Falkland "seemed to have something of which he wished to disburthen his mind, but to want words in which to convey it" (p. 8). The bestial Tyrrel remains forever alien from them largely because his "proficiency . . . in the arts of writing and reading was extremely slender" (p. 17). On the other hand, the divine Mr. Clare writes poetry like an angel. As Caleb's character grows, he takes over the role of narrator, and increasingly his identity becomes concurrent or synonymous with his language. No substantiality of self exists for him without control over words.[16] From his roles as secretary and scholar, he becomes a court-testifier, a letter-writer, a storyteller, a hack who authors imaginary adventures, autobiography, mathematical and political tracts, poetry, essays, and sensational journalism. At a moment when inspiration fails him, he pulls out his "pocket Horace." Finally, after reading much, writing much, and scrutinizing what was "inscribed in legible characters upon [the] countenance[s]" of others, he becomes an etymologist, searching even more meticulously for meaning in individual words (p. 294).

But, at the same time, Caleb's self is being written upon by experience. Sometimes contradictory versions of him take the form of opinion: his master's guilt-engendering words, also ironically the "good words" of a gentleman, cause everyone to believe him guilty of crimes. These opinions so threaten Caleb's sense of self that he is driven intermittently insane. Other erroneous texts of himself take printed form: the cheap broadsides about the notorious Kit Williams, for example, turn up at various crucial points of the action. The discrepancies between Caleb's inner text and the textual accounts of him in the world drive him to distraction: his "mind was bursting with depression and anguish." As false accounts proliferate in volume three, he undergoes a corresponding series of metamorphoses, as if acting out physically the power of language to destabilize or dissolve identity, becoming beggar, farmer's son, Jew, Irishman, cripple, watchmaker, and teacher. He twice is reduced to nakedness and twice renews efforts (as on a kind of *tabula rasa*) to produce new versions of himself. He even changes the accents in which he speaks. While he is reduced to a series of textual variants, Falkland seems silent. And yet, we learn that Falkland, too, has been writing texts: like an omniscient author, he has arranged the plots through which the protagonist struggles. Last of all, Caleb writes the novel of "things as they are" to vindicate his "true" self. Indeed, his urgency over being properly "read" makes the structure of the narrative, as Robert Uphaus notes, not progressively episodic, but obsessive and recapitulatory telling and re-telling.[17]

Also obsessive and recapitulatory is the setting: the landscape and architecture through which the characters move reinforce the psychological mysteries of the narrative. Here Godwin reflects another mode of inquiry into the workings of the mind. A relationship between architectural styles and mental states had received considerable attention by 1750, so that, for example, baroque design was explicitly discussed and accepted as more irrational, more passionate, less reasonable than Palladian.[18] Pope had implied this correspondence between setting or style and sanity or insanity in his praise of Burlington, in the Cave of Spleen, in the *Dunciad*, and elsewhere. The Gothic mode, generally, found its own way of exploiting the projection of psychological states onto the external world. Godwin's setting uniquely evidences his double purpose. On the one hand, it depicts English society and institutions, and Godwin indulges in overtly political digressions about their ills. These ardent harangues attempt realistic detail about

England in the 1790s, with such minutiae as the precise measurements of a particular prison cell. Assorted details lead us through life in village, estate, town, and city. Ostensibly, at least, Godwin supplies an environment for the abstract tenets of *Political Justice*: that human systems can be pernicious; that human beings are perfectible; that circumstance is formative. Yet setting in *Caleb Williams* functions in contradictory ways as well. It becomes the unreal background for the furtive lurkings of characters who re-form circumstance as much as they are formed by it, who seem only as perfectible as their language. The representation of society becomes no more than the play of shadows when characters can render either truth or falsehood "gradually . . . mysterious."

Thus landscape and architecture become visual counterparts to the "secret recesses" of the human mind. Caleb's first "station was in that part of the house which was appropriated for the reception of books" (p. 6). He usually is shut away in some small area: in a closet, behind a bush, at a secluded cottage, in an attic, a thicket, a ditch, a cell. The prison scenes fastidiously account for the increasingly confining chambers that Caleb is forced to know. These dark places are mental landscapes, locations of psychological probing: every discovery about the "select and eternal secret" of Falkland's mind or his own leads Caleb down a long narrow passage to a dim room containing a small window, a closed door, a locked trunk. These "private" areas are "separated," "underground," or "hidden," and they are explored during the time of dream and nightmare. Caleb's endless wandering through the same mental landscape becomes almost self-parodic: "This door led into a narrow passage"; "I determined . . . upon another door at the farthest end of the passage"; "the passage . . . was so narrow . . . that it was but a . . . melancholy light that entered my apartment"; "I had thus opened myself a passage . . . overgrown with brushwood and furze"; "[I] passed along a winding passage that was perfectly dark. At the upper end of this passage was a door"; "I contrived to make out the chief part of its contents by the help of lamp at the upper end of a narrow passage." His only interlude of happiness, it comes as no surprise, occurs in a "wild and romantic" natural setting, "rich and abundant in production."

Further connections link the mental landscapes of *Caleb Williams* to the narrative's double function. Following Caleb's tortuous route, like losing oneself in the shadowy interiors and architectural complexity of Piranesi's *Caraceri*, leads to no obvious exit. Following the exhausting ups and downs of his emotional states becomes, in a sense, agitation for the overthrow of political tyranny. But it is also a journey of self-realization on which the tyranny of language may be overthrown only at the loss of personal identity. For Caleb, dark recesses and cramped spaces conduce to authorship. The locked trunk in Falkland's house illustrates this process: the human mind will inscribe *something* onto a blank space; it will try to fill emptiness with its own desires, with reflections of its needs.[19] This compulsion produces the intense guilt that pervades the novel: guilt that is personal and social; guilt over locking things away and over unlocking them. Guilt in *Caleb Williams* accompanies knowledge: understanding "things as they are" implicates one in the crimes of others; this interaction, as portrayed in the world of Godwin's novel, is not susceptible to change through politics. Even the innocent Laura becomes tainted simply by learning about the murder. "No disorder of the intellect," Johnson cautions through Imlac, "is more dangerous than that which is complicated with the dread of guilt," a potent and ever-present force.

Thus, with ramifications that are both psychological and political, a major preoccupation in *Caleb Williams* (both as a source and an expiation of guilt) is with penning, penetrating, and penance. Writing, piercing/perceiving, and suffering absorb most of the hero's time. In addition to his "penning of these memoirs" and other texts, he desires to penetrate the unknown. He has an "inquisitive mind" that likes to get inside things. Curiosity drives him: "curiosity is a restless propensity," he says. "The spring of action which, perhaps more than any other, characterised the whole train of my life, was curiosity" (p. 4). This quality, Swift said, "enters into the Depth of Things," and is allied with reason's "Tools for cutting, and opening, and mangling, and piercing."[20] Caleb fervently wishes to penetrate the locked trunk, a sexual metaphor and a metaphor for the "secret . . . gloomy recesses of the mind."[21] Furthermore, he at first believes the "fatal trunk" to contain a piercing weapon or "some murderous instrument"; eventually the imagined dagger becomes an equally imagined text: "I am now persuaded," he writes, that the contents are "a faithful narrative . . . written by Mr. Falkland" (p. 315). Indeed, by the end, penning has supplanted penetrating: "I will use no daggers," he exclaims, "with this little engine, this little pen I defeat all his machinations; I stab him in the very point he was most solicitous to defend!" The parallels and conflated meanings are obvious: Tyrrel uses Grimes and his engine to penetrate Emily Melville; Falkland uses Gines to penetrate Caleb; Caleb uses "this little engine, this little pen" to "stab" his enemy.[22]

Caleb pokes and probes his way through the world: he opens the letter from Hawkins (p. 114); he prods Falkland until the latter protests the invasion to "extort all the treasures of my soul" (p. 118). When Caleb does extort the secret of the murder, he exults, "It is out! It is discovered!" He makes inroads into "the most secret paths of the garden" and is "never so perfectly alive as at that moment" (p. 130). Later, he must penetrate prison walls. His false reputation gives him pleasure in only one aspect, its exaggeration of his ability of penetration: Kit Williams is, of course, a "notorious housebreaker," as well as a jailbreaker "no less than five times." The lusty tavern wench loves him because he "made his way through stone walls, as if they were so many cobwebs" (p. 237). He sums up his final plea for innocence by saying that Falkland was "penetrated with my grief" (p. 324).

But, for Caleb, the consequence of entering his master's heart of darkness is to do "an eternal penance" (p. 143). Both members of this symbiotic pair are caught up in the process of invading and keeping out. Both are "too deeply pervaded" with chivalric codes; romantic "poison" has seeped into both. Caleb admits that "plunging headlong" into mystery was "an act of insanity" (p. 132). He finds that he must now harbor his own impenetrable secret, one which he "must never disburthen" (p. 138) and which makes him a "depository" (p. 275). Falkland soon wears "an armour against which all [his] weapons are impotent"; indeed, no one in the novel passively submits to the prying of others. Godwin's prose becomes pervaded with imagery of violation and violent release: Caleb received looks that could tear him to pieces (p. 171) and "could have dashed [his] brains against the walls of [his] dungeon." He "felt the fangs of the tyger striking deep into [his] heart" (p. 240). Concealment and enclosure become the necessary counterparts to penetration. Physical objects represent these counterparts and become progressively more intimate: entrapping objects include claustrophobic rooms, the trunk, the coffin, the naked body; objects used for piercing follow the pattern, so that in prison Caleb works first with tools, then with a single nail, and finally with his teeth.

Of course, Caleb most admires intellectual insight: the outlaw Raymond's "penetration was such that no imposter could hope to mislead him . . . and he confided in that penetration." But lawful society makes men vulnerable; Caleb's "penance" is to be open constantly to discovery by others. He "lies concealed" in London, but the hue-and-cry publishes all his disguises. "Disguise was no longer of use," he admits, because reward money will "sharpen [public] penetration" (p. 270). He attempts a defense of "desperate firmness" yet it does no good (p. 278); disturbingly, his obsession with penetration makes real freedom intolerable: when released from prison, he paradoxically reacts, "The effect which this incredible reverse [freedom] produced upon my mind" is "impossible to express. . . ." Was it for this that I had broken through so many locks, and bolts, and the adamantine walls of my prison . . . that I had racked my invention for expedients of evasion and concealment?" (p. 279). Prison drives him mad, but so does release. Simple political freedom does not satisfy his psychological need for walls to break through. While his heart is "gorged . . . with abhorrence of Mr. Falkland" he hopes his penning will be "digested" or internalized by others. But even writing grows tedious; "the whole world" seems to him as "cold as the torpedo."

In the published ending, Falkland and Caleb both are "pierced" and "penetrated." In the manuscript ending, Caleb's intellectual powers disintegrate into an echo of the famous passage in Swift's "Digression on Madness": "The idea then occurred of mystery, of something which the understanding was incessantly anxious to penetrate . . . but always returned empty, wearied, dissatisfied, unrewarded" (p. 330). The hero hardens into an impenetrable lifeless thing—"a GRAVE-STONE"—and finds there was "nothing in life worth making such a bustle about" (p. 334). Nothing seems terribly sure, except that someone will engrave something on that vacant stone. A further irony is that Caleb's self-destructive obsession—to break into Falkland's trunk, to break out of prison, to see his enemy closed in his coffin—is also the mysterious source of his creativity. Antonin Artaud aptly has observed that "No one has ever written, painted, modelled, built, invented, except to get out of hell."[23] *Caleb Williams* instinctively recognizes that art reflects the best and the worst in a given culture, the brightness and the darkness of the human mind. Like Caleb and Falkland, a symbiotic process is always in effect: concealment and revelation, freedom and bonds, power and submission. The most unsavory kind of experience (murder) and knowledge of that experience is necessary to make Caleb, in the climactic garden scene, wholly "alive."

Perhaps the problem with the bonds between politics and psychology in the novel is that Godwin makes political injustice and emotional agitation so compelling. As life grows more perilous, so his characters deepen and develop into authenticity. Godwin's retrospective account of the composition of *Caleb Williams* clearly emphasizes psychology over politics: "The thing in which my imagination revelled most freely, was the analysis of the private and internal operations of the mind, employing my metaphysical dissecting knife in tracing and laying bare the involutions of motive, and recording the gradually accumulating impulses, which led the personages . . . to adopt the particular way of proceeding in which they afterwards embarked."[24] Godwin, too, pens and penetrates by "dissecting" and "laying bare" what is "internal and private." These "secrets" of human behavior, human identity, and human relationships underlie, but do not depend on, abstract social systems of political justice. Involuted motives and gradually accumulating impulses drive the characters with guilt, fear, and desire, yet do not depend on external institutions of punishment and crime. In *Caleb Williams*, mysterious mental states become tangible, while political states and prison walls become metaphors. The novel shows us things that are very wrong with society, yet offers no way of understanding the members of society that encourages us to trust an ideal. Instead, men live together, influence each other, become more like one another, even as they discover antagonisms and remain mysterious to one another. They are created by and create with language. Godwin writes that, during the "whole period" of composing the novel, his "mind was in a high state of excitement," that he "said to [him]self a thousand times" that his tale would unalterably change ("constitute an epoch in") the "mind of the reader." And so he does inscribe upon us a new awareness of how involuted, receptive, yet impervious we are.

Caleb Williams proposes and subverts rational anarchy, even while it plants the seeds of its destruction. Neither its author, its readers, or its characters experience predominantly rational responses; this is precisely why they fascinate us. Anarchy repeatedly is contradicted by the unending need to make order in language, in stories, in one's sense of self. Every individual seeks meaning in bonds of relationship, as Caleb, for example, searches for father- and mother-figures in Falkland, Collins, Spurrel, Laura, Mrs. Marney, and others. Within relationships and society, a man may suffer, but alone, he is nothing. Caleb comes close to articulating this double bind:

> The pride of philosophy has taught us to treat man as an individual. He is no such thing. He holds, necessarily to his species. He is like those twin-births, that have two heads, indeed, and four hands; but, if you attempt to detach them from each other, they are inevitably subjected to miserable and lingering destruction. (p. 303)

Caleb Williams, with its "twin-births," its double bonds and double binds, urges us toward more general statements about the psychological perceptions worked out in the eighteenth-century novel. Godwin's narrative is, in a way, a compendium of available psychological terms. But it transcends the terms available to it. It dramatizes how thoroughly consciousness of self depends on language and on others. Caleb and Falkland, politics and psychology—these embracively corrosive pairs suggest that the dialogic novel[25] in the eighteenth century (with *Don Quixote* as precedent) re-enacts a process essential to human experience in any century. Cervantes begins with two cardboard characters who eventually pummel each other into life. So, too, English novelists like Richardson, Fielding, Sterne, and Godwin, create pairs of "twinbirth" characters who, during the course of a long, capacious prose narrative, have time to become themselves fully, sometimes to destroy themselves fully. They develop as personalities and as texts; they interact, tell their stories, love and hate, succeed and fail. They do not cause governments to change, nor do they alter permanently the "state" of being human. But they do penetrate temporarily and engage us in the solitary, "secret workings of the human mind."

Thus Godwin the novelist exceeds Godwin as political philosopher. In *Political Justice,* he had argued that "accuracy of language is the indispensable prerequisite of sound knowledge"; in *Caleb Williams,* he celebrates the power of imaginative language to recreate the inaccuracies and uncertainties to which all readers will respond. *Political Justice* sets forth "those general principles of the human mind which are most intimately connected with the topics of political reasoning." His model is a metaphor of a billiards game:

> When a ball upon a billiard board is struck by a person playing and afterwards impinges upon a second ball, the ball which was first in motion is said to act upon the second, though it operates in the strictest conformity to the impression it received. . . .[26]

"Exactly similar to this," he proposes, "are the actions of the human mind"—and so, he reasons, under the doctrine of necessity, "the ideas of guilt, crime, desert and accountableness have no place." Yet in *Caleb Williams*, places of guilt, crime, and accountableness—especially of giving accounts by telling or writing—become the alternative paradigmatic metaphors for the human mind: a prison, a blank slate, a locked trunk, a dark passage leading not to mechanism but to mystery.

NOTES

1. Quotations and page references are to *Caleb Williams*, ed. David McCracken (London: Oxford University Press, 1970).

    Interpretations of *Caleb Williams* typically emphasize either its political or its psychological attributes. Studies of it as a political novel include Harvey Gross, "The Pursuer and the Pursued: A Study of *Caleb Williams*," *Texas Studies in Language and Literature*, 1 (1959), 401-411; James T. Boulton, *The Language of Politics in the Age of Wilkes and Burke* (London: Routledge & Kegan Paul, 1963), pp. 226-232; D. Gilbert Dumas, "Things As They Were: The Original Ending of *Caleb Williams*," *SEL*, 6 (1966), 575-597; David McCracken, "Godwin's *Caleb Williams*: A Fictional Rebuttal of Burke," *Studies in Burke and His Time*, 11 (1969-70), 1442-1452; Gary Kelly, *The English Jacobin Novel 1780-1805* (Oxford: Clarendon Press, 1976), pp. 179-208. Important discussions of the psychological implications of the novel include Rudolph Storch, "Metaphors of Private Guilt and Social Rebellion in Godwin's *Caleb Williams*," *ELH*, 34 (1967), 188-207; Robert W. Uphaus, *The Impossible Observer: Reason and the Reader in Eighteenth-Century Prose* (Lexington: University of Kentucky Press, 1979), pp. 123-136; Alex Gold, Jr., "It's Only Love: The Politics of Passion in Godwin's *Caleb Williams*," *Texas Studies in Language and Literature*, 19 (1977), 137-160. A further important study may be found in Eric Rothstein, *Systems of Order and Inquiry in Late Eighteenth-Century Fiction* (Berkeley: University of California Press, 1975). Several critics have made connections, from various points of view, between the novel's psychological aspects and its concern with "texts," "textuality," or "texture." Some points of mutual agreement and overlap between these studies and the present discussion exist; they seem inevitable to anyone reading *Caleb Williams* with a focus on its affective power. A major distinction is my discussion's intention to work within the terms provided by the novel itself and by eighteenth-century "psychology." I hope that it will be instructive to discover parallel insights between the self-conscious theorists and writers of Godwin's age and the contemporary theorists and critics who have inspired articles including those by Jerrold E. Hogle, "The Texture of the Self in Godwin's *Things As They Are*," *Boundary 2*, 7 (1974), 261-281; Jacqueline T. Miller,

"The Imperfect Tale: Articulation, Rhetoric, and Self in 'Caleb Williams,'" *Criticism* (Detroit, Mich.: Wayne State University Press, 1979), pp. 366-383; James Walton, "'Mad Feary Father': *Caleb Williams* and the Novel Form," *Salzburg Studies in English Literature* 47, (Salzburg: Institut für Englische Sprache, 1975), 1-61.

2. Some excellent discussions of various kinds of "doubles" in *Caleb Williams* occur in the studies by Uphaus, Gold and Storch.

3. An extensive discussion of the importance of the story of Bluebeard's wife, mentioned by Godwin as a source of inspiration for his two central characters, may be found in Alex Gold's "It's Only Love." Gold further clarifies Godwin's distrust of love, its inequities, entanglements, and power struggles, in the ideal political state.

4. Uphaus writes that Caleb and Falkland "imprison one another within their own consciousness, and they alternately escape and pursue one another throughout the remainder of the novel" (p. 129).

5. A fuller discussion of this pair, in many ways parallel to Caleb and Falkland, occurs in my article "Underplotting, Overplotting, and Cor-respondence in *Clarissa*," *MLS*, 11:3 (1981), 61-71.

6. See, for example, David McCracken, "Godwin's Literary Theory: The Alliance Between Fiction and Political Philosophy," *Philological Quarterly*, 79 (January, 1970), as well as Godwin's *Enquiry concerning Political Justice and Its Influence on General Virtue and Happiness*, ed. R. A. Preston (New York: Knopf, 1926), I, p. 179.

7. McCracken's Introduction to the novel, p. xxii.

8. Discussions of eighteenth-century methods and terminology for abnormal psychology occur in Michael DePorte, *Nightmares and Hobbyhorses* (San Marino, Calif.: The Huntington Library, 1974), 3-54; L. J. Rather, *Mind and Body in Eighteenth-Century Medicine* (London: Wellcome Historical Medical Library, 1965); Harold E. Pagliaro, ed., *Irrationalism in the Eighteenth Century*, volume 2 of *Studies in Eighteenth-Century Culture* (London and Cleveland, Ohio: The Press of Case Western Reserve University, 1972), especially George Rosen, "Forms of Irrationality in the Eighteenth Century," pp. 255-288; Lillian Feder, *Madness in Literature* (Princeton, N.J.: Princeton University Press, 1980).

9. See, for example, Feder, Chapter 1.

10. It will be apparent that Pope expresses poetically a common idea: that the ruling passion unrelentingly dominates the unbalanced mind until death.

11. Thomas Hobbes, *Leviathan*, ed. C. B. Macpherson (Harmondsworth: Penguin Press, 1968), especially I. 8, suggests how deeply ingrained these concepts are in the eighteenth-century background. Another echo of Locke, more famous than Caleb's Lockean-Hartleian psychology, is Tristram Shandy's explanatory "Dull organs, dear Sir, in the first place."

12. See Max Byrd, *Visits to Bedlam: Madness and Literature in the Eighteenth Century* (Columbia: University of South Carolina Press, 1974); also Michel Foucault, *Madness and Civilization: A History of Insanity in the Age of Reason*, trans. Richard Howard (New York: Pantheon Books, 1965).

13. For a semiological interpretation of *Caleb Williams* that contrasts the concepts of *telos* and *tabula*, see Hogle's article.

14. John Locke, *An Essay concerning Human Understanding*, ed. P. H. Nidditch (Oxford: Clarendon Press, 1975), pp. 697-706.
15. See Godwin's account of the composition of *Caleb Williams*, reprinted from the preface to the "Standard Novels" edition (1832) of *Fleetwood*, in McCracken's edition, p. 338.
16. Patricia Meyer Spacks, *Imagining A Self: Autobiography and Novel in Eighteenth-Century England* (Cambridge, Mass.: Harvard University Press, 1976). Spacks discusses the role of language in making personal identity "substantial" for eighteenth-century writers.
17. Uphaus, p. 136.
18. Rosen discusses eighteenth-century psychological architecture in Pagliaro, *Irrationalism in the Eighteenth Century*, pp. 273-274.
19. Uphaus describes the trunk as a phenomenological "reading paradigm," illustrating the way in which readers partially produce the texts they encounter.
20. Swift's uses of irony in *A Tale* do not interfere with the parallel qualities associated with curiosity: probing, restlessness, potential danger, disappointment.
21. Gold's article contains a fuller treatment of the trunk as sexual metaphor.
22. Gold, 144.
23. *Antonin Artaud Anthology*, ed. Jack Hirschman, 2nd ed. rev. (San Francisco, Calif.: City Lights Books, 1965), p. 149. Artaud also says artistic creativity is "like the action of forcing one's way through an invisible wall" that must "be undermined and penetrated with a file, slowly and with patience."
24. *Caleb Williams*, p. 339.
25. The relevant theoretical discussion here is the analysis of the dialogic novel in Mikhail Bakhtin, *Problems of Dostoevsky's Poetics*, trans. R. W. Rotsel (Ann Arbor, Mich.: Ardis, 1973), chapters 1 and 4. Also pertinent to an appreciation of *Caleb Williams's* appeal to readers is Roland Barthes, *The Pleasure of the Text*, trans. Richard Miller (New York: Hill and Wang, 1975).
26. See *Political Justice*, IV. 6, in which Godwin treats the idea of necessity and the corresponding functions of the human mind.

Vehicles of Delusion: Swift, Locke, and the Madhouse Poems of James Carkesse

MICHAEL DePORTE

> How fading and insipid do all Objects accost us that
> are not convey'd in the Vehicle of *Delusion?*
> —*A Tale of a Tub*

Delusion, particularly self-delusion, lies at the very heart of *A Tale of a Tub*, where the visions of self entertained by Peter, Jack, the Grubstreet narrator, and a throng of peripheral figures, are radically warped by madness. The question of how madness should affect our notion of personal identity is one to which Locke had recently called attention in the *Essay concerning Human Understanding* by asserting that consciousness alone "makes what we call *self*" (2, 27, 21).[1] Locke's contention stirred much debate, not least for the problem it raised as to what became of identity in madness. Did a man remain the same person if he went mad, or was he transformed into someone else? Christopher Fox has traced the development of the prolonged controversy initiated by Locke's chapter "Of Identity and Diversity," and ably shown how Swift and his friends burlesqued Locke's views in the Scriblerus papers.[2] I should like to suggest here that there is a more searching, if less explicit commentary on Locke's theory of identity in the *Tale*, and to suggest in the process the possible relevance to that commentary of the strange poems James Carkesse published a quarter of a century before Locke's chapter on identity appeared.

Carkesse wrote while a patient at Finsbury madhouse and Bethlehem Hospital. Though Bedlamite poems had been popular since the sixteenth century, Carkesse's verses, entitled *Lucida Intervalla*, are so far as I know the first ever published by an actual inmate. The Tom o'Bedlam songs purport to be intimate accounts of madness, yet invariably they seem written from the outside; they tell us less about insanity than about contemporary attitudes toward insanity. The songs are full of bluster, nonsense, and theatrical whimsy. As a rule the speaker attributes his disorder to a lost love, and there is a calculated extravagance about what he says that betrays someone's idea of delusion, not delusion itself:

> I'le bark against the Dog-Star,
> And crow away the Morning;
> I'le chase the Moon
> Till it be Noon,
> And I'll make her leave her Horning....
>
> I'le Sayl upon a Milstone,
> And make the Sea-Gods wonder
> I'le plunge in the Deep, till I wake asleep,
> And I'le tear the Rockes in sunder.[3]

Such lines aim to astonish and amuse; they cannot be thought the authentic expression of a man suffering from the delusions they describe. More significant still, speakers in the songs routinely declare themselves mad:

> Of thirty bare yeares haue I
> twice twenty bin enraged,
> & of forty bin three tymes fifteene
> in durance soundlie caged,
> On ye lordlie loftes of Bedlam
> with stubble softe & dainty,
> braue braceletts strong, sweet whips ding dong
> with wholsome hunger plenty....

or

> Forth from my sad and darksome Cel,
> And from the deep abysse, of hell,
> Poor *Tom* is come to view the world again,
> To see if he can ease his distemper'd brain.[4]

One need read only a few of Carkesse's poems to appreciate the difference. Carkesse appears to have been committed for stirring up trouble at a dissenting meeting house where he went on a self-appointed mission to "Rout the *Church* of *Englands* Foes" (p. 19).[5] Carkesse himself maintains that he was put in the asylum at the contrivance of his wife, his in-laws, his "*false Friends*"(p. 3), and that he is kept there by the obstinacy of his doctor, a man Carkesse variously depicts as moronic, vicious, and insane. Perhaps the most arresting thing about *Lucida Intervalla* is that while obviously the work of a disturbed mind, almost every poem proclaims its author's sanity. Most frequently, Carkesse insists that commonplace minds have mistaken his genius for madness. To this pedestrian view he will concede no more than that on occasion he pretended madness— as a "*Feat*," he explains in one poem; with some mysterious "design," he confides in another (pp. 4, 45). Yet in all his poems Carkesse contends that he alone can judge rightly who he is and what his motives have been. In light of Locke's belief that consciousness determines personal identity this notion has ramifications worth exploring.

Considering the penetration of Locke's remarks on insanity elsewhere it is disappointing that in his chapter on personal identity he should skirt the issue of what happens to identity in madness. Locke says here that a man may, if he wishes, think he has the same *soul* as Nestor or Thersites, but that unless he is also conscious of all their thoughts and actions he can never claim to be the same person as either of them. "Can he be concerned in either of their Actions? Attribute them to himself, or think them his own more than the Actions of any other Man, that ever existed?" (2, 27, 14). For Locke the answer to the question is self-evident. No man would claim to remember the actions or thoughts of Nestor as if they were his own. No sane man, that is. But what about men who are not sane, men who imagine that they remember such things? After all, in madness the line between memory and fancy may thin out to nothing. One wonders what Locke might have said of cases like those Milton Rokeach studied some years ago of the three men in the Ypsilanti, Michigan state mental hospital who each claimed to be Jesus. Rokeach's idea was to bring them together and see if the meeting might shock them out of their delusional systems. For they would then be confronted, to use his words, "with the ultimate contradiction conceivable for human beings; more than one person claiming the same identity."[6] As a cure the experiment was a complete failure. But as an illustration of the power of delusional identity it was most illuminating. Though the three men were unsettled by the meeting, each quickly devised an explanation for the assertions of the other two that left his own identification with Christ intact. Rokeach's study demonstrates something implicit in Locke's theory which Locke leaves unexplored: if consciousness is made the sole determinant of personality, then altered states of consciousness will produce new identities that must be accounted for.

Locke does, however, offer perceptive conjectures as to how delusions settle on the mind. In his journal entry for 22 January 1678, he notes that the ideas of memory (on which our sense of enduring identity is partly founded) are "like painting after the life"—always falling short; those of imagination, on the other hand, "are usually very bright and cleare in the minde," because they are not "tied to any pattern." The ideas of imagination are so clear, Locke continues, that sometimes they "make impressions as strong and as sensible as those Ideas which come immediately by the senses from externall objects soe that the minde takes one for tother its own imaginations for realitys." When this happens a man goes mad. Locke ventures a further guess that madmen make little use of memory; any idea which strays into consciousness from the past they simply turn over to fancy, which "dresses it up after its own fashion without regard to the original."[7] In the *Essay* Locke points out that madmen do not lose the ability to reason; rather they lose the ability to distinguish the promptings of imagination from those of memory and the senses: "having taken their Fancies for Realities, they make right deductions from them. Thus you shall find a distracted Man fancying himself a King, with a right inference require suitable Attendance, Respect and Obedience" (2, 11, 13).[8]

Nowhere, though, does Locke speculate on the implication these insights into delusion might have for the question of personal identity, except to say that the law quite properly refrains from punishing a man

Lucida Intervalla:

Containing divers

Miscellaneous Poems,

Written at

Finsbury and Bethlem

BY THE

Doctors Patient

EXTRAORDINARY.

By James Carkesse.

--- *semel Insanivimus omnes,*
vpon Dr Thomas Allen.

LONDON,
Printed *Anno Dom.* 1679.

for crimes he commits when insane. The courts thereby make the man into two persons, "which is somewhat explained by our way of speaking in *English*, when we say such a one *is not himself*, or is *besides himself*" (2, 27, 20).[9] In madness, then, a man becomes someone else. But Locke says nothing about who a person is when "not himself," or about what might prompt his disappearance into a new self. One wishes Locke had gone on from his remarks about those who imagine they have the same soul as Nestor or Thersites to say something of Don Quixote.[10] In fairness, however, one should point out that Locke's interest here is not in states of consciousness *per se*; it is in establishing a principle of accountability. As David P. Behan observes, the problem of personal identity for Locke "is the problem of moral ownership over time of substances, thoughts, and actions. Concerned consciousness provides the basis of moral ownership."[11] The consciousness of madmen does not signify in this discussion because Locke does not regard madmen as responsible for their actions or thoughts.

While subsequent critics of Locke were to play up the bizarre possibilities of a theory which locates identity in consciousness, none of them seriously considers what happens to identity in madness either. Isaac Watts does conjure for his readers a picture of Nat Lee in Bedlam imagining himself first Socrates, then Cicero, Caesar, and Virgil, next Luther, and finally Queen Elizabeth; yet only by way of dismissive parody: to show the absurdity of thinking a man might become other persons through changes in consciousness.[12] In some respects, the most dismissive response to the problem comes in a work which echoes Locke's views of consciousness and identity, *An Essay on Consciousness* (1728). The argument has an engaging, if suspect, simplicity. Zachary Mayne, the alleged author, wants to show that consciousness is, as he puts it, "an infallible Assurance of the Reality of our own Being and Existence."[13] Accordingly, he makes consciousness itself a criterion of sanity. One is oneself through consciousness of self alone. Since in madness one loses consciousness of one's usual self the madman cannot be deemed conscious at all, any more than a man is truly conscious in his dreams. Mayne's eagerness to restrict use of the term consciousness to waking, normative states leads him to insist that even if a man were to have a dream which corresponded perfectly to reality he must still regard his dream perceptions as false and the self he perceives in that dream as "an imaginary Being."[14] Mayne solves the riddle of who a man is when he takes leave of his senses by saying, in effect, that he vanishes into the void: he is no one, a figment, an unperson.

This is no answer at all. One can learn more about the nature of deluded consciousness from reading Carkesse. Richard Ellmann has described consciousness as "the movement of the mind both in recognizing its own shape and in maintaining that shape in the face of attack or change."[15] The drama of *Lucida Intervalla* lies in just such movements of mind. As one reads through the volume a dialectic unfolds between Carkesse's assertions of identity and the reported challenges to those assertions by the people who committed him and the keepers who tend him.[16] To Thomas Allen, the doctor, Carkesse is an unfortunate (and troublesome) victim of volatile humors—in short, a typical inmate. If he is to recover his true self he must submit to treatments aimed at restoring those humors to their natural balance: bloodletting, purging, emetics. To himself, Carkesse is someone special, "The Doctors Patient Extraordinary," he styles himself on the title page. What he needs is not treatment, but recognition of his gifts. Carkesse is sure enough of his position to present the doctor's case against him from time to time. "Oh, but, *Parson*, you break the *Wall*, / And *Burglary* you commit," he has Allen exclaim regarding the scene at the dissenting meeting house which led to his confinement, "If I must not this *Madness* call, / I am sure, 'tis want of Wit." Carkesse is ready for him. Allen, poor fellow, has lost the ability to distinguish good from evil:

> For surely, the way to Build up the *Church*,
> Is to pull down the *Chappel* o' th' *Devil*.
> Then throw the House out at Window,
> And lay it flat with the Ground,
> For undoubtedly they Sin do,
> That keep it another year round.
> (p. 11)

In a poem capaciously titled "On his being Seiz'd on for a Madman, only for having endeavoured to reduce Dissenters unto the CHURCH," Carkesse elaborates on Allen's obtuseness and suggests that his own actions were sanctioned by the very highest authority:

> When *Zeal* for *God* inspires the *Breast*,
> Says the *Blind world*, the Man's *possest*;
> And flattering their own cold desire,
> Call *Lunacy*, the *Heavenly Fire*:

> But though their *Eyes* are by the *flame*
> So dasled, they mistake the *Name*;
> Know, that 'twas born with Christ at first
> In *Bethlehem*, and at *Bedlam* Nurst.
> (p. 17)

Christ, too, had been taken for a madman.

Carkesse's predicament is reminiscent of one of Locke's more fanciful hypotheses. Suppose, Locke says, the consciousness of a prince were somehow to enter the body of a cobbler. The cobbler would then be the same person as the prince though no one would recognize his princely identity; "he would be the same Cobbler to everyone besides himself" (2, 27, 15).[17] Carkesse sees himself as a kind of unacknowledged prince. To a friend who sent him a box for his things he writes:

> Yet though a Prince, so low my *Fortune's* sunk,
> That I do want, which you supply, the *Trunk*.
> (p. 44)

Recounting his transfer from Finsbury to Bedlam, Carkesse says that he was taken there by coach like a "Prince" and arrived as a personage more exalted still:

> Their *Emperor* they [the keepers] conduct to his *Bed-chamber*
> And lodge his *Majesty* in *Straw*, like *Amber*. (p. 22)

In poem after poem Carkesse argues that despite appearances he is no mere Bedlamite; he is someone to be reckoned with. Men of superior wit are always liable to be called mad by lesser, envious people like Dr. Allen:

> This makes a Carcase with an *Eagles Eye*,
> Be thought a Fit-for-*Bedlam* Prodigy.
> (p. 24)

Throughout *Lucida Intervalla* Carkesse ascribes exceptional powers to himself, but the source and nature of those powers change in significant respects. In the years before his admission to the hospital Carkesse worked as a clerk in Pepys's office. His career had been shaky at best. He was fired for taking bribes, reinstated, then let go again. In a poem about his marriage Carkesse intimates that the disasters which overtook him as a civil servant, together with a desire to impress his wife, inspired his decision to ordain himself a parson of the Church of England:

> When *Abigail*, by mistake, had *Layman Married*,

In *State Affairs*, 'twas seen, he oft miscarried;
Yet a long time *Nub's* Spouse put on no *Gown*,
But *Hector'd* it, with *Sword* and *Muff*, in *Town*:
Convinc'd at last, though *Poets* him made a *Farce* on,
He'd turn his *Coat*, that *Nab* might have her *Parson*.
                                                           (p. 19)

When first locked up in Finsbury madhouse Carkesse flirted with the idea of becoming a soldier. In the second poem of *Lucida Intervalla*, a petition "to the Duke General of the Artillery Ground Overlookt by Finnes-burrough Mad-house, Where I was Confin'd," Carkesse reflects that though "there's *War* Proclaim'd 'twixt *Armes* and *Gown*" he would rather carry a sword outside the madhouse than preach within (pp. 3-4)—an understandable change of heart for an imprisoned man whose window gave him the constant sight of soldiers coming and going. And as the weeks pass in the asylum, and memory of events before his admission becomes less pressing than the daily duel of wits with his keepers, Carkesse discovers a still more gratifying calling: poetry. The verses he writes prove to him that he is an heir to the splendors of Apollo. If poets once ridiculed his pretensions to be a clergyman, he will turn poet and ridicule Allen's pretensions to practice medicine:

So little *Wit*, so much of *Phlegm* and *Rheume*
Our *Mad-Quack* has, that I may well *presume*
Hither as *Patient* he'l ne're be prefer'd,
To fill the number of the *Madmens* Herd:
Who e're is *Mad*, he first had *Wit* to lose;
Betwixt *Fool* and *Physitian* wink and chuse.
                                                           (p. 31)

Carkesse reflects with satisfaction that Allen will now lose whatever credit he hoped to gain by curing a supposedly crazed parson:

. . . observe how basely *Doc's* defeated
And for *Mad-Parson* with a *Poet* cheated.
                                                           (p. 20)

In poetry Carkesse seems to feel he has found a more potent weapon to defend his self-esteem than in religion. Except for scattered references to the Popish Plot his concern for the church disappears after the first third of *Lucida Intervalla*. Carkesse calls himself poet instead of parson:

In *Bedlam*, best of Universities
The *Poet*, not the *Parson*, takes degrees—
                                                           (p. 50)

and no longer seeks Christian sanctions for his behavior. It is Apollo he invokes, as patron of poets and, when he wishes to appeal over Allen's head, as the ultimate authority on medical issues:

> The truth on't is, my *Brains* well fixt *condition*
> *Apollo* better knows, than his *Physitian*.
> (p. 32)

The thought that Apollo is behind him strengthens Carkesse's resolve to resist treatment, the real aim of which, he suspects, is to deprive him of vocation. "*Wit forswear*, and like me prove but *Dunce*," he makes Allen say in one poem (p. 27). In another, he represents himself as a prisoner of conscience, suffering because he will not betray his new-found cause:

> Desiring his Imprison'd *Muse* t'enlarge
> The *Poet, Mad-quack* mov'd, for his *discharge*.
> He angry answer'd, *Parson*, 'tis too soon,
> As yet I have not Cur'd you of *Lampoon*. . . .
> (p. 51)

There is no evidence that Carkesse ever wrote poetry before or after his confinement. In these poems we see him discovering an identity he can maintain against the assaults of the institution. The delusion that he is a great poet persecuted for his genius sustains him. Having re-made himself as a parson when his career in the navy office foundered, he makes himself over yet again in the asylum. Early in the volume there is a poem addressed to the king in which Carkesse seems to acknowledge his own role in creating these exciting new identities. Referring to the protracted feud he had been conducting with Pepys Carkesse says:

> This *Secretary* I could never Mate:
> But, *Clerk of th' Acts*, if I'm a *Parson*, then
> I shal prevail. . . . (p. 5)

"If" is the crucial word. Carkesse reveals here some momentary uncertainty. He did not prevail against Pepys, but he did not own his error either. Rather he let the idea that he was a parson slip quietly out of mind and evolved another identity more suited to the circumstances in which he found himself. In any case the role of a parson may not have been the most congenial one for a militant Church of England man to defend in a madhouse. Since the publication of Henry More's *Enthusiasmus Triumphatus* (1656) it had been a staple of Anglican polemics to describe dissenters as lunatics who belonged in Bedlam. The traditional association between poetry and madness was far more glamorous. When Allen, evidently a man with a sense of humor, once told Carkesse that the king would soon send Dryden, Rochester, and Buckingham to keep him company, the prospect almost reconciled Carkesse to confinement (p. 51). In his *Essay on Consciousness* 'Mayne' would argue that imagination has no vital role in consciousness.[18] *Lucida Intervalla* suggests, on the contrary, that imagination is central to consciousness and to one's sense of identity.

Carkesse's poems by no means confirm his declarations of genius, but they do tell us much about how the self can be made over in madness, and they open up an intriguing perspective on that far more artful and knowing evocation of madness, *A Tale of a Tub*. Indeed it is tempting for two reasons to think that a copy of *Lucida Intervalla* may have come Swift's way during his years at Moor Park: first, because there are striking parallels between Carkesse's inflated vision of his talents and that of the Grubstreet narrator of the *Tale*; second, because Swift would have seen in Carkesse's claims a perfect illustration of the dangers lurking in Locke's notion of personal identity. *Lucida Intervalla* raises an issue which neither Locke nor those who rushed to attack his theory confronted: to what extent do madmen actively contrive new identities? It was this aspect of the relationship of consciousness to madness which most interested Swift. The peril of madness in the *Tale* is found to lie precisely in its power to alter consciousness of who one is.

The narrator of the *Tale* is not writing from an asylum, but he has spent time there and shares Carkesse's view that genius is generally attended by symptoms the vulgar confuse with simple lunacy. Carkesse addresses a poem to Edward Seymor, speaker of the House of Commons, begging him to send the sergeant-at-arms to "rescue" him from Bedlam (p. 59). The narrator of the *Tale* recommends to the same Seymor that a commission be set up to discover the true abilities of those in Bedlam and to find them proper employment in the world outside (p. 175).[19] To explain *why* men of great parts are so likely to be thought mad Carkesse has recourse to a metaphor suggestive of the theory of sympathetic vibration in the "Digression on Madness":

> ... they are call'd, by *Plot* of *poor* and *rich*,
> *Madmen*, whose *wit's* above the standard pitch.
> (p. 24)

The Grubstreet narrator's explanation is more elaborate, but it is developed from just this musical figure. "There is," he argues, "a peculiar *String* in the Harmony of Human Understanding, which in several individuals is exactly of the same Tuning." If, he continues, "you have the Good Fortune to light among those of the same Pitch, they will by a secret necessary Sympathy, strike at exactly the same time" and you will be hailed as an oracle. Should you, on the other hand, "chance to jar the String among those who are either above or below your own Height, instead of subscribing to your Doctrine, they will tie you fast, call you Mad, and feed you with Bread and Water" (pp. 167-168).

The narrator of the *Tale* is also reminiscent of Carkesse in that his lavish self-regard takes wing from earlier failures. For five years he vainly struggled to make his name as a wit by shining in conversation: "Now, this Disappointment," he confesses, "gave me the first Hint of setting up for an *Author*." Once an author he gains the position of advantage which so long eluded him: "I am grown absolute Master of the Occasions and Opportunities; to expose the Talents I have acquired" (p. 210). Though the narrator lives in squalor approaching that of Bedlam, he too nurses fantasies of literary glory: that in recognition of his genius the "Grandees of *Church* and *State*" have commissioned him to write the *Tale* (p. 39); that he is a purveyor of "momentous Truths" for the "universal Benefit of Mankind" (p. 184); that his work includes and exhausts "all that Human Imagination can *Rise* or *Fall* to" (p. 129); that because of its importance the work will soon be translated into various foreign languages (p. 106); that, in short, his labors have been on so unprecedented a scale as to make him "Secretary" of the universe (p. 123).

While Locke is nowhere mentioned in the *Tale* it seems appropriate that this strutting modern who suffers, he says, from that peculiarly modern complaint—weak memory (pp. 134-135, 92)—and who boasts of having made imagination supreme among his faculties (p. 209), should acquire a new identity in a manner arguably sanctioned by the most modern of philosophers.[20] As Swift presents the narrator's case few readers are apt to think him secretary of the universe or a benefactor of mankind, no matter how vivid his consciousness of fulfilling those roles may be. Still, Locke could be said to deprive us of sure grounds for denying these exalted pretensions by suggesting that through the agency of delusion one might become another person.[21]

Unlike those who were later to see in the matter of deluded consciousness only further proof of the implausibility of Locke's theory, Swift recognized that something important was at stake. The question whether identity is confined to a charmed circle of consciousness is related to the larger question of whether or not there are absolute criteria of truth. Swift regarded Locke's rejection of innate ideas as "dangerous" because it opened the way to an alarming relativism.[22] To say, as Locke had, that values are determined by environment and education, that there are no internal standards of morality common to man, and to press home the argument by noting that some societies consider it virtuous to eat one's enemies, kill one's aged parents, and bury one's children alive (1, 2, 9), is to undermine the assumptions requisite for civilized life. Throughout his career Swift strenuously resisted the notion that moral values might vary according to time and place. He savages the relativism of Locke's follower, Anthony Collins, in *Mr. Collins's Discourse of Freethinking* (1713), and of temporizing churchmen in the *Argument against Abolishing Christianity* (1708). In *Gulliver's Travels* (1726) he makes a point of showing that while customs may differ drastically from country to country behavior should nonetheless be judged by a uniform standard of ethics. Needless to say, the modest proposer may be regarded as a relativist of the most extreme stamp.

Swift no doubt found Locke's theory of personality analogously disturbing insofar as it does away with the notion of fixed individual identity, and seems to bestow a certain legitimacy on delusion with its inference that in the last analysis a person is whoever he thinks he is.[23] In Locke's example of the lunatic who believes himself a king and acts accordingly, the unstated premise is that his delusions will be apparent to everyone save himself and that the awareness others have of his lunacy will severely curtail the scope of his actions. Delusion, in this view, is deplorable, but essentially harmless. For Swift, on the other hand, deception of self is only the first step toward deceiving others. Men like Carkesse are seldom content to cherish their delusions behind locked Bedlam doors; they want people to share them.

Nor are all delusions so transparently foolish as those of the Grubstreet narrator. More times than not madmen are at liberty to influence who they will. And, as Swift makes clear in the *Tale*, delusive transformations of personality involve a malignant alchemy. Consciousness may not affect who a person truly is; all the same, there is no denying the effect it can have on how he is perceived. Once a man makes a proselyte of himself "the Difficulty is not so great in bringing over others; A strong Delusion always operating from *without*, as vigorously as from *within*" (p. 171).[24] Madness, by its very nature, results in psychic imperialism: lunatics, whether fancying themselves conquerors, philosophers, or apostles of new religions, long to impose their delusions on others. If we accept Locke's theory of identity, Swift appears to be saying, how can we demonstrate that a lunatic king, surrounded by people who embrace his delusion, is not in fact a king? Peter calls himself "God Almighty" and "Monarch of the Universe," and he has followers aplenty, followers, moreover, whose faith in several of his chimerical schemes costs them their lives. Those who set sail for his imaginary continent never return; those who trust to the efficacy of his pardons are executed without exception. The crazed Aeolists have equal success in disseminating their belief that foul air is holy spirit, just as Jack's demented rage and spite are taken by his brethren for sure signs of Godliness.

Locke argued that a man mad and a man sane should be considered separate persons because they do not share the same consciousness. Swift allows no such dissociation. Madness in the *Tale* has less to do with the assumption of new identities than with the spectacular elaboration of old ones, as the narrator's remembered scraps of a distasteful past should remind us. The Peter who thinks himself monarch of the universe is only an exaggerated version of the Peter who chafed against the restrictions of his father's will. Jack's craziness dramatizes old grievances against Peter. Having been kept from the will he now reads it with a vengeance; having once truckled to Peter's arbitrary commands he sometimes treats passersby to random acts of violence and sometimes begs them to strike him that he may later boast of heroic sufferings. Madness in the *Tale* is the work neither of humors nor of devils. It is volitional. The vapors which "water the Invention, and render it fruitful" (p. 163), have their source in the "lower Faculties," that is, in the passions.

In Dryden's *The Spanish Friar* there is a scene which illustrates something vitally important to Swift's view of insanity. Torrismond, the hero, is gripped by a mad passion for the queen and will hear no talk of possible cures even from the queen herself. He has no more wish than Carkesse to be cured of what other people think ails him:

> I cannot, nay I wish not to be cured . . .
> There is a pleasure sure
> In being mad, which none but mad-
>   men know.[25]

Swift's madmen in the *Tale* know well the pleasure in being mad, the pleasure of real or imagined power which madness brings, and the pleasure of overturning the rules by which sane men must live. As Peter's inventions, Jack's stratagems, and the contraptions of the Aeolists suggest, madness, for Swift, is a kind of perverse art whereby the madman seeks the control over real things which the artist has over fictive ones. In Carkesse's clumsy attempts to attain glory through fantastic new projections of self we have a Swiftian paradigm of madness. "If we consider," remarks the narrator of the *Tale*, that the choice in life lies "between *Things past*, and *Things conceived* . . . the Question is only this; Whether Things that have Place in the *Imagination* may not as properly be said to Exist as those that are seated in the *Memory*; which may be justly held in the Affirmative, and very much to the Advantage of the former, since This is acknowledged to be the *Womb* of Things, and the other allowed to be no more than the *Grave*" (p. 172). Like the old railway station attendant in *Pale Fire* who comes to believe he is God and begins rerouting the trains, Carkesse "peels off a drab and unhappy past and replaces it with a brilliant invention."[26]

Had Swift recognized that Locke's true concern in his chapter on personal identity was not with who a man *is*, but with what he may be held accountable for, he would, in all probability, still have thought Locke's theory an irresponsible one to espouse: to insist that a man mad should be regarded as a different person than the same man sane is to make madness a license for all manner of crime and folly. As a satirist Swift wished to hold men more accountable, not less. His position in the *Tale* clearly is that people are responsible for their deluded selves inasmuch as those selves are direct expressions of internal forces which they at worst encouraged, at best failed to control. Swift would argue that in Carkesse the "parson" and Carkesse the "poet" we should see primary aspects of Carkesse the man: arrogance, vanity, irascibility, ostentation. To make consciousness the determinant of identity is to cut the self ominously free from external criteria of identification. Swift's madmen know how "insipid" things are when not "convey'd in the Vehicle of *Delusion*" (p. 172). They know, too, that the mind can be made a laboratory of the imagination in which more flattering, often more dangerous, and all too often more successful versions of self are devised.

NOTES

1. John Locke, *An Essay concerning Human Understanding*, ed. Peter H. Nidditch (Oxford: Clarendon Press, 1975).
2. Christopher Fox, "Locke and the Scriblerians: The Discussion of Identity in Early Eighteenth Century England," *Eighteenth-Century Studies*, 16 (1982), 1-25.
3. *Loving Mad Tom: Bedlamite Verses of the XVI and XVII Centuries*, ed. Jack Lindsay (London: Fanfrolico Press, 1927), p. 26.
4. *Loving Mad Tom*, pp. 23, 35.
5. James Carkesse, *Lucida Intervalla: Containing divers Miscellaneous Poems Written at Finsbury and Bethlem* (London, 1679). For a fuller account of Carkesse's life see my introduction to the Augustan Reprint Society edition (Los Angeles, Calif.: Clark Memorial Library, 1979), pp. iii-xi. Page references given for the poetry extracts from Carkesse apply to both the original and the reprint editions.
6. Milton Rokeach, *The Three Christs of Ypsilanti* (New York: Vintage Books, 1964), p. 3.
7. *John Locke (1632-1704): Physician and Philosopher. A Medical Biography with an Edition of the Medical Notes in his Journals*, ed. Kenneth Dewhurst (London: Wellcome Historical Medical Library, 1963), pp. 100-101.
8. In *Nightmares and Hobbyhorses: Swift, Sterne, and Augustan Ideas of Madness* (San Marino, Calif.: Huntington Library, 1974), pp. 12-48, I have discussed how in Locke's day madness comes to be seen as a confusion between images of imagination and those of memory and sensation. Patricia Meyer Spacks observes that though British philosophers from Locke to Reid "recognize the theoretical possibility that the testimony of memory might confuse itself with that of imagination . . . they quickly retreat from the implications of such thinking." *Imagining a Self: Autobiography and Novel in Eighteenth-Century England* (Cambridge, Mass.: Harvard University Press, 1976), p. 3.
9. The possibility of double personality which Locke here opens up was not seriously exploited in literature until the fiction of the nineteenth century. In the first, and in certain respects most powerful, of many double novels in English, James Hogg's *Confessions of a Justified Sinner* (1824), Robert Wringhim *sees* a second self three paces to the left of him wherever he goes.
10. It is worth noting that the problem of identity in madness does not seem to exist

for earlier writers on the mind, most of whom took for granted that people's lives were vulnerable to supernatural intervention. If a devil entered a man and caused him to speak and act as if he were another person there could be no question of whether the man actually was, now, someone else. Rather, something else had become him; he was possessed. A generation before Locke's *Essay* a country doctor named William Drage described a case of what today would be called multiple personality: a young woman speaks in odd voices not her own, voices which shriek blasphemies, urge her to commit suicide, mock visitors, and threaten those who seek to cure her. To Drage the voices are palpably voices of devils; he does not even consider the possibility that they might be disturbed projections of self. (Drage's account is reprinted in *Three Hundred Years of Psychiatry 1535-1860*, ed. Richard Hunter and Ida Macalpine [London: Oxford University Press, 1963], pp. 174-177.) Michael MacDonald has studied the practice of another country doctor, Richard Napier. He points out that delusion does not rank high as a symptom of madness in the clinical records Napier kept between 1597 and 1634 of his mentally unbalanced patients. Reports of visions or otherworldly voices were far less likely to be thought signs of insanity in Napier's day than in Locke's because, MacDonald argues, "Elizabethans believed that the world was vibrant with supernatural forces and invisible beings." Napier himself, according to contemporary biographers, regularly sought the advice of the angel Raphael in diagnosing his patients. *Mystical Bedlam: Madness, Anxiety and Healing in Seventeenth-Century England* (Cambridge: Cambridge University Press, 1981), pp. 157, 16-19.

11. David P. Behan, "Locke on Persons and Personal Identity," *Canadian Journal of Philosophy*, 9 (1979), 69.

12. Isaac Watts, *Works*, ed. George Burder (London, 1810), V, p. 626. This passage was called to my attention by Christopher Fox.

13. *Two Dissertations concerning Sense and the Imagination. With an Essay on Consciousness* (London, 1728), p. 182.

14. *Essay on Consciousness*, pp. 149, 182, 183.

15. Richard Ellmann, *The Consciousness of Joyce* (New York: Oxford University Press, 1977). p.1.

16. Lillian Feder offers a preceptive, sympathetic analysis of Carkesse's plight in *Madness and Literature* (Princeton. N. J.: Princeton University Press, 1980), pp. 156-161.

17. Thomas Reid, one of the most persuasive critics of Locke's theory of identity, argues that knowledge of who we are is the most certain knowledge we have: "The identity of persons has often furnished matter of serious litigation before tribunals of justice. But no man of a sound mind ever doubted of his own identity, as far as he distinctly remembered." Reid does not, however, say anything about the sense of identity possessed by those of *unsound* mind. *Essays on the Intellectual Powers of Man*, Introduction by Baruch A. Brody (Cambridge, Mass.: M.I.T. Press, 1969), p. 341.

18. *Essay on Consciousness*, p. 163.

19. *A Tale of a Tub*, ed. A. C. Guthkelch and D. Nichol Smith, 2nd ed. (Oxford: Clarendon Press, 1958). All citations are to this edition.

20. There would also seem to be some parody of Locke's analysis of the uncertain signification of words, which results from the private associations each man

brings to them (3, 9), in the narrator's instructions for reading books: "Whatever Reader desires to have a thorow Comprehension of an Author's Thoughts, cannot take a better Method, than by putting himself into the Circumstances and Postures of Life, that the Writer was in, upon every important Passage as it flow'd from his Pen; For this will introduce a Parity and strict Correspondence of Idea's between the Reader and the Author" (p. 44).

21. To read Locke in this way is, doubtless, to read him wrong. As mentioned earlier, Locke's concern in discussing the relationship of consciousness to personal identity has to do with defining that faculty of man which appropriates past thoughts and actions to himself and which thereby makes him responsible for them. The history of response to Locke's chapter on identity, however, demonstrates that he is exceedingly easy to misread on this score. Indeed one recent apologist for Locke indirectly suggests that the chapter invites misreading when he asserts that the problems raised by Locke's detractors "*can be made* to disappear" (emphasis mine). M. W. Hughes, "Personal Identity: A Defense of Locke," *Philosophy*, 50 (1975), 169.

22. *The Prose Works of Jonathan Swift*, ed. Herbert Davis, 14 vols. (Oxford: Blackwell, 1939-68), II, 97.

23. Locke seems to have worried about this possibility in other contexts. In the chapter on enthusiasm added to the fourth edition (which appeared in 1700, several years after composition of the *Tale*) Locke is at pains to stress that "the strength of our persuasions" is no evidence of their validity (4, 19).

24. In a lighter vein, Swift has the narrator say that Dryden often confessed "that the World would have never suspected him to be so great a Poet, if he had not assured them so frequently in his Prefaces, that it was impossible they could either doubt or forget it" (p. 131).

25. *John Dryden*, ed. George Saintsbury (New York: A. A. Wyn, 1950), II, p. 144.

26. Vladimir Nabokov, *Pale Fire* (New York: Lancer Books, 1963), p. 162.

The Storied World: The Alloy of Imagination in Otway's Venice Preserved

JOHN DAVID WALKER

Thomas Otway's *Venice Preserv'd, or, A Plot Discover'd* (1682), is a play about alloyed things. The conspirator Renault gives us this dramatic theme in his oration to fellow plotters: "let's call to mind, my dearest Friends, / That there's nothing pure upon the Earth, / That the most valu'd things have most allays."[1] Everything in the play demonstrates the dramatic validity of his remark, even the midnight hour in which significant events occur, that point on the clock where night and morning, today and tomorrow, mingle in an alloy. The hour reminds us that humanity, as Montaigne perceives, is a "patchwork and motley" being;[2] or, as Renault knows, a creation "ne're constant, never certain" (II, 207). In this essay I will attempt to demonstrate three alloys which in the play affect, even shape, human actions. In the *New Organon* (1620), Francis Bacon observes that the mind "forming its notions mixes up [alloys] its own nature with the nature of things."[3] Specifically, in *Venice Preserv'd*, it is the human imagination which alloys "the nature of things," affecting perception to such an extent that what is perceived is often called a "story" or "tale."[4] Second, the imagination is itself alloyed in the play with the nature or quality of the good which it forms and contains. And third, the dramatic effect of the human imagination in shaping the "plot" or "tale" of human life is alloyed with the divine imagination which, as Ralph Cudworth remarks, shapes the greater *"Plot of Divine Providence."*[5]

It is important to my argument that we recall that an alloy may function in two quite different ways. It may work to make a substance strong and useful. In his essay "We taste nothing pure," Montaigne observes that neither gold nor virtue nor pleasure "could be serviceable to life without admixture."[6] It may also, however, serve as an admixture which devalues or lowers the quality of that to which it is added. Throughout *Venice Preserv'd*, Otway tempers action with alloys that function in both ways—either to disvalue or to create value.

Almost everywhere in *Venice Preserv'd* is an appeal to imagination which, alloying perception, shapes the plot or tale or story each character acts out in his human drama. The play begins with Jaffeir and his father-in-law, Priuli, recalling to each other's memory shared events, yet each perceiving those events differently; the middle of the play has Renault recalling for the conspirators their shared past while at the same time impressing upon them images of the destruction of Venice—the last act in their plot of conspiracy; towards the end of the play Belvidera, Jaffeir's wife, attempts to alter the memory her father has of her elopement—"do not call to memory / My disobedience, but let pity enter / . . . and quite deface the impression" (V, 51-53). For Thomas Hobbes, "imagination and memory are but one thing,"[7] and Samuel Gott, an urbane, mid-seventeenth-century Puritan writer, asserts in *The Divine History of the Genesis of the World* (1670), that "there are several . . . Facultys of the Imagination, as Judgement, Ingeny, Memory . . . "[8] An appeal to memory is an appeal to the imagination.

Moreover, the decisive turning point in Jaffeir's life, his betrayal of the conspirators, is brought about in Act IV when Belvidera reshapes his imagination by making him visualize the savagery he has bound himself by vows to commit. She reminds him that her lot may yet be to fall "Victim to the hatefull lust / Of that Infernal Devil, that old Fiend" (IV, 29-30) Renault, who has attempted to rape her. Jaffeir replies, Name, name it not again. / It shews a beastly Image for him to see—the slaughter of the innocents:

> Think thou already hearst their dying screams,
> Think that thou seest their sad distracted Mothers
> Kneeling before thy feet, and begging pity
> With torn dishevel'd hair . . .
> Think thou seest this . . .

> . . . .
> Think too . . .
> What miseries the next day brings upon thee.
> Imagine all the horrours of that night.
> . . . .
> Think what then may prove.
> My Lot! the Ravisher may the come safe. . . .
> (IV, 51-54; 58; 59-61; 63-64)[9]

Jaffeir's response indicates some profound change which now begins in him:

> By all Heavens powers Prophetick truth dwells in thee,
> For every word thou speak'st strikes through my heart
> Like a new light, and shows it how't has wander'd. . . .
> (IV, 69-71)

That this "new light" which radiates through Jaffeir signals a change in the quality of his imagination finds support in a statement made by the seventeenth-century French physician and moralist Marin Cureau de la Chambre in *The Character of the Passions*, translated into English in 1650:

> when this image [of the good] is formed in the imagination, it multiplies in all parts of the Soul, it enlights them and excites after them those which are capable to be moved; Its even very likely that 'tis in effect a refined and purified light. . . .[10]

And again:

> its . . . true, that the image of good is in the imagination, as a light which sheds its rays. . . .[11]

With a similar image, Samuel Gott states:

> the Imagination doth . . . Actualy Irradiate its own Phantasms for the use and service of the Understanding, whereby they become the most spiritual and fitt Objects thereof: and then when the Understanding would Animadvert them, it doth farther Irradiate them by its own most Pure and Mental Light. . . .[12]

For Gott, the imagination and understanding are so interrelated that should "the Imagination be hurt or distempered . . . the Understanding is accordingly disordered,"[13] and their light so alloying one another that it seems an easy step to Pierre Gassendi's earlier observation: "I find no distinction between the understanding and the imagination."[14]

This seems to be Otway's assumption, since Belvidera, in her altering of Jaffeir's imagination, equates *to think* with *to imagine*.

De la Chambre's belief that the image of the good is formed and held by the imagination may help in determining the "new light" Jaffeir experiences. For if the imagination alloys perception of reality, the imagination itself is alloyed by the good which informs it. Towards the end of Act II, Jaffeir calls Belvidera, whose name means "beautiful vision," "the divinest Good man e're possest" (II, 380). Since Belvidera is for Jaffeir his image, his beautiful vision, of the divine Good, we may determine the quality of that good alloying his imagination by looking at his conception of her prior to the "new light."

In the play's first scene, Priuli calls to memory Jaffeir's elopement with Belvidera "At dead of night": "You stole her from me, like a Theif you stole her" (49). Jaffeir reminds him, "Tis to me you owe her" (27), and to justify his claim he describes his rescue of her when, having "sail'd to see / The *Adriatick* wedded by our Duke" (31-32), she was swept overboard. Plunging after her, he

> Redeem'd her Life with half the loss of mine;
> Like a rich Conquest in one hand I bore her,
> And with the other dasht the sawcy Waves,
> That throng'd and prest to rob me of my prize:
> . . . .
> Indeed you thank't me; but a nobler gratitude
> Rose in her soul: for from that hour she lov'd me,
> Till for her Life she paid me with her self.
> (I, 41-44; 46-48)

The imagery defines Belvidera as a treasure that can be stolen or owed or redeemed; a rich conquest tempting to saucy thieves; wealth that can be used to repay Jaffeir for his efforts. Moreover, when Jaffeir and Belvidera meet after the state's foreclosure on his property, he suspects that with the loss of his wealth, Belvidera too may leave him: "If thou art alter'd," he asks, "where shall I have harbour? / Where ease my loaded Heart?" (I, 326-327). Here he imagines himself as a merchant vessel—a ship of fortune—seeking harbor in Belvidera. Similarly, being assured of her constancy, he imagines himself as

> . . . a poor Merchant driven on unknown Land,
> That had by chance packt up his choicest Treasure
> In one dear Casket, and sav'd only that . . .
> (I, 390-392)

He then embraces her as his "precious store" (394), and the equation between worldly treasures and Belvidera is emphatic: like a merchant of Venice he has salvaged from fortune's sea his jewel of great price and "hugs" it with a merchant's love. Jaffeir has confused a sensible good with a divine good.

When the imagination confuses its "divinest Good" with a sensible good, as does Jaffeir's, the potential for moral ruin, Otway suggests, is present. It leads Jaffeir to accept as logical Pierre's "story" of the foreclosure by the state on Jaffeir's property as a *rape* of Belvidera. It leads as well to his joining a conspiracy to revenge the insult, not only to the "Common Good" (I, 211) of Venice, but specifically to his "divine" Good, Belvidera. Both the time and place in which he enters the conspiracy exert a quiet commentary on the spiritual journey he is set upon, following, as he is, a sensible good. He meets Pierre at midnight (that "dead time of Night" he says [II, 72]) on the Rialto, the mercantile center of seventeenth-century Venice, and the occasion makes him think:

> I look as if all Hell were in my Heart,
> And I in Hell. Nay, surely 'tis so with me . . .
> . . . .
> Hell! Hell! why sleepest thou?
> (II, 67–68, 76)

Pierre enters, and the next event completes the carefully-wrought implication that an imagination alloyed by a mutable good risks selling the soul to the world of matter, whose archetypal image is hell. Pierre offers money: "here's something to buy Pins, / Marriage is Chargeable." Jaffeir responds, "I but half wisht / To see the Devil, and he's here already. . . . What must this buy, Rebellion, Murder, Treason?" (II, 98-100, 102).

What he buys is admission into the secret, midnight world of conspiracy, and, with disturbing irony, the price is Belvidera, "A Pledge, worth more than all the World can pay for" (II, 346). The irony persists, for as Belvidera is led away by Renault, so is the "beautiful vision" of Jaffeir's "divine" good. Jaffeir turns away into blindness:

> Oh my Eyes!
> Look not that way, but turn your selves awhile
> Into my heart, and be wean'd all together.

>   My Friend, where art thou?
> *Pierr.* Here, my Honour's Brother.
>   (II, 417-420)

Led by an imagination alloyed with a sensible good, Jaffeir finds at the end of his journey into conspiracy only the blinding darkness of his heart.[15]

In a scene which parallels Jaffeir's selling of Belvidera, and implicitly comments on Jaffeir's action, Antonio, a corrupt Venetian senator, buys *his* way into the graces of the courtesan, Aquilina. Otway thus provides an even bleaker view of what happens ultimately when imagination is alloyed with a sensible good. Antonio disassembles her name—Aquilina—and reassembles it as Queen Nacky and then as Nicky Nacky, while referring to her in the same scene as his Madonna:

> *Nacky, Nacky, Nacky*—how dost do *Nacky?*
> Hurry durry. I am come little *Nacky*; past eleven a Clock, a late hour; time in all Conscience to go to bed *Nacky—Nacky* did I say? Ay *Nacky*; *Aquilina, lina, lina, quilina, quilina, quilina, Aquilina, Naquilina, Naquilina, Acky, Acky, Nacky, Nacky,* Queen *Nacky*—come let's to bed—
> . . . .
> *Madona,* as I take it you are my—you are—thou art my little *Nicky Nacky.* . . .
>   (III, 14-19, 30-31)

If, as John Donne once said, "names are to instruct us, and express natures and essences,"[16] then Antonio's disassembling and reassembling her name in altered form provides an instance of his imagination transforming her into a metaphor of meaning. Nicky Nack refers to the pudendum, and a Nick Nack is a trivial object bought and sold—in his case a whore. Antonio's imagination transforms his Madonna into a knick knack. For him she is "Queen *Nacky*," his "*Madona*," and thus the image of the good which alloys his imagination. The result of such an alloy is the disfiguring of humanity: Antonio subsequently sees her as a toad who will "spit in my Face a little . . . spit in my Face, never so little" (III, i, 91-92); or he sees himself as "a Bull, a *Basan*-Bull, the Bull of Bulls, or any Bull" (82-83); or a dog, "let me be a Dog—and . . . use me like a Dog a little" (98). The comedy is alloyed by the tragedy of debased imaginings. Gian Francesco Pico della Mirandola states in an essay on the imagination that if, yielding to the senses, phantasy shall decline to apply itself to the business of virtue, so great is its power that it afflicts the body and beclouds the mind, and finally brings it about that man divests himself of humanity, and takes on bestiality. Therefore we can without difficulty affirm that not only all the good, universally, but also all the bad, can be derived from the imagination.[17]

Jaffeir does not reach the extent of Antonio's debasement, yet the scene implies that the good his imagination follows leads to this final darkness.

Returning now to the "new light" Belvidera brings to Jaffeir's imagination, we are better able to see the change in Jaffeir as a shift from a sensible to a spiritual good, to a "beautiful vision" that truly is "the divinest good man e're possest." I will mention only a few of the instances in the remainder of the play which suggest the presence of this new perception. First, we should recall Belvidera's plea to her father: "do not call to memory / My disobedience, but let pity enter / . . . and quite deface the impression" (V, 51-53). Pity, compassion, a selfless love deface the images of a sensible good and, it seems, alter the nature of the imagination. When Jaffeir appears before the midnight meeting of the senators, he tells them he has come "in pity / To all those wretches whose unhappy dooms / Are fix'd and seal'd" (IV, 142-144). When he confronts Pierre, Jaffeir begs to be looked upon "with an eye of mercy, / With pity and with charity" to be beheld (IV, 282-283). Remembering his vow to kill Belvidera should he betray the conspirators, he threatens to do so, then throws the dagger away: "by immortal Love," Jaffeir tells her, "I cannot longer bear a thought to harm thee" (IV, 523). Belvidera later tells her father that she was by "love preserv'd" (V, 105), and her phrase links with the title, for *Venice Preserv'd* is "love preserv'd" against the passions of revenge which a mutable good seems inevitably to inspire. The "new light" is then, at least in part, the light of compassion, the self-sacrificing love for the other, which the divine good radiates.

As this "new light" irradiates Jaffeir's darkness, it causes him also to understand the alloyed nature of life. Jaffeir's perception before his change was binary, an either-or. Later he recognizes the presence of human alloy when he asks, "Why was such happiness not given me pure? Why dash'd [alloyed] with cruel wrongs, and bitter wantings?" (IV, 85-86). Towards the close of the play, he has learned the answer.

Parting with Belvidera to join Pierre on the scaffold, Jaffeir blesses her, aware that his blessing wounds like a curse—"Your cruel blessings," Belvidera cries (V, 306). He recalls "the miserable day / We wedded" (V, 256-257), a "curs'd" day (261), though, as he tells her, "man ne'r was bless'd / Since the first pair first met, as I have been" (270-271). The inheritance of Adam and Eve's fall into the knowledge of good and evil, Jaffeir implies, is the alloyed world where, in Montaigne's words, "We taste nothing pure."

And finally when Jaffeir on the scaffold stabs Pierre at Pierre's request, Jaffeir perceives his murder of Pierre and then his own suicide as a ritual sacrifice where the rack is also an altar, Pierre a sacrificial victim, and himself a priest and victim.

> Now, ye curs'd Rulers,
> Thus of the blood y'have shed I make Libation,
> And sprinkl't mingling; May it rest upon you,
> And all your Race .... (V, 469–472)

Through his imagery, his blood, mingled or alloyed with Pierre's on the knife's edge, when sprinkled, as from a hyssop, becomes both a libation in praise of love preserved and a curse which consecrates the Rulers of Venice, who had broken their vow not to execute the conspirators, to divine judgment. Otway, at the same time, draws his audience into his theme, asking them to alloy Jaffeir's greatest loss with his greatest gain.

In his essay "We taste nothing pure," Montaigne quotes "an old Greek verse" and comments on it: "'The gods sell us all the good things they give us.' That is to say, they gave us none pure and perfect, none that we do not buy at the price of some evil."[18] The gift of an imagination alloyed with a spiritual good which Jaffeir has accepted from Belvidera and which has preserved the state from violation and ruin costs Jaffeir his life, the life of his friend Pierre, and, at the end, the life of Belvidera, who dies of a broken heart. Yet in the somber vision of the play, only an imagination alloyed with a spiritual good can preserve the human community. Such preservation, for Otway, is a "most valu'd" thing and thus most alloyed in its cost.

II

The alternate title to *Venice Preserv'd—A Plot Discover'd*—is an obvious reference to the conspiracy to overthrow the Venetian government.

Less obvious, perhaps, though just as meaningful, is Otway's use of "Plot" to refer to a plan, outline, or scheme of a fictional work. This particular "Plot Discover'd," as we have seen, is the "storied" world that imagination alloyed by a sensible or divine good creates. It is also, as I will now argue, the "storied" world of divine providence, or the "*Plot* of *Divine Providence*," as Ralph Cudworth calls it. In his *True Intellectual System of the Universe*, published four years before Otway's play, Cudworth sees "The Evolution of the World" as "a *Truer Poem*" in which all of us are

> Histrionical Acters [sic] upon the Stage, who notwithstanding insert something of our *Own* into the *Poem* too; but God *Almighty*, is that *Skilful Dramatist*, who always connecteth that of ours which went before, with what of his follows after, into good *Coherent Sense*; and will at last make it appear, that a *Thred* of exact *Justice* did run through all. . . . [19]

The divine imagination, in other words, composing the dramatic poem of the world, is the constant alloy of all human plots and designs, providing whatever value they may have in the overall "*Coherent Sense*" of the divine play. It is this "Plot" which is also "Discover'd" in *Venice Preserv'd*.

Isaac Barrow observes that on the world's stage "Divine and human influences are so twisted and knit together that it is hard to sever them."[20] In ways which reflect this difficulty, Otway ranges through degrees of complexity to discover for his audiences the plot of providence alloying the plot of conspiracy. When Jaffeir, acting upon the changed imagination Belvidera has created in him, stands before the entrance to the senate, he says, "Now the Lot's cast, and Fate doe what thou wilt" (IV, 105). After revealing the names and plans of the conspirators to the senate, he again says, "Now Fate thou hast caught me" (IV, 177). Jaffeir senses that in rejecting one plot, he has entered into another—the plot evoked in Cudworth's and Barrow's statements. That indeed Jaffeir has, Otway indicates in a variety of ways. The senate is assembled at this midnight hour because, as Priuli tells them,

> we stand
> Upon the Very brink of gaping ruine,
> Within this City's form'd a dark Conspiracy,
> To massacre us all . . . .
> . . . .

>   nay the hour too, fixt;
> . . . .
>   from unknown hands
> I had this warning . . . .
>   (IV, 117-120, 122, 124-125)

The fact of a conspiracy (if not the details) is discovered through "unknown hands," at the very moment Jaffeir is about to do the same.

Otway runs a dramatic risk of dulling the effect of Jaffeir's revelation, unless we are being asked to see his action as being "twisted and knit" with that of the "*Skilful Dramatist*" whose "overruling hand,"[21] or "special hand," "interposing . . . hand," "insensible hand," or "immediate hand"[22] is composing the plot of providence. Barrow argues "that in truth there is not in the world any occurrence meerly fortuitous, or fatal (all being guided and wielded by the powerful hand of an All-wise, and Almighty God) . . . wherefore upon every event, we should, raising our minds above all other causes, discern and acknowledge God's hand."[23] Those "unknown hands" which discovered the conspirator's plot coincidentally with Jaffeir's discovery seem analogous to the "insensible hand" of God in whose plot Jaffeir has willingly taken the role of protagonist.

The antagonists whose counter plot must be defeated and assimilated are the conspirators. They think of themselves as "Men like Gods" (II, 139), "Men separated by the Choice of Providence, / From the gross heap of Mankind" (II, 224-225), and thus empowered to bring apocalyptic judgment on Venice. Renault in fact imagines Venice "Burning with flames rather from Heav'n than ours" (III, ii, 377). In this context, the midnight settings are symbolic, for that hour is traditionally the hour of apocalypse, the "*Meridies noctis . . . that noone of night*" as John Donne describes.[24] Thomas Wilson defines midnight in *A Complete Christian Dictionary* (London, 1678): "Mid-night. The time of mens most secure Rest . . . when they say, *Peace and safety, then cometh sudden destruction.*" A sense of "profound repose" runs through Renault's midnight charge to the conspirators:

> Are not the Senate lull'd in full security,
> Quiet and satisfy'd, as Fools are always!
> Never did so profound repose forerun
> Calamity so great. . . . (III, ii, 358-361)

But the senate is assembled, the conspiracy is discovered, and instead it is the conspirators themselves who are "lull'd in full security":

> Nay our good Fortune
> Has blinded the most piercing of Mankind:
> Strengthen'd the fearfull'st, charm'd the most
> suspectful, confounded the most subtle: for we
> live....
> (III, ii, 361-364)

> How often on the brink of some discovery
> Have we stood tottering, and yet still kept our ground
> So well, the busiest searchers ne'r could follow
> Those subtle Tracks which puzzled all suspition....
> (III, ii, 351-354)

The conspirator's midnight sense of security preceding their "sudden destruction" should also be understood in other contexts from providential literature. Isaac Barrow, for instance, observes that "when pestilent enterprises ... are brought to a head, and come near to the point of being executed; the sudden detection ... doe argue the ever vigilant Eye, and the all-powerful Hand to be engaged.... [God] often doth suffer it to grow on to a pitch of maturity, till it be ... ready to be hatched ... then in a trice he snappeth and crusheth it to nothing...."[25] And Robert South declares: "so many politic conceptions, so elaborately formed and wrought, and grown at length ripe for delivery, do yet, in the issue, miscarry and prove abortive; for, being come to the birth, the all-disposing providence of God denies them strength to bring forth."[26] South's image echoes in Bedamore's statement to Pierre, "the Deed's near Birth" (II, 257); but providence, through those "unknown hands" and through Jaffeir, alloys their plot and brings instead sudden destruction upon the conspirators.

The most complex strategy Otway uses to suggest the altered effects of human actions and perceptions when alloyed by the divine imagination is in the structural designs of the play. The linear progression of the play's action is expressed principally in the movement of the conspiracy from secrecy to exposure and in Jaffeir's "descent" from the community of Venice into the "hell" of the conspirator's society and his return to Venice. There is in addition another structure, reflective or ring-like rather than linear, where events in the first half of the play are mirrored in the second half. This structure appears in Jaffeir's actions and incidentally (though touchingly) in Belvidera's. For instance, Jaffeir's movement towards conspiracy is prompted by Pierre's description of the foreclosure on Jaffeir's property as a metaphoric rape of Belvidera (I, 232-249); his movement out of conspiracy begins with Belvidera's account of Renault's real attempt to rape her (III, ii, 179-193). Jaffeir agrees to meet Pierre at midnight (I, 301-305), then, in a prayer, asks heaven why he has "sence to know the Curse that's on" him (I, 314); after Belvidera's account of attempted rape, he agrees to meet her at midnight, followed by a prayer in which he contemplates his "curst . . . Condition" (III, ii, 209-213). This reflective structure continues in the scene between Jaffeir and Pierre before the senate, for their language reaches back to remind us of the play's opening scene between Jaffeir and Priuli. Pierre's question, "Hast thou not wrong'd me?" (IV, 313), recalls Priuli's: "Have you not wrong'd me?" (I, 7); and Priuli's remembrance of his generosity towards Jaffeir and Jaffeir's betrayal of it through his "theft" of Belvidera is echoed in Pierre's recollection and accusation:

> when first my foolish heart took pity
> On thy misfortunes, sought thee in thy miseries,
> Reliev'd thy wants, and rais'd thee from thy State
> Of wretchedness . . . .
> . . . .
> All I receiv'd in surety for thy truth,
> Were unregarded oaths; and this, this dagger,
> Given with a worthless pledge [Belvidera], thou since
> hast stoln. . . .
> (IV, 355-358, 360-362)

Belvidera's last scene at the close of the play reflects events in the first act. Jaffeir has asked her, "When in a Bed of straw we shrink together, / And the bleak winds shall whistle round our heads; / . . .Wilt thou then / . . . shelter me with Love?" (I, 367-370). Her answer—"Oh I will love thee, even in Madness love thee" (I, 371)—is dramatically recalled in her final scene where she shrinks before a whistling wind her mind cannot bear:

> come to bed!
> Prithee my Love. The Winds! hark how they whistle!
> And the Rain beats: oh how the weather shrinks me!
> (V, 482-484)

Memories of Jaffeir and Pierre then rise like ghosts in her imagination: "help me! / They have hold on me, and drag me to the bottom" (V, 507-508). The word "bottom" here as elsewhere in the play refers to the sea's depths, and the image of Belvidera drowning recalls (with an ironic twist) her rescue from the sea which Jaffeir describes to Priuli in Act I.

This reflective, ring-like structure alloys the linear in this sense: like Dante's pilgrim who finds redemption only through the experience of hell, Jaffeir's journey into conspiracy, motivated by an imagination alloyed with a sensible good, is imaged as a descent into hell where, undergoing a conversion in which his imagination becomes alloyed with a divine good, he sees his mind's "sickness" (III, ii, 93), and returns to save Venice. Events in that descent are mirrored in his ascent out of conspiracy, the difference being that, alloyed with a divine good, his imagination responds to the events in opposite ways. Alloyed with a divine good, Jaffeir enacts the central paradox of the plot composed by the imagination of God, "that *Skilful Dramatist*," that the way up is the way down. The mirroring of events in his journey into and out of hell is the saving alloy for Jaffeir that turns descent into ascent.

Imagination which alloys the perception of things, the nature of the good which alloys imagination, and the divine imagination which alloys all human designs, bringing them into the plot of providence, are the "most valu'd things" which Otway dramatically develops in his last and finest tragedy. I should like to add one other alloy in conclusion. The seventeenth century paralleled Venice with Venus. In a prefatory poem to *A Survey of the Signorie of Venice* (1651), James Howell declares:

> Venus *and* Venice *are great Queens in their degree,*
> Venus *is Queen* of Love, Venice *of* Policie.

More explicitly, Howell develops the comparison: "it may be well thought that the Goddesse *Venus* and the Cittie of *Venice* had one kind of procreation being both engendred of the Sea; It is also very likely Aphrodite . . . had her Original out of the white Spume which *Neptune* casts upon those little gentle Ilands whereon *Venice* makes her bed."[27]

Venice preserved is in the play Venus or love preserved. In Otway's perception, the very existence of the city of man, no matter how crippled with frailties and vain imaginings, implies an ever-present and preserving alloy of compassionate human love, like that of Jaffeir's and Belvidera's, even though it costs no less than life itself. Perhaps this alloy is truly for Otway the "most valu'd" thing.

NOTES

1. Thomas Otway, *Venice Preserv'd*, in *The Works of Thomas Otway*, ed. J. C. Ghosh (Oxford: Clarendon Press, 1932), II, p. 247. Quotations from the play are from this edition. Citations to act and lines will be incorporated in the text of the essay.
2. Michel de Montaigne, "We taste nothing pure," in *The Complete Works*, trans. Donald M. Frame (Stanford, Calif.: Stanford University Press, 1948), p. 511.
3. *The Works of Francis Bacon*, ed. James Spedding, *et al.* (New York: Hurd and Houghton, 1869), VIII, p. 45.
4. See, for example: I, 228, 268; II, 176; III, ii, 130, 132; IV, 43, 150, 417; V, 516. For the use of *story* to mean fiction as well as history in the seventeenth century, see Bruce W. Wardropper, "*Don Quixote*: Story or History," *Modern Philology*, 63 (1965), 1-11.
5. Ralph Cudworth, *The True Intellectual System of the Universe* (London, 1678), p. 670.
6. Montaigne, *The Complete Works*, p. 510.
7. Thomas Hobbes, *Leviathan*, ed. Michael Oakeshott (Oxford: Blackwell, n. d.), p. 10.
8. Samuel Gott, *The Divine History of the Genesis of the World* (London, 1670), p. 456. For an informative discussion of Gott, see J. Max Patrick, "Puritanism and Poetry: Samuel Gott," *University of Toronto Quarterly*, 8 (1939), 211-226.
9. This appeal to the imagination, both in technique and rhetoric, is strikingly similar to one made by the anonymous writer of *An Appeal from the Country to the City For the Preservation of his Majesties Person, Liberty, Property, and the Protestant Religion* (London, 1679), p. 2: "Imagine you see the whole Town in a flame, occasioned ... by the Popish malice ... fancy, that amongst the distracted Crowd, you behold Troops of Papists, ravishing your wives and Daughters, dashing your little Childrens brains out against the walls ... represent to yourselves ... imagine you see ... fancy you behold ... Women running with their hair about their ears. ..."
10. Marin Cureau de la Chambre, *The Character of the Passions* (London, 1650), p. 48.
11. De la Chambre, pp. 49-50.
12. Gott, *Divine History*, p. 449.
13. Gott, *Divine History*, p. 450.
14. *The Selected Works of Pierre Gassendi*, ed. and trans. Craig B. Brush (New York: Johnson Reprint Corporation, 1972), p. 25.
15. For discussion of the Scholastic and Neostoic view that imagination conceives only a sensible good and is thus apparently a principle of error, see Anthony Levi, S. J., *French Moralists: The Theory of the Passions* (Oxford: Clarendon Press, 1964).
16. John Donne, *Essays in Divinity*, ed. Evelyn Simpson (Oxford: Clarendon Press, 1952), p. 23.

17. Gian Francesco Pico della Mirandola [nephew of the famous Pico], *On the Imagination*, trans. Harry Caplan (New Haven, Conn.: Yale University Press, 1930), p. 43.
18. Montaigne, *Complete Works*, p. 510.
19. Cudworth, *True Intellectual System*, pp. 879-880.
20. *The Works of the Learned Isaac Barrow* (London, 1700), I, p. 131.
21. Robert South, *Sermons Preached Upon Several Occasions* (Oxford: Clarendon Press, 1823), I, p. 245.
22. Barrow, *Works*, I, p. 137; II, pp. 103, 126, 125.
23. Barrow, III, p. 45.
24. *The Sermons of John Donne*, ed. George Potter and Evelyn Simpson (Berkeley: University of California Press, 1955), II, p. 350.
25. Barrow, *Works*, I, pp. 135-136.
26. South, *Sermons Preached*, I, pp. 246-247.
27. James Howell, in *A Survey of the Signorie of Venice* (London, 1651), p. 32.

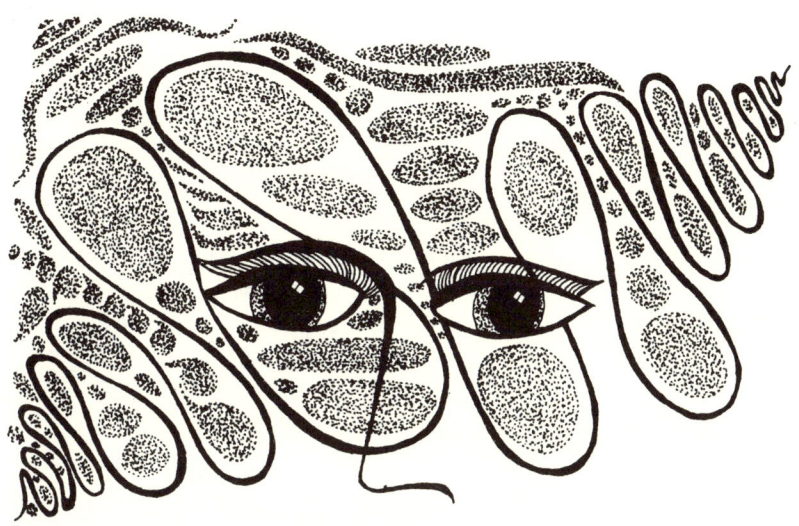

Association, Madness, and the Measures of Probability in Locke and Hume

JOHN P. WRIGHT

While it played an important part in subsequent philosophical thought,[1] the final chapter of Book II of Locke's *Essay concerning Human Understanding* has been disregarded or disparaged by major twentieth-century Locke scholars. For example, James Gibson wrote that this chapter, which is entitled "Of the Association of *Ideas*,"

> was only added as an afterthought, in the fourth edition of the *Essay*. The use which is then made of Association [is] as merely a principle by which we can explain some part of the oddness and extravagance of men's opinions and actions. . . .[2]

Gibson argues that Locke's primary interest in the *Essay* was in cognitive consciousness in so far as its "natural tendency" was "towards knowledge."[3] Aaron writes in a similar vein when he claims that the chapter was not central to Locke's thinking for he "only uses it to account for aberrations from the normal."[4] In this paper I shall take on three tasks. In the first place I shall argue that the chapter plays a more integral role in Locke's thought than is suggested by these comments of Gibson and Aaron, and by the silence of other commentators. I shall explain why, nevertheless, the chapter does appear to be at odds with a central thesis espoused in earlier editions of the *Essay*. Secondly, I shall speculate on the sources of two of the main ideas developed in the chapter and explain Locke's own original contribution to the topics discussed. Finally, I shall show the importance of Locke's chapter for one eighteenth-century writer, namely David Hume. I shall show how their reflections on association of ideas can help us understand the relations between the epistemological writings of these authors.

THE ASSOCIATION OF IDEAS AND THE REST OF THE *ESSAY*

I think that Gibson and Aaron are correct in claiming that Locke's central goal was to establish those positive conditions in the mind which lead us toward knowledge and rational belief. In describing his task in the introductory chapter of the *Essay*, Locke writes that he is going

> to search out the *Bounds* between Opinion and Knowledge; and examine by what Measures, in things, whereof we have no certain Knowledge, we ought to regulate our Assent, and moderate our Perswasions.[5]

His ultimate aim is to establish a normative epistemology[6]—one which tells us what exactly we can be certain about and how we *ought* to regulate our belief in those matters about which we cannot be certain. At the same time it must be recognized that the whole of the *Essay* is written against the background of Locke's conviction that nonsense, error, and ignorance are far more prevalent among men than clarity and a careful weighing of evidence. In his introductory chapter Locke also writes that he is going to set down

> the Grounds of those Perswasions, which are to be found amongst Men, so various, different and wholly contradictory; and yet asserted some where or other with such Assurance, and Confidence, that he that shall take a view of the Opinions of Mankind, observe their Opposition . . . may perhaps have Reason to suspect, That either there is no such thing as Truth at all; or that Mankind hath no sufficient Means to attain a certain Knowledge of it.
> (1, 1, 2)

His task is to counter a kind of skepticism which arises from a reflection on the fact that the world is full of opinions which, while mutually contradictory, are upheld by their proponents with absolute assurance. There is evidence which suggests that the whole problem of human understanding arose when Locke and some of his friends were discussing "the principles of morality and revealed religion."[7] At least it is clear that the heated disputes of his comtemporaries on these topics were never very far from Locke's mind while he was writing the *Essay*.

While Book IV of the *Essay* is primarily concerned with the establishment of a normative epistemology, the other three books include important reflections on aberrant thinking. In Book I, Locke identifies a principle—that of innate ideas—which he thinks has been used to establish the worst sorts of prejudices. In Book II, where Locke is primarily concerned to identify the source of our ideas, he includes four chapters apart from that on association in which he discusses the ways in which our ideas may be faulty.[8] In another chapter—"Of Power"—Locke devotes a number of sections to the discussion of the errors human beings make about good and evil.[9] In Book III and elsewhere he is concerned to identify a major source of confusion in our thinking—namely, the misuse of words. Even Book IV includes a whole chapter devoted to "Wrong Assent or Errour"[10] and another wholly devoted to the discussion of the delusions of religious fanatics.[11]

The chapter on association itself has its roots in an earlier chapter of Book II, as well as in some entries in Locke's Journals for 1666, 1677, and 1678.[12] It begins with the reflection that while we find it easy to recognize what is "Extravagant in the Opinions, Reasonings, and Actions of other Men," we are often unable to recognize such extravagances in ourselves. We are able to employ the "Authority of Reason" in order to condemn the unreasonableness of others but are unable to recognize our own absurd beliefs, reasoning patterns, and behavior (2, 33, 1). Locke tells his reader that he has discovered that this blindness to reason has "the very same Root" and depends on "the very same Cause" to which he had earlier attributed madness (2, 33, 3). In the earlier chapter, "Of Discerning," Locke argued that madmen, unlike imbeciles, have not "lost the Faculty of Reasoning." In fact madmen, "having joined together some *Ideas* very wrongly ...

mistake them for Truths; and they err as Men do, that argue right from wrong Principles." One madman wrongly fancies himself a king, but he correctly reasons that he should have "suitable Attendance, Respect and Obedience." Another believes that he is made out of glass and draws the correct inference that he should take suitable precautions to prevent his brittle body from breaking (2, 11, 13). The thesis that the madman's reason is wholly intact is clearly formulated in the 1677 Journals, where Locke remarks that "Madnesse seems to be noething but a disorder in the imagination, and not in the discursive faculty."[13] In both of these discussions of madness, Locke notes that many men who are sane in other respects may, on some particular topic, be "as frantik, as any in *Bedlam*." While he does not employ the term "association of ideas" for the cause, he notes that either a "sudden very strong impression" or the "long fixing his Fancy upon one sort of Thoughts" will cause "incoherent *Ideas*" to be "cemented together so powerfully, as to remain united." This powerful connection of ideas seems to be the source of the "wrong Propositions" which madmen mistake for truth (2, 11, 13).

However, Locke makes far stronger claims about the scope of the principle of association in the new chapter which he added to the fourth edition of the *Essay*. There he writes that it is this principle which accounts for the "Irreconcilable opposition between the different Sects of Philosophy and Religion." Such a claim is hardly insignificant given his stated aims in the introductory chapter of the book. Moreover, Locke claims that association is the source of absurdity, error, and even our inability to reason. The principle

> gives Sence to *Jargon*, Demonstration to Absurdities, and Consistency to Nonsense, and is the foundation of the greatest, I had almost said, of all the Errors in the World; or if it does not reach so far, it is at least the most dangerous one, since so far as it obtains, it hinders Men from seeing and examining.   (2, 33, 18)

In short, he is claiming that it is really this cause which underlies the various forms of misguided thinking which he has identified throughout the *Essay*.

While Locke never attempts to show in detail how a wrong association of ideas underlies such sources of controversy as the "uncertain use of Words,"[14] it may not be difficult to sketch such an account. One would have to show how the indeterminate use of language results from the fact that distinct ideas are "so coupled" in men's minds "that they always appear there together, and they can no more separate them in their Thoughts, than if they were but one *Idea*" (2, 33, 18). Some such account may be illuminating in explaining, for example, the confounding of different ideas under one name which Locke discusses in chapter 29 of Book II of the *Essay*. Similarly, when Locke says that this operation of the mind prevents one "from seeing," he may mean that it stands in the way of intuitive knowledge itself; a failure to separate ideas would make one treat as identical what is really distinct. Perhaps, as has been suggested recently, this is what Locke thought the Cartesians had done with the ideas of space and body.[15] Both of these explanations are quite compatible with Locke's original discussions of these topics.

Why then do we have the uneasy feeling, with Gibson and Aaron, that the chapter on association introduces a new thesis which is in some way incompatible with the rest of the *Essay*? I would suggest that it is because we see a kind of determinism underlying such a psychological explanation.[16] The problem seems particularly acute in the case of Locke's discussion of belief, where he insists that "Our assent ought to be regulated by the grounds of Probability."[17] As John Passmore has recently pointed out, if "ought" implies "can," then Locke's claim appears "to entail that we are free . . . to regulate, or not to regulate our assent."[18] Does Locke's psychological explanation of error not tend to undermine the freedom and responsibility of those who fail to regulate their assent by the rational means of measuring probabilities?

Locke's claim that it is association which prevents us "from seeing and examining" seems to be in opposition to earlier reflections, which appear in the penultimate chapter of the *Essay*, that we ourselves are responsible for the failure to examine the evidence for any proposition. Locke wrote that

> *We can hinder both Knowledge and Assent, by stopping our Enquiry,* and not employing our Faculties in the search of any Truth. If it were not so, Ignorance, Error, or Infidelity could not in any Case be a Fault. (4, 20, 16)

Locke also made the ability to examine evidence the crux of the account of human freedom which he developed in the revised second edition version of the chapter "Of Power":

> The mind having in most cases, as is evident in Experience, a power to *suspend* the execution and satisfaction of any of its desires, . . . is at liberty to consider the objects of them; examine them on all sides, and weigh them with others. In this lies the liberty Man has; and from the not using of it right comes all that variety of mistakes, errors and faults which we run into, in the conduct of our lives, and our endeavours after happiness. (2, 21, 47)

Here Locke is claiming that our freedom lies in our ability to *examine* whether the fulfilment of a given desire will lead to true happiness. We are responsible for a misuse of this freedom which results in a failure to judge rationally. When, in the fourth edition of the *Essay*, he suggests a psychological account of our failure to pursue reason, Locke appears to be undermining our responsibility.

The problem of determining Locke's view on the relation between "error" and "will" is compounded when we consider that he also holds that we are, in an important sense, forced to believe *what is true*. This is what Gibson meant when he pointed out that, for Locke, the mind has a natural tendency toward knowledge. Locke's view here is essentially Cartesian.[19] In his *Principles of Philosophy*, Descartes had written that

> we are naturally so inclined to give our assent to things which we manifestly perceive that we are not able to doubt *when we perceive in this way*.[20]

Similarly, Locke wrote that

> When the Agreement of any two *Ideas* appears to our Minds, whether immediately, or by the Assistance of Reason, I can no more refuse to perceive, no more avoid knowing it, than I can avoid seeing those Objects, which I turn my Eyes to, and look on in daylight. (4, 20, 16)

For both authors the understanding wholly determines the will in those cases where we perceive some internal relation of ideas. It is this Cartesian theory that Locke extended to the realm of probabilities. By a "probability" Locke meant a proposition in which the connection of ideas is not directly perceivable; such a connection is considered *likely* to be true given certain relevant reasons or measures of probability (4, 15). Just as "we cannot hinder our Knowledge, where the Agreement is once perceived" so we cannot withhold our belief "where the Probability manifestly appears upon due Consideration of all the Measures of it" (4, 20, 16). On Locke's view a correct measure of probability compels our assent. Thus he seems committed to the view that we are forced to believe in a given proposition as "the certainty of Observations, . . . the frequency and constancy of Experience, and the number and credibility of Testimonies" (4, 15, 6) in its favor become overwhelming. Gibson seems to be right when he says that Locke assumes "a general correspondence" between "the psychological influence of the objective conditions of belief and their logical value."[21] The attempt to give a psychological explanation of error and ignorance in terms of the association of ideas seems to be at odds with this schema. Thus Locke appears to be committed to the view that we are compelled to believe *both* in the case where overwhelming evidence leads us to truth *and* in the case where subjective factors of association lead us to embrace error. In the last section of this paper I shall argue that this fact is important in understanding Hume's development of Locke's theories.

Locke held that human freedom lies in the power to consider more evidence just in those cases in which the will is not determined by objective factors—for he wanted men to be responsible for those false beliefs which they adopt before considering the evidence. However, even in the early editions of the *Essay* Locke recognized that there are strong psychological factors which hinder a man from considering evidence. The very chapter in which Locke claims that rational grounds of belief compel assent is concerned with "Wrong Assent, or Error." In this chapter Locke lists a number of *"wrong measures of probability."* This list of factors which interfere with our ability to appreciate the evidence is hardly added as an afterthought, as some commentators have implied. The first factor which Locke mentions is the use of "principles" which are based on "doubtful and false" propositions (4, 20, 7). The specific principles which he mentions are those which form the foundations of religion, such as the "Romanist" principle that one "must believe as the Church . . . believes, or that the Pope is infallible." On the basis of such a false measure of probability a man is prepared to believe what goes against "the clear Evidence of his Senses." He will "believe that to be Flesh, which he sees to be Bread" (4, 20, 10). Or an *"Enthusiast"* who is "principled, that he or his Teacher is inspired, and acted by an immediate Communication of the Divine Spirit" will never be able to consider rational evidence against his doctrines. Locke describes in this chapter how, through constant repetition in childhood such principles are "fastened by degrees" in the understanding and "are at last . . . riveted there by long Custom and Education beyond all possibility of being pull'd out again." The origin of such principles is not considered by adults but "they look on them as the *Urim* and *Thummim* set up in their Minds immediately by GOD Himself."[22] This account, which parallels Locke's earlier discussion of supposed innate practical principles,[23] even seems to presuppose the theory of association of ideas. In these discussions Locke argues that principles of reasoning which connect truth with the authority of a church, a man, a party, or a country become the foundation for absurd beliefs which are impervious to rational evidence.

Yet it is certainly true that in the first two editions of the *Essay* Locke was hesitant to admit that such irrational beliefs were entirely beyond the responsibility of the persons who held them. While the beliefs which are based on "wrong Principles" cannot "be moved by the most apparent and convincing Probabilities" nevertheless they can be uprooted when men are "so candid and ingenuous to themselves, as to be persuaded to examine . . . those very *Principles*" (4, 20, 10). Another of the wrong measures of probability—"Predominant Passions or Inclinations"—would also *appear* to presuppose a form of psychological compulsion. Locke cites the case of the man who is passionately in love and is therefore unable to accept the evidence showing the infidelity of his mistress. Yet this avoidance of the evidence is still characterized as a "power" a man has to "suspend and restrain" his inquiries. Did Locke himself go against the evidence of human irrationality in order to support his theoretical conviction that men are responsible for their errors, as John Passmore has suggested?[24] However we answer this question, we must recognize that, in the additions he made to the fourth edition of the *Essay*, Locke acknowledges in an *unqualified* way that there are positive conditions in the human soul which restrain free inquiry.

In the chapter "Of the Association of *Ideas*" Locke presents his explanation as one which accounts for the fact that there really are men who, while they hold entirely absurd views, do not "impose wilfully" on themselves "and knowingly refuse Truth offer'd by plain Reason." These men "pursue Truth sincerely; and therefore there must be something that blinds their Understandings, and makes them not see the falsehood of what they embrace for real Truth" (2, 33, 18). In these cases there is clearly a compulsion to accept error. Moreover, it is clear that Locke holds that association does not merely distort our cognitive faculties but directly affects the will itself. For Locke writes that association accounts not only for habits of thought "in the Understanding" but also for habits "of Determining in the Will" (2, 33, 6).

It is important to note that Locke's reflections on association are fully compatible with two main concerns of his overall philosophy—namely toleration and education. The reflection that we all hold false principles which cannot be uprooted by reason should make us less eager to impose those principles on other people; it should also make us more tolerant of the irrational convictions of others.[25] Moreover, Locke clearly recognized that the power to eradicate such irrational beliefs lay in changing the methods of educating young children. In his *Conduct of the Understanding,* Locke writes that he "can see no other right way of principling" children whose future life will allow them to inquire into truth, "but to take heed . . . that, in their tender years, ideas that have no natural cohesion come not to be united in their heads."[26] In this work, as well as in his *Some Thoughts Concerning Education,*[27] Locke stresses the harmful effects of associations inculcated in early childhood. In the final analysis the responsibility for ridding society of erroneous beliefs lies with the educators of young children.

SOURCES OF THE CENTRAL IDEAS IN THE CHAPTER

In a letter to William Molyneux in April of 1695, Locke discusses various items he is thinking of adding to a new edition of the *Essay*:

> I think I shall make some other additions to be put into your latin translation, and particularly concerning the Connexion of *Ideas*, which has not, that I know, been hitherto consider'd and has, I guess, a greater influence upon our minds, than is usually taken notice of.

This is an apparent reference to Locke's reflections on association which later appeared in the fourth edition of the *Essay* in 1700. Locke's words imply not that he is the first to consider such a connection of ideas, but clearly that he thinks his predecessors have underestimated the extent of its influence on the mind. In the letter Locke also discusses some proposed additions on enthusiasm: these remarks anticipate the other new chapter which Locke added to the fourth edition of the *Essay*. The other discussion in the letter, which we shall find relevant, concerns Locke's criticism of Malebranche's view that we see "all things in God." Locke notes that he has almost completed his study of Malebranche's philosophy.[28] For my purposes it is only important to note that Locke was reading parts of Malebranche's philosophy around the time he wrote this letter to Molyneux. I believe that this letter contains some important hints about the sources of the ideas developed in the chapter "Of the Association of *Ideas*."

I have not yet mentioned what I take to be one of the most distinctive ideas developed in Locke's chapter. We have seen that even in earlier editions of the *Essay*, Locke gives education and custom as the cause of prejudice. But in the chapter on association he says that he is going to "look a little farther" in order to trace it "to the root it springs from" (2, 33, 3). He goes on to note that "Chance or Custom" produce a "Connexion of *Ideas*" which have no "natural Correspondence and Connexion one with another" (2, 33, 5). Here Locke clearly contrasts the *natural* connection of ideas which it is "the Office and Excellency of our Reason to trace" with the sort of incoherent connection of ideas which is, for him, the result of association. But Locke is not content merely to distinguish the faculty of mind responsible for association from the faculty of reason; he goes on to present a psycho-physiological description which, he says, "may help us a little to conceive of Intellectual Habits." According to Locke,

> Custom settles habits of Thinking in the Understanding, as well as of Determining in the Will, and of Motions in the Body; all which seems to be but Trains of Motion in the Animal Spirits, which once set a going continue on in the same steps they have been used to, which by often treading are worn into a smooth path, and the Motion in it becomes easy and as it were Natural.

He goes on to say that such a cause appears also to explain why

> A Musician used to any Tune will find that let it but once begin in his Head, the *Ideas* of the several Notes of it will follow one another orderly in his Understanding without any care or attention, as regularly as his Fingers move orderly over the Keys of the Organ to play out the Tune he has begun.... (2, 33, 6)

I think it is clear that in this chapter, in explaining the association of ideas, Locke has set aside his original resolution not "at present" to "meddle with the Physical Consideration of the Mind" (1, 1, 2).

I do not think there can be much question about one important source for Locke's psycho-physiological account of the association of ideas. In chapter 5 of Book II of his *Recherche de la Vérité*, Malebranche discussed what he called "causes of the connection between ideas and [brain-] traces."[29] Malebranche went on to distinguish certain sorts of "connections which are not natural." One of the causes of such connections between brain traces and hence between their corresponding ideas is

> the identity of time in which they were imprinted in the brain, for it suffices that several traces have been produced at the same time, in order that they can only be reawakened together. For the animal spirits, finding the pathways of all the traces which are made at the same time open, continue their way through them because they can pass there more easily than other places in the brain.
> (*Recherche*, I, p. 223)

Malebranche also noted how repetition of stimuli produces deeper traces in the brain and how this results in the easier flow of animal spirits:

> we imagine things more strongly to the degree that these [brain-] traces are deeper and better engraved, and the animal spirits pass there more often and with greater violence . . .: When the spirits have passed that way several times they enter with greater facility. . . . This is the most usual cause of the confusion and falsity of our ideas. (*Recherche*, I, p. 275)

In Eclaircissement VII, Malebranche gave an example of the sort of "intellectual habits" which were explained by such mechanisms:

> The facility to play certain instruments which certain persons acquire . . . [is formed in so far as] the pathways through which their spirits flow are smoother and more united by the habit of exercise. . . . (*Recherche*, III, p. 69)

But the pathways which the animal spirits cut through the solid substance of the brain can also be the source of mental aberrations. In the third part of Book II of the *Recherche* Malebranche writes about the "strong imagination" which results from a certain condition of the brain. This condition makes it susceptible to very deep footsteps and traces which so fill the capacity of the soul that they prevent it from carrying its attention to other things than those which these images represent.[30]

Some of these people are "entirely mad" and unable to converse with other people, but there are others whose ideas are less bizarre and who suffer from a less serious form of the same ailment. These theories of Malebranche closely parallel those which are to be found in Locke's chapter on association of ideas. It seems clear that Locke was not only finding material to criticize in his reading of Malebranche during the 1690s.[31]

Of course it would be wrong to say that Locke merely adopted Malebranche's theory of the association of ideas. The natural connections between ideas which Malebranche wants to contrast with these non-natural connections are those which (in Locke's words) "depend upon our original Constitution, and are born with us" (2, 33, 7). Locke allows for the existence of connections which are natural in this sense but tends to downplay their importance. He is really concerned to contrast associational connections with those which are objective and established by reason. It is these latter which *Locke* calls natural connections of ideas. This clear contrast between associational and rational connections of ideas is, it seems to me, distinctive in Locke's account. Locke, even more than Malebranche, is concerned to stress that the non-natural associational connections are the source of errors in our thinking. It is in this way that he wants to show that association has "a greater influence upon our minds, than is usually taken notice of."

Locke's reflections on the nature of madness have had any number of sources, for his basic views on this topic seem to represent those prevalent in his own day. Galen had claimed that mental derangement is usually caused by *both* "improper imagining and incorrect reasoning," but he does give one example of a man who had a severe delusion but was otherwise quite rational.[32] However, Henry More reports that many physicians define melancholy in terms of deranged imagination:

> it is most observable in *Melancholy* when it reaches to a disease, that it sets on some one particular absurd imagination upon the Mind so fast, that all the evidence of Reason to the contrary cannot remove it, the parties, thus affected in other things being as sober and rational as other men.[33]

More notes in particular that Daniel Sennert, one of the most respected medical authorities of the day, defined melancholy "from this very Effect of it." Locke may well have directly derived his theory that madness is a disorder of the imagination (madness and melancholy were commonly conflated) from Sennert, whose collected works were in his library. More describes a number of cases of deluded imagination, derived from different authors. The case cited by Locke, that of the man who thought he was made out of glass and took all the rational precautions, appears to have its origin in the writings of the sixteenth-century French physician André du Laurens.[34]

But Locke's own extension of the theory of madness to the more general discussion of prejudice in the chapter on association of ideas may well have been sparked by his reading of Henry More himself. Locke would probably have read or re-read More's popular *Enthusiasmus Triumphatus* in 1695 when he was working on both chapters which were eventually added to the fourth edition of the *Essay*. In this work More asks why the enthusiast's claim to divine inspiration is impervious to reason. He argues that the origin of this delusion is "the enormous strength and vigour of the Imagination" which makes "men become mad or fanaticall whether they will or no." Thus the enthusiast is not really responsible for his behavior. Something "captivates [his] *Imagination*" and "carries it . . . out of the reach or hearing of that more free and superiour Faculty of *Reason*" (p. 5). More goes on to reflect on the nature of madness for the specific purpose of "weakening . . . the authority of the bold Enthusiasts" (p.9). He suggests that the reason people believe the enthusiast's claim to divine inspiration is that apart from this one delusion, he is perfectly rational. But once people realize that he is suffering from the disease discussed by Sennert and others, his authority will be undermined. More's claim that religious enthusiasm was a form of madness became a weapon in the Anglican rationalists' "attacks on Dissenters for the next one hundred years."[35] In his chapter "Of Enthusiasm" Locke follows More's account quite faithfully. In the chapter on association of ideas, however, he seems to want to employ More's parallel between madness and fanaticism in a more general way to undermine the authority of *any* absurd thinking patterns which are impervious to reason. He also gave a far more specific account, that which he found in Malebranche, of the mechanisms by which the absurd thinking patterns are produced.

LOCKE VS. HUME ON ASSOCIATION

In his discussion of his own book in the *Abstract of . . . A Treatise of Human Nature*, Hume wrote that

> if any thing can intitle the author to so glorious a name as that of an *inventor*, 'tis the use he makes of the principle of the association of ideas, which enters into most of his philosophy.[36]

This principle plays a key role in Book I of the *Treatise* itself, where Hume's central purpose was to "explain the principles and operations of our reasoning faculty, and the nature of our ideas."[37] The central aim of Hume's philosophy of the understanding was to show that our scientific reasoning processes and our judgments about the nature of reality have their roots in the principles of human nature—especially the association of ideas. He argued that *all* measures of probability—the valid as well as the invalid ones—arise from this principle. According to Hume, the very same cause which Locke used to explain error and illusion is the ultimate source of the highest degree of probability—that which is based on our belief in cause and effect.

There is, one must admit, a good deal of irony in Hume's story. Locke tried to undermine prejudice by showing that it has the same ancestry as madness. He tried to explain how they both could exist in a mind that was otherwise rational and yet not yield to the authority of reason. But Hume appears to show that what Locke really uncovered was the sordid background of reason itself. Its roots, like those of madness and prejudice, lie in custom and habit.

Let me briefly reconstruct Hume's story. In Book IV of the *Essay*, Locke had proposed a series of measures by which the "several degrees" of assent "are, or ought to be *regulated*" (4, 16, 1). The highest degree of probability is based on "the regular proceedings of Causes and Effects in the ordinary course of Nature." Locke proposed the rule that

> what our own and other Men's constant Observation has found always to be after the same manner, that we with reason conclude to be the Effects of steady and regular Causes. . . .   (4, 16, 6)

As we saw earlier, Locke held that correct measures of probability compel our assent. In the passage we are now discussing he goes on to argue that "constant Observation" actually produces the belief in causation. Locke writes that

> Probability upon such grounds carries so much evidence with it, that it naturally determines the Judgment, and leaves us as little liberty to believe, or disbelieve, as a Demonstration does. ...
> (4, 16, 9)

Now Hume apparently asked himself why this should be so—why we should be forced to believe on the basis of what Locke calls constant observation or "the frequency and constancy of Experience" (4, 15, 6). Hume's answer was that

> The idea of cause and effect is deriv'd from experience, which presenting us with certain objects constantly conjoin'd with each other, produces such a habit of surveying them in that relation, that we cannot without a sensible violence survey them in any other.[38]

Hume claims that there is a close connection between this habit of thought from which our ideas of cause and effect are derived, and the principle of association of ideas:

> As the habit, which produces the association, arises from the frequent conjunction of objects, it must arrive at its perfection by degrees, and must acquire new force from each instance, that falls under our observation. ... 'Tis by these slow steps, that our judgment arrives at a full *assurance*.
> (*Treatise*, p. 130; italics are mine)

According to him, our belief in the "probability of causes" increases with the frequency of observations because the latter gradually produces a stronger association of ideas.

The close connection between Hume's discussion of the probability of causes and that of Locke is indicated by his use of terms such as "assurance." Locke had used this term to mark the highest degree of probability which results from an invariant conjunction (*Essay*, 4, 16, 6). In the passage we have just quoted from page 130 of the Selby-Bigge edition of the *Treatise*, Hume clearly uses the explanatory mechanisms of Locke's chapter on association of ideas to give an account of the origin of this "assurance." It seems clear that Hume was quite self-consciously setting Locke's philosophy on its head. In the *Treatise* he argues extensively that the same principles are operating in the case of "prejudice"—or, more generally, in the case of what he calls "unphilosophical" probabilities—as in the case of rational or "philosophical" probabilities. For Hume, the right measures of probability operate through the same principles of human nature as the wrong ones. Hume wrote that "all reasonings"—he means all probabilistic reasonings—"are nothing but the effects of custom."[39]

But may we not ask whether, even if Hume is right about the origins of our criteria for rational assent, this really undermines the central thesis of Locke's *Essay*. Has Hume not merely proposed and answered a question which is different from that which interested Locke—a question about *origins* of our probabilistic reasonings? Unlike Hume, Locke was primarily interested in telling people just what they could be certain about and what criteria they ought to use to regulate their assent. Locke's interest centered on *normative*—not naturalistic—epistemology. The *origin* of the criteria of rational assent is irrelevant to such a project. In their respective works on "human understanding" Locke and Hume were primarily engaged in very different philosophical enterprises.

Such an answer, while it is not wholly without merit, cannot be accepted without qualification. For, while we must acknowledge that the focus of the discussion in each of their books differs, it is still true that Locke tried to base his normative probabilistic epistemology on some sort of psychological foundation. We have just noted that Locke purports to establish the rational connection between constant observation and our judgments of cause and effect on the ground that the former "determines" the latter. In fact, in the same paragraph in which this discussion occurs, Locke denies that one can produce normative rules of belief in just those cases where the evidence does *not* naturally determine one's judgment:

> The difficulty is, when Testimonies contradict common Experience, and the reports of History and Witnesses clash with the ordinary course of Nature, or with one another.... [In such cases] 'tis impossible to reduce to precise Rules, the various degrees wherein Men give their Assent.   (*Essay* 4, 16, 9)

Hence, it seems that Locke himself tried to base his normative epistemology on the psychological influence of the available evidence. But if, as Hume seems to have shown, such psychological influence is based on the same principles as lead to false measures of probability, then a major support for Locke's epistemology is undermined.

Moreover, it is also true that Hume attempted to found a normative epistemology on naturalistic principles and despaired at the results. While it is not always recognized, it is clear that Hume tried to establish what he called "general rules" by which to determine the relations of cause and effect in nature.[40] Such rules clearly go beyond the natural principles of the understanding, though in an important sense they are based on them. However, at the end of Book I of the *Treatise* Hume reports that a systematic application of these general rules has left him in despair. He claims to have shown that it is the enlivening of ideas, which is based on the principle of association of ideas,

> which makes us reason from causes and effects; and 'tis the same principle, which convinces us of the continu'd existence of external objects, when absent from the senses. But tho' these two operations be equally natural and necessary in the human mind, yet in some circumstances they are directly contrary, nor is it possible for us to reason justly and regularly from causes and effects, and at the same time believe the continu'd existence of matter. (*Treatise*, p. 266)

It is the systematic rule-governed use of our causal reasonings which, according to Hume, undermines our natural belief in the existence of matter.

Yet, at the same time, we must recognize that Hume's despair does not arise from his naturalistic account of our causal reasonings itself. Fundamentally, Hume's goals are fully compatible with those of Locke's *Essay*. In spite of the fact that he sought an associational basis for our belief in causality, Hume thought that he could distinguish correct from incorrect measures of probability. In Part 4 of Book I of the *Treatise*, Hume gives a formula for distinguishing the legitimate from the illegitimate use of natural principles. Here he claims that those beliefs which arise from the observation of causal patterns in nature are based on "principles which are permanent, irresistable, and universal." More importantly, beliefs based on these principles are required for the survival of the human species: they are "the foundation of all our thoughts and actions, so that upon their removal human nature must immediately perish and go to ruin" (*Treatise*, p. 225). When we rely on the observation of a constant conjunction *in nature*, we rely upon a principle without which human beings would not survive. On the other hand, the associations which arise from education—those which arise from artificial conditioning—often have no survival value. They are "neither universal nor unavoidable in human nature" (*Treatise*, p. 226). Thus Hume gives us a basis to distinguish two kinds of belief which have their roots in custom—those which arise from an "artificial" occasioning cause and those which arise from a "natural" occasioning cause (*Treatise*, p. 117). It is only when it produces associations on the basis of the latter sort of cause that "custom" provides a source of legitimate beliefs. For it is only in that case that one is dealing with principles which are essential to the survival of the species.[41]

It is also important to stress the fact that, while Hume sought to show the origin of our scientific causal reasoning in natural principles, he thought that such reasoning transcends such principles. It is easy to lose sight of this when one reads passages of Book I of the *Treatise* like the one where Hume claims that "all reasonings are nothing but the effects of custom." Such passages seem to suggest that all human enquiry is merely a function of the mechanistic processes of assocation. If his intent were really to reduce all reasoning to association, Hume would certainly be undermining that realm of freedom which always remained central in Locke's epistemology—namely, the ability to continue our inquiry and look for more evidence in those cases where there is no compulsion to believe. On such a view the construction of rules of knowledge and belief would become irrelevant. But I think that this interpretation is based on a clear misunderstanding of Hume's own philosophy. Like Locke, Hume recognized an important distinction between associational and rational thought. He acknowledged a use of reason which while it is, in some essential sense, dependent upon custom, is not based solely on that principle. Hume defined causality as both a natural and a philosophical relation (*Treatise*, p. 170). In so doing he recognized a distinction between a purely associational operation of the mind and one which operates reflectively and systematically by the use of established criteria. Moreover, Hume was careful—in fact more careful than Locke—to note that, in our rational scientific enquiries, we operate by means of reflective rules which can be in opposition to the most natural processes of the understanding. These rules are arrived at through reason and reflection—that is, "on our experience of [the] operations [of our understanding] in the judgments we form concerning objects." They allow us "to distinguish the accidental circumstances from the efficacious causes" (*Treatise*, p. 149; cf.

p. 173). Hume recognized that the systematic discovery of causes in nature depends upon more than the mechanistic processes of association of ideas.

Indeed, it is clear that Hume adopted the essential features of Locke's normative account of our probabilistic reasonings—more systematically than did Locke himself. Locke had claimed that "constant Experience makes us sensible" of the causal processes of mind and body,

> though our narrow Understandings can comprehend neither. For when the Mind would look beyond those original *Ideas* we have from Sensation or Reflection, and penetrate into their Causes, and manner of production, we find still it discovers nothing but its own short-sightedness. (2, 23, 28)

Now Locke is not entirely consistent in his acceptance of this view. There are passages in the *Essay* where he appears to claim that we have some sort of *a priori* insight into the operations of matter and mind. For example, Locke claimed that "it is as repugnant to the *Idea* of senseless Matter, that it should put into it self Sense, Perception, and Knowledge, as it is repugnant to the *Idea* of a Triangle, that it should put into it self greater Angles than two right ones" (4, 10, 5). Moreover, at one point he even seems to suggest that we have some sort of insight that new motion comes into the world through the activity of minds: he tells his reader that "the active power of Moving . . . is much clearer in Spirit than Body," and he thinks it is possible that this power of adding motion to the universe may be "the proper attribute of Spirits" (*Essay*, 2, 23, 28). The theory that new motion can only come into the world through the activity of minds was in fact central in the natural theology of Newton and Clarke—a theology which Hume sought to undermine in his famous *Dialogues Concerning Natural Religion*. Hume thought that through a systematic application of the principle that "experience alone can point out . . . the true cause of any phenomenon" we can discover that there is no more reason to think that minds are the source of new motion in the universe than that bodies are.[42]

It is important to remember that in his *Treatise of Human Nature* Hume sought to justify the principle that constant experience provides the only basis for belief in causality by showing that the principle is firmly implanted in human nature. He argued that our probabilistic reasoning has its roots in custom and association, and claimed that we do not need any understanding of the causal process itself in order to draw inferences from causes to effects and from effects to causes. By showing how constant experience gives us complete assurance without any *a priori* insight, Hume hoped to define, even more clearly than Locke, the bounds between knowledge and opinion. Hume hoped to show that whatever legitimacy there is in our probabilistic reasonings comes from the fact that they are rooted in human nature.

Thus, in the final analysis, we must recognize that Hume's associational account was meant to support rather than undermine our probabilistic reasonings. However, it is also clear that, since Hume's day, most of his readers have seen the negative skeptical side of his thought as predominant in his early philosophical writings. His own contemporaries, who would have read the *Treatise* with Locke's *Essay* in mind, must certainly be forgiven for having seen him as undermining rather than providing a foundation for our probabilistic reasonings. For the principle in which Hume sought to root such reasonings is the very principle which, according to his own view as well as that of Locke, is also the source of prejudice and the inability to think rationally.

NOTES

An earlier draft of this paper was prepared for and presented to the International Colloquium on the Historical Study of John Locke, Rutgers University, 13-17 June, 1983. I am indebted to other participants for their helpful comments and suggestions. I am especially indebted to Tom Lennon, Henry Schankula, John Yolton, and Christopher Fox for their help at different stages of this work. This work was supported by a grant from the Social Sciences and Humanities Research Council of Canada.

1. See Maurice Mandelbaum, *History, Man, and Reason* (Baltimore, Maryland: Johns Hopkins University Press, 1971), pp.147-162; and Martin Kallich, *The Association of Ideas and Critical Theory in Eighteenth-Century England* (The Hague: Mouton, 1970). Locke's theory of association of ideas would have been known to many in the eighteenth century through its appearance under this heading in Ephraim Chambers, *Cyclopaedia: or, an Universal Dictionary of Arts and Sciences* (London, 1728). But its most spectacular eighteenth-century appearance is surely as the foundation for the thoughts of Laurence Sterne's *Tristram Shandy*. See M. V. DePorte, *Nightmares and Hobbyhorses* (San Marino, Calif.: Huntington Library Press, 1974) for a good discussion of the importance of Locke's theory in Sterne's work.
2. James Gibson, *Locke's Theory of Knowledge and its Historical Relations* (Cambridge: Cambridge University Press, 1917), pp. 235-236.
3. Gibson, p. 140.
4. Richard I. Aaron, *John Locke*, 3rd. ed. (Oxford: Clarendon Press, 1971), p.141.

5. *An Essay concerning Human Understanding*, ed. Peter H. Nidditch (Oxford: Clarendon Press, 1975), 1, 1, 3. Textual references in this form are to book, chapter, and section numbers.
6. Throughout this paper I have used the expression 'normative epistemology' even though my concern is largely with the second of Locke's goals—that which concerns probability rather than knowledge. Strictly speaking 'epistemology' means 'theory of *knowledge*.' Locke clearly distinguishes knowledge from probability: the latter is only "likeliness to be true" (4, 15, 3) and unlike the former does not involve the perception of "a constant, immutable, and visible connexion" between ideas (4, 15, 1). I would like to say that my major concern here is with Locke's normative 'probabology'—but unfortunately (or fortunately) there is no such English word. It is also important to bear in mind that Locke has no interest in probability in its statistical sense.
7. Noted by James Tyrrell in his copy of the *Essay*, now to be found in the British Library. See Maurice Cranston, *John Locke, a Biography* (London: Longmans, 1957), pp. 140-141. Also Locke's "Epistle to the Reader," *Essay*, p.7. In his *John Locke and the Way of Ideas* (Oxford: Clarendon Press, 1956) John Yolton has shown that the views of his contemporaries on these principles form the essential backdrop to the polemic against innate ideas in Book I of the *Essay*.
8. Chapter 29, "Of Clear and Distinct, Obscure and Confused *Ideas*"; chapter 30, "Of Real and Fantastical *Ideas*"; chapter 31, "Of Adequate and Inadequate *Ideas*"; chapter 32, "Of True and False *Ideas*."
9. *Essay*, 2, 21, 56-70.
10. *Essay*, 4, 20.
11. "Of Enthusiasm", *Essay*, 4, 19.
12. See the transcription of Locke's Journal entry for Friday, 5 November 1677, in Kenneth Dewhurst, *John Locke (1632-1704), Physician and Philosopher* (London: Wellcome Institute, 1963), p. 89. Compare the entry for Saturday, 22 January 1678 (Dewhurst, pp. 100-102).

    On page 70 Dewhurst interprets Locke's entry for Wednesday, 15 July 1676 (MS. Locke f. 1, p. 320), as follows: "Query whether mania be not putting together wrong ideas and so making wrong propositions from them, notwithstanding the reason be right? But madness is a fault in the faculty of reasoning." Thus it *appears* that Locke held the opposite of his later view of madness. But, as Henry Schankula has pointed out to me, this interpretation of Locke's entry (which was partly written in shorthand) is quite misleading. The word Dewhurst has given as "madness" is in fact "fatuitas," which should be translated as "silliness" or "folly." Hence, the entry is fully compatible with Locke's later views. On page 20 of *Nightmares and Hobbyhorses* Michael DePorte has been misled by Dewhurst's mistranslation.
13. Dewhurst, p. 89.
14. In the addition to his "Epistle to the Reader" in the fourth edition of the *Essay*, Locke had claimed that "the greatest part of the Questions and Controversies that perplex Mankind [depend] on the doubtful and uncertain use of Words" (p. 13). At first sight, Locke appears to be making irreconcilable claims about the fundamental cause of error: I am suggesting here that the psychological account in terms of association may well be the more basic.

15. H. A. S. Schankula, "Locke, Descartes, and the Science of Nature," *Journal of the History of Ideas*, 51 (1980), 477.
16. See DePorte, *Nightmares*, pp. 23-24.
17. This is Locke's marginal summary of *Essay* 4, 16, 1.
18. "Locke and the Ethics of Belief," *Proceedings of the British Academy*, 64 (1980), 186. This paper, which was given as the Dawes Hicks Lecture in 1978, contains a fascinating discussion of Book IV of the *Essay*. I am indebted to Passmore's study for my own reflections in this part of the paper.
19. Gibson (note 2) says that "Locke is at every point in disagreement" with Descartes's theory (p. 138). He is clearly wrong here. For a good account of Descartes's theory of judgment see Hiram Caton, "Will and Reason in Descartes's Theory of Error," *Journal of Philosophy*, 72 (1975), 87-104. It is certainly true that Descartes insists that the will is required in order to affirm any proposition. Nevertheless when we *choose* between two contraries, this is only the lowest form of liberty; on the other hand, he writes that "if I were always to know clearly what is true and what is good, I would never have any difficulty deciding what judgment and what choice I ought to make; and thus I would be entirely free, without being indifferent." See his *Meditationes de Prima Philosophia*, in *Oeuvres de Descartes*, ed. Charles Adam and Paul Tannery, new presentation by C.N.R.S. (Paris, 1973), vol. VII, p. 58; vol. IX-1, p. 46; Meditation 4. For Descartes, the highest freedom arises when I am self-determined by what he calls "natural knowledge."
20. *Principia Philosophiae*, in *Oeuvres de Descartes*, vol. VIII-1, p. 21; vol. IX-2, p. 43; Principle I-43.
21. Gibson, p. 140. From a twentieth-century point of view, it would have been more accurate to speak of "epistemological" rather than "logical" value here (see note 6). However, as James G. Buickerood's paper, "The Natural History of the Understanding: Locke and the Rise of Facultative Logic in the Eighteenth Century," *History and Philosophy of Logic*, 6 (1985), 157-190 shows us, the eighteenth-century sense of the word "logic" encompasses theory of knowledge.
22. See *Essay*, 4, 20, 9. The Urim and Thummim are to be found on the breastplate of the high priest as symbols of judgment. They are supposed to provide Divine guidance in times of national crisis. See Exodus 28, 30.
23. See *Essay*, 1, 3, 25-27. Here Locke regards as especially harmful the principle "That Principles [themselves] ought not to be questioned." In his *Conduct of the Understanding*, originally intended as an additional chapter to the *Essay*, Locke gave the following list of first principles commonly appealed to by men: "the founders or leaders of my party are good men, and therefore their tenets are true; it is the opinion of a sect that is erroneous, therefore it is false; it hath been long received in the world, therefore it is true; or it is new, and therefore false." See *Locke's Conduct of the Understanding*, ed. Thomas Fowler, 2nd ed. (rpt. New York: Lenox Hill, 1971), Section VI, p. 16.
24. See Passmore, 201-202. Passmore tends to concentrate on the case of the passionate man and examines with care the chapter "Of Enthusiasm." He argues that Locke ultimately concludes that the irrational man must be blamed for his lack of love of truth. But this solution does not seem possible in the light of what Locke

says at *Essay* 2, 33, 18. Here he clearly asserts that such a man does not intentionally deceive himself.

25. Locke's first *Letter Concerning Toleration* was published in 1689, one year before the first edition of his *Essay*. Locke's main aim was to encourage the toleration of those who differ from oneself in matters of religion.
26. Locke, *Conduct*, Section XLI, p. 89.
27. See *The Works of John Locke*, (London, 1823; rpt. Darmstadt, 1963), IX, Section 138, pp. 129-130. In this work Locke discusses the inculcation of the belief that evil spirits come out when it is dark, an example he also employed in the *Essay* (2, 33, 10).
28. *The Correspondence of John Locke*, ed. E. S. De Beer (Oxford: Clarendon Press, 1979), V, pp. 350-353. Locke's study of Malebranche was posthumously published under the name "An Examination of P. Malebranche's Opinion of Seeing All Things in God."
29. Nicolas Malebranche, *Recherche de la Vérité*, ed. G. Rodis-Lewis, in *Oeuvres de Malebranche*, ed. André Robinet, volumes I-III (Paris, 1962), vol. I, p. 216. Hereafter this work will be referred to as *Recherche* with the volume number and the page. All translations from the *Recherche* are my own.
30. *Recherche* I, 323. The word I have here translated as "footsteps" is "vestiges" in the original. In A. Boyer's *The Royal Dictionary Abridged* (London, 1700; rpt. Menston: Scolar Press, 1971), the French *"Vestige"* is translated as "step, foot-step, vestiges, ... sign, mark, remain, vestige."
31. Michael DePorte suggests another possible source for Locke's psycho-physiological account, namely Thomas Willis's *Two Discourses Concerning The Soul of Brutes* (which was first published in 1672, two years before the first edition of Malebranche's *Recherche)*. See *Two Discourses*, trans. S. Pordage (London, 1683; rpt. Gainesville, 1971), pp. 201-202; also *Nightmares and Hobbyhorses*, pp. 50-51, n. 54. The attribution of the error to custom seems to be common to Locke and Malebranche, but not to Willis (at least in the passage to which DePorte calls our attention). The talk of a "smooth path" and "easy" motion in Locke also seems clearly to be derived from Malebranche. But most importantly, while both Locke and Malebranche stress that the animal spirits move in an *ordered* way in producing absurd and erroneous connections of ideas, Willis stresses their *disordered* movements. He thinks that the animal spirits produce "unaccustomed notions" (p. 202) because they are "driven beyond their orders and wonted passages" (p. 203). Both Locke's language and central thought seem to me to be closer to Malebranche than Willis. Malebranche clearly read Willis (see *Recherche* I, 193, where he discusses Willis's views on the location of the common sense, memory, and imagination), but Willis's own views on the role of the animal spirits and the formation of corporeal ideas are likely to be derived either directly or indirectly from Descartes's *Treatise of Man* (which was first published posthumously in 1662). See René Descartes, *Treatise of Man*, ed. and trans. Thomas S. Hall (Cambridge, Mass. Harvard University Press, 1972), pp. 86ff.
32. Claudii Galeni, *De Symptomatum Differentiis*, in *Opera Omnia*, ed. C. G. Kuhn (Leipzig, 1824; rpt. Hildesheim, 1965), VII, pp. 60-61. I am indebted to Paul Potter for finding and translating the relevant passage of Galen for me.

33. Henry More, *Enthusiasmus Triumphatus; or a Brief Discourse of the Nature, Causes, Kinds, and Cure of Enthusiasm* (London, 1662; rpt. with an introduction by M. V. DePorte, Los Angeles: Clark Memorial Library, 1966), p. 8.
34. More, p. 9. Both of Locke's examples which I cited on page 106 were given by Descartes in his first Meditation. Descartes writes of those whose "brain is so troubled and obscured by the black vapours of bile that they assure us constantly they are kings, though they are very poor" and of those who "imagine" that they "have a body which is made out of glass." See *Oeuvres de Descartes,* vol. IX-1, p. 14. While Descartes does not explicitly note that the faculty of reason of madmen is intact, the distinction between the faculties of reason and imagination is very important in his philosophy. It is interesting to note that Robert Burton, a well-known early seventeenth-century writer on melancholy, claims that the primary disorder of imagination affects reason when the disease lasts for any time. See his *The Anatomy of Melancholy,* ed. Holbrook Jackson (London: Dent, 1932), I, pp. 171-172.
35. See DePorte's introduction to *Enthusiasmus Triumphatus,* p. vi, and *Nightmares and Hobbyhorses,* pp. 38ff. Also see Phillip Harth's *Swift and Anglican Rationalism: The Religious Background of a Tale of a Tub* (Chicago, Ill.: University of Chicago Press, 1961), and Roy Porter, "The Rage of Party: a Glorious Revolution in English Psychiatry?," *Medical History,* 27 (1983), 35. Henry Schankula has called my attention to the fact that Locke's reflections on the close connections among enthusiasm, imagination, and madness go back to his 1682 Journal. (See the entry for Sunday, February 19, MS Locke, f.6, 1682, pp. 20-24.)
36. David Hume, *An Abstract of a Book lately Published; Entituled, A Treatise of Human Nature, & c.: Wherein the Chief Argument of that Book is farther Illustrated and Explained,* in *A Treatise of Human Nature,* ed. L. A. Selby-Bigge, rev. P. H. Nidditch, 2nd ed. (Oxford: Clarendon Press, 1978), pp. 661-662. For a discussion of the reasons for attributing this anonymous work to Hume, see P. H. Nidditch, *An Apparatus of Variant Readings for Hume's Treatise of Human Nature* (Sheffield: University of Sheffield, 1976).
37. David Hume, *A Treatise of Human Nature,* p. xv.
38. *Treatise,* p. 125.
39. *Treatise,* pp. 143-155, esp. p. 146 and p. 149. When he speaks strictly about the highest degree of certainty—that which arises from an invariant conjunction of causally related items—Hume speaks of *proofs* as opposed to *probabilities.* He criticizes Locke for adopting a twofold distinction between demonstrative and probable reasoning, but his objection does not reach beyond the verbal impropriety of saying "that it is only probable all men must die, or that the sun must rise tomorrow" (See *Enquiries Concerning Human Understanding and Concerning the Principles of Morals,* ed. L. A. Selby-Bigge, rev. P. H. Nidditch, 3rd ed. [Oxford: Clarendon Press, 1975], p. 56fn. and *Treatise,* p. 124). For Locke himself had written that "these Probabilities rise so near to *Certainty,* that they govern our Thoughts as absolutely, and influence our Actions as fully, as the most evident demonstration" (*Essay,* 4, 16, 6). Hume adopts the essence of Locke's view when he distinguishes two kinds of relations between objects—those which are discoverable merely by a comparison of ideas and those which cannot be so discovered (*Enquiry* p. 25). In the *Treatise* Hume clearly adopts Locke's distinction between demonstration, which involves the discovery of "a constant, immutable

... connection" between the intermediate ideas, and probability, which involves the discovery of an intermediate connection which is "not constant and immutable, or at least is not perceived to be so" (*Essay*, 4, 15, 1 and 3, and *Treatise*, pp. 69-73).

40. *Treatise*, pp. 173-175. See Tom L. Beauchamp and Alexander Rosenberg, *Hume and the Problem of Causation* (New York: Oxford University Press, 1981), pp. 52ff.

41. For a more extended discussion of Hume's use of this argument and its historical roots see John P. Wright, *The Sceptical Realism of David Hume* (Minneapolis: University of Minnesota Press, 1983), pp. 221ff.

42. *Dialogues Concerning Natural Religion*, ed. Norman Kemp Smith, 2nd ed. (Edinburgh: Nelson, 1947), p. 146. Also see Wright (note 41), especially section 16, pp. 161-174.

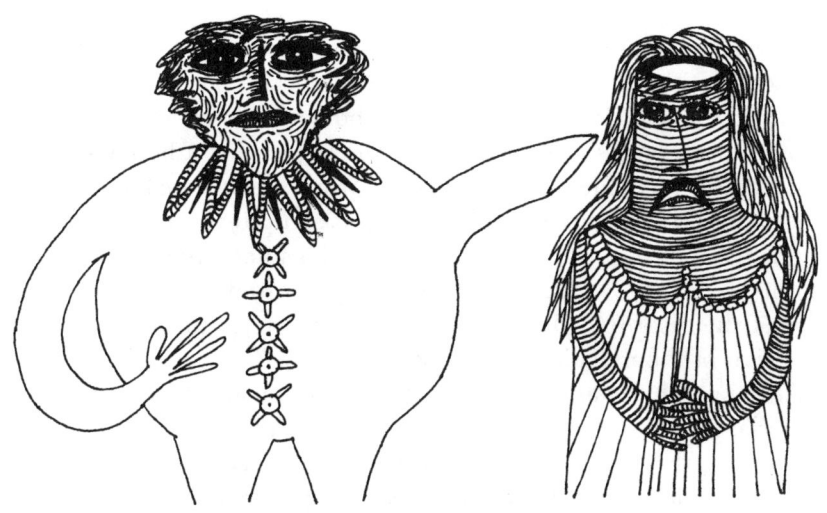

Belinda's Hysteria: The Medical Context of *The Rape of the Lock*

JOHN F. SENA

Pope's Belinda is undoubtedly one of the most thoroughly examined coquettes in literary history. We have pried into her love life with both the Baron and the sylphs, we have looked over her shoulder at the card table, we have spied on her as she applied her cosmetics, we have even peeked at her petticoats.[1] Indeed, we have left her with very little mystery. Yet we have ignored the nature and significance of a major event in her life—the hysterical fit she experiences after the Baron cuts her lock. Belinda's hysteria, it will be seen, is a realistic depiction of a fashionable eighteenth-century malady which reflects not only Pope's knowledge of contemporary medicine but his ability to employ medical theories for characterization and satiric purposes.

Before examining Belinda's hysteria, however, it may be helpful to discuss briefly the contemporary conception of the disorder. Hysteria or melancholia was probably the most common affliction experienced by eighteenth-century women.[2] "Of all chronic diseases," wrote

Thomas Sydenham, a physician described by Lady Mary Wortley Montagu as the English Hippocrates, "hysteria . . . is the commonest . . . as to females, if we except those who lead a hard and hardy life, there is rarely one who is wholly free from [it]. . . ."[3] Although hysteria was a daily fact of life for many women, ironically no one knew exactly what it was. Its causes were so diverse, its symptoms so numerous, its characteristics so amorphous, that physicians and laymen alike were unable to define—with any degree of accuracy and precision—the nature of the disorder. "Like a globule of mercury," to quote a recent historian of the malady, "it escapes the grasp."[4]

Although physicians were not able to agree on an exact definition of hysteria, there were several broad areas of accord among them. In general terms, they considered hysteria to be a functional or behavioral disorder which arose from the effects of physical or psychological stimuli on the brain and nervous system. Furthermore, they agreed that the malady was most prevalent, as Sydenham implies, among women who did not work or exert themselves physically, among women who led a sedentary or refined life—among women, in other words, of the upper class.[5] Finally, while all upper-class women were susceptible to the disorder, there was also a general belief that women who were celibate—virgins and widows—were especially prone to attacks of hysteria.

The theory that celibate women are most susceptible to the affliction arose from the ancient belief that hysteria was caused by a disfunction of the uterus.[6] According to Hippocrates, prolonged continence caused the uterus to become dry and light. The uterus, which he thought capable of wandering throughout the body, would then rise in the chest in search of moisture. The rising uterus, he averred, was responsible for the sensation of choking or suffocation that hysterics claimed they experienced. If the uterus traveled to the head it could cause pains in the eyes and nose, as well as a general feeling of drowsiness.[7] Galen, writing in the second century A.D., also posited a causal relationship between sexual abstinence and hysteria. Based on his observations of a woman who was free from hysteria during her two marriages but who suffered from severe attacks during her periods of widowhood, Galen theorized that the uterus produced a semen, analogous to the semen of a man, which must be expelled through sexual intercourse if mental and physical health are to be maintained.[8]

Advocating a two-thousand-year-old theory, Robert Burton in his Brobdingnagian *The Anatomy of Melancholy* (1621) reiterated the relationship between celibacy and hysteria. In a section of the *Anatomy* devoted to the hysteria of "Maids, Nuns, and Widows," he reasoned that the "menstruous blood" and the "fuliginous exhalation of corrupt seed" of celibate women produced black vapors which ascended to the brain and caused melancholia. Although he endorsed several types of cures, he recommended marriage as the best remedy for hysteria: "But the best and surest remedy of all, is to see them well placed, and married to good husbands . . . that's the primary cause, and this the ready cure, to give them content to their desires."[9] Although Burton's physiological explanation of the effect of celibacy—like the explanations of Hippocrates and Galen—may seem naive to us today, the causal relationship between sexual abstinence and hysteria is not without basis. "The association of hysteria with the female generative system was," as Ilza Veith reminds us, "in essence an expression of awareness of the malign effect of disordered sexual activity on emotional stability."[10]

At approximately the time that Burton was writing his monumental work, the theory that hysteria was a uterine disease was being combined with the theory that the cerebral area was also involved in its etiology. The work of Thomas Willis, in particular, a physiologist and neuroanatomist, had a profound impact in establishing what was to become the dominant eighteenth-century view that hysteria was primarily an affliction of the brain and nervous system. Central to Willis's theory—as well as to eighteenth-century physicians who followed him—was the role of animal spirits in producing the mental, emotional, and physical symptoms of hysteria. Animal spirits were thought to be the vital link between the mind and the body. Consisting of a thin, delicate fluid, they were believed to carry data from the five senses through the nervous system to the brain, as well as the impulses of the brain to the various parts of the body.[11] When the composition of the animal spirits was altered from a *"spirituous-saline"* state to "an acetous or sharp disposition" (which Willis also called "corrosive"), that chemical change, he averred, was capable of producing the violent physical convulsions, rapid emotional shifts, and absurd hallucinations of hysterics.[12] Although he and the eighteenth-century physicians who wrote under his influence posited the primacy of the nervous system and the brain in causing hysteria, it should be added that neither he nor his followers ruled out the womb entirely as a cause for the affliction. The womb can induce hysteria, he thought, when the menses do not flow freely, a condition which may occur when "the provocations of *Venus* or Lust" are restrained.[13]

As a mixed malady of mind and body, then, hysteria was probably the most gruesome affliction that could befall an eighteenth-century woman. Physically, the sufferer was likely to experience, according to Richard Blackmore, intestinal convulsions, stomach sickness, loss of appetite, vomiting, difficulty in breathing, palpitations of the heart, fainting, vertigo, giddiness, impaired vision, and crying. Often the hysteric is thrown, he suggested, into a violent convulsive fit—resembling an epileptic fit— in which the face becomes disfigured, limbs move involuntarily, and the victim falls to the ground, beating her breast and biting her tongue.[14] Psychologically, it was generally believed that the sufferer was likely to experience fear, anger, sadness, anxiety, depression, and paranoia. Hysterics "brood over trifles," according to Sydenham, "cherishing them in their anxious and unquiet bosoms. Fear, anger, jealousy, suspicion, and the worst passions of the mind arise without cause."[15]

In addition to experiencing a wide variety of emotions, hysterics were also likely to undergo violent and abrupt shifts in their emotional state. They could rapidly alternate between elation and depression, intense rage and deep lethargy. It was not uncommon for "violent laughter and profuse weeping," according to John Ball, author of the widely-read *The Modern Practice of Physic* (1760), to "succeed each other by turns."[16] "They love without measure," wrote Sydenham in the *Epistolary Dedication* (1681-82), "those whom they will soon hate without reason." In fact, their emotional instability became for Sydenham one of the most obvious and fascinating manifestations of the malady. With hysterics, he added wistfully, "there is no moderation. All is caprice."[17]

As horrible and painful as the physical and psychological effects of hysteria were, an even worse fate ultimately awaited its hapless victim. If not brought under control, hysteria, it was believed, could result in insanity. Since the animal spirits were responsible for reporting the data gathered by the senses to the brain, any disruption of them could result in the imagination presenting images to the mind that bore little resemblance to the objects perceived. Thus hysterics were likely to experience hallucinations, delusions, and fantasies; to "think they see, hear, smell, and touch, that which they do not."[18] Often the delusions of an hysteric were so overwhelming that the sufferer was convinced, as we shall see later, that she had been transformed into a different form and substance. In view, then, of the gruesome physical, emotional, and mental effects of the malady, one can well understand the remorse and horror of Capt. Booth when he learned that his beloved Amelia had developed hysteria:

> "These fatigues, added to the uneasiness of her mind, overpowered her weak spirits, and threw her into one of the worst disorders that can possibly attend a woman; a disorder very common among the ladies, and our physicians have not agreed upon its name. Some call it fever of the spirits, some a nervous fever, some the vapours, and some the hysterics."
> "O say no more," cries Miss Matthews; "I pity you, I pity you from my soul. A man had better be plagued with all the curses of Egypt than with a vapourish wife."
> "Pity me! madam," answered Booth; "pity rather that dear creature who, from her love and care of my unworthy self, contracted a distemper, the horrors of which are scarce to be imagined. It is, indeed, a sort of complication of all diseases together, with almost madness added to them."[19]

While Fielding used medical notions of hysteria in this brief passage to elicit pity for the sufferer, the malady could also be employed by an artist in a more elaborate and sustained fashion for decidedly unsentimental purposes. Nowhere is this more clearly to be seen than in the period's most famous mock-heroic poem, *The Rape of the Lock*.

Obviously, *The Rape of the Lock* is not a poem about hysteria. Pope is more concerned with moral and ethical issues than with medicine. Yet it is also evident that he employs the medical lore of hysteria in his characterization of Belinda. Belinda is depicted as experiencing an hysterical attack after her lock of hair is cut, suffering a number of the symptoms we have seen described by the physicians. In addition to providing his heroine with a fashionable adornment to her personality, Pope's use of hysteria, it will be shown, has a thematic function in the work as well, one which is aptly suited to his satiric purposes in *The Rape of the Lock*.

Even before she experiences her hysterical attack, Belinda, it should be noted, would probably have been recognized by an informed reader as the type of woman especially susceptible to the disorder. She is, for instance, a member of the upper class; as such, the idle and luxurious life she leads conforms fairly closely to the pattern that physicians thought would make a woman prone to hysteria. Burton, for example, declared that the women most vulnerable to melancholia are "noble virgins [and] nice gentlewomen, such as are solitary and idle, live at ease, lead a life out of action and employment, that fare well, in great houses and jovial companies."[20] Robert James, author of one of the most popular medical dictionaries of the period, added that hysteria was prevalent among those "whose affluence of Fortune permits them to indulge in Ease and Indolence; who sleep much, and that long in the Morning . . . who drink copiously of warm liquors, as Tea."[21] We see then, that before Belinda suffers the disastrous "rape" that gives her an hysterical fit, she is depicted as being a prime candidate for the disorder.

In addition to the natural propensity of female members of the *beau monde* to hysteria, Belinda's association with Rosicrucian sylphs would have also been perceived as making her particularly susceptible to the malady. In Rosicrucianism, virginity is a prerequisite for salvation.[22] Although Pope has inverted Rosicrucian theology in the poem, making women the central figures and men their tempters, the notion remains that one must abstain from sexual intercourse in order to exist after death as an immortal spirit.

If celibacy, especially in light of Rosicrucian theology, is important to Belinda, it is also, as we have seen, one of the most prevalent—and certainly one of the most traditional—causes of hysteria. Regardless of the medical predilections of the practitioner, whether he believed in the humoral medicine of Hippocrates or the iatrophysical medicine of Willis and James, whether he believed the the disease arose from the womb or from the cerebrum, virtually all physicians posited a causal relationship between sexual abstinence and hysteria. It is likely, then, that given the widespread knowledge of this particular cause of hysteria, a contemporary reader would have recognized in Belinda's virginity a condition which, like the idle and luxurious life she leads, would make her especially vulnerable to hysterical attacks.[23]

Belinda's susceptibility to hysteria is translated into an actual hysterical fit—described with medical accuracy—when the Baron cuts her lock of hair. Losing a lock of hair would seem an adequate provocation for hysteria in terms of eighteenth-century medicine, for physicians theorized that the malady could be brought on by "any accident occasioning sudden surprise,"[24] by the "passions of the mind, and by every considerable emotion, especially those brought on by surprise."[25] Immediately after Belinda receives her sudden surprise, Umbriel, "a dusky melancholy Spright," descends to the Cave of Spleen and pleads with the local deity to help him make Belinda a melancholic sufferer. The Goddess of the Cave obliges by giving him a bag and a vial which contain a number of the emotional and physical symptoms we have seen ascribed to the malady in medical works. The bag, which he breaks over Belinda's head, contains "Sighs, Sobs, and Passions, and the War of Tongues," recalling Burton's remarks that one is likely to hear "tears, sighs, and groans, and grievous miseries" from melancholic women, or that the malady often leaves women "grieving, sighing, weeping, and discontented."[26] Likewise the contents of the vial—"fainting Fears, / Soft Sorrows, melting Griefs, and flowing Tears"—which he next breaks over Belinda, also reflect the consensus of medical opinion that an hysteric will generally experience "sighing and sobbing," "fainting away," and "dreadful anguish of mind."[27] The Baron's destruction of her emotional stability, then, followed by the contents of Umbriel's bag and vial, consign Belinda to that large group of eighteenth-century women afflicted with hysteria.

Hysterics were, as we have seen, notorious for the intensity of their emotions as well as the "Fickle, Wavering, and Unconstant" nature of their emotional responses.[28] The violence of Belinda's passions and the rapidity with which her passions change suggest the emotional intensity and instability that physicians ascribed to hysterical women. Belinda, for instance, alternates between excessive anger and excessive depression, two of the most common emotions experienced by hysterics. For the first three cantos she is depicted as a vivacious coquette who harbors a "mighty rage" in her bosom toward men. After her lock is cut, however, she undergoes a sudden emotional transformation and becomes deeply depressed, languid, and grief-stricken. Umbriel finds her in the arms of Thalestris, "Her Eyes dejected and her Hair unbound." When he disperses on Belinda's head the hysterical contents of the bag he has received from the Goddess of the Cave, Belinda experiences another radical emotional change and now no longer remains listless and lethargic but instead "burns with more than mortal Ire." When he next breaks the vial which contains additional hysterical symptoms, she once again undergoes a rapid emotional transformation: "Her Eyes half-languishing, half-drown'd in Tears; / On her heav'd Bosom hung her drooping Head." The lugubrious Belinda, however, is soon changed once again back into the "fierce *Belinda*" and the "incens'd *Belinda*" as she vents her spleen on the Baron. She finally subdues her antagonist's "manly Strength" by blowing snuff at his nose and thus provoking an orgasmic sneeze. It is appropriate that her final victory is depicted in sexual terms, since it was the symbolic loss of her virginity to a man who wished "no more than on his Foe to die" that occasioned her hysteria.

While Belinda is experiencing her hysterical attacks, several other women are presented who are also afflicted with the malady. The Goddess of the Cave of Spleen, for instance, is depicted as lying pensively in a grotto "screen'd in Shades from Day's detested Glare," troubled with a pain in her side and a severe headache—two common symptoms of hysteria.[29] The Goddess is accompanied by two handmaidens, "*Ill-nature*" and "*Affectation.*" "*Ill-nature*," suggesting the austere and melancholic nature of Puritan worship, is seen holding prayers "for Mornings, Nights, and Noons" in her hands and lampoons in her bosom,[30] while "*Affectation*," representing all those who feign melancholy, is depicted languishing on a "rich Quilt." Although Pope's Cave is filled with many such unusual sights—"glaring Fiends," "Snakes on rolling Spires," "Lakes of liquid Gold"—perhaps the most extraordinary spectacle of all is the procession of hapless victims of hysterical insanity:

> Unnumber'd Throngs on ev'ry side are seen
> Of Bodies chang'd to various Forms by *Spleen*.
> Here living *Teapots* stand, one Arm held out,
> One bent; the Handle this, and that the Spout:
> A Pipkin there like *Homer's Tripod* walks;
> Here sighs a Jar, and there a Goose-pye talks;
> Men prove with Child, as pow'rful Fancy works,
> And Maids turn'd Bottels, call aloud for Corks.
> (IV, 47–54)

This passage reflects the seventeenth- and eighteenth-century medical theory that the disordered animal spirits of one who has suffered from prolonged melancholia may cause the imagination to present perverse images to the brain with such vigor that one will experience the delusion that his or her body has been transformed into a different form and substance. Thus "some *Melancholick* persons undergo imaginary *Metamorphoses*," according to Willis, and believe "themselves to be Dogs or Wolves, and have imitated their ways and kind by barking or howling; others have thought themselves dead, desiring presently to be buried; others imagining that their bodies were made of glass, were afraid to be touched lest they should be broke to pieces."[31] Richard Blackmore, a physician whose patients included numerous melancholics, noted in *A Treatise of the Spleen and Vapours* (1725) that "some will by no means be convinced, but that they are entirely formed of Glass, and that by the next Knock or Jog on any solid Objects, they shall break all to pieces. . . . One has believed himself to be Millet-Seed, another a Goose, or a Goose-Pye. And once a Man filled with Strong Drink, feared to render it by Urine, lest he should drown the World by a Deluge."[32] Nicholas Robinson, a fellow of the Royal College of Physicians, added that it is not uncommon for some melancholics to be persuaded that "their Bodies are transform'd into Swans, Geese, Glasses, Tea Cups, etc. and act with the very same Regard to their Friends and Acquaintances, as if their Bodies had actually suffer'd such a Metamorphosis."[33] Pope's insane hysterics, then, are not products of the poet's imagination as much as they are an artistic rendering of contemporary medical cases.[34]

Although Belinda is not among the "Unnumber'd Throngs" which Pope specifically enumerates, the concept of metamorphosis, implicit in her hysteria, is a vital element in her depiction throughout the poem. She wishes to avoid undergoing, for instance, the relatively ordinary and natural change from virginity to sexual initiation so that she may undergo the extraordinary and unnatural change from a human to an hermaphroditic sylph. As a sylph she would, in turn, be capable of changing into whatever shape and form that she wished: "For spirits, freed from mortal laws, with ease / Assume what sexes and what shapes they please" (I, 69–70). Although she never achieves her desired metamorphosis from a coquette to a sylph, she does, however, transform herself from a mortal to a "Goddess" at her toilette. This change is, in turn, made possible by the use of metamorphosed substances—Arabia which has been transformed into perfume, and the tortoise and elephant which have been changed into combs. Her proudest possession is also depicted in terms of metamorphosis. Her lock of hair changes from a mere physical attribute at the beginning of the poem, to a symbol of virginity which the Baron cuts, to a celestial body—"a sudden Star"—when it rises into the heavens, to a specific celestial body—"*Venus*"—to, finally, a heavenly sign of Belinda's immortality, for we are told that the star with its "radiant Trail of Hair" shall inscribe forever Belinda's name in the firmament. Although I do not wish to argue that these transformations are derived exclusively from medical lore—for the concept of bodies changing shapes is a recurring theme in Western literature from at least the time of Ovid—I do wish to suggest that Belinda's metamorphoses, viewed in the context of Pope's medical interests, represent a skillful blending of literary motif and medical theory.

In addition to inflicting Belinda with an hysterical attack, Pope also recommends, allusively, a cure for her malady. Immediately after the Baron cuts Belinda's lock with his "glitt'ring *Forfex*," he launches into an hyperbolic passage on the power of steel:

> What Time wou'd spare, from Steel receives its date,
> And Monuments, like Men, submit to Fate!
> Steel cou'd the Labour of the Gods destroy,
> And strike to Dust th' Imperial Tow'rs of *Troy*;
> Steel cou'd the Works of mortal Pride confound,
> And hew Triumphal Arches to the Ground.
> What Wonder then, fair Nymph! thy Hairs shou'd feel
> The conqu'ring Force of unresisted Steel?
> (III, 171–178)

While the Baron is obviously comparing in mock-epic fashion his scissors to the heroic implements of war, the passage has an additional implication in terms of Belinda's hysteria. "Steel," a generic term for medicines containing iron or steel, was one of the most widely recommended cures for hysteria and melancholia. Willis, for instance, in addition to encouraging melancholic sufferers to drink "spaw-Waters coming from Iron," included in his *Two Discourses Concerning the Soul of Brutes* (1672) the precise formulae for making steel medicines in various forms: "Vitriol of steel," "syrup of Steel," "extract of Steel," "filings of Iron."[35] Sydenham also believed that steel and chalybeate medicines (medicines containing salts of iron) were the most efficacious nostrums for curing hysteria, recommending to the sufferer a tasty concoction made by "steeping iron or steel filings in cold Rhenish wine."[36] Even medical dilettantes endorsed the use of steel. Mr. Bickerstaff in *Tatler*, No. 80, for instance, prescribes "the Cold Bath, with a Course of Steel" to a man suffering from the spleen, while the melancholic George Gloom in *Spectator*, No. 547, is advised to take a "Course of *Steele*" for his ailment.[37] In exalting over his victory, the Baron may also therefore be punning on Belinda's hysterical condition, reminding her that "the conqu'ring Force of unresisted Steel" is able to provoke as well as cure an hysterical fit.

It is evident, then, that Pope made extensive use of medical theories of hysteria in his depiction of Belinda. By adding a medical dimension to her personality, by reflecting in her delineation the major elements of the most prevalent affliction of the eighteenth century, he increased the complexity of her characterization as well as her interest and fascination among contemporary readers. Pope's readers could take delight, presumably, in diagnosing from a comfortable distance the symptoms of a malady that in real life they would view with alarm and trepidation.

Although the concept of hysteria contributes to the richness of Belinda's depiction, Pope also uses the malady, as I have suggested, for satiric purposes. Through hysteria, for instance, he attacks the hypocrisy of women who would use a sickness to achieve their selfish objectives. As a fashionable disorder—one associated especially with the upper classes—hysteria was a malady which some women affected as a means of raising or preserving their social status. Still others used the fact that hysteria occasioned erratic and unpredictable behavior as a convenient rationale to explain their fickle and irrational conduct. When Lucy, for instance, wishes to explain her outrageous behavior to Polly in *The Beggar's Opera*, she merely attributes it to an attack of the spleen: "Dear Madam, your servant. I hope you will pardon my passion when I was so happy to see you last. I was so overrun with the spleen that I was perfectly out of myself. And really, when one hath the spleen, everything is to be excused by a friend."[38]

Pope attacks hysterical poseurs primarily through his depiction of "*Affectation*," one of the handmaidens of the Goddess of the Cave of Spleen. "*Affectation*," like the hypocritical pretenders to the malady, feigns the most obvious symptoms of hysteria. She wears a "sickly Mien," pretends to faint and languish, and rehearses how "to lisp, and hang the head aside." For her, and the "Fair ones" like her, the spleen is not the dreadful disorder described by Capt. Booth, but is instead an excuse to exhibit a new "nightdress" (dressing gown) to their beaux. In fact, the spleen is for them a nightdress, an attractive and useful outer covering that may be removed at will. While it is likely that Pope would have had deep sympathy for women genuinely afflicted with hysteria, it is also likely that, to a man who described his life as "this long disease," he reserved an especial contempt for those who used sickness as a convenient means of cloaking hypocritical and egoistic behavior.

In addition to satirizing the hypocritical behavior of some women, Pope also employs hysteria to suggest the frailty and weakness of human nature. Although the physical effects of hysteria made it an unpleasant malady, it must be remembered that it was the mental and emotional symptoms of the disease that rendered it a particularly dreaded affliction for Pope's contemporaries. In an age which considered equanimity, self-discipline, and moderation in behavior among its ideals, hysteria caused violent emotional outbursts, erratic behavior, and loss of self-control. In an age which valued reason and order, it disrupted the rational process and made the mind a slave to unrestrained passions and terrifying hallucinations. The very mental and emotional effects, then, that made the malady a baleful affliction also made hysteria an appropriate vehicle for attacking overly optimistic and complacent attitudes toward human nature. Belinda's hysteria is a vivid reminder of both the existence of violent passions and destructive impulses within our nature as well as our inability to prevent them from breaking through the thin veneer of civilized behavior and social decorum.

The medical implications of hysteria also made it particularly well-suited for Pope's general attack on pride. The two emotions which comprise Belinda's hysterical fit—anger and depression—were widely associated with insanity. In fact, to Thomas Hobbes those two emotions constituted the two general types of madness: there is a "Madnesse," he wrote in *The Leviathan*, "called RAGE, and FURY," and there is a "Madnesse commonly called MELANCHOLY." Insanity, in turn, was generally believed in the seventeenth and eighteenth centuries to stem from pride. Hobbes, for instance, averred that "*Pride*, and *selfe-conceipt*" were responsible for producing one type of madness, the madness of

"RAGE, and FURY," for if one's pride is affronted, anger results, which then leads to a state of uncontrollable rage and fury.[39] Richard Steele went even further and declared in *Tatler*, No. 127, that pride or excessive self-esteem is responsible for all mental disorders. After visiting Bedlam Hospital and observing the "havoc in the brain" and "disorder in the imagination" engendered by pride, he avowed that he could make a "proud man a lunatic in three weeks time."[40] As a medical theorist, Willis tried to provide a physiological explanation for the association between pride and insanity. To Willis any agitation of the animal spirits which caused them to break out of the vessels which carried them and "cut for themselves, everywhere in the Brain, new little spaces or walks," could result in insanity. While various physical and psychological factors could provoke this condition, so too could pride:

> The Corporeal Soul swelling up with an opinion and pride of its own excellency, lifts up itself, and endeavours on every side to expand or stretch itself forth most amply, beyond the border or sphere of its body, the Animal Spirits being tumultuarily [sic] called into the Head, will not be contained within their wonted bounds, but being there broken and diversly reflected, by reason of their too much excretion, are compelled into new and plainly devious tracts; wherefore, both they being thrust forth from the course of their proper emanation, and also from the nervous Liquor, do quickly acquire a sharp and incitative Disposition, as was said but now, for that reason *Madness* follows.[41]

Belinda's pride, then, would have been recognized by Pope's contemporaries as the ultimate cause of her hysterical madness. In fact, the causal sequence described by Hobbes from pride to anger to rage and fury broadly describes Belinda's movement from her overweening pride, which has convinced her that she is superior to men, to her anger, rage, and fury at having that hierarchy inverted by the loss of a lock of hair. By recalling the close alliance between pride and insanity, Pope is able to remind his audience that to be proud is to live a life of madness, to live within a subjective world, within the confines of self, cut off from the moral and behavioral norms of society. Pride is ultimately for Pope but another form of insanity.

In addition to satirizing hypocrisy and pride, Belinda's hysteria permits Pope to undermine the entire world of Hampton Court. The presence of hysteria in both Hampton Court and the Cave of Spleen invites us to see a similarity between the modes of behavior in those two places. Thus, the hypocrisy of "*Affectation*," the foolishness of men who are convinced that they are pregnant, the sexual excesses of maids calling for corks, the vanity of women who become irate over a pimple, are not confined to the Cave of Spleen, but are reflections of the irrational and absurd conduct that may also be found at Hampton Court. Indeed, the general grotesque and nightmarish quality of the Cave may suggest Pope's vision of the true nature of life at Hampton Court, the life that lies hidden beneath the splendor and magnificence of its outer trappings. Ironically the pastoral goddess of Hampton Court, by having an hysterical attack and providing a bond between the Court and the Cave, destroys the pristine purity of her own world.[42] Hysteria, as well as the Baron's scissors, cracks the frail China jar.

It may also be added that the symptoms and effects of hysteria—as conceived by Pope and his contemporaries—helped to define for the eighteenth century the nature and character of women. Hysteria, as we have seen, was characterized by violent passions, emotional instability, and inconsistency of mood. Since both physicians and laymen considered the disorder to be a virtually universal affliction among women, it is probable that the age conceived of those traits as constituting the basic behavioral pattern of all women. In fact, those characteristics are precisely the traits that Pope attributes to most of the women he depicts in *Moral Essay II, To a Lady*. Furthermore, the close association between hysteria and insanity may have caused women to be perceived by themselves as well as by men as being mentally weak, constantly in danger of crossing the thin partition into unreason. Hysteria, then, as it appears in *The Rape of the Lock* and as it was understood by the age did little to raise either the image or self-esteem of women. Rather it served to lend medical credence to the timeworn notion that women were erratic and fickle creatures barely capable of holding on to the small measure of reason they possessed.

NOTES

1. See, for instance, Hugo M. Reichard, "The Love Affair in Pope's *Rape of the Lock*," *PMLA*, 69 (1954), 887-902; W. K. Wimsatt, "The Game of Ombre in *The Rape of*

the Lock," *RES*, ns 1 (1950), 136-43; Earl R. Wasserman, "The Limits of Allusion in *The Rape of the Lock*," *JEGP*, 65 (1966), 425-44; and the remarks of Geoffrey Tillotson on Belinda's card playing and his notes on her garments in *The Rape of the Lock*, ed. Geoffrey Tillotson, in *The Poems of Alexander Pope*, Twickenham Edition, 3rd ed. (New Haven, Conn., and London: Yale University Press and Methuen, 1962), vol. II. All quotations from *The Rape of the Lock* are from this edition and will be cited in the text by canto and line reference.

2. There were several terms—melancholy, spleen, vapour—that were used interchangeably with hysteria in the eighteenth century. Ironically, these names derive from humoral medicine, a collection of medical theories that was largely rejected by eighteenth-century physicians. The term "melancholy" (which derives from the Greek word for black bile) arose from the humoral theory that an excessive amount of black bile was responsible for the malady. According to humoral medicine it was the function of the spleen to extract black bile from the blood. Since a malfunction of that organ would result in a superabundance of black bile, the malady was also called "the spleen." "Vapours" arose from the humoral theory that if the body temperature suddenly increased, which may be caused by improper diet, physiological sickness, or immoderate passions, black bile which had gathered in the lower abdomen would burn. The vapors of the burned bile would then rise to the cerebral area where they would adulterate the animal spirits and thus bring on an attack of melancholy or hysteria. Since these various terms were interchangeable in the eighteenth century, I have regarded them as synonyms in my essay.

3. *Epistolary Dissertation* (1681-82), in *The Works of Thomas Sydenham*, trans. R. C. Latham (London, 1848-50), II, p. 85.

4. Ilza Veith, *Hysteria: The History of a Disease* (Chicago: University of Chicago Press, 1965), p. 1. William Cullen reflected the general opinion of eighteenth-century physicians when he declared that "The many and various symptoms which have been supposed to belong to a disease under this appellation, render it extremely difficult to give a general character or definition of it" (*First Lines of the Practice of Physic* [1777], ed. John Rotheram [Philadelphia, 1792], II, p. 257).

5. "For seldom should you see an hired servant, a poor handmaid, though ancient, that is kept hard to her work and bodily labour, a coarse country wench, troubled in this kind . . . " (Robert Burton, *The Anatomy of Melancholy*, ed. H. Jackson [London: Dent, 1964], I, p. 417. See also Robert James, *A Medicinal Dictionary* (London, 1745), "Hysteria."

6 "Hysteria," it should be remembered, derives from the Greek word "hystera," which means "uterus."

7. For Hippocrates' general discussion of hysteria see his work, *On the Diseases of Women*. The cures he recommended reflected his belief in the theory of the wandering uterus. Fetid smells, he thought, should be applied to the nose to repel the uterus, while perfumed aromatics should be placed near the vagina to attract the uterus to its proper place.

8. *De locis affectis* (Venice, 1541), Lib. VI. I wish to express my indebtedness to Prof. Veith's excellent study of hysteria for my brief discussion of Hippocrates and Galen.

9. Burton, I, pp. 414-417.

10. Veith, p. 2. For a recent consideration of "hysteria" and some qualifications of Veith's account, see John P. Wright, "Hysteria and Mechanical Man," *Journal of the History of Ideas*, 41 (1980), 233-247, especially p. 235, n. 14.

11. Animal spirits, described by Richard Mead as "a thin, volatile Liquor" of great power and elasticity (Introduction to *A Mechanical Account of Poisons* [1702], in *The Medical Works of Richard Mead* [Dublin, 1767], p. xiv), were an object of scientific faith rather than scientific fact. The basis upon which physicians argued for their existence was that without them "no man could ever explain the Modus of the Union" between the mind and the senses (Edward Strother, *An Essay on Sickness and Health* [London, 1725], p. 436). It was the consensus of medical opinion that animal spirits circulated in a manner not unlike that of the blood. Rather than using arteries and veins, however, they traveled either along the nerves or in thin tubes especially created for their movement. Large quantities of these spirits were constantly being manufactured by the body, for they were the *sine qua non* of life; without them all thought, sensation, and locomotion would cease.

12. *Two Discourses Concerning the Soul of Brutes* (1672), trans. S. Pordage (London, 1683), p. 188. The changes in the animal spirits that produce melancholy are, according to Willis, similar to the changes that cause insanity, for melancholy and insanity are for him "so much akin, that these Distempers often change, and pass from one into the other . . ." (p. 201). Eighteenth-century physicians posited a virtually endless number of physical and psychological factors that could adversely alter the animal spirits and bring on melancholic or hysterical attacks. Among the more common physical factors were poor digestion, weak muscle tone, viscid body fluids, a general delicacy of body, obstructions in the stomach, bowels, liver, or spleen, salt in the blood, retention of blood in the uterus, moist air, the "pollution of cities" brought on by "sulphureous and Bituminous fires," improper diet, even English commerce. A sudden shock or surprise, prolonged grief, disappointment, and anxiety were among the most prevalent psychological conditions that could have a baleful effect on animal spirits.

13. Willis, p. 192. For eighteenth-century reiterations of this view, see James, "Hysteria," and Cullen, pp. 259, 261.

14. "An Essay Upon the Spleen," in *Essays Upon Several Subjects* (London, 1717), II, pp. 203-04. See also Sydenham, pp. 85-88; James, "Hysteria." The numerous symptoms of hysteria and their similarity to the symptoms of other disorders made hysteria one of the most difficult afflictions for an eighteenth-century physician to diagnose. Physicians, in fact, often compared hysteria and melancholy to Proteus, the shape-changing god of the sea, because their manifestations were always changing, continuously shifting from one part of the body to another, while constantly mimicking other diseases. See Sydenham, p. 85, and John Purcell, *A Treatise of Vapours and Hysteric Fits* (London, 1702), pp. 1-2.

15. Sydenham, p. 89. For the psychological symptoms of the disorder, see Blackmore's "An Essay Upon the Spleen," pp. 203-204; Robert Whytt, *Observations on the Nature, Cause, and Cure of those Disorders Commonly called Nervous, Hypochondriac, or Hysteric* (Edinburgh, 1765), pp. 101-103.

16. *The Modern Practice of Physic* (London, 1760), II, p. 229.

17. Sydenham, p. 89.

18. Burton, I, p. 384.

19. Henry Fielding, *Amelia* (1751), ed. Ernest Rhys (London, 1930), Bk. III, chapter 7.
20. Burton, I, p. 417.
21. James, "Hysteria."
22. For a discussion of Pope's use of Rosicrucianism, see "Appendix B" of the Tillotson edition of *The Rape of the Lock*, and Wasserman, "The Limits of Allusion in *The Rape of the Lock*."
23. In one of the best-known descriptions of any hysteric in eighteenth-century fiction, Tobias Smollett also insists on the virginal status of the sufferer. Narcissa's aunt in *Roderick Random* (1748) is a "maiden of forty years" who is filled with contempt for "the male part of the creation." To underscore her celibacy, Smollett makes her, like Belinda, a follower of Rosicrucianism: "she professes the principles of Rosicrucius, and believes the earth, air, and sea are inhabited by invisible beings, with whom it is possible for the human species, to entertain correspondence and intimacy, on the easy condition of living chaste" (*Roderick Random*, in *The Novels of Tobias Smollett* [Oxford: Blackwell, 1925-26], 2: chapter XXXVIII).
24. Whytt, p. 115.
25. Cullen, p. 259.
26. Burton, I, p. 416.
27. See Cullen, p. 258; Purcell, pp. 4, 8.
28. Purcell, p. 8.
29. For an excellent discussion of the scientific backgrounds to the Cave of Spleen, see Lawrence Babb, "The Cave of Spleen," *RES*, 12 (1936), 165-176.
30. Richard Baxter epitomized the seventeenth-and eighteenth-century view of the relationship between the Puritans and melancholy when he declared "*Spiritus Calvinianus est spiritus melancholicus*" (*Saint or Brute*, in *The Practical Works*, ed. William Orme [London, 1830], X, p. 60). See also Henry More, *Enthusiasmus Triumphatus* (1656); C. M. Webster, "Swift and Some Earlier Satirists of Puritan Enthusiasm," *PMLA*, 48 (1933), 1141-1153; George Rosen, "Enthusiasm: 'a dark lanthorn of the spirit,'" *Bulletin of the History of Medicine*, 42 (1968), 393-421.
31. Willis, pp. 188, 200. See also Babb, "The Cave of Spleen."
32. *A Treatise of the Spleen and Vapours* (London, 1725), pp. 161-162.
33. *A New System of the Spleen, Vapours, and Hypochondriack Melancholy* (London, 1729), p. 230.
34. Smollett also has Narcissa's aunt undergo a series of startling metamorphoses. When Roderick calls on her one morning, he is informed by the maid that she has chosen to remain in bed because she "actually believed herself a hare beset with the hunters; and begged a few greens to munch for her breakfast." At one time, he is told, she imagined herself transformed into "a piece of furniture." She had even considered herself to be a human fire extinguisher. She prophesied that the conflagration of the apocalypse was at hand and could only be extinguished by her urine, which she refused to evacuate even to the point of endangering her life (chapter XXXIX).
35. Willis, pp. 196-197.
36. Sydenham, pp. 97-98.

37. Note, of course, the pun on the name of one of the authors of the *Spectator*.
38. *The Beggar's Opera*, ed. Edgar V. Roberts (Lincoln: University of Nebraska Press, 1969), 3: viii, 1-5. Attacks of the spleen could even be used by coquettes, according to Anne Finch, as a means of capturing the heart of a Beau:

    > The careless Posture, and the Head reclin'd;
    > The thoughtful and composed Face
    > Proclaiming the withdrawn and absent Mind,
    > Allows the Fop more liberty to gaze;
    > Who gently for the tender Cause enquires:
    > The Cause indeed is a defect in Sense;
    > But still the Spleen's alledg'd, and still the dull pretence.

    ("The Spleen," st. V in *The Poems of Anne, Countess of Winchilsea*, ed. Myra Reynolds [Chicago, 1903].)

39. *The Leviathan*, ed A. D. Lindsay (London: Dent, 1965), Part I, chapter 8.
40. Swift, too, ascribed madness to pride by depicting the insane philosophers in *A Tale of a Tub* as victims of inordinate self-esteem and egotism: "For, what Man in the natural State, or Course of Thinking, did ever conceive it in his Power, to reduce the Notions of all Mankind exactly to the same Length, and Breadth, and Height of his own?" (*A Tale of a Tub*, ed. A. C. Guthkelch and D. Nichol Smith, 2nd ed. [Oxford: Clarendon Press, 1958], p. 166).
41. Willis, p. 203.
42. For a discussion of the pastoralism of Hampton Court, see Murray Krieger, "The 'Frail China Jar' and the Rude Hand of Chaos," *Centennial Review of Arts and Sciences*, 5 (1961), 176–194.

A TREATISE

OF THE

Spleen and Vapours:

OR,

HYPOCONDRIACAL

AND

HYSTERICAL AFFECTIONS.

WITH

Three DISCOURSES on the Nature and Cure of the CHOLICK, MELANCHOLY, and PALSIES.

Never before Published.

WRITTEN BY
Sir *RICHARD BLACKMORE*, Kt. M. D. and Fellow of the Royal College of Physicians in *London*.

LONDON:
Printed for J. PEMBERTON at the *Buck* and *Sun* over-gainst St. Dunstan's Church in *Fleet-street*. MDCCXXV.

Addison and Hutcheson: Literary Theory and the Psychology of the Audience

ROBERT L. MONTGOMERY

Seventeenth-century literary theory is often understood to be characterized by attention to rules and questions of form, but it also exhibits an increasingly powerful emphasis on the interests of the audience. Early in the next century with Addison's essays on the pleasures of the imagination these interests overtook and at least partially obscured the older critical preoccupation with matters of form and theme. Hutcheson's thinking on aesthetics and poetry, often considered closely tied to Addison's views of imaginative pleasure, shows a greater interest in formal questions, while Addison's most surprising and original contribution to the history of theory is his almost complete indifference to literary form as the center of critical focus. What he has to say in the essays on "The Pleasures of the Imagination," as well as in the earlier pieces on wit, the ballad and epic, *Paradise Lost*, and tragedy, is always written from the point of view of a critic whose main concern is with literary or artistic affect. He expresses just this point of view when he supposes that a classical or Roman style in architecture is preferable to the Gothic, noting "the Greatness of the Manner in the one, and the Meanness in the other." In seeking the cause, he says: "The Reason I take to be, because in these Figures [the round and the convex] we generally see more of the Body, than in those other Kinds" (*Spectator* 415).

Addison's motive was to educate his contemporaries away from styles he considered trivial, fussy, or (and this is more important) inclined to divide the attention of the mind. He was not in any sense of the word an objective student of the viewing or reading sensibility. But the task he set himself required, if not a fully developed systematic psychology, at least a set of reasonably coherent propositions about the makeup of mental reactions and about our capacity not just to respond to art but also to fashion experience within the mind.

There is general agreement today that most of his psychological concepts are drawn from Locke. Clarence D. Thorpe, in his account of Addison's theory of imagination, relates it back to Descartes and Hobbes, and it is not difficult to find the origins of his view of sense experience as the basis of mental experience in medieval and Aristotelian faculty psychology.[1] But conventional faculty psychology reached him sufficiently modified to allow him to think differently. Renaissance literary theory asked that poetry induce specific and predicted reactions in the audience based on the belief in a system of sequential response from sense perception through imagination to reason and will. The terms in use—"delight," "instruction," "persuasion," "moving"—point to the motive of effecting a particular and intended concept, attitude, or mode of behavior in the reader. What is hoped for is virtuous behavior or acceptance of a truth arrived at by means of an attractive image. One thinks of Sidney's classic statement of the way in which Virgil's account of Aeneas carrying Anchises in the wrack of Troy should move the reader to a kindred piety. The theory behind Sidney's example supposes responses that may be simple or complex, but in any case involve the orderly sequential influence of the artistic image over several powers of the mind, and poet, poem, and reader are linked by a foreordained series of events in a chain of command leading to moral consequences meant to be profound and durable. Imaginative literature and its concrete images embody and make visible concepts already shaped to our imagination and understanding. Their affective properties, which primarily come from the reader's ability to "see" what the poet is talking about, are fashioned to attract him to the truths he is asked to accept.[2]

Addison also proposes the reader's imagination as a mode of seeing, but pleasure is no longer simply a means to persuasion. It is the end of art, the purpose for which it is designed, a purpose implicit in

Addison's much-quoted statement about the imagination: "we have the Power of retaining, altering and compounding those Images, which we have once received, into all the varieties of Picture and Vision that are most agreeable to the Imagination. . . ."[3] I shall later deal more at length with the passage in which this statement occurs. What is of interest here is that Addison leaves out any sense of such experience leading beyond itself. He promises nothing beyond the mind's satisfaction in picturing objects to itself. What is involved is a psychology of response to art and nature as stimuli, as occasions for experience rather than interpreters of experience. The mind is filled with objects, possessed by them, and given over entirely, if Addison's prescription is followed, to a single coherent sensation. In his essay on the soul, *Spectator* 600, he says, "The Soul consists of many Faculties, as the Understanding, and the Will, with all the Senses both outward and inward; or to speak more Philosophically, the Soul can exert herself in many different ways of Action. . . ." Each faculty has proper objects in the world outside the mind and can take satisfaction in responding to them. Addison's psychology is not at all concerned with behavior; it is exclusively a psychology of perception.

It would be surprising if Addison were to depend upon a psychology in which mind and nature were not coordinate. But unlike the theorists of the Middle Ages and Renaissance he does not believe that the separate faculties can be located in actual regions of the brain, nor does he arrange them in any sequence of perception and intellection: "as the whole Soul acts in the Exertion of any of its particular Powers, the whole Soul is happy in the Pleasure which arises from any of its particular Acts. For notwithstanding, as has been before hinted, and as it has been taken Notice by one of the greatest modern Philosophers,[4] we divide the Soul into several Powers and Faculties, there is no such Division in the Soul it self, since it is the whole Soul that remembers, understands, wills, or imagines." And finally: "The Soul does not care to be always in the same bent. The Faculties relieve one another by Turns, and receive an Additional Pleasure from the Novelty of those Objects, about which they are conversant."

Addison and his successors saw the audience responding to both mimetic and expressive forms. One kind of pleasure resulted from the opportunity to compare the artificial copy with its natural original. As Addison puts it, "this Secondary Pleasure of the Imagination proceeds from that Action of the Mind, which compares the Ideas arising from the Original Objects, with the ideas we receive from the Statue, Picture, Description, or Sound that represents them" (*Spectator* 416). But he understood that this ancient and familiar concept was subject to complications. Statuary might be close to the object it represented, but as we turn to two dimensions in painting and then to words, the grounds of reference and hence of comparison move from the universal or natural to the conventional. With language we come upon an arbitrary, cultural basis for likeness: "Colours speak all Languages, but words are understood only by such a People or Nation."

He is not, however, concerned to explore the role of convention in taste apart from noting in *Spectator* 409 that people can be educated and habituated to certain styles. Instead he draws attention to a form of pleasure that does not involve comparisons at all, and investigates the way in which the mind "converses" with objects at a distance. It is often noticed that he places the imagination between the external senses and understanding (*Spectator* 411), distinguishing it from the mere physical experience of the external world and the contemplation of significance, and because he is talking about the pleasures we gain from these "faculties," he establishes a scale from the "gross" pleasures of sense to the more "refined" sort in the understanding. But the pleasures of the imagination have the advantage of ease and at the very least are equal in intensity to the more rational or deliberative kind. Moreover, Addison throughout the series on the "Pleasures of the Imagination" pretty strictly confines his discussion to mental experience which is modeled on the senses, and mostly on sight. The only difference between primary and secondary pleasures of the imagination is that the primary are based on the direct viewing, while the secondary "flow from the Ideas of visible Objects, when the Objects are not actually before the Eye, but are called up into our Memories, or form'd into agreeable Visions of Things that are either Absent or Fictitious" (*Spectator* 411).

The last or "fictitious" alternative is the escape clause, the hint that lets us know that Addison's concept of psychological pleasure is more complex than it seems. First of all, though he never abandons the making of comparisons as one major source of aesthetic delight, he includes something quite different, a moving of the mind away from present reality. In describing the ease with which we can enjoy a landscape, he provides an account of the dynamics of visual affect which goes beyond any kind of mimetic connoisseurship:

> It is but opening the Eye, and the Scene enters. The Colours paint themselves on the Fancy, with very little Attention of Thought or Application of Mind in the Beholder.... A man of a Polite Imagination ... can converse with a Picture, and find an agreeable Companion in a Statue. He meets with a secret Refreshment in a Description, and often feels a greater Satisfaction in the Prospect of Fields and Meadows, than another does in the Possession. It gives him, indeed, a kind of Property in every thing he sees, and makes the most rude uncultivated Parts of Nature administer to his Pleasures: So that he looks upon the World, as it were, in another Light....

In this same seminal essay Addison has already noted that "by this Faculty a Man in a Dungeon is capable of entertaining himself with Scenes and Landskips more beautiful than any that can be found in the whole Compass of Nature." He is thus deeply committed to a concept of imaginative pleasure as compensation for the inadequacy of the natural and social worlds, as well as for our physical limitations as human beings. Indeed *Spectator* 411 ends on a medical note, celebrating "delightful scenes" as an antidote to grief and melancholy. And in *Spectator* 412, discussing the appeal of "greatness," he observes: "The Mind of Man naturally hates every thing that looks like a Restraint upon it, and is apt to fancy it self under a sort of Confinement, when the Sight is pent up in a narrow Compass.... On the contrary, a spacious Horison is an Image of Liberty, where the Eye has Room to range abroad...." This version of imaginative experience amounts to a psychology of space and motion.

Although one wonders sometimes if Addison seriously recognizes any artistic standard other than the criterion of pleasure, there is an anchor both in classical styles and in certain classes of object. He acknowledges that all manner of things can provide pleasure, but he wishes to limit "polite" pleasure to the visual contemplation of objects, either directly or through the media of the arts, and to three modes: greatness, novelty, and beauty. What he does not wish to circumscribe is the extent or direction of our response to objects which seem to us to possess these characteristics. This deliberate avoidance of affective limits goes hand in hand with his distaste for "false" or "mixt" wit, poems involving verbal games, epigrams, "Gothic" poetry and architecture, and the like. These, he says contemptuously, are "quaint." In some cases they may lead only to an analytical response, and the pleasure we may take in them is brief. On the positive side he looks everywhere for affective values involving power, astonishment, duration. The point is made in one of the papers on *Paradise Lost* where he observes of Milton's use of simile and allusion: "he never quits his Simile till it rises to some very great Idea, which is often foreign to the Occasion that gave Birth to it. The Resemblance does not, perhaps, last above a Line or two, but the Poet runs on with the Hint, till he has raised out of it some glorious Image or Sentiment, proper to inflame the Mind of the Reader, and to give it that sublime kind of Entertainment, which is suitable to the Nature of an Heroic Poem" (*Spectator* 303).[5]

The drift of Addison's thought away from mimetic criticism also involves the notion that beauty and deformity are really subjective determinations: "There is not perhaps," he says, "any real Beauty or Deformity more in one piece of Matter than another. . . ." (*Spectator* 412).[6] This is a loaded statement of an issue that Addison by no means resolved and that bedeviled aesthetic criticism at least for another two generations. And Addison, when he writes about objects, tends to speak of them as having fixed qualities in spite of his reading of Locke, though he does not, so far as I am aware, confidently assert that beauty is a quality in objects, except to note that each species of creature "is most affected with the Beauties of its own kind." It is only on this one point that he implies that imaginative pleasure may involve a desire for possession.

When Hutcheson discusses the arts and matters related to them, like Addison he does so from the point of view of their effect on the audience or viewer, and like Addison, as we shall see, he resorts to a kind of psychology to explain certain consequences of his aesthetic doctrine. But it is a distortion of Hutcheson's position to think of him as one of Addison's followers or as proposing the same kind of affective psychology, for notwithstanding their mutual dependence on Locke, the consequences are quite different.

Hutcheson's system, first articulated in *An Inquiry into the Original of Our Ideas of Beauty and Virtue* (1725), argues for an ideal or primary concept of beauty expressed in an innate sense of beauty in the human soul.[7] In the moral realm the sense of beauty is balanced by an analogous sense. Both senses are "natural," that is instinctive.[8] Both provide the individual with a fundamentally positive orientation towards the material and social worlds—the key concept on the aesthetic side is Hutcheson's belief that our perception of beauty is independent of the motives of possession or utility and involves self-interest only to the extent of providing the means to a kind of gratification that is an end in itself. As Hutcheson remarks in *An Inquiry*, "Had we no such *Sense* of Beauty and Harmony; Houses, Gardens, Dress, Equipage, might have been recommended to us as convenient, fruitful, warm, easy; but never as *beautiful*."[9] The qualities to which the sense of beauty responds are "uniformity amidst variety, " a concept he devotes a good deal of the early pages of the *Inquiry* to illustrating in various kinds of object. But he is careful to point out that, although such qualities do exist in all sorts of objects and situations, without a special sense or faculty to perceive or elicit them there would not be what we call beauty. Uniformity amidst variety is not a definition of beauty, but simply the cause of perception to which we give the name. Two other points need to be mentioned: our sense of beauty operates spontaneously and independently of the will, and it is also independent of possession or utilitarian interest.

Hutcheson's theory of a special sense of beauty has spectacular implications. First, as a recent critic has noted, he attempts to divorce the sense of beauty totally from sense experience, which he associates with the knowledge of the scientist and the dead analytical skills of the critic:[10]

> Let everyone here consider, how different we must suppose the *Perception* to be, with which a Poet is transported upon the Prospect of any of those Objects of *natural Beauty*, which ravish us even in his Description; from the cold lifeless *Conception* which we imagine in a *dull Critick*, or one of the *Virtuosi*, without what we call a *fine Taste*. This latter Class of Men may have greater Perfection in that Knowledge, which is deriv'd from external Sensation; they can tell all the *specifick Differences* of Trees, herbs, Minerals; they know the *Form* of every Leaf, Stalk, Root, Flower, and Seed of all the Species, about which the Poet is often ignorant: And yet the Poet shall have a much more delightful Perception of the Whole; and not only the Poet but any Man of a fine Taste. (*Beauty*, I, XII)

This radically separates Hutcheson's psychology from that of Addison, and seems as well a break in the long tradition descending from Aristotle of associating imagination with seeing. One of the difficulties in Hutcheson's account of affective experience is that he never really gets around to describing what the perception of beauty does to the sensibility. Addison, as we have seen, outlines what he considers a normal inner response to greatness, novelty, or beauty, attempting to convey what it feels like to be pleased with objects of those kinds. What Hutcheson seems to offer is much less palpable, simply a kind of noticing that this or that can be beautiful or not. He is more definite in stating the objective conditions which touch our special senses than he is in defining their affective consequences.

As a result, in order to understand what Hutcheson is doing, we need to examine the way he thinks about two issues. The first has to do with our response to what he calls relative beauty, that in which we compare an object of art with an original; the second involves his theory of the pleasure we find in tragedy.

Our idea of absolute or ideal beauty involves only the perception of uniformity amidst variety.[11] Relative beauty is that "which is apprehended in any *Object*, commonly consider'd as an *Imitation* of some Original: And this *Beauty* is founded on a *Conformity*, or a kind of *Unity* between the Original and the Copy" (*Beauty*, IV. I). More carefully and positively than Addison, Hutcheson proposes a psychology of response which seems to require a standard, and if Thorpe is correct in arguing that Hutcheson does not subscribe to Shaftesbury's notion of an innate standard of perfection, nevertheless Hutcheson, in describing the way in which we appreciate a work of art, resorts to a mimetic process that seems as he develops it to depart from his notion that our pleasure is spontaneous and unreflective. He continues:

> The Original may be either some Object in *Nature*, or some *establish'd Idea*, for if there be any known *Idea* as a Standard, and Rules to fix this Image or Idea by, we may make a *beautiful Imitation*. Thus a *Statuary*, *Painter*, or *Poet*, may please us with an HERCULES, if his Piece retains that *Grandeur*, and those marks of *Strength*, and *Courage*, which we imagine in that Hero.
>
> (*Beauty*, IV. I)

This last statement suggests that other qualifications of his notion of a standard of original beauty may be necessary. He does not acknowledge that once the mind takes pleasure in comparing two things—unless the comparison is simply a matter of size, color, shape, or other kinds of physical detail—something besides sensation is bound to be involved. The example of Hercules would suggest that the concept of imitation as Hutcheson proposes it is a very definite complication for his theory: the work of art becomes almost an imitation of the audience's concept. There is clearly an expectation antecedent to aesthetic experience upon which pleasure depends, and this expectation may involve a moral idea, as well as other kinds of standard (grandeur or strength).[12]

We can delight in "relative" or "comparative" beauty even though the thing imitated is not in itself beautiful. (It should be kept in mind that Hutcheson occasionally shifts his terms without notice, as here. Moreover, he frequently translates absolute beauty as "harmony" or "proportion," terms which he considers equivalent to uniformity amidst variety.) Here accuracy seems to determine pleasure, or even novelty. The pragmatist in Hutcheson seems to have the upper hand:

> And farther, to obtain *comparative Beauty* alone, it is not necessary that there be any Beauty in the Original; the Imitation of *absolute Beauty* may in the whole make a more lovely Piece, and yet an exact Imitation shall still be *beautiful*, tho the Original were entirely void of it: Thus the *Deformitys* of old Age in a Picture, the *rudest Rocks* or *Mountains* in a *Landskip*, if well represented, shall have abundant *Beauty*, tho perhaps not so great as if the Original were *absolutely beautiful*, and as well represented: Nay, perhaps the *Novelty* may make us prefer the representation of Irregularity.
> (*Beauty*, IV. I)

It is also worth noting that this concession to the experience of the senses, if that is what it is, allows Hutcheson to vindicate certain formalist principles that we might have expected him to leave entirely aside. This occurs when he turns to poetry specifically. Poets, he asserts, should attempt relative, rather than original beauty, for when it comes to the depiction of human character, complete moral perfection is not credible. Absolute beauty in the context of poetry becomes the province of the rhythmical qualities of artistic language, whereas figurative language (metaphor, simile, allegory) belongs to relative beauty (*Beauty*, IV. II-III).

In an effort to maintain "pleasure" as the controlling term in his discussion of affect, Hutcheson argues that the absence of beauty, relative or absolute, is not painful: many objects are unpleasant to the senses, but as to our *Sense* of *Beauty*, no Composition of Objects which give not unpleasant simple Ideas, seems positively unpleasant or painful of itself, had we never observ'd any thing better of the Kind. *Deformity* is only *the absence of Beauty,* or *deficiency in the Beauty expected in any Species:* Thus *bad Musick* pleases *Rusticks* who never heard any better, and the *finest Ear* is not offended with *tuning* of Instruments if it be not too tedious, where no *Harmony* is expected.

(Beauty, VI. I)

It is not clear whether Hutcheson is aware how far he has modified his first account of the sense of beauty, but on the basis of this latest passage it is difficult to understand how the external senses are not involved, and the interesting concept of expectation cannot exist in a void. It requires a context (the concert at which instruments are tuned) and previous experience, perhaps something like Addison's notion that we develop our taste through exposure to the best authors. Hutcheson has entered rather difficult territory, for he continues to propose that the sense of beauty is essentially apart: like the external senses, the internal sense is a "natural" power of perception, "or *Determination* of *the Mind* to receive necessarily certain Ideas from the Presence of Objects" *(Beauty,* VI. X). And yet the later pages of this essay (VI. XI and XII) are devoted to a discussion of the ways in which our experience of beauty may be modified by association of ideas, education, and custom, all of them influences that rock our aesthetic appreciation off center. The actual experience of beauty might seem to be a matter of the degree to which the psychological makeup of the individual corrodes the function of the internal sense.

Does this fairly represent Hutcheson's position? Aware that taste is various, he accounts for it by arguing that the habit of association, not in itself a capacity to experience beauty, may influence us either to prefer one kind of beauty over another or even to believe that something is beautiful which is not. Hutcheson contends that the association of ideas, though it may temper or distort our sense of beauty, is not to be confused with it. It is the capacity of association that makes us think of groves or woods as melancholy or solitary, for example. Association accounts for the imposition of certain ideas of feeling upon neutral matter. "And this is often the Occasion both of great Pleasure and Pain, Delight and Aversion to many Objects, which of themselves might have been perfectly indifferent to us: but these *Approbations, or Distastes,* are remote from the Ideas of *Beauty,* being plainly different

Ideas" (VI. XI).

We might agree that not all delight and aversion is bound up in objects that can be thought beautiful, but on the other hand such ideas might be. It would then be very difficult logically or empirically to say that association is not involved in the perception of beauty as it is in other perceptions. When he discusses education and custom in the next section, Hutcheson suggests that they may enlarge "the Capacity of our Minds to retain and compare the Parts of complex Compositions. And then if the finest Objects are presented to us, we grow conscious of a Pleasure far superior to what common Performances excite" (VII. III). Though he continues to insist that the sense of beauty is still separate and prior, by this time the distinction seems forced and open to the charge that the basic sense of beauty must be sharply divided from the mental processes that are involved in actual and particular aesthetic perceptions. But the problem is not just one of inadequate psychology: it is also a matter of a definition of beauty so general and abstract as to be ultimately elusive. Finally, by allowing himself to be drawn into the vexing problem of diversity of taste, Hutcheson has postponed an equally difficult matter: how can the sense of beauty, which seems to be primarily a matter of perceiving structural relationships, explain our delight in portrayals of human character and human experience?

Hutcheson is aware that what most art represents is not an ideal but an image of behavior or character that matches the expectations of the audience. This issue is close to the problem raised by affective criticism of the kind embraced by Addison, whose psychology as we have seen is founded in the notion of art as the means of entry into an internal landscape. The papers on "The Pleasures of the Imagination" do not deal with our response to dramatic or fictional characters, and his essays on *Paradise Lost,* ballad and epic, and wit, are primarily concerned with the impact of style and technique on the reader. From the point of view of affective criticism the most persistent problem is tragedy and our pleasure in it: how can we take delight in the representation of events that in themselves are distressing?[13] Addison's answer is simply the flat assertion that terror and commiseration "leave a pleasing Anguish in the Mind" *(Spectator* 40). As we have already seen, he does not divide and separate responses to art categorically, resting content to suppose that many different kinds of things give pleasure.

Hutcheson's assignment of responses to separate senses forces him to abandon the idea of integrated perception he theorizes for the sense of beauty. Though he admits degrees of beauty, the same sense allows us to register relative beauty by means of "resemblance" (this includes metaphor, simile, and "likeness") and measures and cadence, which are instances of absolute beauty (IV. III), but it is not until he is well into the second treatise, *An Inquiry concerning Moral Good and Evil* (here referred to as *Moral*) that there is any sustained discussion of literature, and when he does embark on such a discussion, he divides what we might call the technical features of poetry from character and action. As a result, it is the "moral sense" (at a higher level than the sense of beauty, but like it in being spontaneous and instinctive) that is the "Foundation . . . of the chief Pleasures of POETRY." His remarks are, I believe, a deliberate effort to supply the deficiencies in Addison's too exclusive concentration on natural scenery and material objects as the content of art and source of imaginative delight:

> We hinted, in the former Treatise, at the Foundation of Delight in the *Numbers, Measures, Metaphors, Similitudes*. But as the Contemplation of *moral Objects*, either of *Vice* or *Virtue*, affects us more strongly, and moves our Passions in a quite different and more powerful manner than *natural Beauty*, or what we commonly call *Deformity;* so the most moving Beautys bear a relation to our *moral Sense*, and affect us more vehemently, than the Representations of *natural Objects* in the liveliest Descriptions. *Dramatic* and *Epic* Poetry, are intirely address'd to this *Sense*, and raise our Passions by the Fortunes of *Characters*, distinctly represented as *morally good* or evil. . . . *(Moral*, VI. VII)

But of course the moral sense takes in much more than poetry, so what Hutcheson seems to be offering is simply a psychology of feeling which may be directed to real as well as fictional human events. The emotion he chooses to discuss is compassion, which is basic to his theory of naturally benevolent feeling. Compassion is spontaneous, antecedent to advantage or "interest," and needs exercise, a prompting that Hutcheson illustrates in what must be one of the oddest examples in modern philosophic discourse. It is, he says, a *"natural,* kind *Instinct* [in human beings], to see Objects of *Compassion,* and to expose themselves to this Pain when they can give no reason for it; as in the Instance of *publick Executions*" (*Moral*, V. VIII).

He adds that "This same Principle leads Men to *Tragedies;* only we are to observe, that another strong reason of this, is the *moral Beauty* of the *Characters* and *Actions* which we love to behold." Such a statement suggests that some motive other than pleasure is involved, but to avoid inconsistency he drops "moral beauty" into the discussion without ever explaining it. Perhaps it involves the perception of friendship, love, and benevolence, or in tragedy or romance the spectacle of characters overcoming natural evils such as labor, hunger, thirst, poverty, or danger (*Moral*, VI. I). The moral sense accounts for our pleasure in dramatic and epic poetry especially. We can find an echo of Addison in a brief reference to *enargeia:*

> Where we are studying to raise any *Desire*, or *Admiration* of an Object *really beautiful*, we are not content with a *bare Narration*, but endeavour, if we can, to present the *Object* it self, or the most *lively Image* of it. And hence the *Epic Poem*, or *Tragedy*, gives a far greater Pleasure than the Writings of *Philosophers,* tho both aim at recommending *Virtue*. The representing the Actions themselves, if the Representation be *judicious, natural,* and *lively,* will make us admire the *Good,* and detest the *Vitious,* the *Inhuman,* the *Treacherous,* and *Cruel,* by means of our *moral Sense,* without any Reflections of the *Poet* to guide our Sentiments. (*Moral*, VI. VII)

Such response is analogous to that effected by the sense of beauty, not just in spontaneity but also in the power to appreciate accurate and skillful representation. Furthermore, there is a hint that he recognizes that the moral sense may also encompass something like Addison's pictorial imagination. But we are not told whether the instinctive reaction to good and evil is somehow different from that which detects accuracy or not. All this passage allows us is the conclusion that Hutcheson's psychology, when it involves the perception of the human in literature, is a process of assigning value, though not as the consequence of deliberation, reflection, or reasoning.

This effort in the *Inquiry* may have seemed to Hutcheson less than definitive, for in *An Essay on the Nature and Conduct of the Passions and Affections* (1728) he returns to tragedy, which he discusses under the third of the five different senses he assigns to the human sensibility. These senses are in ascending order: the external senses, the sense of beauty,[14] the "public sense," the moral sense, and the sense of honor. The arrangement is hierarchical, the first three being spontaneous and not under the control of the will, while the last two are both less universal and in part the product of conscious reflection. It is the third, or public sense—"our Determination to be pleased with the *Happiness* of others, and to be uneasy at their *Misery*"—and the fourth, which observes "the Actions of Agents some way *attached* to each other," that he associates with our taste for tragedy.

To some extent Hutcheson's theory of tragedy is a rehashing of Aristotle's explanation of the need for the morally imperfect protagonist: the misfortune of a virtuous character merely shocks us, or in Hutcheson's words, "If the Evil befals him, we feel the contrary Passions, *Sorrow*, *Dissatisfaction* with Providence, and *Suspicion* of the Reality of Virtue" (p. 73). If protagonists are flawed, then there must be some logical connection between their moral nature and what happens to them in the play: "An imperfectly evil Character, threatened by an Evil greater than is necessary to make him relent and reform, or by a greater Calamity, which has no direct tendency to reform him, instead of raising *Desire* toward the *Event*, raises *Aversion;* his escaping it raises *Joy*, and his falling under it raises *Pity*, a species of Sorrow." Only by recalling that in the *Inquiry* Hutcheson had argued that compassion is an instinct that requires exercise can we consider that he is still concerned with pleasure as a general concept to describe affective responses to art. For one thing, these responses are complex. The same work may evoke several "passions" at once: "When an imperfect good Character, by an evil Action, procures the highest Misery to himself: this raises these complicated Passions, *Pity* toward the Sufferer; *Sorrow* for the State, *Abhorrence* of Vice, *Awe* and *Admiration* of Providence as keeping strict Measures of Sanctity and Justice" (p. 78).

Further complications in our responses to tragedy occur if we examine the fourth sense, which is concerned with human social relationships: our feelings for one character may be quite the opposite of those for another (pp. 81ff). It is clear by this time that attention to the psychology of response has prompted Hutcheson to a considerable modification of the relatively simple concept of aesthetic experience with which he began. Yet perhaps we can find an implicit continuity in the remarks on tragedy, for what they seem to be getting at is the concept that our responsive feelings, whether of pleasure or aversion, are governed by a standard of justice, whether moral or aesthetic and material. Some instinct for fitness, he seems to be saying, allows us to react to structural, social, or moral relationships. Unlike Hume, he does not openly propose that tragedy appeals to us because the various elements of artistic representation are "naturally . . . delightful to the mind."[15]

If Hutcheson falls short of describing our responses to literature and to objects of beauty, he does assert their variety and their order, and he relates types of response to classes of object. What these responses amount to is a set of predispositions that are first of all natural powers which work prior to desire, will, and reason—almost, in his repeated insistence that they are determined, prior to consciousness. (Hutcheson insists that we respond to objects of beauty without knowledge of their specific ingredients as causes; he does not make quite the same point for the moral sense and it is difficult to see how we could find an action good without some notion of the nature of the goodness to which we respond.) In the second place, these responses can be modified, often rather drastically, by time and experience. Repeated exposure to an object we find beautiful at first and perhaps second encounter may eventually leave us indifferent, and the experience of other objects might well totally change our perception (*Beauty*, VII. II). These are concessions Hutcheson has to make if he attempts to adhere to Locke in any manner and if he wants to be at all realistic about the vagaries of taste, which by the time he is writing is an unavoidable issue. Yet it *is* a concession because his prior motive has established, in contradiction to Hobbes and Mandeville, ideal modes of perception that are automatic and benevolent as standards against which to estimate individual mental events. It amounts to a belief registered on the level of sensation and perception that the world is fundamentally ordered and good.

Addison's proposals about the ubiquity of pleasure and its final causes take somewhat similar directions, but they are offered much more tentatively.[16] Addison, as I have tried to suggest, is more detailed about certain classes of what he considers common affective reactions, and in contrast to what Hutcheson offers, his psychology of pleasure appears more coherent. But this is so because he attempts much less, for Hutcheson, having first divided perceptions into separate classes and then turned his attention to tragic and epic poetry, seeks to show that our responses to a single work are complex, involving distinct and separate items as well as different levels of structural relationship within the work. Given these ambitions, a concept of pleasure does not synthesize or comprehend affect, primarily I suspect because of the overriding concern to insist on the primacy of feeling and to further limit that feeling to decisions of value.

Finally, we have noted that Addison offers a psychology of release, of mental movement away both from the actual present and even from the object that provokes response in the first place. The effect of Hutcheson's thinking is the opposite: if anything, by submitting feeling to value he ties it rigidly to the objects that prompt and also to objects—I am talking now of relative beauty—that are mimetic of something else. The result is to validate aesthetic and moral objects that have certain formal properties and to propose formal kinds of transaction between these objects and our sensibilities. The theories of both men with their attendant psychological "systems" anticipate the clearer vision of Hume.

NOTES

1. Clarence DeWitt Thorpe, "Addison's Theory of the Imagination as 'Perceptive Response,'" *Papers of the Michigan Academy of Arts and Sciences*, 21 (1936), 509-530; see also his "Addison and Hutcheson on the Imagination," *ELH*, 2 (1935), 233. The latter essay overemphasizes the similarities between the psychological systems of the two. See also Lee Andrew Elioseff, *The Cultural Milieu of Addison's Literary Criticism* (Austin: University of Texas Press, 1963), pp. 161–191.
2. *An Apology for Poetry*, ed. Geoffrey Shepherd (Manchester: Manchester University Press, 1973), pp. 119-120. For discussions of Sidney's theory of literary affect, see my *The Reader's Eye: Studies in Didactic Literary Theory from Dante to Tasso* (Berkeley and Los Angeles: University of California Press, 1979), pp. 117–141.
3. *Spectator* 411. My text is Donald F. Bond's edition of *The Spectator* (Oxford: Clarendon Press, 1965), 5 vols.
4. The reference is to John Locke.
5. This essay also records Addison's belief that the point of a "comparison" (a simile or metaphor) is not minute exactness or correspondence. He quotes Boileau ("Critical Reflections on Longinus," #5): "Comparisons, says he, in odes and epic poems are not introduced only to illustrate and embellish the discourse, but to amuse and relax the mind of the reader, by frequently disengaging him from too painful an attention to the principal subject, and by leading him into other agreeable images." Such views as this suggest that the comments of Wimsatt and Brooks to the effect that Addison offers a too literal version of imitation are a bit overdrawn. See *Literary Criticism: A Short History* (New York: Knopf, 1957), pp. 255–256.
6. In *Spectator* 413, Addison asserts that "Light and Colours, as apprehended by the Imagination, are only Ideas in the Mind, and not Qualities that have any Existence in Matter." See Locke, *An Essay concerning Human Understanding* (2, 8, 10–13).

7. But not, as he insists more than once, innate ideas. As I have mentioned, Addison does not think of the imagination as a faculty, but Hutcheson in his last work, *A System of Moral Philosophy* (London, 1755), I, p. 15, pointedly equates the sense of beauty with Addison's imagination. In "Addison and Hutcheson on the Imagination" (note 1), Thorpe discusses this matter in detail.

8. In *An Essay on the Nature and Conduct of the Passions and Affections* (London, 1725), pp. 4-6, Hutcheson multiplies the inner senses to four, making, with the outer senses, a total of five sensory powers. As Peter Kivy notes, he risks postulating a separate sense for every category of perception: *The Seventh Sense: A Study of Francis Hutcheson's Aesthetics and Its Influence in Eighteenth-Century Britain* (New York: Burt Franklin, 1976), pp. 32–34.

9. Hutcheson's *An Inquiry into the Original of Our Ideas of Beauty and Virtue* (London, 1725), consists of two parallel essays, the first, entitled "An Inquiry concerning Beauty, Order, etc.," I have shortened to *Beauty* for purposes of reference; the second, entitled *An Inquiry concerning Our Ideas of Moral Good and Evil*," I have shortened to *Moral*. I quote from the third, corrected edition of 1729. References to this work are to section and paragraph, for readers who have other editions available. The quotation here is from *Beauty*, I, XVI.

10. For a thorough discussion of this point, see Ermanno Migliorini, *Studi sul pensiero estetico di Francis Hutcheson* (Padua: Liviana Edetrice, 1974), pp. 11–17.

11. Ideal beauty is not mimetic. The issue of whether Hutcheson believes the objects of perception to possess the qualities we find or whether they are fictions of the perceiving mind is discussed by Caroline Wilkes Korsmeyer, "Relativism and Hutcheson's Aesthetic Theory," *JHI*, 36 (1975), 319–330. She understands him as trying to resist the claims of aesthetic relativism.

12. There is obscure acknowledgment of this difficulty in *Beauty*, IV. VI, where he talks of "a *just Representation* of Manners or Characters as they are in *Nature*." It is hard to know how we could decide such justness without bringing prior experience and judgment to our perception. Still, Hutcheson thinks of our senses as prior to experience or the effects of association.

13. See, for example, Baxter Hathaway, "The Lucretian 'Return upon Ourselves' in Eighteenth-Century Theories of Tragedy," *PMLA*, 62 (1947), 672-689, and W. P. Albrecht, *The Sublime Pleasures of Tragedy: A Study of Critical Theory from Dennis to Keats* (Lawrence: University of Kansas Press, 1975).

14. At this point Hutcheson refers directly to Addison on "The Pleasures of the Imagination" and says that the sense of beauty gives us "*Pleasant Perceptions* arising from *regular, harmonious, uniform* Objects; as also from *Grandeur* and *Novelty*" (p. 5).

15. David Hume, "Of Tragedy," in *Of the Standard of Taste and Other Essays*, ed. John W. Lenz (Indianapolis: Bobbs-Merrill, 1965), p. 35.

16. In *Spectator* 413, Addison supposes that God has formed our souls to admire Him and His creation and for our recreation. But Addison's language is inexact and leaves in doubt as to whether we are presented with a universe already beautiful or with the capacity to endow it with beauty, as if it were a black and white etching to which we are meant to supply the colors: "he has made every thing that is beautiful in all other Objects pleasant, or rather has made so many Objects appear beautiful, that he might render the whole Creation more gay and delightful. . . . Things would make but a poor Appearance to the Eye, if we saw them

only in their proper Figures and Motions: And what Reason can we assign for their exciting in us many of those Ideas which are different from any thing that exists in the Objects themselves, (for such are Light and Colours) were it not to add Supernumerary Ornaments to the Universe, and make it more agreeable to the Imagination?"

Accounting for Dreams in *Clarissa*: The Clash of Probabilities

JANET E. AIKINS

> A Dream, therefore, is a motion or fiction of the Soul.
> —Artemidorus

Shortly after Clarissa has been drugged, raped, and begins plotting her escape from Sinclair's nightmarish house, Lovelace dreams a "very odd dream" about her. Within it, Dorcas, who is an "artful servant in the vile house,"[1] uncharacteristically assists Clarissa to flee in the coach of a "grave matronly lady" who has stopped at a grocer's across the street. The vehicle takes them to a "sumptuous dwelling" near Lincoln's Inn Fields that is "replete with damsels who wrought curiously in muslins, cambrics, and fine linen." As Clarissa offers her rescuer a "dismal account of her wrongs and sufferings," the old lady is strangely transformed into the "famous Mother H.," a friend of the evil Sinclair's. In bed that night with Clarissa, Mother H. is again transformed, this time into a "young person of the other sex" who is none other than Lovelace. Despite her "grief, and surprise" at this occurrence, Clarissa is actually consoled to find that she is in bed with her rapist and not a stranger. Following these events, a "strange promiscuous huddle of adventures" results in Clarissa's giving birth to a boy and thereby feeling rewarded for her suffering, resuming her grandfather's estate, and being reunited with Norton, her old nurse. In this happy situation, Anna Howe comes to visit, bears Lovelace a "charming girl," and the two babies grow up and marry. After narrating these "incongruous" happenings, Lovelace tells Belford that he "awoke . . . in great disorder" and that he "rejoiced" to find that it had only been a dream.

Terry Castle is one of several critics who have attempted to interpret this enticing text, and she regards Lovelace's "daytime 'revery'" as a curiously ironic emblem of the dreamlike structure of the novel itself. When narrated to Belford, she explains, it serves as a "ribald tale," "a good yarn," "a shapely narrative." It is literally a reflection of the entrapment and rape that have already occurred, and it becomes a nightmarish prophecy of Clarissa's future or a plan by which Lovelace can abduct and rape her a second time. Yet combined with Clarissa's ensuing escape it constitutes an Aristotelian *peripateia*, a turn of the plot in which power shifts to Clarissa, who is now transformed into "someone suspicious, streetwise, savvy." Finally, it serves as *deus ex machina* for Richardson, the sentimental plotter, who needed a way to remove Clarissa from the brothel to a more fitting setting for her exemplary death. In arguing the coexistance of these contrary views of the episode, Castle asserts that "reading itself is transformed into a dreamlike, recursive process" since "any proposition we make about the 'plot' of *Clarissa* is instantly convertible into its opposite." Similarly for William B. Warner, the text "seems to have become the reader's plaything."[2] The fitting emblem for the "line" of plot is no longer Aristotle's extended piece of thread but, in Castle's terms, a Möbius strip where two faces perpetually collapse into one.

While these arguments are extremely appealing, they are not quite accurate. For example, there are earlier moments than the dream itself when Clarissa emerges as a "plotter,"[3] and surely her departure from home or her rape are more typically experienced as turning points. Apart from its hypothesis about the hallucinatory experience of reading *Clarissa*, Castle's essay is an attempt to formulate the "meaning" of Lovelace's dream itself. As such it attests to our irresistible desire to posit theories of meaning not only about this dream, but about the other two that are narrated, one by Clarissa and another by Lovelace. In 1733 Andrew Baxter wrote that dreaming is "a strange phaenomenon, and appears to be altogether unaccountable";[4] and Lovelace himself calls dreams "unaccountable things." So why do we and the characters in this novel persist in our dizzying attempts at interpretation? Even more perplexing, why should Richardson have stumped us with these contradictory, nocturnal brain teasers in a fiction which he hoped would "maintain that air of probability, which is necessary to be maintained in a story designed to represent real life"?[5] Dreaming is of course a part of "real life," yet if interpreted as prophecy or as pictorial summary of the novel's major themes,[6] as many commentators wish, the dreams surely constitute the sorts of miraculous or fabulated events typical of the romance tradition from which Richardson hoped to depart. My point is that the dreams are important to the novel precisely because they simultaneously tempt us to analysis and remain uninterpretable; that is, they cannot be definitively unraveled as allegory, prophecy, or even emblems of the plot, yet they invite both characters and readers to try solving what Clarissa calls the many "pregnant puzzles" of the novel.

If we must have an analogy, the process of reading this narrative is not best compared to dreaming but to the problematic experience of dream interpretation, a subject of well-established interest in Richardson's day. Although Freud's birth was generations away, the eighteenth century expressed a fascination with dreams for two main reasons: dreams seemed evidence of a spiritual, supernatural world, and they invited speculation about human nature. Reveries were regarded both as products of the self and as predictors of the future, and they drew attention from several perspectives. Psychology or psychoanalysis as disciplines did not yet exist, but the "art" of dream interpretation or "oneirocriticism" found its way into the writings of philosophers, physicians, historians, theologians, and antiquarians. The history of dream analysis is thus important to the history of ideas since it exposes a radical difference between the configuration of intellectual disciplines in the eighteenth century and ours today. For literary scholars this tradition is also significant, since it informed the outlook of the readers who confronted "the novel" for the first time.

Terry Castle's approach to Lovelace's dream is Freudian. She writes, "Like all dreams, Lovelace's vision has to do most profoundly, not with the either/or, but the both/and"; Castle then argues that *Clarissa* as a narrative structure apes the "syntax of dreams" in which "apparent contraries merge."[7] Terry Eagleton treats us to a similar construction:

> This baffling, bottomlessly interpretable dream-text ... exhibits

one striking general feature: what, after Freud, we may call the 'polymorphous perversity' of Lovelace himself. Mother, father, child, lover; transsexuality; sibling and parental incest: in a dizzying exchange of positions, a constant process of splitting, projection, condensation and displacement, Lovelace comes in his dream to assume all these roles and practices in turn, with the same protean movement which marks his pen. The dream reveals Clarissa as unconscious mother-figure for Lovelace. . . . She bears him a son, who is at once Lovelace's own son and Lovelace himself, so that in a common Oedipal fantasy he triumphantly becomes his own father. By the end of the dream, he has successfully resolved his relationship with the ambivalently threatening and nurturing mother, reaffirmed his own masculine power by impregnating Clarissa, and punctured her own infuriating narcissism in the process. It is no wonder that Lovelace, having reified Clarissa to the phallus, stands in such awe of her.[8]

Despite the insights these two critics bring to Richardson's text, few eighteenth-century readers could have accepted an oneirocriticism that transformed Clarissa into a phallus or that regarded the strange merging of contraries in dreams as a challenge to our waking notions of "reality." Instead, the received tradition of dream interpretation suggested an approach to the reveries of *Clarissa* that we must examine without a Freudian overlay in order to discern it fully and not dismiss it as "primitive." To discover the tradition, we must turn to the writers who created it.

Some eighty years before *Clarissa*'s publication, Philip Goodwin, "a Preacher of the Gospel," urged oneirocriticism on a somewhat hesitant audience by citing secular and religious precedents from both ancient and modern times. He wrote, "a Dream is a close covered *Dish* brought in by *night* for the *Soul* to feed on; And is it not meet for a man, after to uncover the *dish*, to see and know upon what Meat he hath eaten?"[9] His somewhat defensive stance echoes Thomas Hill who in 1576 had complained, "great pitty it were that so noble a knowledge, so necessarye to all men be trodden under fote." A century after Hill, Lowde published his translation of Moses Amyraldus's *A Discourse Concerning the Divine Dreams Mention'd in Scripture* (1676) with the opening statement, "I could wish that I had not so much to plead for the seasonableness of the Discourse, in an Age where Infidelity on the one hand, & Fanatical Enthusiasm on the other, seem to divide the greater part of the World." In 1696, shortly after the publication of Thomas Tryon's important *Treatise of Dreams and Visions,* John Aubrey wrote about various kinds of supernatural phenomena and expressed his wonder that "*Hermetick Philosophy* hath lain so long untouched" while "Natural Philosophy" had drawn so much attention in the previous fifty years. In 1738 Thomas Branch defiantly insisted that "No intelligent Persons" could regard the phenomenon of dreaming as "useless or trifling" since it affords vital proof of the soul's existence in a separate state.[10] Perhaps one of the most important documents on the subject was Andrew Baxter's "An Essay on the phaenomenon of Dreaming" in *An Enquiry into the Nature of the Human Soul* (c. 1733). Although it may first have appeared in 1733, it came out in second and third editions in 1737 and 1745, exactly at the time that Richardson was writing *Clarissa.* Warburton would later comment that Baxter's "noble demonstration has been neglected" precisely because he wrote of dreaming, yet the many published responses to Baxter's essay suggest an inaccuracy in Warburton's comment.[11]

Thus, despite the felt need to defend the seriousness of the enterprise, from the seventeenth century onward a genuine interest in the "art" of dream interpretation persisted. Between 1606 and 1740, Artemidorus's treatise on the subject went through twenty-four English editions. Artemidorus, Cardan, and Synesius were among the accepted authorities, but even the more recent writings of William Lilly, Amyraldus, and Tryon went through many reprintings and revisions.[12] Authors as diverse as Thomas Hobbes, Joseph Glanvill, Robert Burton, and Joseph Addison all felt compelled to comment on dreams at some point in their writings, perhaps in response to the contemporary appeal of the subject. While oneirocriticism clearly interested philosophers, physicians, and theologians, the existence of eighteenth-century chapbooks of dream interpretation also suggests its appeal in more frivolous circles. One such work recommends it as an activity for "such as have much leisure Time on their Hands," and especially for women.[13] Accompanying the interest in dreams, a belief in apparitions, second sight, and supernatural intervention was common throughout the seventeenth and into the eighteenth century; the 1720s and '30s, for example, witnessed the popularity of Duncan Campbell, a deaf and mute fortune-teller, dream interpreter, and quack doctor whom Addison could not take seriously and yet regarded as one of the London rarities not to be missed.[14] For modern scholars this ongoing though apparently trivial fascination with dreams is important, for it reveals that a faith in unseen, elusive worlds paradoxically coexisted with a growing interest in the powers of perception through the senses.[15]

II

We do not possess evidence of Richardson's familiarity with oneirocriticism. That he may have read about the subject or discussed it with such friends as George Cheyne is likely, since he chose to incorporate three relatively elaborate dreams into the text of *Clarissa*. Yet his exact knowledge of the subject remains uncertain. Defining a supposed "general view" of dreams is also a risky business, since dream analysis hovered on the fringes of serious intellectual investigation. No one can say, with certainty, what a given reader of *Clarissa* in the 1740s and 50s would have believed about dreams. For these reasons it is important to survey a range of published material from the seventeenth and eighteenth centuries in order to sense contemporary attitudes.

In the writings on dreams, the first task was typically to define them and probe their causes. Artemidorus, for example, believed the dream to be "a motion or fiction of the Soul"; his translator's striking choice of the word "fiction" strangely accentuates the falsehood of dreams within a treatise whose very purpose was to defend their significance. As we shall see, this paradox runs through much of the literature on the subject and informs *Clarissa*, for Richardson invites us to take its narrated dreams seriously while recognizing them to be "fictions of the soul." Thomas Nashe described the dream more cynically as "nothing els [sic] but a bubling scum or froath of the fancie, which the day hath left undigested." Perhaps sensing the limitations of his own metaphor, he went on to compare our visions of the night to daytime arrows that are "ouer-drawne" and fly past their mark, to the tremblings that criminals feel even after the hand of the executioner has been removed, and to the dazzlings of our eyes after we come out of the bright sunlight. Hobbes more simply called dreams "the imaginations of those that sleep," while Tryon regarded them as "discourses and incorporeal Sights of the Soul, being in sleep, loosened from the heavy Fetters of the

Body and sense." Tryon's metaphor implies that the soul can both see and talk by means other than the physical, yet Richardson's great friend and physician, George Cheyne, insisted that dreaming was merely confused and imperfect thinking.[16] Discussion about the causes of dreams was elaborate, but basically three major theories prevailed through the seventeenth and into the eighteenth century: dreams are prompted either by the physical or temperamental leanings of our individual bodies (natural dreams), by particular happenings of the day or temporary conditions such as disease, diet, or posture during sleep (animal dreams), or by supernatural intervention (celestial dreams).[17]

Among those who advanced physiological theories were Robert Burton and Thomas Nashe who saw dreams as the effect of melancholy, and Timothy Nourse who argued that the mind's operations receive "a kind of fuliginous Tincture" from vapours that actually "fill the Brain in time of Sleep." Many writers, including Hill, argued that the frequency of dreams depended on one's age, while Sir Thomas Browne attributed much to diet: "Cato who doated upon cabbage might find the crude effects thereof in his sleep. . . . Pythagoras might have more calmer sleepes if he totally abstained from beanes. Even Daniel, that great interpreter of dreams, in his leguminous dyet seems to have chosen no advantageous food for quiet sleeps."[18] In 1728, Chambers's *Cyclopaedia* under "Ephialtes" explained the nightmare or Incubus as a delusion resulting from sleeping on one's back. By the eighteenth century few would have accepted the old theory, mentioned by Hill, that "the ayre is the outward cause of dreames, because in the first it receiveth the impression of the starres, and, after touche on the bodies of men and beastes"; writers from Hill through Tryon agreed, however, that physicians can make good use of dreams in diagnosing diseases.

In addition to these physical or mechanical hypotheses, theories of supernatural causes persisted into the eighteenth century. Whether they spoke of good or evil spirits, devils, angels, or God himself, almost all writers on the subject, including the skeptical Hobbes, acknowledged the possibility of divine or diabolical intervention by this means.[19] Joseph Glanvill, for example, wrote, "'tis easie to give an account of *Dreams*, both *Monitory* and *Temperamental, Enthusiasms, Fanatick Extascies*, and the like" as the direct result of "Angelical Incouragements" or influence upon our imaginations from "other

Worlds"; and Jean François Balthus claimed that "it is certain the Devil can cause Dreams." Belief in supernatural dreams did not preclude more mechanical explanations, however. Thomas Tryon broadly listed seven diverse causes of dreams as follows: bodily constitution, profession, the planets, diet, evil spirits, visits of good angels, and God himself.[20] Richardson was aware of at least the angelic theory, for shortly after her rape, Clarissa contrasts her "*lost* self" with the more fortunate Anna who can still enjoy "conversing with saints and angels" during "unbroken, unstarting slumbers" (III, 321). Richardson might well have read Tryon who spoke in almost the same words of the "secret converse of Angels and Souls," or John Aubrey whose *Miscellanies* contains a whole chapter on "Converse with Angels and Spirits." Richardson would surely have sympathized with Daniel Defoe, who complained that "modern Wits . . . allow no God or Providence, no invisible World, no Angelick kind" who conduct "a secret Correspondence with our embodied Spirits." Baxter's treatise may even have influenced Richardson's remark, for it reasserted the notion that all dreams are "prompted by separate immaterial Beings."[21]

However, the modern concept of unconscious wish fulfillment, which recent commentators have applied to Lovelace's dream, played no part in contemporary discussions. What did sometimes appear was the view that our conscious thoughts and desires of the day influence our dreams of the night, yet this idea was not explored as an important indicator of the operation of the psyche but merely mentioned in passing as one of the less signigicant causes of dreams. For example, in a marginal note on Cicero, Thomas Newton wrote, "Dreames, commonlie represent to us in Sleepe, those thinges wee most earnestlye delighted in and devised waking." Similarly, in 1724 Justicia (Eliza Haywood) insisted that we should ignore the ordinary dreams that merely result from "our Desires of the Day" and instead turn our attention to the dreams prompted by "our Guardian Angels" and which carry true "Signification."[22]

As today, dreams were regularly acknowledged to be wild and improbable in structure, often organized by principles of association.[23] Lovelace himself remarks that the metamorphoses of dreams happen "quick as thought" and not according to logic, as a "strange promiscuous huddle of adventures" (III, 250). Several writers noted the size distortion in dreams; Thomas Branch even employed a mathematical metaphor to argue that "the Soul can *add* and *multiply*, and *magnify*" in sleep.[24] The author of the first essay on consciousness, alleged to be Zachary Mayne, spoke of the imagination in dreams as if it were an irresponsible person or naughty child:

> because at such Times [the imagination] acts quite alone, as having no Controul, or Curb and Restraint upon it, it is then most truly itself; and so shews us what Opinion we are to have of it. There is nothing so foolish and absurd, so preposterous and inconsistent, or so wild and extravagant, that it is not then capable of. For in short, it runs a-muck at every thing; never recollects itself, or stops to consider and reflect what it is a doing; nor has any the least Regard to Probability, or even Possibility, but couples and joins Things that are the most heterogeneous and incongruous, and the most contrary and averse to one another in Nature.

A treatise of 1731, published posthumously from a manuscript by Ralph Cudworth, argues that the "Phantastical Power of the Soul" in sleep is analogous to the imagination which produces waking dreams, or fantasies, as they would be called today. Whether waking or sleeping, "the Fancy, being not commanded or determined by the Will, roves, and wanders, and runs at random; and spins out a long Thread or Concatenated Series of Imaginations or Phantasms of Corporeal Things, quite different from those things which our outward Senses at the same time take notice of." Cudworth insists that some people more than others are prone to such associatively-structured waking dreams, and clearly Lovelace would be among them.

Cudworth also describes the way in which daytime fantasies can produce actual dreams, and such an experience happens to Lovelace within *Clarissa*. "There is little doubt," writes Cudworth, that

> if a Man should suddenly fall asleep in the midst of one of these Waking Dreams, when his Fancy is roving and spinning out such a long Series of Imaginations, those very Imaginations and Phantasms would *of course* become Dreams, and run on, and appear not as Phantasms or Imaginations only of things nonexistent, but as Perceptions of things really existent, that is, as Sensations.[25]

This phenomenon is precisely what prompts Lovelace's first dream. His letter describing the experience begins, "Tired with a succession of fatiguing days and sleepless nights, and with contemplating the precarious situation I stand in with my beloved, I fell into a profound reverie; which brought on sleep; and that produced a dream; a fortunate dream" (III, 248).

Yet despite the awareness of the wildness of dreams, a few commentators including Cudworth notably insisted that dreaming is a *"real phaenomenon"* moving "beyond the license of the *Painter* or the *Poet's* imagination," since while we are actually dreaming, the effect is the same as that of reality itself, unlike reading a poem or seeing a painting in which we are aware of artifice. The alleged Mayne wrote, "in Dreaming, we never wonder at the most strange and surprising Objects and Accidents, and which, awake, would amaze and astonish us." Cudworth insisted that dreams are "true Sensations" because "the Soul is as really affected, and hath as lively Images, Ideas and Phantasms of Sensible Things as existent then, as when we are awake, and many times is really Sensible of violent and exquisite Pain, which is a Real Sense, though it be but a Phantastical Thing; and immediately vanishes away upon our awakening."[26] Many people tried to explain why dreams "seem" so very real while we are asleep, including Hobbes who insisted that dreams could seem even more real than our waking thoughts since in dreaming the senses do not distract us.[27] The convincing appearance of dreams was of course what caused Descartes to question the reality of all sense perception, and in 1692 one commentator remarked, "if there be so great an *uncertainty* in our *Knowledge*, of our being asleep or awake, that it was worth the Disquisition of so great a Philosopher as *Des Cartes*, with so solemn a Face of *Seriosity*, I know not, whether there be so material a *Distinction* betwixt our Dreams, and being awake, as the generality of the *World* imagines." As we shall see, both Clarissa and Belton assert a similar faith in the continuity between dreamed and actual worlds. Andrew Baxter even went so far as to argue that poets such as Homer and Ovid make use of dreams in literature "to preserve probability" and aid them in following nature.[28]

In this context, Daniel Defoe's *An Essay on the History and Reality of Apparitions* (1727) reflects an important change in the accepted ontology of dreams, and this shift directly bears on our view of the dreams in *Clarissa*. Sir Thomas Browne and Locke had argued that if a man is either mad or sleepwalking when he commits a crime, or if he commits it within a dream, he is not morally responsible for it since he is literally "beside himself" or not his own person. Hobbes had made the point that a person should be excused for committing a crime that was suggested to him by a dream.[29] These writers assume that dreams do not figure in a person's responsibility for moral action; they are not a part of personal identity since, according to Locke, identity resides in consciousness and dreams occur when we are asleep. In *Paradise Lost*, Book IV, Milton dramatized the innocence of the dreamer of evil thoughts; the sleeping Eve is clearly not responsible for originating the notions (Phantasms and Dreams) that Satan, "Squat like a Toad," inspires by whispering in her ear. Defoe, however, recorded an important modification of this idea. He discussed the phenomenon of dreaming of committing adultery or robbing an unprotected child, and he asserted that people who have such visions are responsible for their dreamed actions just as if they were real. Defoe's *Essay* describes one such victim: "I robb'd it, *says he*, in my Imagination, and deserve as much to be hang'd for it, as if I had actively committed the horrid Fact at noon-day."[30] This passage suggests that people were beginning to view dreams as a feature of personal identity so that moral or legal responsibility actually extended to "thought workings" as well as to real actions. An important corollary to this view is the notion that we can and should seek self-knowledge through our dreams. Sir Thomas Browne, Moses Amyraldus, and Owen Felltham briefly mention this idea, and Philip Goodwin even calls it a duty, yet only Tryon's *Pythagoras* attempts to be a full "Science of *Dreams*," arguing that internal self-knowledge precedes all external awareness.[31]

Tryon most fully laid out this "new" kind of learning several years later in his treatise, *The Knowledge of a Man's Self*. In a passage that is reminiscent of Clarissa's self-probings, he wrote: "the first step to all *Real Vertue*, and *Useful Knowledge*, is, for every Person to turn the Eye of his Mind inwards, and there to search and learn *Himself*." In a fascinating section of the essay which asserts that the English are the best glass-makers and that mirrors "imitate the Orbs of the celestial Powers," Tryon argues that dreams, states of madness, and reflections in mirrors "are all three Brethren, and concurring Witnesses testifying the strange and unaccountable power of a Man's Soul." He claims that both dreams and images in glasses show us "the condition of Eternity," for within them "near and far off is the same, and a thousand years as one day; that is, there is neither Time, Place, nor Progression of Time in Eternity."[32]

Here Tryon dignifies the old superstition about the mysterious powers of mirrors simply by asking us to take it seriously. Hill had used mirrors as a metaphor, claiming that dreams are "the loking Glasses of the body" in that they "foreshewe" the future through the intervention of spirits. Hobbes, in a passage which caught Henry More's attention, argued that superstitious fears of ghosts typically arise from foolish extensions of this very analogy. Yet Tryon, in all seriousness, claims that dreams, mad delusions, and reflections in mirrors all "shew the magical power of the Soul," and they do so because of the illusory quality of the experience they offer: "each of these make something appear, and to be essential where there is nothing, and to be dreadful or pleasant, rejoyce or afflict, as if all were real." Like Baxter, Burthogge, and Defoe, Tryon thereby invests the illusory nature of dreams and mirrored reflections with an ontological significance. Dreams are important precisely because they are "fictions" of the soul. Moreover, these fleeting phenomena are so powerful that by looking in mirrors pregnant women can "impress the 'complectional ideas' of what they see" onto their unborn children.[33] Yet the essence of such experience remains transitory so that when it comes to memory, a person actually "retains a much better idea of himself from the Contemplation of his Picture, than from his representation in a Glass." It is tempting to imagine that Richardson knew Tryon's views when we read Clarissa's description of seeing her mother's face reflected in a mirror: "I thought, by the glass before me, I saw the *mother* in her softened eye cast towards me: but her words confirmed not the hoped-for tenderness" (I, 89). Despite her mother's subsequent verbal coldness, the mirror tells the reader, if not Clarissa, that a motherly sympathy is indeed present in this scene.

The startling apparent reality of dreams was acknowledged by Hobbes and others who nevertheless felt that dreams were to be disregarded; Tryon departed in insisting on the usefulness of the phenomenon as a vehicle for self-knowledge. He and others attributed the moving force of dreams to the imagination which remains awake when "all the Mind's other Faculties," including judgment and memory, "are benum'd and lifeless."[34] While "Mayne" was suspicious of the faculty, Tryon had great respect for it since the continuous operation of the imagination during sleep connects it with the soul, with eternity, and with God. In his treatise on dreams Tryon devoted a whole chapter to considering "*why* Dreams *are always Represented as actually Present*" in which he explained that "the Soul in *Dreams* . . . is as it were already in Eternity" where there is "neither time nor place, night nor day, . . . for things in Eternity go not on by degrees or by progressions."[35] As "Mayne" or even Hobbes might say, cause and effect progressions are notions only of the waking mind, so that to analyze dreams by such rules is to apply to them systems by which they do not in fact operate, a lesson that Lovelace fails to learn, as we shall see.

In a sense, Tryon's concept of a mysterious, elusive self waiting to be understood approaches a theory of the unconscious, a view that might perhaps be latent in the writings of both Joseph Glanvill and Henry More. In speaking of the operation of the imagination Glanvill writes: "'tis not from an Impress directly from without, but the Prime and Original Motion is from within our Selves: Thus the Soul it self sometimes strikes upon those Strings, whose Motion begets such and such Phantasms." Similarly, Henry More asserts that both visions and dreams are "Fantasms impressed on the Imagination, not by any free Act or Excitation of our selves, but in a Way merely passive"; therefore, according to More, "the Question is not concerning the Principle from whence, or the Manner how these divinatory Impresses come, but what they represent or signifie."[36] In his extension of Glanvill's idea, More is less interested in questioning how an individual mind produces its dreams than in understanding the ones that have already occurred. Both writers suggest that the soul operates by a will of its own, creating its fictions at the prompting of supernatural agents; dreams are thus involuntary, as Baxter reminds us. Goodwin, Nourse, Parker, Felltham, Defoe, Tryon, and "Mayne" all made a special point of insisting that the soul or at least its imaginative faculty remains active during sleep, when we are not aware of it. Yet while the self has no active control over the creations of the soul, we are nonetheless responsible for our dreams as unconscious reflections of our "*inwardest* minds*,*" to borrow Clarissa's phrase. The main concern of many of these writers was to find a way, through dreams, to prove the continued persistence of the soul, and yet taken as a whole their remarks inadvertently hint at the notion of the unconscious as we would define it today.

An author through whom Richardson would most certainly have encountered many of these views was Joseph Addison. When Anna

Howe mentions the cave of Trophonius (I, 248), a footnote refers us to the *Spectator* where Addison uses this legendary interpreter of dreams as one of his correspondents and also mentions Duncan Campbell.[37] Addison was of two minds about dreams. He saw them as potentially instructive, cited his own dreams to lend authority and "probability" to his essays, claimed that they prove the soul to be active in sleep, and anticipating Richardson's Belton, compared the moment of death to a dreamlike state in which we commune with God. In *Spectator* 487 he wrote, "Dreams may give us some Idea of the great Excellency of an Human Soul, and some Intimations of its Independency on Matter." In describing the soul's "wonderful Power," he wrote, "She converses with numberless Beings of her own Creation, and is transported into ten thousand Scenes of her own raising. She is herself the Theatre, the Actors, and the Beholder." Furthermore, regarding the existence of **supernatural dreams he insisted, "the matter of Fact is I think incontestable, and has been looked upon as such by the greatest Writers,** who have been never suspected either of Superstition or Enthusiasm." Nevertheless, Addison was also disdainful of fortune-telling through dreams, and he warned against "pursuing the Imagination through all its Extravagancies, whether in Sleeping or Waking."[38] In this sense Addison's words embody the fundamentally ambivalent attitude toward dreams of nearly all who write about them in the period, even including the deranged William Freke who implied the complexity of oneirocriticism by writing an "Allegorick Dictionary," a "Divine Grammar," and an "Alphabet" for dream interpretation with a dedicatory epistle addressed to God.[39]

III

In approaching the dreams within *Clarissa*, it is important to remember that the various treatises which urge us to make use of reveries all highlight the difficulty and uncertainty of doing so. As Owen Felltham writes, "Every *dream* is not to be regarded; nor yet are *all* to be cast away with *contempt.*" The major problem is to detect what sort of revery we have had. In general, those inspired by supernatural agents are worthy of our attention and are either prophetic or allegorical. However, we ought not to heed the "vain delusions" that are merely physiological reactions, except of course to diagnose disease. Though the terms may vary, these basic notions run through much of the literature. Artemidorus's "speculative" dreams, Saunders's "conjectural" dreams, and Freke's "literal" dreams predict the future or comment on actual events that are occurring in our lives. By contrast, Artemidorus's "allegorical" dreams, Saunders's "ambiguous" dreams, and Freke's "allegorick" dreams are structured symbolically to hide an abstruse secret.[40] Some writers more elaborately divide dreams into five types: the actual dream which "discovers truth in a hidden Figure"; the vision, when a person "really sees awake, what he did asleep"; the oracle or revelation made to us by an angel or saint and telling us to perform God's will; the phantasy or vain imaginative experience; and the apparition or a nocturnal vision that frightens us. Only the first three of these types were viewed as "true" in any sense.[41]

Philip Goodwin's *Mystery of Dreams, Historically Discoursed* offers the most unusual system. Many writers attempted to show how to interpret dreams by a kind of short story approach, briefly narrating many examples of actual reveries from those of Cicero through Sir Christopher Wren.[42] Goodwin, on the other hand, wrote a manual distinguishing five separate kinds of dreams by their effects upon us, and his method suggests a fundamental difference between Lovelace's sexually satisfying dream and Clarissa's terrifying nightmare. Goodwin speaks of false dreams that delude us intellectually, filthy dreams that physically defile us (when Satan makes use of our bodies to indulge in perversions that he cannot otherwise experience since he lacks a body of his own), and idle or vain dreams that merely waste time and energy. These three types are all prompted by Satan, and Lovelace's revery would be among them. God, on the other hand, stimulates "Troublesome and Affrighting Dreams" like Clarissa's as well as "Profitable and Instructive Dreams, " both of which are "explicatory" and "applicatory." Moses Amyraldus shared with Goodwin a desire "not to report histories, but to make Theological and Rational Reflexions upon this matter." His *Discourse* also advances a theory of historical progression and cautions readers that although "divine" dreams did occur in Biblical times, the era in which such dreams were possible has passed; dreams prompted by angels still do occur, Amyraldus claims, but he insists that those who believe themselves inspired by God himself are most typically the victims of "Hypochondriack Vapours."[43]

All of the works I have mentioned share the view of Artemidorus, that in spite of the "*mixed* and *compounded*" wildness of dreams, those which are divinely inspired can nevertheless be interpreted, for "as in all other things there is an *order* and *dependence*" in them; yet the difficulty of performing such analysis "is a great *grief* to many." Hill claims that dream interpreters must, like poets, be "naturall prophetes" and possess a special knowledge of "similitudes" or the art of knowing "how to discuss from like to like." Thus Philip Goodwin warns, "from Dreames so considered, a man may make no certain *Theses*, or infallible conclusions, yet a man may gather probabilities, and may give a great guess." As Tryon sees it, the soul probes the mysteries of dreams "without long tedious study, . . . without toil of Logical demonstrations, or perplexity of Syllogisms and Problems." A French treatise comments: "the Rules of dreaming are not general, . . . but often according to times and persons, admit of various interpretations." Hill believes that dream interpreters came to be called "conjecturers" because their art depends not only on wisdom but on the ability to "conjecture cunninglye." Following Hill, Tryon advises, "all who would be worthy of this sublime Knowledge and Gift of true Dreams, must keep a pure . . . Spirit and Imagination . . . like a clear Glass, or calm limpid spring of water, wherein you may behold the true Images of things." He warns that "if the same be . . . stirred or agitated, then you perceive nothing but confused Figures."[44] Even the firm believer in witchcraft, Joseph Glanvill, warns against "Hypocritical Imposters" or "Enthusiasts" who are deceived by their own "*raptures, extasies*, and *deliquiums* of sense, in which every *dream* is taken for a *Prophecy.*"[45]

Interpreting dreams is thus as difficult as being what Richardson called an "attentive reader" of *Clarissa*. What an intelligent layman like Richardson might assume is that dreams are indeed to be taken seriously but that we are mistaken to seize too quickly upon facile interpretations of them. Many dreams are indeed nothing more than worthless delusions with physiological causes, and to mistake them for divine prophecies is to commit a prideful mistake. Yet at the same time dreams can be important reflections of our deepest selves since they are the "fictions" created by our souls when in possible communication with both good and evil spirits. Unfortunately, however, we lack a system of infallible rules for interpreting and applying them. Though dreams had always seemed puzzling, even conscious states of mind were beginning to seem problematic by the time Richardson wrote his novel. For example, in 1742 Henry Fielding noted that it takes an "accurate Observer" to penetrate the disguises of false character that men inevitably assume.[46] Both Fielding's essay on the "Knowledge of the Characters of Men" and the literature of dream interpretation reflect the increasing eighteenth-century interest in multivalent reality and in new kinds of probabilistic thought. According to Paul Korshin, characters no longer acted predictably; to formulate a judgment of character either in literature or in courts of law one now had to gather reliable evidence and remain aware that all such judgments involve a degree of calculated risk.[47] Even Clarissa herself reveals an awareness of such complexity when she speaks of her "*inwardest* mind." Her use of the phrase implies a concept of a multivalent self with several realms of operation that do not always function in concert and yet that all offer legitimate knowledge.

IV

The problematic nature of knowledge and perception in *Clarissa* is never more clear than when we try to interpret the narrated dreams. Clarissa's dream, for example, cannot be definitively analyzed as an allegory or emblem of plot action since it offers several possible readings. Commentators have turned to it for hints about Clarissa's future, yet the dream is strikingly inefficient as a prophecy about the heroine since its visual details force us to experience Lovelace's perspective rather than her own: we accompany him as he discovers a plot against him by the Harlowes, turns his rage against Clarissa, carries her to a churchyard, stabs her to the heart, tumbles her into a deep grave with two or three half-dissolved carcasses, throws in the dirt and earth upon her with his hands, and tramples it down with his feet.[48] Presumably the stab has been fatal, yet Clarissa oddly narrates the dream as if she were still conscious. In this sense the incident peculiarly fulfills her often stated preference to be "buried alive" rather than marry Solmes. Yet since she describes none of the unpleasant physical or mental sensations that she would literally feel in such a state, the dream does not effectively forecast her suffering. It is misleading as a prophecy of external events, since it confirms an earlier suggestion that

Lovelace will actually commit murder. Some critics interpret it as the symbolic soiling or rape of Clarissa, but we can do so with certainty only in retrospect. If we regard the "two or three half-dissolved carcasses" in the grave as Lovelace's former conquests, we encounter logical problems since Clarissa does not know the details of Lovelace's history, though she might well project such thoughts or be warned of them by an angel. Nor is the dream needed as a general warning of future woe, since Clarissa and others have assured us several times already that fleeing her family will make her situation worse, and when the dream occurs she is about to do so.

The dream's failure to convey a single, separable meaning is a result not only of its internal structure, but also of its rendering and placement within the epistolary narrative. We do not actually dream with Clarissa and so experience her fantasy as reality; instead, we hear her narrate the revery and are therefore constantly aware of it as a fiction which her soul has unconsciously and involuntarily created. We thus experience not the dream but an act of remembering and interpreting it that contributes to one of the novel's most critical climaxes.

At this moment the motion of the plot has come to a halt since Clarissa and her family have reached an impasse in their struggle over Solmes. Anna Howe writes: "The strings cannot long continue thus overstrained. They must break, or be relaxed" (I, 417-418). These words are followed by Clarissa's announcement that she has "done . . . the most rash thing that ever I did in my life" (I, 425)—she has written to Lovelace that she will flee to his aunts. Yet she tells Anna that her "*inwardest* mind" has experienced such "strange forebodings" that she has now decided to remove the rash letter from its hiding place before Lovelace can receive it. Because the narrated dream is placed in the very next letter we read and gives us a new kind of knowledge from another part of Clarissa's "self," it plays a vital role in the impending breaking of strings.

To understand the dream's importance here we must remind ourselves that as the novel opened, Anna asked Clarissa to tell her story so as to clear her reputation in the face of strange rumors, and in response Clarissa promised to provide "facts," and as many as possible, so that we will understand the truth. Yet as Clarissa herself points out, certainty of knowledge, particularly of the "self," is deeply open to question; "the *Heart of man is deceitful above all things*," wrote Tryon, echoing scripture.[19] Detailed evidence is less important than credibility, as Korshin would remind us, and Clarissa's candor seems vaguely dubious during the first quarter of the novel. For example, along with Anna Howe and Clarissa's family we often suspect that her feelings for Lovelace amount to far more than "a conditional kind of liking," as she insists.[50] Up to now such doubts have not seemed crucial, yet upon her clearly reprehensible decision to leave home we suddenly need a new sort of indicator of her attitude since this action for the first time seriously threatens our belief that she has behaved as well as anyone could. Curiously Clarissa's dream gives us just such an indicator.

Though critics have said that in their improbable structure and timelessness the narrated dreams of the novel resemble the waking fantasies in which Lovelace often indulges,[51] I would argue that they are unique in reflecting the action of the imagination when the powers of judgment have ceased as they can only do in sleep. Because dreams are involuntary, as Andrew Baxter pointed out, they are reliable in ways that other reports of experience are not. Thus, the narrated dreams in Clarissa possess an ontological status that is fundamentally different from all other epistolary acts within this fiction. Following Tryon, Lovelace reminds Belford (II, 42) that dreams reveal secrets. Clarissa may tell us that she has taken a wrong step in agreeing to seek refuge in Lovelace's family, but only the dream which echoes her waking reluctance to leave home allows us to forgive her for this error. For once we see with certainty that Clarissa has hidden nothing from us or from herself. She freely narrates a dream which if anything hints at the error in her recent decision. The first quarter of the novel is remarkable for its lack of an implied authorial point of view, and the dream is the mechanism for creating such a guide since it authorizes us to feel strongly that Clarissa is virtuous just as she is on the verge of making a serious mistake. Immediately after her account of the dream, Clarissa writes to Anna, "The man, my dear, has got the letter!" and her words cause the string to snap. With the "getting" of the letter by Lovelace, Clarissa's reprehensible action takes place though the dream has entirely exonerated Clarissa herself from responsibility for it.

By affirming Clarissa's credibility, the revery alters our continuing experience of the novel. The doubts we have had of her sincerity not only cease in the future but appear to have been wrong in the past, though we actually have no new solid evidence one way or the other.

Here we engage in a process that Anna later labels "retrospecting" or the reverse calculation of probabilities. She explains that she and Clarissa have often "retrospected" their acquaintances by forming guesses "from their present appearances, outside and in," of the "figures they made" at some previous time.[52] Retrospection is not the discovery of the truth but the fabulation of probable fictions of the past. After the dream we reprocess our memory of the doubts we have had about Clarissa as a reliable narrator so that we judge in her favor, something we can only do because the evidence has been genuinely contradictory. This helps explain how Richardson creates a character who strikes us as potentially fallible and therefore convincing, and yet whom we accept in the end as entirely "virtuous, noble, wise, and pious" (IV, 119), to quote Belford. Near the close of the novel we feel a truth in Lovelace's claim that she is the only woman in the world who can say that she is not "artful" (IV, 135), despite all of our previous experience of her as a "plotter." We can thereby see that the novel's ontology will indeed appear dreamlike of we make the mistake of trying to judge Clarissa out of her eighteenth-century context, by standards of fixed character portrayal or consistently reliable narration. The dreams within the novel are most suggestive if we regard them not as containers of meaning but as parts of a larger narrative fabric that creates evolving meaning as we progress through the work. It was perhaps from Richardson that Austen learned to create a Knightley whom we initially respect as we would a father to Emma and eventually accept as her lover.

Our experience with Clarissa's revery teaches us how to interpret Lovelace's two dreams, for again we experience not the dreams but their narration by the dreamer, a point not discussed by the critics who attempt Freudian readings of them. Although Clarissa thinks "slightly" of dreams, she narrates hers to Anna, without any attempt at analysis, simply because it caused her to wake "in great terror . . . in a cold sweat, trembling, and in agonies." She leaves the reader to recognize that it is what Goodwin might call an affrighting dream, sent by God. As such it is potentially interpretable as a sign to a virtuous dreamer to correct evil or promote good in the world. Clarissa, however, does not offer an assessment of the dream's meaning but instead draws our attention to its powerful affective force and her own frank avowal of it. She asks herself, "Why should I, who have such *real* evils to contend with, regard *imaginary* ones?" Yet clearly Clarissa does "regard" her dream or take its effect on her seriously, and the boundaries between imagination and reality thereby lose their usual significance, although they clearly do exist. On his deathbed Belton makes almost the same point when he angrily insists that fearful dying men are not "fantastic dreamers" who have become unable to distinguish reality from imagination. Instead, they have gained a special awareness of the connection between these two realms; for the dying, "the evils *before* thee, and *with* thee" which are unseen by others are nonetheless "more than the effects of the imagination" (IV, 150). These words not only remind us of Baxter or Burthogge's insistence on the "reality" of dream experience but they bear on Lovelace as a dream interpreter since Belton speaks them only pages before Lovelace offers his faulty analysis of his second dream.[53]

Lovelace does not allow himself to feel the effects of his dreams as Clarissa and Belton do. Instead, he characteristically searches them for allegorical and prophetic meaning, and in doing so he is deceived by his own "*deliquiums* of sense."[54] His daytime revery is what he calls a "fortunate dream" that he will use as "the means to effect" (III, 248) his aims by reenacting it in life. That is, he will attempt to direct upcoming events according to the somewhat fantastic plot that the dream has sketched, including the "strange metamorphosis" of a kind old lady into the infamous "Mother H." and then into a "young person of the other sex" who turns out to be Lovelace, after which a strange "huddle of adventures" ends with Clarissa and Anna's each bearing Lovelace's children, a "charming girl" and a "charming boy" who ultimately "intermarry" (III, 250-251). Lovelace rightly calls this "a very odd dream," yet he insists that "it is not altogether improbable that something like it may happen" since he intends to use it as a script for his treacherous dealings with Clarissa. Here Addison's words about the foolish use of dreams come to mind. Thomas Hill had warned that it is "a rash matter to Judge of unknowen matters," and the 1690 edition of Artemidorus comments, "it were *fondness* for any *man* to think, that *monstrous* and impossible things should happen as the *Dreamer* hath seen them," yet this is precisely what Lovelace does. The 1722 edition of Artemidorus even outlines the very kind of error Lovelace is about to commit as dream interpreter: it describes the suffering of the person who is led by his dream to hope for a certain turn of events, only to be disappointed, although the actions that ensue actually do fulfill the terms of the dream by an alternate reading. Lovelace is oblivious to these possibilities. He is so pleased with the use he intends to make of his revery that he even plans to write a book upon the subject (III, 245 and 253).[55] Ultimately, however, his "great faith in dreams" (III, 254) fades as his plans fail, and he concludes that he "shall nevermore depend upon those . . . illusions of a fancy depraved, and run mad" (III, 255).

Despite his resolution, Lovelace does again depend on dreams, for he also interprets his second one "to his own liking" (IV, 572), this time as a prophecy of his marriage to Clarissa. Along with Belford who offers to give another, less favorable interpretation (IV, 156), we instantly recognize that Lovelace's analysis is wishful thinking. He even admits that he dislikes Morden's threat to him in the dream and that he is perplexed to find himself "tumbling over and over through the floor into a frightful hole, *descending* as she *ascends*" (IV, 158). In his daytime revery he revealingly admits that he "forgot to tell" us the part of the dream in which Clarissa is so stricken with grief that she attempts suicide (III, 251). In both instances Lovelace willfully ignores information his own imagination reveals and so reassures us that whatever worldly tortures are ahead for our heroine, she is spiritually beyond his power. Thus his dreams cannot frighten us as grisly prophecy, to borrow Castle's term, particularly if we are sensitive to the vagaries of dream analysis as they were highlighted in seventeenth- and eighteenth-century treatises. Instead, Lovelace's dreams in combination with his own discussions of them powerfully expose the nature of the man himself.

V

The various attempts to account for dreams within this novel reveal a telling clash between two concepts of probability, only one of which the text imposes on its readers. Lovelace believes in the formal rules of art, yet in applying such rules to dreams he violates the accepted views on oneirocriticism. Though he comments that dreams happen "as quick as thought" and "confine not themselves to the rules of drama" (III, 250), he tries to transform his first dream into a drama in his own life.

His notion of probability respects the laws of cause and effect as dramas typically do, and by extending these rules from art to life he feels that he can shape the future.[56] He characterizes himself as a puppeteer controlling the Harlowe family. The causes of their behavior may lie "in their malignant hearts," as he puts it, yet he feels that he can "guide the effects" because he views "probability" as a dynamic system (II, 100; II, 182). Marriage will repair any injury he may have caused Clarissa, for he asks, "Is not the catastrophe of every story *that ends in wedlock accounted happy*, be the difficulties in the progress to it ever so great?" (III, 281). Here, being "accounted" happy is equivalent to being happy. Even in his letters he writes what he calls a "narrative of my progressions towards bringing" his schemes "to effect" (II, 337), and he apologizes for a letter in which he indulges in a fantasy since the letter is "not a narrative one, or a journal of proceedings" (III, 320).

Causally connected, controllable, accountable systems of "proceedings" constitute reality for Lovelace. The "probable" is that which can be anticipated. He is thus understandably perplexed that a chance rainstorm and the accidental negligence of Sinclair's nymphs are what allow Clarissa to escape him, for he says, there "was much more luck than probability" that such events would occur (III, 319). Lovelace too slavishly follows principles akin to those of David Hume in trying to predict and thereby control the future by calculating the frequency of past events.[57] If, on the other hand, we calculate probability in retrospect as Clarissa does, the escape by means of a chance rainstorm will seem far less miraculous than a carefully plotted escape by our innocent heroine.

Terry Castle is right that a kind of "purposiveness" typifies Clarissa's behavior after Lovelace's daytime revery, yet we must not overlook the critical distinction between Clarissa's plotting and that of Lovelace. He seeks to accomplish certain objectives by employing the predictability of dramatic probability. By contrast, Clarissa calculates probabilities only to avoid evil. She anticipates the folly of marrying either Solmes or Lovelace and tries to avoid both without contriving a serious alternative.[58] She lives by a principle which she articulates at the very start of her story: "Who can command or foresee events? To act up to our best judgments at the time, is all we can do" (I, 92). As in assessing our dreams, we can only make guesses about our futures based on whatever evidence we currently possess; we must constantly revise old guesses and make new ones as events take place. We do not anticipate coincidental rainstorms, but after they have occurred we accept them as part of a probable reality. Lovelace's approach clearly gives him less power: his impulse to interpret the meaning of his second dream also causes him to misinterpret Clarissa's allegorical letter at the very same moment. Despite all of his love of metaphorical thought, he is ill-equipped to recognize a true allegory when it is before him. Clarissa herself sums up this clash between kinds of probability (the predictable versus the retrospective, the effective versus the affective, the artistic versus the natural); she says that Lovelace is indeed the "author" of her calamities, yet he "could not have been the author of them but for a strange concurrence of unhappy causes" (IV, 259).

We can now see that the process of reading *Clarissa* is not dreamlike nor is this novel, by implication, an indictment of the stable order of the world. If anything, reading *Clarissa* is analogous to the art of dream interpretation as it was understood in Richardson's time. We try out alternate theories of meaning about events that are so elusive and contradictory that they finally resist being accounted for by any single, fixed perspective on truth. Yet we do not lose faith that just beyond the boundaries of our perception lies a truth awaiting our discovery. Our pleasure in reading comes from recognizing curious connections among events currently being described, events already experienced and that the current narrator may or may not be aware of, and guesses we make about the future. It makes little difference whether we are correct in our guesses about either the future or the past, since new information will simply allow us to reprocess the old.

We explore a range of interpretations, anticipations, and echoings of the dreams throughout *Clarissa* without attaching conclusive "meaning" to them, as Lovelace would prefer. For example, we may notice an ironic visual and verbal parallel between Mrs. Sinclair's actual death and the heroine's dreamed one; in her revery, Clarissa is "tumbled" into her grave with several "half-dissolved carcasses," while Sinclair ends up in a "tumbled" deathbed, surrounded by what Belford calls the "contaminated carcasses" of her young ladies. Similarly, each of the various theories about the dreams as prophecy seems apt at one time or another, although the dreams themselves do not function as prophecy within the narrative.[59]

While our reading thus involves a series of continually revised hypotheses, we end with a sense, however illusory, that we know what we have experienced. Dreams are indeed "fictions of the soul," to use Artemidorus's phrase, but they are nevertheless to be taken seriously, as "real" phenomena; and Richardson's "fiction" makes a parallel demand. Its plot is finally not a Möbius strip or plaything for the ingenious reader; as Belton might insist, our experience of it is more than the capricious effect of our imagination. Clarissa is our wholly innocent and virtuous heroine who dies of a broken heart; Lovelace is the nasty villain who tortures her mercilessly; and Richardson's art at tempting us to endless "retrospections" and anticipations is what transforms such a simple and trite story into the fascinating and compelling novel that *Clarissa* is.

NOTES

1. *Clarissa*, 4 vols. (London: Dent-Everyman's Library, 1932), I, p. xvi. Further references are listed by volume and page number within the text.
2. Terry Castle, "Lovelace's Dream," *Studies in Eighteenth-Century Culture*, Vol. 13, ed. O M Brack, Jr. (Madison Wis.: University of Wisconsin Press, 1984), pp. 29–42; and William Beatty Warner, *Reading Clarissa* (London and New Haven, Conn.: Yale University Press, 1979).
3. See, for example, *Clarissa*, I, p. 349.
4. Andrew Baxter, "An Essay on the phaenomenon of Dreaming" in *An Enquiry into the Nature of the Human Soul*, 3rd ed. (London, 1745), II, p. 9. The first edition of this work is thought to have appeared in 1733.
5. *Clarissa*, IV, p. 564. Richardson used the phrase, "air of probability," from the first edition of his novel onward. In his chapter on *Clarissa*, R. F. Brissenden writes that "Richardson was the first English writer to demonstrate that an extended piece of naturalistic prose fiction could be a major work of art." See *Virtue in Distress* (New York: Barnes and Noble, 1974), p. 163.
6. For such interpretations see Margaret Anne Doody, *A Natural Passion* (Oxford: Clarendon Press, 1974), p. 239; Warner, pp. 14–17; and Carol Houlihan Flynn, *Samuel Richardson: A Man of Letters* (Princeton, N.J.: Princeton University Press, 1982), p. 32.
7. "Lovelace's Dream," p. 39, and Terry Castle, *Clarissa's Ciphers: Meaning and Disruption in Richardson's "Clarissa"* (London and Ithaca, N.Y.: Cornell University Press, 1982), p. 35.
8. Terry Eagleton, *The Rape of Clarissa: Writing, Sexuality and Class Struggle in Samuel Richardson* (Minneapolis: University of Minnesota Press, 1982), pp. 62–63.
9. Philip Goodwin, *The Mystery of Dreams, Historically Discoursed* (London, 1658), "Epistle Dedicatory."

10. Thomas Hill, "The Preface to the Reader" in *The Moste Pleasaunte Arte of The Interpretation of Dreames* (London, 1576):Moses Amyraldus, "The Epistle Dedicatory" in *A Discourse Concerning the Divine Dreams Mention'd in Scripture*, trans. Ja[mes] Lowde (London, 1676); John Aubrey, *Miscellanies* (London, 1696), p. 1; and Thomas Branch, *Thoughts on Dreaming* (London, 1738), p. 1. Aubrey's *Miscellanies*, which contains a chapter on "Dreams," came out in a second edition in 1721. For a survey of some of the major views on dreams at the time of *Clarissa's* publication see "Enquiry into the Causes of Dreams," *Gentleman's Magazine*, 24 (1754), pp. 36–37.

11. See Warburton's letter of 3 March 1759 in *Letters from a Late Eminent Prelate to One of his Friends* (London, c. 1793), p. 208. Works written in response to Baxter's essay include John Jackson, *A Dissertation on Matter AND Spirit with Some Remarks on a Book Entitled An Enquiry into the Nature of the Human Soul* (London, 1735); Thomas Branch, *Thoughts on Dreaming* (London, 1738); Vincent Perronet, *A Second Vindication of Mr. LOCKE* (London, 1738); [Joseph Wimpey], *Remarks On a Book, intitled, An Enquiry into the Nature of the Human Soul* (London, 1741); and the anonymous *A Letter to the Author of a Book Entituled An Enquiry into the Nature of the Human Soul* (London, 1741). William King mentions A. Baxter in *The Dreamer* (London, 1754), p. v., as does J. Richardson in *Thoughts upon Thinking, or, a New Theory of the Human Mind* (London, 1755), p. 21.

12. Authors who refer to Artemidorus, Cardan, Synesius, and others as the major authorities include Thomas Nashe, "The Terrors of the Night Or, A Discourse of Apparitions"(London, 1594),in *The Works of Thomas Nashe*, ed. Ronald B. McKerrow and rpt. and rev. F. P. Wilson (Oxford: Basil Blackwell, 1958), I, p. 361; Robert Burton, *The Anatomy of Melancholy*, ed. Floyd Dell and Paul Jordan-Smith (New York: Tudor Publishing Co., 1927), pp. 140 and 466; Henry More, "The Immortality of the Soul" in *A Collection of Several Philosophical Writings*, 2nd ed. corr. and enlarged (London, 1662), p. 40, and *Synopsis Prophetica* (London, 1706) in *The Theological Works of the most Pious and Learned Henry More* (London, 1707), p. 535; and Thomas Tryon, *Pythagoras His Mystical Philosophy Reviv'd; or, The Mystery of Dreams Unfolded* (London, 1691), p. 8. I have examined three different editions of Artemidorus: Artemidorus, *The Interpretation of Dreames*, trans. Robert Wood, 4th ed. corr. (London, 1644); Artemidorus, *The Interpretation of Dreams*, trans. Robert Wood, 10th ed. (London, 1690); and Artemidorus and other authors, *The Interpretation of Dreams*, 20th ed. (London, 1722), which compiles ideas of several unidentified writers. Often it is difficult to identify the actual author of a given work. For example, the anonymous editor of *A Groatsworth of Wit for a Penny; or, The Interpretation of Dreams* (London, c. 1750) attributes the volume to Mr. Lilly "whose works are so well known." Thomas Tryon's treatise on dreams appeared in 1689, 1695, and possibly 1700 as *A Treatise of Dreams and Visions*, by Philotheos Physiologus. The edition to which this paper refers carries Tryon's name as the author and is called *Pythagoras His Mystick Philosophy Reviv'd; or, the Mystery of Dreams Unfolded* (London, 1691). In 1706–07 it was published in an altered form, without his name and in two parts called *Nocturnal Revels: or, A General History of Dreams* (London, 1707) and *Nocturnal Revels: or, A Universal Dream-Book* (London, 1706). See also John Booker, *Nocturnal Revels; or, A Universal Dream-Book* (London, 1767). For other useful references see Manfred Weidhorn, *Dreams in Seventeenth-Century English Literature* (The Hague: Mouton, 1970).

Accounting for Dreams in *Clarissa* 193

13. [William Lilly], *A Groatsworth of Wit for a Penny; or, The Interpretation of Dreams* (London, c. 1750), p. 2. See also *Dreams and Moles With their Interpretation and Signification* (London, c. 1750) and *The High German Fortune-Teller Laying down True Rules and Directions By which Both Men and Women Know Their Good and Bad Fortune* (London, n.d.). All three of these works were published in Aldermary Churchyard, Bow Lane. For later editions see William Lillie, *A Groatsworth of Wit for a Penny; Or, The Interpretation of Dreams*, 11th ed. corr. (Newcastle, c. 1770) and *Nine Pennyworth of Wit for a Penny; Or, the most exact and approved Fortune Teller* (Newcastle upon Tyne, n.d.).

14. See Rodney M. Baine, *Daniel Defoe and the Supernatural* (Athens: University of Georgia Press, 1969), p. 138. See also *The History of the Life and Adventures of Mr. Duncan Campbell* (London, 1720); Justicia, *A Spy upon the Conjuror: or, a Collection of Surprising Stories* (London, 1724); Justicia, *The Dumb Projector* (London, 1725); Duncan Campbel, *The Friendly Daemon, or the Generous Apparition* (London 1726); *Secret Memoirs of the late Mr. Duncan Campbell* (London, 1732); and *The History of the Life and Adventures of Mr. Duncan Campbell*, 3rd ed. corr. (London, 1739). These works are variously attributed to Daniel Defoe, William Bond, and Eliza Haywood (Justicia).

15. Samuel Parker, for example, objected to the Cartesian or Malebranchian view that dreams challenge the authority of the senses. See *Six Philosophical Essays* (London, 1700), pp. 82–83. Following Tryon and others, but differing from Richard Baxter, Parker insisted that the soul is active in sleep although we are not conscious of its activity. See "Of the Soul" in *Essays on Divers Weighty and Curious Subjects* (London, 1702), pp. 162–163, and Richard Baxter, *The Immortality of a Mans Soul, And the Nature of it, and other Spirits* (London, 1682), pp. 37–38. In *The Gentleman's Magazine*, 24 (1754), p. 36, the writer objects to George Cheyne's belief that the soul does not think or dream during sound sleep, a view that was perhaps derived from Locke (John Locke, *An Essay concerning Human Understanding*, ed. Peter H. Nidditch [Oxford: Clarendon Press, 1975], 2, 1, 10–19).

16. Artemidorus (1690), p. 7; Nashe, p. 355; Thomas Hobbes, *Physics*, in *The English Works of Thomas Hobbes*, ed. William Molesworth (London, 1839; reprinted Scientia-Aalen, 1962), I, p. 396; and Tryon, p. 194. Addison echoes Tryon in *Spectator* 487. George Cheyne's views on dreams are discussed in *The Gentleman's Magazine*, 24 (1754), 36–37.

17. This "threefold division of Dreams" as natural, animal, or celestial appears in the 1722 edition of Artemidorus. However, it may have originally come from David Person, "Of Sleepe and Dreames," in *Of Varieties* (London, 1635), pp. 251–253. Other writers simply distinguish between natural and supernatural dreams; see Goodwin, pp. 13–14, and Hobbes, *Leviathan*, in *The English Works of Thomas Hobbes*, III, p. 658.

18. Burton, p. 466; Nashe, p. 355; [Timothy Nourse], *A Discourse of Natural and Reveal'd Religion* (London, 1691), p. 310; and Sir Thomas Browne, "On Dreams," in *Works*, ed. Geoffrey Keynes (London: Faber and Faber Ltd., 1931), V, p. 400. See also John Trenchard, *The Natural History of Superstition* (London, 1709), pp. 11–13, 23, and 40. In light of Browne's remark it is amusing to note that Thomas Tryon believed in a vegetarian diet.

19. Hobbes felt that people would be better fitted for civil obedience if superstition

were generally given up, yet he expressed a belief in the prophetic dreams of the Bible. See the *Leviathan*, in *Works*, III, pp. 10 and 360–362.

20. Glanvill, *Essays on Several Important Subjects in Philosophy and Religion* (London, 1676), p. 52; Balthus, *An Account of M. de Fontenelle's History of Oracles* (London, 1709), p. 142; and Tryon, *Pythagoras*, pp. 48–49. Following Amyraldus, Richard Saunders outlined the causes of dreams as three: physiology, angels, or God. See Saunders, *Physiognomie . . . with The Subject of Dreams Made Plain*, 2nd ed. enlarged (London, 1671), pp. 258–260. See also Artemidorus, Hill, Browne, Person, Goodwin, *Spectator* 487, and *The Gentleman's Magazine*, 24 (1754), p. 36.

21. Tryon, p. 78; [Daniel Defoe], *An Essay on The History and Reality of Apparitions* (London, 1727), p. 218; and A. Baxter, p. 45.

22. See Thomas Newton, trans., *Fouure Severall Treatises of M. Tullius Cicero* (London, 1577), p. 122, and *A Spy upon the Conjuror*, p. 27. See also John Beaumont, *An Historical Physiological and Theological Treatise of Spirits, Apparitions, Witchcrafts, and Other Magical Practices* (London, 1705), p. 252, and Branch, p. 81.

23. Nashe, p. 356; Goodwin, p. 5; Hobbes, *Physics*, p. 399, *Leviathan*, p. 12, and *Tripos* in *The English Works of Thomas Hobbes*, IV, pp. 11–12; and A. Baxter, p. 63. Baxter used this point to argue that dreams cannot therefore be the products of our own souls, but must be stimulated by "separate immaterial Beings" since our souls would surely recognize and reject improbable happenings as unnatural. The writer of "Enquiry into the Causes of Dreams" in *The Gentleman's Magazine* refers to this idea and perhaps had Baxter in mind.

24. Branch, pp. 5–9; Browne, p. 186; Nashe, p. 376; and Goodwin, p. 12.

25. Anon., *Two Dissertations Concerning Sense and the Imagination. With an Essay on Consciousness* (London, 1728), p. 80, and Ralph Cudworth, *A Treatise Concerning Eternal and Immutable Morality* (London, 1731), pp. 113–115.

26. Baxter, p. 9; *Two Dissertations*, p. 204; and Cudworth, p. 116. See also Timothy Bright, *A Treatise of Melancholy*, newly corr. and amended (London, 1611), pp. 143–145; Richard Burthogge, *An Essay upon Reason, and the Nature of Spirits* (London, 1694), p. 88; and Goodwin, p. 12.

27. Hobbes, *Tripos*, pp. 13–14 and *Physics*, pp. 396 and 401–402; More, "The Immortality of the Soul," pp. 37–38, and "Enthusiasmus Triumphatus," in *A Collection*, pp. 3 and 19–20; Glanvill, *Essays*, p. 52; Tryon, pp. 194–195; Nourse, pp. 309–310; Parker, "Of the Soul," pp. 162–163; and *Two Dissertations*, p. 187.

28. [Charles Gildon], *The Post-boy rob'd of his mail: or, the Pacquet Broke Open* (London, 1692), p.109, and Baxter, pp. 95–96. See also Anthony, Earl of Shaftesbury, *Characteristics of Men, Manners, Opinions, Times* (1711), ed. John M. Robertson (Indianapolis and New York: The Bobbs-Merrill Co., 1964), II, pp. 275–276, and John Hughes, "On the Pleasure in Being Deceived," in *Poems on Several Occasions With Some Select Essays in Prose* (London, 1735), p. 261. "On the Pleasure of Being Deceived" was written in 1701.

29. Browne, p. 186; Hobbes, *Leviathan*, pp. 286–287; and John Locke, *Essay*, 2, 27, 20. See also Beaumont, p. 222.

30. Defoe, pp. 209–210.

31. Browne, p. 185; Amyraldus, p. 130; Owen Felltham, *Resolves: Divine, Moral, Political*, 12th ed. (London, 1709), p. 125; Goodwin, p. 20; and Tryon, pp. 45–46 and

57. Felltham, like Tryon, calls dream interpretation a "science," p. 128.

32. Thomas Tryon, *The Knowledge of a Man's Self* (London, 1703–04), II, 26–27, and III, 236, 238, and 252. In this context it is interesting to remember that Clarissa goes temporarily mad after the rape. See also Locke (*Essay*, 2, 1, 15) for a comparison of the fleeting images in looking glasses to the "*useless sort of thinking*" that the soul does not retain.

33. Tryon, *The Knowledge of a Man's Self*, III, pp. 236–239 and 250–252.

34. [Mayne], p. 79. See also Burton, p. 140; Hobbes, *Physics*, p. 396; Amyraldus, Chapter 1; and Tryon, *Pythagoras*, p. 20, for example.

35. Tryon, *Pythagoras*, pp. 219, 16, and 220–221. Hobbes makes a similar point in *Physics*, pp. 400–402, as does Bright, pp. 144–145.

36. Glanvill, *Essays*, p. 52, and More, *Synopsis Prophetica* (London, 1706) in *The Theological Works of the most Pious and Learned Henry More* (London, 1707), p. 535.

37. Richardson refers to *Spectator* 599. See also *Spectators* 487, 505, 586, 587, 593, 597, and 598 in *The Spectator*, 5 vols., ed. D.F. Bond (Oxford: Clarendon Press, 1965). In the 1688 London translation of *The History of Oracles, and the Cheats of the Pagan Priests*, 2 parts, Fontenelle speaks of Trophonius as one of the most famous interpreters of dreams. See pp. 126–128.

38. See *Spectator* 487. Andrew Baxter referred to Addison's use of dreams as a means of giving authority and probability to his arguments. See Baxter, pp. 98–99, 62, and 140, and *Spectators* 505 and 598.

39. William Freke, *Lingua Tersancta* (London, 1703), *The Fountain of Monition and Intercommunication Divine* (London, 1703), and *The Divine Grammar* (London, 1703). Henry More's ambivalence is interesting, for in *Enthusiasmus Triumphatus* he wrote, "*he that regardeth Dreams, is like him that catcheth at a shadow*" (p. 20), and yet in *Synopsis Prophetica* he relied on the oneirocritics for help in interpreting the visions of Daniel (p. 535). The *Dictionary of National Biography* implies that Freke was deranged by mentioning the "increasing craziness" of his writings and commenting that his recorded dreams "constitute the autobiography of a diseased imagination."

40. See Felltham, p. 126; Artemidorus, 1690, p. 1; Saunders, p. 260; and Freke, *The Divine Grammar*, Chapter 1. See also Defoe, p. 211; *A Spy upon the Conjuror*, p. 28; and J. B., *The Prophetical Dream* (London, 1746), pp. 4–5.

41. See Artemidorus, 1722, pp. 2–3, and March de Vulson Sieur de la Colombière, *The Court of Curiosity*, 3rd ed. trans. (London, 1681), p. 2.

42. For writers who use the "short story approach," see Thomas Bromhall, *A Treatise of Specters* (London, 1658), 3rd Book; Joseph Glanvill, *Sadducismus Triumphatus* (London, 1681); Richard Baxter, *The Certainty of the Worlds of Spirits* (London, 1691); John Aubrey, *Miscellanies* (London, 1696); William Turner, *A Compleat History of the Most Remarkable Providences* (London, 1697), Part 1, Chapter VIII; Beaumont, Chapter IX; Artemidorus, *The Interpretation of Dreams*, 20th ed. (London, 1722); and *The Dreamer's Vade Mecum* (London, 1808).

43. Amyraldus, pp. 126 and 113, and Defoe, p. 203. William Turner disagrees, however. See Turner, p. 47, and Beaumont, p. 229.

44. Artemidorus, 1690, p. 110; Goodwin, "Epistle Dedicatory"; Tryon, *Pythagoras*, pp. 231 and 182; and de la Colombière, p. 6.

45. *Philosophia Pia* (London, 1671), pp. 58–59. For a survey of the history of this debate see Branch, *Thoughts on Dreaming*, p. 2.

46. Henry Fielding, "An Essay on the Knowledge of the Characters of Men" in *Miscellanies by Henry Fielding, Esq.; Volume One*, ed. Henry Knight Miller (Middleton, Conn.: Wesleyan University Press, 1972), p. 155.

47. Paul J. Korshin, "Probability and Character in the Eighteenth Century" in *Probability, Time, and Space in Eighteenth-Century Literature*, ed. Paula R. Backscheider (New York: AMS Press, 1979), pp. 63–77. Korshin argues that this attitude was paralleled by a development in jurisprudence. While a witness's testimony was accepted as true in the seventeenth century, during the eighteenth century the witness's natural credibility gradually shrank so that quantities of detailed evidence were no longer as important as establishing the credibility of the speaker.

48. The odd use of Lovelace's point of view in the dream is even more striking if we compare Clarissa's revery to that of Harriet Byron in *Sir Charles Grandison* discussed by Margaret Anne Doody in "Deserts, Ruins and Troubled Waters: Female Dreams in Fiction and the Development of the Gothic Novel," *Genre*, 10 (1977), 539–544.

49. See Tryon, *Pythagoras*, pp. 6–7; Korshin, p. 74; and Margaret J. Osler, "Certainty, Scepticism, and Scientific Optimism: The Roots of Eighteenth-Century Attitudes Towards Scientific Knowledge" in Backscheider, *Probability*, pp. 3–28. Clarissa would certainly have agreed with Tryon on the importance of self-knowledge, for she blames her error in fleeing with Lovelace on her own lack of awareness of herself (I, 486–487).

50. See Warner, Part I, chapter 1 for an extensive discussion of Clarissa's duplicity as a narrator.

51. For an essay that takes such an approach see Maximillian E. Novak, "The Extended Moment: Time, Dream, History, and Perspective in Eighteenth-Century Ficton" in Backscheider, *Probability*, pp. 152 and 158.

52. Anna later demonstrates the process when she revises her understanding of Clarissa's entire story using only a few pieces of new evidence concerning Lovelace's evil nature and the "devilish house" in which he has placed her (III, 7).

53. Belton's death is in fact the occasion which temporarily draws Belford away from his role as major narrator at the end of the novel, thereby allowing Lovelace to "hunt" Clarissa again before our very eyes and to narrate his own dream and his interpretation of it to us directly. Also, Belton's words about the experience of dying curiously echo Clarissa's earlier response to Aunt Hervey who had reprimanded her for having "so apprehensive an imagination." Clarissa had insisted that "whatever we strongly imagined, was, in its effects at the time, *more* than imaginary, although to others it might not appear so" (I, 372). We are urged to grant that reality for Clarissa is whatever her mind perceives, though we as readers only partially experience her perspective. Again, the argument here parallels that of Andrew Baxter and Ralph Cudworth about the "reality" of the phenomenon of dreams.

54. Lovelace has a love of discovering allegory and metaphor (see for example IV, 167) even where they do not exist, as his fanciful attempt to decipher the iconography on his marriage certificate reveals (III, 180). Elsewhere he tries to apply a spider-and-fly metaphor to his relations with the Harlowes, but then wonders

whether the comparison "will not . . . do as well for the *entangled girls*" as for his relations with their parents (II, 23). He therefore has the capacity to recognize that the analysis of allegory is not at all a simple matter, yet he fails to put two and two together.

55. See Hill, "Epistle Dedicatory"; Artemidorus, 1690, p. 113 and 1722, p. 7. In describing his plans for a book, Lovelace distorts the titles. He says, "*Glanville of Witches* and Baxter's *History of Spirits and Apparitions*, and the *Royal Pedant's Demonology*, will be nothing at all to *Lovelace's Reveries*." The actual works in question are, most probably, Glanvill's *A Blow at Modern Sadducism* (London, 1668), later printed with a letter by Henry More and called *Sadducismus Triumphatus* (London, 1681); Richard Baxter's *The Certainty of the Worlds of Spirits* (London, 1681) or *Of the Nature of Spirits* (London, 1682), which was a reply to More in the former work; and King James I, *Daemonologie* (London, 1597). There is a certain irony in Lovelace's last choice, since King James wrote of the devil's ability to delude or "illude" us with dreams and of the power of witches to render men impotent.

56. He calls "marriage" the true "dramatic recompense" and comments that the "comedy" of his dealings with Clarissa can be made to end happily after all with their wedding (III, 410–411). These remarks have led one critic to comment that Lovelace's error was in trying to impose a comic form onto what was essentially a tragic situation. See William J. Palmer, "Two Dramatists: Lovelace and Richardson in *Clarissa*," *Studies in the Novel*, 5 (1973), 7–21.

57. David Hume, "Of Probability," in *Enquiries Concerning Human Understanding and Concerning the Principles of Morals*, ed. L. A. Selby-Bigge, 3rd ed. rev. by P. H. Nidditch (Oxford: Clarendon Press, 1975), p. 58.

58. Clarissa vividly describes to Anna the future she imagines that her marriage to Lovelace would all "too probably" bring (III, 519–521), and she concludes with a question, "What then . . . can I wish for but death?" She does not actively seek death, as she tells her doctor, but allows it to come upon her as it will.

59. This phenomenon shares certain affinities with what Gérard Genette describes as the analepses and prolepses which account for the "temporal omnipresence characteristic of Proustean narrative." See *Narrative Discourse: An Essay in Method*, trans. Jane E. Lewin (Ithaca, New York: Cornell University Press, 1980), p. 41.

Coalescence: David Hartley's "Great Apparatus"

STEPHEN H. FORD

Recent commentators on David Hartley have considered the mechanical and passive character of his view of the human mind, and the unity of the two parts of his work. Most writers, however, have not noticed the role played by coalescence in his conception of the mind and its ethical and religious development.[1] "Coalescence" is a key word in Hartley's *Observations on Man, His Frame, His Duty, and His Expectations*.[2] In his account of the acquisition of knowledge coalescence is the process by which intellectual ideas are generated from ideas of sensation. In his ethical and religious observations coalescence is the process by which the ultimate goal of human happiness is attained.

Hartley provides a comprehensive causal analysis of man in a hierarchy of approaches, from neurophysiology to metaphysics: "All that great *Apparatus* for carrying us from Body to Mind, and from Self-love to the pure Love of God, which the Doctrine of Association opens to View" (II, 387). In Hartley's view, the mental contents of sensations and ideas have a physical basis in the world and the human organism, and they are amenable to a simple explanation. Intellectual ideas, of which language and logic are instances, are derived from sensations by means of association and coalescence. There is a hierarchy of six classes of intellectual pleasures and pains: imagination, ambition, self-interest, sympathy, theopathy, and the moral sense. These pleasures aim at happiness, which ethics approximates through benevolence, but which religion accomplishes through resignation to God (II, 284). Man can be happy only by coalescing with God, who is infinite, and therefore, alone real. Appearance is false, because finite: God, the cause of all causes, annihilates appearance. He is the center or point towards which all things move, and in which alone man can rest. God is the abyss that absorbs all. There is no human unity of consciousness, for God is the sole consciousness that permeates and vanquishes appearance, including human intellectual ideas. There is no co-inherence or reconciliation of the finite and the infinite or of time and eternity. There is no repetition of the infinite in the finite mind: there is unity without multeity; there is the void of the infinite. God is the vortex into which the human mind vanishes.

Hartley presumes the distinctness of the mind from the body, the mental from the corporeal, and vibrations from feelings. Feelings are the contents of the mind, and they are divided into two sorts, sensations and ideas. Sensations are the immediate effects of impressions made by objects upon the body, the neurophysiological nature of which limits the capacity for sensation.[3] The sufficient repetition of a particular kind of sensation, seeing apples, for example, causes the disposition to remember or imagine an apple when none is perceptually present.[4] The simple idea of sensation is a vestige of, and resembles, the antecedent sensations of apples. In turn, simple ideas cause complex ideas; for example, the conception of a perfect apple or the appreciation of the figurative expression, "apple of one's eye." The crucial distinction between ideas of sensation and intellectual ideas is that the latter are complex: "It will appear in the Course of these Observations, that the *Ideas of Sensation* are the Elements of which all the rest are compounded. Hence *Ideas of Sensation* may be termed *simple, intellectual* ones *complex*" (I, ii). "Coalescence" is the name of the process whereby intellectual ideas are formed from ideas of sensation, and, ultimately, from sensation.

"Feeling" is ambiguous between "affect" and "cognition": all the contents of the mind are feelings in both senses, though the proportions vary. Hartley discusses the six classes of intellectual pleasures rather than intellectual ideas, for the chief importance of intellectual endeavor is the attainment of happiness. All pleasures and pains are feelings; all feelings (meaning sensations and ideas) "seem to be attended with some degree either of *Pleasure* or *Pain*" (I, iii). The affectivity must be high for the idea to be called a pleasure or pain: ideas whose affectivity has diminished through frequent repetition are mere ideas. "Burn," for example, is attended with a disagreeable feeling (I, 145), and Hartley concedes that in a general way all words may be attended with ideas or internal feelings (I, 278). The affective character of sensations and ideas indicates that man's fundamental motivation is the desire for happiness, which is pleasure. Pleasure is produced through sensations and ideas. Each stage of affective and cognitive development is preparatory for the next. A diminution of affectivity at the level of pleasures of the imagination, for example, is proximately transitional to the pleasures of ambition and ultimately transitional to the love of God. The pleasures of sensation lead to the intellectual pleasures that culminate in benevolence for men and animals, and, ultimately, love for God.[5] The fundamental motivation of the human being is the desire to rest in the infinite: this state is achieved through ever-descending cycles of pleasure followed by ennui, driving man down into the all-absorbing object of desire, the infinite, which Hartley calls "God." Human conduct is the "endless Grasping after Infinity" (II, 247). Cognition is subordinate to affectivity.

"Coalescence" is linked with "cause" in Hartley's observations. These investigations belong to the fields outlined in seven branches of knowledge. The sixth and seventh branches are natural philosophy and religion. The former is the application of mathematics, logic, and philology to natural phenomena. Natural philosophy includes in its parts "Medicine and Psychology, or the Theory of the human Mind, with that of the intellectual Principles of Brute Animals" (I, 354). Elsewhere he speaks of "the Analysis of the Mind" (I, 351). The analysis is a causal one: by "cause" he means that the same effect must result from the same set of previous circumstances. The principle of causality applies universally, extending to human acts:

> By the Mechanism of human Actions I mean, that each Action results from the previous Circumstances of Body and Mind, in the same manner, and with the same Certainty, as other Effects do from their mechanical Causes; so that a Person cannot do indifferently either of the Actions A, and its contrary a, while the previous Circumstances are the same; but is under an absolute Necessity of doing one of them, and that only. (I, 500)

"Mechanical" and "necessary" are linked with "cause." Motives, the chief of which is self-interest, and is directed ultimately to the infinite, are the causes of actions (I, 502). "Coalescence" is a causal expression, and names the causal principle by which intellectual ideas are derived from the single source of sensation.

By making sensation the sole source of intellectual ideas, mediated by ideas of sensation, Hartley excludes innate ideas, instinct, and reflection as sources.[6] Intellectual ideas are distinguished from sensory ideas by being complex. They differ in their manner of production, not in their source. On this point of theoretical simplicity he disagrees with John Locke: "First, then, It appears to me, that all the most complex Ideas arise from Sensation; and that Reflection is not a distinct Source, as Mr. *Locke* makes it" (I, 360).[7] Since ideas are both affective and cognitive, varying in proportion to the extent that frequent repetition has dulled their affectivity, all pains and pleasures arise from the pleasures and pains of sensation (I, 417 and 490; II, 213). Sensation, the source of all ideas, falls on the mental side of the great gulf between the body and the mind. The causal analysis of human conduct is deterministic, because the same set of preceding circumstances must bring about the same effect. The account is not materialistic, for the origin, sensation, is mental.

Sensation is itself causally explained by reference to antecedent circumstances: physical objects leave impressions upon the human body. Sensation is not identified with the vibrations or motions impressed upon the nervous system. The best account in physiological terms of the formation of sensations and ideas may be that vibrations cause them. The doctrine of association stands in a causal relation to the doctrine of vibrations: "One may expect, that *Vibrations* should infer *Association* as their Effect, and *Association* point to *Vibrations* as its Cause" (I, 6). Hartley does not, however, endeavor to go beyond a body-mind parallelism in his analysis.

Hartley offers a number of considerations of why it is difficult to be more precise concerning the mind-body relationship. The brain is not fully understood: he speaks of "the unknown internal Structure of the Brain, the great Instrument of Sense and Thought" (II, 361). A different physiological account of the nervous system is possible (I, 416 and 503), though he considers his account of the nerves as solid "capillaments" to be superior to the view that they are hollow tubes. The presumption of a body-mind dualism would have to be modified by the admission of an infinitesimal body mediating the connection between the nerves and the mind: he would have to surrender the claim that the nerves are the immediate instrument of sensation (I, 34). It may not be possible to discover the way in which vibrations are connected with sensations and ideas. They may be correlatable without one being able to specify which is the cause of which (I, 33), or whether vibrations are the physical causes, the occasional causes, or non-essential accompaniments of sensations (I, 511). Hartley denies that he is a materialist, for sensations and ideas cannot be ascribed to matter (I, 33). He denies as incompatible with the project of a causal analysis the hypothesis that the body is directly determined in its tendencies by a rational agent that produces effects not accountable in mechanistic terms (I, 266-267). Any account, then, must be mechanical.

Hartley claims that he has not attempted to characterize the connection, the efficient causal regularity, between the soul and body: "However, there remains one Chasm still, *viz.* that between Sensation, and the material Organs, which this Theory does not attempt to fill up. An immaterial Substance may be required for the simplest Sensation" (II, 383). Elsewhere he does endeavor to close the gap by suggesting that sensations are localized in the brain, and that a specific region of the brain is "originally fitted to receive, and, as one may say, sympathize with, such Vibrations as are likely to be impressed upon them in the various Incidents of Life" (I, 42). He also speaks of the various regions of the brain having a texture suited to specific vibrations. The optic and aural nerves, for example, cannot replace one another; nerves, too, are predisposed to vibrate. Each region has its own natural vibrations: impressions caused by an object produce vibrations of a kind that will, with sufficient repetition, change the natural vibrations of a particular region of the brain to the preternatural vibrations correlated with a particular sensation and its derivative ideas (I, 60-61). The gap, however, may not be closed if an immaterial substance must mediate the transfer from the physical to the mental. Hartley, then, is not certain concerning the manner of the relationship between the corporeal and the mental. The relevant propositions are "true, in a very useful practical Sense, yet they are not so in an ultimate and precise one" (I, 34). He is prepared to advance his account of the genesis of intellectual ideas without the doctrine of vibrations as the neurophysiological basis (I, 416).

The superiority of the doctrine of vibrations consists in the greater ease with which vibrations are propagated along solid, rather than hollow, nerves: "The *Vibrations* hereafter to be described may more easily be conceived to be propagated along solid Capillaments, so uniform in their Texture as to be pellucid when singly taken, than along hollow *Tubuli*" (I, 17). The mode of propagation is "in some such manner as Sound runs along the Surfaces of Rivers, or an electrical Virtue along hempen Strings" (I, 88).

All ideas are produced from sensation by a single process, association, which consists in the single principle of contiguity: groups of ideas are successive or synchronous. He achieves an economy of explanation by extending the application of association from habit and custom to the whole range of human conduct. Reasoning is an associative product: "But I have endeavoured to show in these Papers, that all Reasoning, as well as Affection, is the mere Result of Association" (I, 499). Association, he remarks, is "the Power of Habit" (I, 96). He wishes, however, to preserve the distinction between intellect and sensory perception: to do so he must at some point introduce a further explanatory principle. Coalescence is that principle.

Hartley claims that the analysis of the mind is a quantitative causal analysis, and he proposes that mathematics is the explanatory mould into which "the History and Analysis of the Sensations, Motions, and Ideas" (I, 416) should be cast. Quantity is the primary category into which all others may be reduced:

> It appears also not impossible, that future Generations should put all Kinds of Evidences and Inquiries into mathematical Forms; and, as it were, reduce *Aristotle's* ten Categories, and Bishop *Wilkins's* forty *Summa Genera*, to the Head of Quantity alone, so as to make Mathematics and Logic, Natural History, and Civil History, Natural Philosophy, and Philosophy of all other Kinds, coincide *omni ex parte*. (I, 351)

With sensation as the single source, and association as the single process, Hartley intends to give an analysis of the intellectual ideas and their pleasures and pains, distinguishing ideas of sensation from intellectual ideas by the pair of expressions "simple" and "complex." "Coalescence" is paired with "complex." "Coalescence" replaces "reflection" as the crucial expression in a purely quantitative analysis of mind, and marks the secondary principle of explanation needed in psychology.

To the extent to which there is a neurophysiological parallel to mental phenomena the quantitative analysis can be expressed both in terms of the psychological doctrine of association, and in terms of the physiological doctrine of vibrations and vibratiuncles (minuscule vibrations in the nerves produced by vibrations induced by impressions upon the nervous system). The frequency of the occurrence of vibrations to produce vibratiuncles (dispositions to vibrate, corresponding to ideas), and the frequency of occurrence required to cause fatigue or fading (the loss of affectivity accompanying the final stage of formation of a new complex idea) are the factors. The neurophysiological account is basic, for the genesis of sensations and ideas is constrained by the nature of the nervous system. This account may be sufficient; words, heard or seen, are treated as impressions, *i.e.* physical items (I, 268). From the vantage point of infinity, which alone is real, both accounts are false. For the limited purpose of elucidating what we mean by intellectual ideas Hartley calls them complex ideas, and to explain complexity he uses the key expression "coalescence."

An intellectual idea is a coalescence of simple ideas:

> And, upon the Whole, it may appear to the Reader, that the simple Ideas of Sensation must run into Clusters and Combinations, by Association; and that each of these will, at last, coalesce into one complex Idea, by the Approach and Commixture of the several compounding Parts.
>
> It appears also from Observation, that many of our intellectual ideas, such as those that belong to the Heads of Beauty, Honour, moral Qualities, *&c.* are, in Fact, thus composed of Parts, which, by degrees, coalesce into one complex Idea.
>
> And as this Coalescence of simple Ideas into complex ones is thus evinced, both by the foregoing Theory, and by Observation, so it may be illustrated, and farther confirmed, by the similar Coalescence of Letters into Syllables and Words, in which Association is likewise a chief Instrument. (I, 74–75)

"Coalesce" is paired with "commixture" and "complex," and is distinguished from "cluster," "combination," "simple," and "association." Coalescence is the final step in the formation of complex ideas: a single idea is formed from a number of ideas.

The primary characteristic of a coalescence is that the single whole "appears to bear no Relation to its component Parts" (I, 322). That an intellectual idea is indeed complex can be determined by attending to the cluster of ideas about to coalesce. Personal beauty, for example, is a complex idea:

> The reciprocal Influences of our Ideas upon each other, and the endless Variety of their Combinations, are eminently conspicuous in this Article; the Strength of Desire here rendering the Associations, with the several Steps previous to the perfect Coalescence of the Ideas associated, more visible than in most other Cases.
> (I, 436–437)

The doctrine of the association of ideas makes it possible to understand coalescence, for the steps leading to the formation of complex ideas can be reversed:

> It is of the utmost Consequence to Morality and Religion, that the Affections and Passions should be analysed into their simple compounding Parts, by reversing the Steps of the Associations which concur to form them. (I, 81)

One can introspect the onset of coalescence in one's own case, or examine the circumstances likely to produce complex ideas in another's case:

> these several particular Pleasures coalesce into a single general one, in which the compounding Parts cannot be discerned separately from each other, and which consequently appears to have no Relation to its several compounding Parts; unless when by a particular Attention to, and Examination of, what passes in our Minds, we lay hold of the last compounding Parts before their intire Coalescence, or reason upon the Causes of these Pleasures, by comparing their Growth, and the Changes made in them, with the concomitant Circumstances. (I, 433)

The fusion or coalescence of parts into a whole is inferred by noticing that the parts are in the process of fusing. Hartley's analysis of the mind is of particular importance for him for morality and religion, the complex ideas of which are a particular kind of coalesced idea.

Coalescence, however, applies not only to the formation of complex, intellectual ideas, but to sensations as well. The illustration that he gives of coalescence is the taste of a compound medicine:

> Thus, in a very compound Medicine, the several Tastes and Flavours of the separate Ingredients are lost and overpowered by the complex one of the whole Mass: So that this has a Taste and

> Flavour of its own, which appears to be simple and original, and like that of a natural Body. (I, 75)

The compound taste is nonetheless a sensation, not the vestige or trace of a sensation. The compound medicine can, of course, be analyzed, and each ingredient separately tasted. A recipe for the medicine allows one to produce the distinctive flavor: the taste is not analyzable by inspection, but knowing the recipe enables the investigator to discover the way in which the complex but original taste is formed.

Taste is a paradigm of coalescence and its role in the development of the human mind from the sensations and pleasures of the body: the

> Pleasures of the Taste, considered as extending itself from the Mouth thro' the whole alimentary Duct, are very considerable, and frequently repeated; they must therefore be one chief Means, by which pleasurable States are introduced into the Brain, and nervous System. These pleasurable States must, after some time, leave Miniatures of themselves . . . . When Groupes of these Miniatures have been long and closely connected with particular Objects, they coalesce into one complex Idea, appearing, however, to be a simple one; and so begin to be transferred upon other Objects, and even upon Tastes back again. . . . And from this way of Reasoning it may now appear, that a great Part of our intellectual Pleasures are ultimately deducible from those of Taste. . . .
>
> The social Pleasures seem, in a particular manner, to be derived from this Source; since it has been customary in all Ages and Nations, and is, in a manner, necessary, that we should enjoy the Pleasures of Taste in Conjunction with our Relatives, Friends, and Neighbours.
>
> . . . And thus it may appear, that there ought to be a great reciprocal Influence between the Mind and alimentary Duct, agreeably to common Observation; which is farther confirmed by the very large Number of Nerves distributed there. (I, 166-167)

The bodily pleasures of eating are repeated frequently. That we enjoy dining with others shows that the pleasure is not purely a pleasure of sensation, but a complex of pleasures: the pleasures of benevolence towards those with whom we dine, and the pleasures of refined and edifying conversation upon wholesome topics tend towards the improvement of the mind in its grasping towards the infinite source of human happiness. The path of progress for the mind arises in the alimentary canal and in the social context of feeding.

Language illustrates and confirms coalescence, for letters coalesce into syllables and words (I, 75): a child first learns the alphabet, and then is able to read without spelling (I, 319). Language is analyzable "up to a few simple Sounds" (I, 75). It develops as feelings, both cognitive and affective, are associated with sounds and marks. Being able to read without spelling is a result of the formation of an indivisible idea:

> And when Association has so far cemented the component Parts of any Aggregate of Ideas, Pleasures and Pains, together, as that they appear one indivisible Idea, Pleasure or Pain, the Child must be supposed by an analogous Association to have learnt to read without spelling. (I, 319)

The cementing into an indivisible idea is the process of coalescence. Being able to read is a result of being able to form intellectual ideas. Coalescence is followed by a decrease in affectivity so that the newly formed whole becomes a mere idea, and becomes the means for a further development in language. Language is "the principal Means by which we make intellectual and moral Improvements" (I, 287). The importance of language training for children, therefore, cannot be underestimated, for "Children may be formed and moulded as we please" (II, 453).

Metaphor and figurative language generally represent the stage in linguistic coalescence where the affectivity produced by the cementing of the components is most pronounced. Indeed, the metaphors of "live," "dead," and "moribund" draw attention to the affectivity of language. Ordinarily, metaphors die and become new literal expressions through the entire decay of the affective component. In this way language grows:

> Many, or most common Figures, pass so far into literal Expressions by Use, *i.e.* Association, that we do not attend at all to their figurative Nature. And thus by degrees figurative Senses become a Foundation for successive Figures, in the same manner, as originally literal Senses.
>
> It is evident, that if a Language be narrow, and much confined to sensible Things, it will have great Occasion for Figures: These will naturally occur in the common Intercourses of Life, and will in their Turn, as they become literal Expressions in the secondary Senses, much augment and improve the Language, and assist the Invention. (I, 292–293)

He thinks that dead metaphors can be revived, and that they are revived by renewing their affectivity by comparing the metaphorical meaning with the foundational literal meaning, which meanings have coalesced and faded into the new or secondary literal meaning:

> Now figurative Words seem to strike and please us chiefly from that Impropriety which appears at first Sight, upon their Application to the Things denoted by them, and from the consequent Heightening of the Propriety, as soon as it is duly perceived. For when figurative Words have recurred so often as to excite the secondary Idea instantaneously, and without any previous Harshness to the Imagination, they lose their peculiar Beauty and Force; and, in order to recover this, and make ourselves sensible of it, we are obliged to recal [sic] the literal Sense, and to place the literal and figurative Senses close together, that so we may first be sensible of the Inconsistency, and then be more affected with the Union and Coalescence. (I, 429)

One is first struck with the inconsistency of calling Herod a fox—for Herod is a man, not a fox. One is next impressed by the appropriateness of the remark, for both Herod and a fox are crafty (by analogy). Figures of speech cease to be figures when they do not elicit this pair of responses. Craftiness is the secondary idea of "fox" in "Herod is a fox." Should "fox" come to mean "crafty," it would be a new literal meaning bypassing "animal." The original literal meaning has coalesced with the secondary, now new literal meaning. The restoration of the original figurative meaning requires that one regain the original literal sense of "fox" and read "Herod is a fox" as "Herod is impossibly both a fox and a man, and he is, analogous to a fox (or, 'fox' in lore), crafty." The inconsistency lies in implying that Herod is not a human being; the union and coalescence lie in suppressing the zoological sense of "fox," accentuating its emblematic meaning. Coalescence furthers the development of language through combining components, even incompatible ones, to create a new expression. The repetition of the new expression leads to a decay of its affectivity, that is, its beauty. The only word that does not lose its power to affect the mind, according to Hartley, is "God," a word which dominates all the words brought into relation with it.

Language exemplifies the limitation of coalescence. The great variety of the components associated and aggregated may prevent intellectual ideas, essentially complex, from coalescing together. Letters "adhere closer together" in words than words do in sentences (I, 77). In infinity, everything coalesces into infinity or God. Within the domain of appearance, inhabited by sensations and ideas, there are sentences that are coalescences, which Hartley explains neurophysiologically. Association, he claims, is the "general Law, according to which the Intellectual World is framed and conducted" (II, 21). In the case of logic he appeals beyond the doctrine of association to the doctrine of vibrations to account for the notion of logical necessity. Logic, according to Hartley, is the foundation of all science, and must itself be certain. Certainty is explained by coalescence: "This *summum Genus* is the necessary Coalescence of the Subject with the Predicate" (I, 359). The basis of all knowledge is the identity of subject and predicate: "A is A." The self-evidence of this identity is grounded in neurophysiology; language and logic are treated non-mentally:

> The necessary Coalescence just spoken of carries its own Evidence with it. It is necessary from the Nature of the Brain. . . . And we need only inquire into the History of the Brain, and the physiological Influences of Words and Symbols upon it by Association, in order to see this. I am also inclined to believe, that the Method here proposed of considering Words and Sentences as Impressions, whose Influence upon the Mind is intirely to be determined by the Associations heaped upon them in the Intercourses of Life . . . will cast much Light upon logical Subjects. . . . (I, 359-360)

Logical necessity is to be explained neurophysiologically by reference to the nature and operation of the nervous system and the brain. Logic is to be explained in quantitative terms with respect to the vibrations or physical motions in the brain. "Impressions" belong to the physical side of the mind-body divide, for they are the motions caused to the nervous system by objects. In this case the objects are the words and sentences spoken, considered as impressions that produce vibrations in the hearer. The canons of correct reasoning are the laws, the descriptive laws, of the manner in which the brain works. "Coalescence" implies "identity." In principle, all sentences should collapse into a single identity for a mind so constituted that there are no limits to its capacity for uniting a range of particulars. A timeless mind would entertain a single true statement. This discussion of logic and language shows that Hartley does suppose that a neurophysiological and quantitative analysis is possible, basic, and sufficient.

"Coalescence" is a central expression in ethics and religion, for the pleasures of the love of God and man represent the higher stages in human affective and cognitive development. The pleasures of the intellect, from imagination to the moral sense, are based on the pleasures of sensation; they are the ones of which we are first capable (II, 213). They alone are original, and are the common source for the intellectual pleasures (I, 417). The higher pleasures presuppose the lower pleasures; the lower pleasures coalesce with the higher so that the higher are the sum of the antecedent components. These components are no longer discrete, and so appear to bear no resemblance to the aggregate of the sensible pleasures constituting them (II, 213). They affect the entire nervous system instead of being confined to one region as sensible pleasures are (II, 214). The ingredients of the pleasures of honor and ambition "are so mixed amongst one another, as hardly to be discernible separately" (I, 455). The love of God, the ultimate goal of human intellectual development, is a coalescence of a great variety of sources, including naked self-interest, whether gross, refined, or rational:

> The Love of God is, according to this Theory, evidently deduced in part from interested Motives directly; *viz.* from the Hopes of a future Reward; and those Motives to it, or Sources of it, in which direct explicit Self-interest does not appear, may yet be analysed up to it ultimately. However, after all the several Sources of the Love of God have coalesced together, this Affection becomes as disinterested as any other; as the Pleasure we take in any natural or artificial Beauty, in the Esteem of others, or even in sensual Gratifications. (I, 490)

The doctrine of association is a method of analyzing a whole to show that it does indeed consist of parts, contrary to all appearance. Coalescence, then, is not an instance of association, but a phenomenon to be understood by an analysis of the associations that serve as the cause of, because antecedent to, the coalescence. Coalescence is the apparatus that is disclosed by associative analysis. While the love for God is a coalescence, one of its sources, gross self-interest, seems evident: the motivation to benevolence, piety, and the moral sense is the approbation of God, the greatest of honors (II, 264). The love of God appears, then, to fall under the pleasure of ambition.

The progress from the pleasures of sensation to the love for God is effected through the alternation of coalescence and fading. With the fading of the pleasure into a mere idea, the desire for ultimate happiness remains unsatisfied (I, 489-490): the mere idea, along with the pain of dissatisfaction, leads to the formation of the next level of pleasure. It is not possible to advance to the ultimate pleasure of loving God by endeavoring to achieve ultimate happiness through renewing pleasure at a lower level, denying its subordinate character. It is an error, for example, to value knowledge for itself (I, 298). It is neurophysiologically determined that human beings may mistake the object that produces ultimate happiness. It is dubtful that one remains mistaken, for Hartley thinks that divine causality is ineluctable in its operation upon the human frame:

> It appears likewise, that all Aggregates of Pleasure, thus collected by them all [i.e., by the means of happiness], must, from the Mechanism and Necessity of our Natures, and of the World which surrounds us, be made at last to centre and rest upon Him who is the inexhaustible Fountian of all Power, Knowledge, Goodness, Majesty, Glory, Property, &c. So that even Avarice and Ambition are, in their respective Ways, carrying on the benevolent Designs of Him who is *All in All*. (I, 463)

The collections of pleasure finally center and rest in their source by coalescing with it. The fading of the subordinate pleasures is the chief means by which the human being is directed from the pleasures of sensation at the circumstances through the converging series of the more valuable, because intellectual, pleasures. The pleasures of the imagination, for example, the pursuit of literature (II, 243), take a good deal of time to develop and practice; there are too many of them to develop fully, and their frequent repetition breeds boredom:

> The frequent Repetition of these Pleasures cloys, as in other Cases: And though the whole circle of them is so extensive, as that it might, in some measure, obviate this Objection; yet the human Fancy is too narrow to take in this whole Circle, and the greatest Virtuosos do, in fact, seldom apply themselves to more than one or two considerable Branches. (II, 242)

The intellectual pleasures generally, with the exception of the love of God, require renewal if their affectivity is not to fade completely (I, 275). The capacity for intellectual pleasure is neurophysiologically determined. As Hartley puts it: "our Capacity for receiving Pleasure depends upon our Associations, and upon the State of the medullary Substance of the Brain ..."(II, 274). The central difficulty for Hartley's view is to reconcile the satisfaction of man's ultimate desire for the infinite with his limited capacity for enjoyment.

The fading of the pleasures of the imagination directs man to the next inward circle and, finally, to God. The wide range of the pleasures of the imagination, their unlimited character, appeals to, but cannot satisfy, the longing for ultimate happiness. The need for renewal of the pleasures proceeding from the imagination should be recognized to be the sign that one should press inwards and downwards to God, the sole adequate object of man's desire:

> It may be remarked, that the Pleasures of Imagination point to Devotion in a particular manner by their unlimited Nature. For all Beauty, both natural and artificial, begins to fade and languish after a short Acquaintance with it: Novelty is a never-failing Requisite: We look down, with Indifference and Contempt, upon what we comprehend easily; and are ever aiming at, and pursuing, such Objects as are but just within the Compass of our present Faculties. What is it now, that we ought to learn from this Dissatisfaction to look behind us, and Tendency to press forward; from this endless Grasping after Infinity? Is it not, that the infinite Author of all Things has so formed our Faculties, that nothing less than himself can be an adequate Object for them? (II, 246–247)

This "endless Grasping after Infinity," the dissatisfaction of the aesthetic mode of life, motivates one to pursue God. It is an essential stage in the growing recognition of which mode of life is the proper one. While the frequent repetition of the pleasures of the imagination produces pain (I, 397), the pleasures of religion can be repeated without palling, for they are infinite (I, 398). Religion is of ultimate concern to human beings, for God alone can satisfy man's "endless Grasping after Infinity," affording him true rest. Religion is the sole criterion of the value of all pleasure (I, 442). Benevolence, for example, may be pursued nearly without limit, and it can be improved by piety and the moral sense, producing a diminution of selfishness (II, 286). Compassion, one aspect of benevolence, arises from selfishness coalescing with the uneasiness of another's misery (I, 475).

The moral sense is superior to benevolence, for it not only improves benevolence but goes further inward to its infinite center. The moral sense is the crowning intellectual achievement, for it is "the Sum total of all the rest, and the ultimate Result from them" (I, 497), and consists in "the pure Love of God, as our highest and ultimate Perfection, our End, Centre, and only Resting-place, to which yet we can never attain" (I, 497). Religion comprehends all other knowledge and their pleasures (I, 367). Benevolence is perfected through love of God: "we are led by the Love of good Men to that of God, and back again by the Love of God to that of all his Creatures in and through him . . . "(II, 283). Nonetheless, God is attained finally, and there cannot ultimately be a return from God. While benevolence and its pleasures bear repeating, they are not pure. Benevolence is but a goad to God: "And yet Disappointments must sometimes happen to the purest Benevolence; else our Love of God, and Resignation to his Will, which is the highest Principle of all, could not be brought to Perfection" (II, 284). The love of God is superior to benevolence. Benevolence produces the social happiness of a community, the mystical body of Christ, to which political communities are analogous in being collections of individuals (II, 306–307), where happiness circulates ceaselessly from one sentient being to the next (II, 287). Language is the way in which happiness unites the individuals of the society: "by means of a perfect and adequate Language, they might be like new Senses and Powers of Perception to each other, and both give to and receive from each other Happiness indefinitely" (I, 320). This compound body of sentient beings constitutes a society of individuals, and individuals they remain in the enjoyment of felicitous rapport. Ultimate happiness for Hartley, however, is not social; man grasps for the infinite, and coalescence with it.

"Centre" is a key model-expression for God (I, 463 and 497; II, 282, 310, 313, 328), and is connected with the claim that God, the infinite, alone is a cause or creator, and real. The causality that is the subject of Hartley's natural philosophy of man is not genuine causality at all, for human judgments, being finite, are always false. Hartley's observations are a meditation to develop resignation. God unites with, and becomes, all human ideas. All ideas vanish into the idea of God:

> God is our Centre, and the Love of Him a Pleasure superior to all the rest, not only on account of the Mixture of Pain in all the rest, . . . but also because they all point to it, like so many Lines terminating in the same Centre. When Men have entered sufficiently into the Ways of Piety, God appears more and more to them in the whole Course and Tenor of their Lives; and by uniting himself with all their Sensations, and intellectual Perceptions, overpowers all the Pains; augments, and attracts to himself, all the Pleasures. Every thing sweet, beautiful, or glorious, brings in the Idea of God, mixes with it, and vanishes into it. For all is God's; he is the only Cause and Reality; and the Existence of every thing else is only the Effect, Pledge, and Proof, of his Existence and Glory.
> (II, 312–313)

The course of human life is not only an enlargement of the capacities for enjoying the pleasures of the intellect as a human activity, but it is an invasion by the divine into the human sphere. All the pleasures of sensation and the intellect, in so far as they have the qualities of ultimate happiness, being sweet and beautiful ideas, "bring in" and "mix" with the idea of God, and "vanish" into the idea of God. There is no difference for Hartley between saying that God is the center or that God appears, and saying that something mixes with the idea of God. All ideas, then, including the ideas of the self, sink into the infinite. There are not, then, individual human minds, being finite, distinct from the single infinite mind, any more than there could be two distinct infinite beings. Finite beings vanish into the infinite vortex.

The model of the infinite as a series of lines converging on the center of the infinite perfection and happiness (II, 213) can be exchanged for a three-dimensional model. Hartley speaks of God as a fountain, and as an abyss: "All Meditations upon God, who is the inexhaustible Fountain, and infinite Abyss, of all Perfection, both natural and moral" (I, 497). The infinite wells up into its finite creatures and draws them down an ever-narrowing funnel of "higher" pleasures by pain to the final rest of resignation and annihilation. We ought not to be satisfied with ourselves, says Hartley, paradoxically, "till we arrive at perfect Self-annihilation, and the pure Love of God" (II, 282). Self-annihilation corresponds to becoming "*Partakers of the Divine Nature*" (II, 312). Since all will be absorbed into the divine, the divine alone is permanent:

> and that as we advance in Perfection, the Associations relating to

> the one only, ultimate, infinite Cause, must at last overpower all the rest; that we shall pay no Regards but to God alone; and that all Resentment, Demerit, Sin and Misery, will be utterly annihilated and absorbed by his infinite Happiness and Perfections. For our Associations being in this, as in many other Cases, inconsistent with each other, our first gross and transitory ones must yield to those which succeed and remain. (I, 506–507)

The only association that could remain is the idea of God, for the infinite overpowers whatever is finite, whether finitely good or finitely evil.

The infinite being alone has the real and correct viewpoint for making judgments. Judgments made finitely are "false and delusive":

> Different finite Beings form different Judgments according to their different Experiences, and ways of Reasoning. Who therefore shall be made the Standard? Not the inferior Orders certainly. And, if the superior, we shall not be able to rest, till we conclude, that all that appears to all finite Beings, is false and delusive; and that the Judgment of the infinite Being is the only true real Judgment. (II, 422)

That one must be infinite in order to make correct judgments vitiates Hartley's entire project, unless he has grounds for supposing that he can make the judgment that the judgment of God alone is true and real. Hartley does make this claim; for he speaks of taking "our Station in the Divine Nature, and view[ing] every thing from thence, and in the Relation which it bears to God" (II, 310).

Viewing everything from the divine standpoint is approximated in finite experience in that finite capacities are enlarged throughout life, and this development makes it possible to unite "different and opposite Sensations into one" (II, 27). Indeed, should our capacities be sufficiently large, all sensations, causally connected, would be "esteemed one Sensation" (II, 27), for they are only relatively simple, being infinitely divisible, and consisting of successive and coexistent parts (I, 56; II, 27). Time is overcome in infinity, and since causality (excluding divine causality because it is atemporal) is a temporal relation between cause and effect, there is in infinity no sensation at all. Infinity or reality is purely intellectual:

> For all Time, whether past, present, or future, is present Time in the Eye of God, and all Ideas coalesce into one to him; and this one is infinite Happiness, without any Mixture of Misery, *viz.* by the

> infinite Prepollence of Happiness above Misery, so as to annihilate it; and this merely by considering Time as it ought to be considered in Strictness, *i.e.* as a relative Thing, belonging to Beings of finite Capacities, and varying with them, but which is infinitely absorbed in the pure Eternity of God. Now the Appearance of Things to the Eye of an infinite Being must be called their real Appearance in all Propriety. (II, 28)

Association is a temporal process; coalescence is an instantaneous formation of a whole. Without time, all ideas coalesce into one, a single, complex intellectual idea, whose component parts cannot be distinguished. No analysis, being temporal, could be performed. The idea, infinite happiness, is predominantly affective. Not only are there not sensations in God, there are not ideas either, but a single idea. If, as Hartley suggests, finite beings can take up a position in the divine nature, nothing distinguishes my position in the divine nature from your position, and from the divine nature itself.

Hartley in one place speaks of consciousness as the accompaniment of thoughts and actions: "that Consciousness which accompanies our Thoughts and Actions, and by which we connect ourselves with ourselves from time to time" (I, 390). He accounts for assenting to a proposition as the addition of the feeling associated with the word "truth" to the proposition (I, 324). Analogously, there is a feeling of selfhood:

> Thus, suppose a Person, whose nervous System is disordered, to turn his Thoughts accidentally to some barely possible Good or Evil. If the nervous Disorder falls in with this, it increases the Vibrations belonging to its Idea so much, as to give it a Reality, a Connexion with *Self*. For we distinguish the Recollection and Anticipation of things relating to ourselves, from those of things relating to other Persons, chiefly by the Difference of Strength in the Vibrations, and in their Coalescences with each other. (I, 401)

Hartley firmly rejects the expression "unity of consciousness"; he claims the physical-mental duality would be overcome through the union of vibrations with mental contents:

> In like manner the Unity of Consciousness seems to me an inconclusive Argument. For Consciousness is a mental Perception; and if Perception be a Monad, then every inseparable Adjunct of it must be so too, *i.e.* Vibrations, according to this Theory, which is evidently false. Not to mention, that it is difficult to know what is

meant by the Unity of Consciousness. (I, 512)

On the contrary, that consciousness produces a monad is evidently true for Hartley, and he has made it quite clear what the unity of consciousness is. The coalescence of the physical with the mental, and the absorption of the physical by the mental, is precisely what takes place in the infinite mind of God: God is the Monad and the presiding rational agent in Hartley's metaphysics. A unity of consciousness is implied by his claims that human beings can participate in the divine nature, and can see things as God does. It is not possible for appearance to maintain its separate existence. There is no distinction between the thought of the infinite mind and the mind itself: the idea of God is God. Consciousness is infinite, and annihilates the finite. Things resist consciousness, but only apparently. In the Eye of God all is coalesced.

The problem of unity in Hartley's thought arises from his conception of unity as coalescence. His own principle of distinguishing efficient causes from final causes, and his program of discovering causal regularities through attending to efficient causes in the fields of medicine and the analysis of the mind, are overthrown by his conception of the divine and the relationship of God to man. Since God is "the Cause of Causes, the one only Source of all Power" (I, 508), then finite selfhood cannot ultimately be sustained. We should realize, says Hartley, "that God is the sole Spring of all Action" (II, 321). To suppose that human beings are agents is to impugn divine sovereignty. True humility requires that we reject the doctrine of philosophical free will, "For philosophical Free-will supposes, that God has given to each Man a Sphere of Action, in which he does not interpose; but leaves Man to act intirely from himself, independently of his Creator . . . " (II,268). Human mental acts of thought, reflection, and reasoning are likewise actions whose cause is God. The supernatural inspiration of the Scriptures is not different in kind from other acts, "it being evident from obvious Reasonings, as well as from the foregoing Theory, that the natural Workings of the Mind are not to be distinguished from those, which a Being that has a sufficient Power over our intellectual Frame, might excite in us" (II, 82). The mind-body parallelism with which Hartley ostensibly begins, and his account of the acquisition of knowledge through engagement with the world by means of objects impressing traces in the brain, is an unsatisfactory account of the human mind. It is unsatisfactory because it is inconsistent, not because the doctrines of vibrations and association are mechanical, necessitarian, or empirically false. The attempt to give an account of the mind and the body, as Hartley does, is inconsistent with the postulate of a presiding rational agent who alone is the real cause. Hartley prizes, not mathematics, but the certainty of intuitive knowledge that mathematics represents. The foundation of all knowledge is the coalescent identity of subject and object, best exemplified by the idea of God, not by the logical statement, "A is A." God alone knows all things timelessly and therefore intuitively. The quest for happiness is the quest for certainty; it is achieved when the finite mind takes its station in the divine nature, though in fact it never has been outside. Since the finite mind is no more than its ideas, grounded, not in brain traces, but in God, there are not in reality finite minds at all. All apparent reality, according to Hartley, must be understood as coalescing with, and vanishing into, the idea of God. The idea of God has no other content than God; for the greater annihilates the smaller.

There is no community within God; for we could not distinguish the members of that community:

> For, if we suppose more than one, it is plain, since the Attributes of infinite Power, Knowlege, and Goodness, include all possible Perfection, that they must be intirely alike to each other, without the least possible Variation. They will therefore intirely coalesce in our Idea, *i.e.* be one to us. Since they fill all Time and Space, and are all independent, omnipotent, omniscient, and infinitely benevolent, their Ideas cannot be separated, but will have a numerical, as well as a generical, Identity. (II, 30)

Coalescence implies numerical identity. There is no community within God; there cannot be community with God. The coalescence of the idea of God with all other ideas, by the same token, implies that there is only one idea. Hartley's conception of God's unity as an undifferentiated whole constitutes the fundamental objection to his thought. The last word about man and God is not "coalescence."[8]

NOTES

1. James Engell, *The Creative Imagination: Enlightenment to Romanticism* (Cambridge, Mass.: Harvard University Press, 1981), pp. 67–68 and 170–171; Thomas McFarland, *Coleridge and the Pantheist Tradition* (Oxford: Clarendon Press, 1969), p. 312. Also see note 8 below.
2. David Hartley, *Observations on Man, His Frame, His Duty, and His Expectations*, 2 vols. (London, 1749; rpt. Hildesheim: Georg Olms Verlagsbuchhandlung, 1967). All further references are to this edition, giving volume and page numbers.
3. *Observations*, I, "Introduction", p. ii. Hartley says that we may overestimate our capacity for pleasure and happiness, which capacity "depends upon our Associations, and upon the State of the medullary Substance of the Brain; and consequently that it must fail often" (II, 274).
4. Hartley suggests a "thousand joint Impressions" (I, 68).
5. Of animals Hartley says, "if they should be Partakers of the same Redemption as well as of our Fall, and be Members of the same mystical Body, this would have a particular Tendency to increase our Tenderness for them" (II, 223).
6. For instance, "the Pleasures of Honour and Ambition are not of an original, instinctive, implanted Nature, but derived from the other Pleasures of human Life, by the Association of these into various Parcels, where the several Ingredients are so mixed amongst one another, as hardly to be discernible separately" (I, 455).
7. John Locke, *An Essay concerning Human Understanding*, ed. P. H. Nidditch (Oxford: Clarendon Press, 1975), pp. 127–128.
8. Along with the work on Hartley cited in note 1, also see the following:
   Appleyard, J. A. *Coleridge's Philosophy of Literature: The Development of a Concept of Poetry 1791–1819.* Cambridge, Massachusetts: Harvard University Press, 1965. Hartley's *Observations* is unified by the moral and religious principles made explicit in the second part. The account is inadequate because of its denial of personal freedom (pp. 27–28). "Coalescence" is not noted. Against the claim that an account of the conditions of perception is offered, but not of the connection of things, I suggest that Hartley's claim that God is the only cause implies that these distinct issues are inseparable, if not identical, in this context (p. 45).
   Christensen, Jerome. *Coleridge's Blessed Machine of Language.* Ithaca, N.Y.: Cornell University Press, 1981. The first three chapters are devoted to Hartley and his importance for Coleridge: "Observations on Hartley," "Hartley's Influence on Coleridge," and "The Marginal Method of the *Biographia Literaria.*" It is suggested that Hartley's mechanism is "developmental": vibrations and God are co-present through each stage, and the transitions are "ostensibly qualitative" (p. 53). Hartley endeavored, but failed, to achieve unity, for his particular account of knowledge endangers his moral and theological holism (p. 84). I suggest that "coalescence" expresses both of these topics, with the difference that Hartley's theological holism annihilates his epistemology. I was led by Christensen's title to search for an associative counterpart: deridably they trope like fantastic tools.
   Delkeskamp, Corinna. "Medicine, Science, and Moral Philosophy: David Hartley's Attempt at Reconciliation." *The Journal of Medicine and Philosophy*, 2 (1977), 162–176. Hartley's account of human acts is insufficient for the ascription of praise and blame (174–175). I suggest that an examination of Hartley's

attempt should take account of his claim that difficulties arise only if the popular language of liberty is mixed with the philosophical language of necessity (*Observations*, II, 56 and 58).

Fairchild, Hoxie N. "Hartley, Pistorius, and Coleridge." *PMLA*, 62 (1947), 1010-1021. The unity of Hartley's *Observations* is defended, for his "pseudo-mystical pantheism" is continuous with the theories of association and brain processes (1018-1019).

Ferg, Stephen. "Two Early Works by David Hartley." *Journal of the History of Philosophy*, 19 (1981), 173-189. Two anonymous works earlier than the *Observations* are Hartley's, including *An Introduction towards an Essay on the Origin of the Passions* (London, 1741) and another work usually attributed to James Long, titled *An Enquiry into the Origin of the Human Appetites and Affections, Shewing How Each Arises from Association* (London, 1747). Ferg points out that the two-language argument is a qualified free-will position. Hartley, therefore, did not totally abandon libertarianism in embracing necessitarianism (187-188). These two works are important for the contribution they make to the study of the development of Hartley's thought (188).

Gingerich, S. F. "From Necessity to Transcendentalism in Coleridge." *PMLA*, 35 (NS 28) (1920), 1-59. Unity is a constant in Coleridge's religious philosophy from the necessitarian phase to the transcendentalist phase. Freedom of the will, and other transcendent qualities, make possible a unity with God superior to the unity effected through a necessary and necessitated deity (59). Coleridge's conception of unity, I would argue, differs from Hartley's as perichoresis differs from coalescence.See *Theology*, 99 (January, 1986), 20-24.

Giuntini, Chiara. "Attrazione e associazione: Hartley e le leggi della natura umana." *Rivista di Filosofia*, 71 (1980), 198-229. Hartley's *Observations* is a unity. There are references to Marsh and Oberg (202-203). The coalescence of simple ideas implies that the mechanism of association has been transformed into a chemistry of the mind (222).

Hatch, Ronald B."Joseph Priestley: An Addition to Hartley's *Observations*."*Journal of the History of Ideas*, 36 (1975), 548-550. In his edition of Hartley, Priestley made prominent the notion of self-annihilation that Hartley had conjectured. The two-language approach to the freedom of human acts is a correct one, one that Hartley himself fails to observe when he makes God the sole agent (549). The addition is to be found in *Observations*, II, 267-269.

Haven, Richard. "Coleridge, Hartley, and the Mystics." *Journal of the History of Ideas*, 20 (1959), 477-494. *Observations*, I, 74-75, which contains "coalescence," is cited. Mechanistic psychology is Hartley's proposed rational and analytical support for the ideas of the annihilation of the self and union with God. There is no discussion of "coalescence" (481-482).

Kallich, Martin. *The Association of Ideas and Critical Theory in Eighteenth-Century England: A History of a Psychological Method in English Criticism*. The Hague: Mouton, 1970. "Coalescence" is glossed as "fusing," but its possible importance for Hartley's account is not discussed (p. 121).

Lamb, Jonathan. "Language and Hartleian Associationism in *A Sentimental Journey*." *ECS*, 13 (1979-80), 285-312. Attempts to connect Hartley to Sterne's views of language.

Leslie, Margaret. "Mysticism Misunderstood: David Hartley and the Idea of Progress." *Journal of the History of Ideas*, 33 (1972), 625-632. Hartley held a doctrine of the spiritual progress of the individual rather than one of social progress (with one exception). Coalescence is an irreversible process by which complex vibrations are formed from simple vibrations (631). *Observations,* II, 28 is cited, where Hartley says of God, " . . . all ideas coalesce into one to him" (Leslie, 632). No link is drawn between the first mention of coalescence in the formation of ideas from sensation, and the second mention in the characterization of the divine mind.

Marsh, Robert. *Four Dialectical Theories of Poetry: An Aspect of English Neoclassical Criticism.* Chicago, Ill.: The University of Chicago Press, 1965. Chapter four, "Hartley and the Providence of God," includes material from the following published articles.

―――. "Mechanism and Prescription in David Hartley's Theory of Poetry." *The Journal of Aesthetics and Art Criticism,* 17 (1959), 473–485.

―――. "The Second Part of Hartley's System." *Journal of the History of Ideas,* 20 (1959), 264–273.

Hartley's *Observations* is a unity; for the analysis of the mind in part one presupposes the theological doctrine of man's Fall in part two (pp. 267–268). Coalescence is restricted to mathematics (p. 266). No connection is made with the concluding citation from *Observations,* II, 313: "Every thing sweet . . . brings in the Idea of God, mixes with it, and vanishes into it . . ." (p. 273). There is no comment concerning "mixes" and "vanishes."

Oberg, Barbara Bowen. "David Hartley and the Association of Ideas." *Journal of the History of Ideas,* 37 (1976), 441–454. The association of ideas supersedes Hartley's physiology (445). The analytic technique is independent of the larger religious scheme into which every detail must fit (452). Coalescence is not mentioned, though reference is made to the absolute coincidence of ideas in mathematics (451). The means by which the transformation from the human to the divine takes place is secondary to the fact that it does (453). The means, I would suggest, is coalescence.

Piper, Herbert. "The Pantheist Sources of Coleridge's Early Poetry." *Journal of the History of Ideas,* 20 (1959), 47–59. Hartley's thesis is that the process of moving by means of sense impressions to God takes place in the individual (53).

Popkin, Richard H. "Joseph Priestley's Criticism of David Hume's Philosophy." *Journal of the History of Ideas,* 15 (1977), 437–447. Priestley found in Hartley an explanation of the human mind, and he derived his theology from Hartley's chiliastic views (437).

Rand, Benjamin. "The Early Development of Hartley's Doctrine of Association." *Psychological Review,* 30 (1923), 306–320. Hartley's association psychology should be dated to 1746: he should be regarded as "the first pronounced physiological psychologist" (313).

Shelley, Bryan Keith. "The Synthetic Imagination: Shelley and Associationism." *The Wordsworth Circle,* 14 (1983), 68–73. There is agreement with M. H. Abrams's remark that coalescence was forced upon associationists (70). Hartley's chemical union is not a synthesis (71).

Waples, Dorothy. "David Hartley in *The Ancient Mariner.*" *The Journal of English and Germanic Philology,* 35 (1936), 337–351. The poem is the complete exemplification of Hartley's psychology; for all seven stages of the system, from the pleasures and pains of sensation to the ones of the moral sense, may be discerned.

Warren, Howard C. *A History of the Association Psychology.* New York: Charles Scribner's Sons, 1921. Only the first part of *Observations* is examined (p. 51). Tucker in his *The Light of Nature Pursued* (1768) was the first to describe the associative synthesis as a transformation, a coalescence: Hartley did not think that any transformation occurred (pp. 262–263). No remarks are made about the occurrence of "coalesce" in "coalesce into one complex idea" (*Observations*, I, 74–75). See Warren, pp. 54–55.

Wheeler, Kathleen M. *The Creative Mind in Coleridge's Poetry.* Cambridge, Mass.: Harvard University Press, 1981. The introduction, "The Struggle with Associationism," describes Hartley's conception of the mind as one based upon materialism (p. 8).

Yolton, John W. *Thinking Matter: Materialism in Eighteenth-Century Britain.* Minneapolis: University of Minnesota Press, 1983. An important book, which discusses Hartley's physiological explanations of thought and action, his theory of vibrations, and his influence on Priestley. Yolton (pp. 151n., 181) supports Ferg's attribution to Hartley of *An Enquiry into the Origin of the Human Appetites and Affections* (London, 1747).

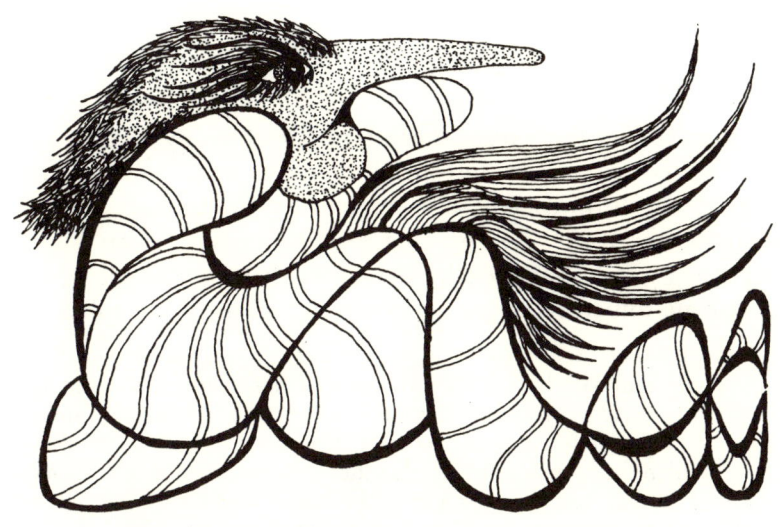

Eighteenth-Century Spleen

WILLIAM B. OBER, M.D.

> "In sooth, I know not why I am so sad."
> *(Merchant of Venice)*

In one iambic pentameter line, ten Anglo-Saxon monosyllables, Shakespeare lays open the problem of sadness, melancholy, and depression. Antonio does not know the reason for his low spirits and cannot find an objective cause for them. That is the critical distinction between reactive depression, which has a reasonable external cause, and more serious emotional disorders. Melancholia is no longer a fashionable term in psychiatry; today's vocabulary speaks of endogenous depression, be its root hereditary, biochemical, or unknown. The etymology of melancholy (black bile) carries the stigma of Galenic humoral theories of disease that dominated medical thinking well into Elizabethan and Jacobean times. It was only after the Restoration that slowly, unevenly, and tentatively was humoral theory replaced by ideas of mental and emotional disease that later evolved into nineteenth- and twentieth-century concepts and interpretations.

A brief glance at Elizabethan-Jacobean melancholy will suffice as a background for eighteenth-century conceptual changes. In *A Treatise on Melancholie* (1586), the first monograph in English on a psychiatric subject, Timothy Bright (1551?–1615), physician to St. Bartholomew's Hospital 1585–91, distinguished unnatural from natural humors. The unnatural humor of melancholy affected the mind without "empairing of the nature thereof; or decay of any facultie therein ... but such a disposition, and such discontentment, as a false stringed lute, giveth to the musician: or a rough and evill fashioned pen, to the cunning writer...."[1] Recognizing that melancholia is an emotional disturbance unaccompanied by dementia, Bright, like his predecessors, had no difficulty assigning its organic basis to the spleen:

> that melancholick humor ... for the most part is settled in the spleane, and with his vapours anoyeth the harte and passing up to the brayne, countersetteth terrible objects to the fantasie, [and] causeth it without externall occasio[n], to forge monstrous fictions ... which the judgement taking as they are presented by the disordered instrument, deliver over to the harte, which hath no judgment or discretion in it self, but giving credit to the mistaken report of the braine, breaketh out into that inordinate passion, against reason.... [D]arkness & cloudes of melancholie vapours rising from that pudle of the spleane obscure the clearnes, which our spirites are endued with.... [T]he brayne hath plentifully drunke of that spleneticke fogge....[2]

Put simply, the heart, being the seat of emotions but not endowed with reasoning capacity, reacts to stimulus from the brain which has been deranged by noxious vapors rising from the spleen. The brain, so disturbed by these vapors, perceives reality incorrectly, and the cycle of emotional disturbance is reinforced. The primary seat of organic pathology is the spleen's failure to excrete melancholic humors properly, a failure of metabolic clearance.

An anatomic basis for Bright's theory was Banister's description (1578) of the route by which melancholy vapors are conveyed: "[A] short vessel, whereby the splene belcheth up malyncholye into the ventricle," (i.e. stomach).[3] Alas for Banister's skill at dissection, the splenic vein empties into the portal vein and thence to the liver, where no doubt it can collect the black bile of melancholy. There is no direct connection between the spleen and the stomach, heart, or brain.

Thomas Walkington's *Optick Glasse of Humors* (1607) added astrological influences to the concept of splenic melancholy, "borne under leaden *Saturne*."[4] Bright and Walkington were eclipsed by Burton's *Anatomy of Melancholy* (1621), also based on classical humoral theories. Burton classified melancholy into a number of types, depending on a long list of possible causes; he described in detail the lover's melancholy and religious melancholy, and devoted special attention to the melancholy of scholars and statesmen. The last was not a novel idea. Earlier, Lemnius had noted the problems of

> Magistrates and Officers ... or Studentes which at unseasonable times sit at their Bookes and Studies. For through overmuch agitation of the mynd, natural heart is extinguished, & the Spirits as well Animall as Vitall, [become] attenuated and vanish away: whereby it cometh to passe, that after their vital iuyce is exhausted, they fall into a Colde & Drye constitution.[5]

This notion can be traced back to Ficino, the fifteenth-century Florentine who resurrected Aristotle's idea that men of letters are melancholy either from innate temperament or become so from their studies.

Burton's approach to melancholy was more literary and historical than anatomical or physiological, but he assigned to the spleen the seat of *hypochondriacal melancholy,* a term that dominated seventeenth-century vocabulary, roughly equivalent to "a moderately disabling endogenous depression" in twentieth century usage. The symptomatology of melancholy was well known even before Bright and Burton. In the *Castel of Helth* (1534), Sir Thomas Elyot assigned "madnesse, fallynge sickness, bleedynges, quynces, poses, hoorsenes, coighes, lepries, scabbes, [and] ache in the joyntes" to melancholia; later writers expanded the list to include frenzy, hydrophobia, lycanthropy, epilepsy, *chagrin d'amour,* and almost any manner of irrational behavior. Bright, Walkington, and Burton all suffered from episodes of melancholy; their interest in the condition stemmed from their experiences with it, and their writings are in part an attempt at self-treatment or at least an effort to come to an understanding of their personal situations. Shakespeare's acquaintance with Bright's *Treatise* and assimilation of some of its phrases into *Hamlet* has been thoroughly explored by John Dover Wilson.[6]

Bright abandoned medicine, took holy orders, and became a clergyman in Yorkshire; both Walkington and Burton were ordained ministers, and religious melancholy was a prominent theme in Jacobean writing, as is exemplified in Burton's description:

> poor distressed souls ... religiously given, [who] have tender consciences, [whom] every small object affrights ... the very inconsiderate reading of Scripture itself, and misinterpretation of some places of it, as "Many are called but few are chosen." ... They doubt of their election ... torture and crucify themselves, [that]

they are almost mad, and all they get by it is this, [that] they lay open a gap to the devil by desperation to carry them to hell. But, the greatest harm of all proceeds from those thundering Ministers, a most frequent cause they are of this malady.[7]

Many writers attributed melancholia to the teaching of the Puritans and other enthusiastic sects and claimed that Puritans were themselves melancholics.[8] In 1618 the Synod of Dort, dominated by right-wing Calvinists, had confirmed such doctrines as predestination not conditional on belief, Christ's not dying for all mankind, man's total depravity, and the lack of remission of sin by contrition or confession. Though the Synod's canons applied strictly only to the Dutch Reformed Church, religious conservatives in Britain took them to heart. The disastrous psychological effects of believing in man's worthlessness and his eternal damnation can be seen in *God's Plot*,[9] the autobiography and journal of the Rev. Thomas Shepard (1605–49) who was converted to Puritanism while a student at Emmanuel College, Cambridge. He emigrated to Cambridge, Massachusetts in 1634 where he served as pastor of the First Church and unofficial chaplain to Harvard College. *God's Plot* is an unrelieved litany of self-doubt, feelings of inadequacy and guilt, total despair, the account of himself by an unhappy man certain of his dreadful impending doom. Many pious men and women of the period suffered from similar psychological wounds.

Burton also related sexual abstinence to melancholy. Arguing that "menstruous blood" and the "fuliginous exhalation of corrupt seed" in celibate women produced black vapors that ascended to the brain, he recommended marriage: "But the best and surest remedy of all, is to see them well placed, and married to good husbands . . . to give them content to their desires."[10] But Burton does not consider the example of celibate men or men without available sexual outlets and the psychological effects of such a condition.

Another Jacobean voice, this one from the colonies, was Anne Bradstreet (1612–72), who married a nonconformist minister and emigrated to Massachusetts in 1630. Her poem *Of the Four Humours in Man's Constitution* (circulated in manuscript by 1642, published in England in 1650) is based on classical theories of the four elements and four humors:

> If I be partial judged or thought to err,
> The melancholy snake shall it aver,
> Whose cold dry head more subtilty doth yield,
> Than all the huge beasts of the fertile field.
> . . . .
> Likewise the useful spleen, though not the best,
> Yet is called a bowel well as the rest:
> The liver, stomach, owe their thanks of right,
> The first it drains, of th' last quicks appetite.
> Laughter (though thou say malice) flows from hence,
> These two in one cannot have residence.

The humor of melancholy and the elements of coldness and dryness traditionally associated with it are attached to the snake, i.e. serpent, suggesting temptation and sexual guilt. (For "subtilty" read deceitfulness.) Like her Elizabethan predecessors, Bradstreet locates melancholy's seat in the spleen which, she believes, drains bile from the liver and stimulates the appetite, certainly a eupeptic assignment, but she finds it contradictory that the emotions of both laughter and malice should be situated in the same organ.

Perhaps William Strode's popular poem *Melancholly* (circa 1630) owes its inspiration to Burton:

> Then, stretch your bones in a still gloomy valley,
> There's nothing daynty, sweete, save Melancholly.

But Milton's *Il Penseroso,* written in the same decade, resembles no phenomenon described by Burton. His "divinest Melancholy" is a personification in praise of the contemplative life without any clinical overtones. Other sporadic literary allusions can be traced to Burton at the time when his book was widely read. Killigrew's *Pandora* recalls his humoral psychology and comments on melancholy as a fashionable pose: "Only some fumes from his heart, make his head addle. 'Tis called the spleen of late, and much in fashion." The vogue increased, for in 1690 Sir William Temple noted that "Our country must be confess'd to be what a great foreign physician called it, the region of the Spleen." Elizabethan melancholy had been rebaptized Spleen, and Temple's geographical allocation of it to England foreshadowed George Cheyne.

The first breach with the humoral tradition was made by Thomas Willis (1621–75) whose three major monographs, *Cerebri Anatome* (1664), *Pathologiae Cerebri et Nervosi* (1667), and *De Anima Brutorum* (1672) were the first steps toward "modern" neuroanatomy, neurophysiology, and neuropsychiatry. Details of his career may be found in Isler's biography,[11] and Dewhurst has recently published his Oxford lectures and casebooks.[12] We must credit Willis, first, for attempting to localize nervous diseases by correlating clinical signs with postmortem examination of the brain. Needless to say, as anatomical and experimental methods have been refined during the past three centuries, localization of cerebral function has become more precise, and many of Willis's ideas must now be reckoned as first approximations, but he did assign the "rational soul" to the cerebrum and the noncognitive, involuntary functions to lower centers. He coined the term *Neurologie* to describe such scientific observations, and that discipline remains largely such observations today. Willis and his successors attempted to construct an organic concept of nervous diseases. Their ideas were a development from the "mechanical man" viewed as an hydraulic system in the light of Harvey's demonstration of the circulation of the blood. "Animal spirits" circulated in nerves much as did blood in vessels. Much ink was spilled in attempting to define the nature of the fluid and determine whether nerves were hollow or solid.[13]

Second, Willis was the first to deny categorically the theory handed down from antiquity that either the humors or the uterus with its conjectured migrations through the body, its malpositions, or its dysfunctions had anything to do with the syndrome of hysteria, for which melancholy, hypochondria, vapors, and spleen were then essentially synonymous. He assigned hysteria to the brain and nervous stock, firmly establishing it as a neuropsychiatric entity.

Third, based on clinical observations, Willis found no difference between hysteria, then thought to be exclusively a disease of women, and hypochondria, then thought to be a disease exclusively of men. Even though Sydenham echoed this view a decade later, confusion on the point persisted in both medical vocabulary and theory until well into the middle of the eighteenth century. Even as late as the 1890s Charcot and Freud felt impelled to publish case reports of hysteria in men to make the point anew.

Fourth, Willis believed that nerves were solid structures, not mere

CEREBRI ANATOME:

CUI ACCESSIT

NERVORUM DESCRIPTIO

ET USUS.

STUDIO

THOMÆ WILLIS, ex *Æde Christi*
Oxon. M. D. & in ista Celeberrima
Academia Naturalis Philosophiæ Professoris *Sidleiani.*

LONDINI,
Typis *Ja. Flesher,* Impensis *Jo. Martyn* & *Ja. Allestry*
apud insigne Campanæ in Cœmeterio
D. *Pauli.* MDCLXIV.

DE ANIMA BRUTORUM
QUÆ
Hominis Vitalis ac Sensitiva est,
EXERCITATIONES DUÆ.
PRIOR PHYSIOLOGICA
Ejusdem Naturam, partes, Potentias
& Affectiones tradit; *Cuvier*
ALTERA PATHOLOGICA
Morbos qui ipsam, & sedem ejus Primariam,
NEMPE N° 3340.
CEREBRUM & NERVOSUM
GENUS afficiunt, explicat, corúmque
THERAPEIAS instituit, cum Figuris Æneis.

STUDIO
THOMÆ WILLIS M. D. Natural.
Philosophiæ Profess. *OXON.* nec non inclyti
Medic. Colleg. Londin. & Societ. Reg. Socii.

LONDINI,
Prostant apud Gulielm. *Wells,* & Rob. *Scot,* 1675.

hollow tubes that conveyed humors. To them he assigned the function of conduction, which is in fact the case. He developed the idea that nerves conducted "animal spirits" that were distilled from arterial blood by the cerebral cortex and transmitted them throughout the body via peripheral nerves to regulate physiology in health and disease. It might be argued that animal spirits were little more than the old-fashioned humors given a new name, but if we think of this conduction theory in terms of the twentieth-century concept of an electrical impulse with depolarization and repolarization of the fibers, it represents a significant conceptual advance. The first glimmerings that neural impulses are electrical had to wait, of course, for the experiments by Volta and Galvani over a century later.

Fifth, like previous observers Willis recognized the difference between voluntary and involuntary motion. He identified as "the intercostal nerve" the trunk of ganglia and fibers that runs parallel to the vertebral column along the ribs, now labelled the sympathetic chain, a major component of the autonomic nervous system. To this structure Willis correctly assigned many of the vegetative functions that figure so prominently in psychosomatic symptomatology, *viz.* vasomotor and visceral phenomena. By dividing the fibers that lead from the vagus nerve to the heart, he produced changes in cardiac rate and rhythm, even to the point of syncope, thereby establishing the neurological basis for "swooning."

One feature of Willis's neurophysiology that has proved a stumbling block for later readers, indeed that engendered controversy in his own time, was his association of "animal spirits" with "explosive particles," which he thought were localized chiefly in ganglia. To collisions of these he attributed the convulsive fit which he claimed was a cardinal sign of hysteria. In retrospect, he probably included cases of what we would now call temporal lobe epilepsy, hence the confusion. Yet as late as the 1890s Charcot wrote about "hysteroepilepsy," a term discarded in the twentieth century as the distinction between organic and functional diseases sharpened. For Willis the symptoms of hysteria were much the same as those of melancholy; his chief point of distinction seems to have been the convulsive fit. He attributed melancholy to a "Passion of the Heart" as it affected the brain:

> *Melancholy* . . . is a complicated Distemper of the Brain and Heart:

> For as *Melancholick* people talk idly, it proceeds from the vice or fault of the Brain, and the inordination of the Animal Spirits dwelling in it; but as they become very sad and fearful, this is deservedly attributed to the Passion of the Heart. . . . But we cannot here yield to what some *Physicians* affirm, that *Melancholy* doth arise from a *Melancholick* humour. . . . Melancholy being a long time protracted, passes oftentimes into Stupidity, or Foolishness, and sometimes also into Madness. . . . [14]

Willis also denied firmly that the spleen or its disorders had any relationship to melancholy, nor at any point did he refer to Burton whom he had known at Oxford, a *praeteritio* that did not escape his contemporary readers. The transition from simple melancholia to profound depression had been recognized by previous writers, but Willis recognized, albeit not clearly, the relationship between melancholia and mania—that they approach each other by the analogy of their nature and they can change into one another. He compared their relationship to combustion in which either smoke or flame might be emitted, smoke often being followed by outbursts of flames, flames often subsiding into smoke. His casebook for 1650 records such a case,[15] and Calmeil,[16] writing in 1845, credits it as the first recorded example of manic-depressive psychosis, though Falret[17] did not describe *la folie circulaire* until 1854, and the term manic-depressive did not become part of accepted psychiatric vocabulary until Kraepelin's *Lehrbuch* appeared at the end of the nineteenth century. Although previous writers had considered "frenzy" as one of the symptoms of melancholia and in 1390 Gower had written of the spleen as the seat of both melancholy and laughter, Willis was the first to note the cyclical alteration of affect as a medical syndrome.

Writing only a decade after Willis's *De Anima Brutorum*, Thomas Sydenham (1624-1689) accepted some but not all of Willis's ideas. An astute clinical observer and bedside teacher, Sydenham did not have Willis's interest in dissection or experimentation. He noted that hysteria and hypochondria accounted for as much as one-third of all patients with chronic disease. The vocabulary suggested a distinction between the two conditions, but his sound clinical judgment led him to recognize that no real difference existed:

> however much antiquity may have laid the blame of hysteria on the uterus, hypochondriasis (which we impute to some obstruction

of the spleen or viscera) is as like to it as one egg to another. True indeed, it is that women are more subject than males. This, however, is not on account of the uterus.[18]

Exit the womb and re-enter the spleen. Not only did Sydenham's parenthetical comment restore the spleen to its former dignity, it also discounted Willis's concept that both conditions were neuropsychiatric in origin. Sydenham, the clinician, was on firmer ground when he described his patients:

> their mind sickens more than the body. An incurable despair is so thoroughly the nature of this disease, that the very slightest word of hope creates anger. The patients believe that they have to suffer all the evils that can befall humanity. . . . They have melancholy forebodings. They brood over trifles, cherishing them in their anxious and unquiet bosoms. Fear, anger, jealousy, suspicions, and the worst passions of the mind arise without cause. Joy, hope, and cheerfulness . . . find no place at all in their spirits . . . there is no moderation. All is caprice. They love without measure those whom they will soon hate without reason.

Sydenham's victims of splenic or visceral obstruction were people with chronic, low grade, episodic mood depression. They were unhappy and made people around them, their families and friends, unhappy. Sydenham continues:

> it is neither the maniac nor the madman that we write about . . . those who thus suffer are persons of prudent judgment, persons who in the profundity of their meditations and the wisdom of their speech, far surpass those whose minds have never been excited by such stimuli. . . . not without reason has Aristotle observed, that melancholy men are of the greatest genius.[19]

The last sentence gave new life to the old canard, and its consequences were to be seen in all walks of life and in many forms of literature.

Willis's rejection of the spleen as the seat of melancholy found few adherents for some decades. Writing in 1690, Sir William Temple, a rational thinker and skeptical observer, noted:

> In the course of my life I have often pleased or entertained myself with observing the various and fantastical changes of the diseases generally complained of, and the remedies in common vogue, which were like birds of passage, very much seen or heard of at one season, and disappeared at another. . . . When I was very young, nothing was so much feared or talked of as rickets among children,

and consumptions among young people of both sexes. After these, the spleen came in play, and grew a formal disease.[20]

To a large extent the content of emotional disease is colored by the social context in which it occurs. Within our lifetime, Auden's "Age of Anxiety" has been replaced by an age of depression. Eighteenth-century spleen has reappeared as twentieth-century alienation—touched, perhaps, with nostalgia. Viewing the sociology of mental disease, Foucault's *Madness and Civilization*[21] develops the thesis that the growth of publicly maintained madhouses to sequester the insane was based on the effect of such diseases on the body politic rather than on medical considerations. Bethlehem Hospital was founded in the thirteenth century to care for the sick poor; it was not until late in the seventeenth century that its beds were chiefly occupied by psychiatric patients, and it became Bedlam. The first Act of Parliament to separate pauper lunatics from disorderly persons, idle rogues, vagabonds, and beggars dates from 1714 (12 Anne c.23). Then, even as today, the question of who was confined was often decided on social or economic grounds, how much trouble the patient was to his family, or whether he could afford private care.

As a rule, victims of the spleen were not considered mad nor were they confined, but our knowledge of the malady comes from accounts of patients who could afford medical attention or those literate enough to write about it. A touching account of private confinement is the poem *Lucida Intervalla* (1679) by James Carkesse, a clerk in Pepys's office at the admiralty who became deranged and was placed in a private asylum opposite Bethlehem Hospital. He did not attribute his improvement to the medical care he received:

> Who e'er is *Mad*, he first had *Wit* to lose:
> Betwixt *Fool* and *Physitian* wink and chuse.[22]

Unlike Carkesse, most victims of the spleen remained in the bosom of their families and in the circle of their friends, much to the discomfiture of all concerned. Though many consulted doctor after learned doctor, there are almost no statements to show that any but transient improvement took place under medical treatment.

Relating medical notions to their literary expression imposes problems on the reader. Eleanor Sickles argues:

> Who shall decide whether a given poem is sincere sentiment or fashionable sentimantality? And what is melancholy? How is one to distinguish its nuances, the boundaries between its moods, the point where it merges into mere lack of levity on one frontier or into mental derangement on another? Nor is it always easy or even possible to tell how much of a poet's manner and substance is due to the literary fashions and philosophical ideas of the day.[23]

No single rule or simple solution can resolve individual cases, but selected poetic ideas and images can be related to established biographical facts. For example, following Burton, Pope's cave of spleen is filled with vapors, and following Sydenham's description of headache and pain in the side (i.e. the hypochondrium) as cardinal symptoms, Pope's personification of the goddess Spleen lies with "Pain at her side, and Megrims in her head." That Belinda should suffer an hysterical fit after the Baron cuts off her lock of hair is reasonable in the context of eighteenth-century medical beliefs; the malady could be precipitated by "any accident occasioning sudden surprise."[24] Pope suffered from kyphoscoliosis and secondary cardio-pulmonary disease as well as other assorted illnesses. It is not unreasonable to conjecture that he was familiar with headache and flank pain, and if he ascribed them to Spleen, he chose an image that conformed to one school of medical opinion of his day.

In like fashion, Swift's headaches and episodes of vertigo, attributed by most observers to Menière's syndrome, colored some of his attitudes, but in the only passage that deals directly with spleen he satirically describes a Yahoo's hysterical fit:

> a Fancy would sometimes take a *Yahoo*, to retire into a Corner, to lie down and howl, and groan, and spurn away all that came near him, although he were young and fat, and wanted neither Food nor Water; nor did the Servants imagine what could possibly ail him. And the only Remedy they found was to set him to hard Work, after which he would infallibly come to himself.... here I could plainly discover the true Seeds of *Spleen*, which only seizeth on the *Lazy*, the *Luxurious*, and the *Rich*.[25]

It was commonly agreed that the disease was more frequent among the idle rich, especially ladies of leisure with nothing to occupy them but trivial social obligations. Neither Pope nor Swift wore his spleen upon his sleeve, yet both suffered from occasional episodes of melancholy that were far from posture or affectation. Possibly the irony had entered too deep in their souls for them to permit themselves the self-indulgence of a fit of hysterics or even self-pity, at least not in print. To observe the world detached, through a set of satiric lenses, may offer some protection against the outward manifestations of depression. Moreover, unhappy as each of them may have been on occasion, neither felt that he had compromised the ideals and goals set by his ego; feelings of inferiority, inadequacy, failure, or self-reproach are not to be found in their psyches, and that too is a safeguard against "those terrible dreams that shake us nightly." Whatever Pope or Swift may have experienced in private, neither gave any public encouragement or support to the spleen. We can learn more about the eighteenth-century literary expression of spleen from writers of lesser stature whose psyches were more fragile.

Moore has dubbed the first half of the eighteenth century the Age of Melancholy, and a sequence of medical and literary publications marks it so.[26] In 1702, the year of Queen Anne's accession, John Purcell, a London physician, published *A Treatise of Vapours*,[27] little more than a restatement of humoral theories, including convulsive disorders with hysteria and assigning "fits of the vapours" to "the Stomach and Guts; whereof the Grumbling of the one and the heaviness and uneasiness of the other generally preced[e] the Paroxysm." He stated that the disease was the most common ailment of the time, a view so influential that a second edition appeared in 1707. Part of the book's popularity may be due to the fact that Queen Anne suffered from the malady, and, apart from John Radcliffe, the only physician in London independent enough of favor to refuse to take her vapours seriously, her physicians consulted gravely among themselves and prescribed all manner of remedies, none of which modified her unhappiness. The Queen's ailments and personality were much discussed by society gossips and coffee-house wits; a taste for the vapours may well have been the only fashion this madly unchic Stuart monarch set.

Literary comment did not lag. Essays by Addison and Steele in *The Spectator* discussed the ailment seriously and gave it a national character, "a kind of Demon that haunts our Island" (*Spectator* No. 387) and described it as "a Complication of all the Diseases incident to human Nature . . . called the Spleen" (*Spectator* No.558). Innumerable com-

A TREATISE OF Vapours,

OR,

𝔥𝔶𝔰𝔱𝔢𝔯𝔦𝔠𝔨 𝔉𝔦𝔱𝔰.

CONTAINING

An Analytical Proof of its Causes, Mechanical Explanations of all its Symptoms and Accidents, according to the newest and most Rational Principles: Together with its Cure at large.

By *John Purcell*, M.D.

LONDON,
Printed and Sold by *H. Newman* at the *Grasshopper* in the *Poultry*, and *N. Cox* at the *Bible* without *Temple-Bar*, 1702.

A TREATISE OF THE HYPOCHONDRIACK AND HYSTERICK PASSIONS

Vulgarly call'd the HYPO in MEN and VAPOURS in WOMEN;

In which the SYMPTOMS, CAUSES, and CURE of those DISEASES are set forth after a Method intirely new.

The whole interspers'd, with Instructive Discourses ON THE Real ART of PHYSICK it self;

And Entertaining Remarks on the Modern Practice OF PHYSICIANS AND APOTHECARIES:

Very useful to all, that have the Misfortune to stand in need of either. In Three Dialogues.

By B. DE MANDEVILLE, M. D.

*Scire potestates herbarum, usumque medendi
Maluit, & Mutas agitare inglorius artes.*
Æneid. Lib. XU.

LONDON: Printed and Sold by *Dryden Leach*, in *Eliot's* Court, in the *Little-Old-Baily*, and *W. Taylor*, at the *Ship* in *Pater-Noster-Row*. 1711.

ments, many by visitors from the Continent, testified to the distinctively national character of the disorder, and average British subjects accepted melancholy as a badge of their way of life. To suffer from spleen was socially acceptable. Indeed, because Aristotle had considered it a mark of intelligence, to own to the disease suggested the sufferer was a person of consequence. Farquhar's *The Beaux' Stratagem* (1707) makes the point one of social distinction when Archer, disguised as a valet, momentarily forgets his assumed role and remarks that his physician had recommended he drink tea "for a remedy against the spleen," to which Mrs. Sullen's rejoinder is, "I had thought that distemper had been only proper to people of quality."

A Dutch physician, Bernard Mandeville (1670?–1733), better known for his *Fable of the Bees*, found London a profitable place to practice psychosomatic medicine. His *Treatise of the Hypochondriack and Hysterick Passions*[28] (1711) was cleverly cast as a dialogue between Philopirio, a physician, and Misodemon, his patient. As is often the case with dialogues, the text is discursive and reaches no conclusion, though many contemporary ideas are discussed. Most memorable is Mandeville's account of his own melancholy when he labored under the delusion he had contracted syphilis, even to believing his nose and palate had been destroyed. Circumlocutory as Mandeville is, the book found an audience sufficient to warrant a third edition by 1730.

Also dating from the first decade of the eighteenth century was *The Spleen, a Pindarique Ode*, first published anonymously (1701), then later (1709) under the author's name, Anne Finch, Countess of Winchilsea.[29] More than any single literary work of the period, it captures the variety and contrariety of melancholy, its symptoms, its anatomic referents, and the difficulty in comprehending it. The ode begins interrogatively:

> What art thou, SPLEEN, which ev'ry thing dost ape?
> Thou Proteus to abus'd Mankind,
> Who never yet thy real Cause could find,
> Or fix thee to remain in one continued shape

and a few lines further the Countess describes melancholia's familiar symptoms:

> Trembling sometimes thou dost appear,
> Dissolved into a Panick Fear;

> On Sleep intruding dost thy Shadows spread,
> Thy gloomy Terrours round the silent Bed,
> And croud with bolding Dreams the Melancholy Head;
> Or, when the mid-night Hour is told,
> And drooping Lids thou still dost waking hold,
> Thy fond delusions cheat the eyes;
> Before 'em antick Spectres dance
> Unusual Fires their pointed Heads advance,
> And aiery Phantoms rise.

Fear and trembling, insomnia and hallucinations; these are the daily (or nightly) lot of the victim. The Countess recognizes that the symptoms are psychogenic:

> Falsely, the Mortal Part we blame
> Of our deprest and pond'rous Frame.

She distinguishes between the spleen as an organ and "spleen" as a state of mind. Alluding to her own predicament, she assigns some of her melancholy to marital discord, and biographically that may have been the case. Her husband had been Gentleman of the Bedchamber to James II, and she had been Maid of Honour to Mary of Modena. With the Revolution of 1688 they lost their places at court, were in disfavor, and lived in modest retirement. A decade or more of frustration and failure to regain status may well have induced friction between them. She cites her struggle against episodic depression and its inhibiting effect on her writing:

> O'er me alas! thou dost too much prevail:
> I feel thy Force, whilst I against thee rail;
> I feel my verse decay and my crampt numbers fail.
> Thro' thy black jaundice I all Objects see,
> As dark and terrible as Thee,
> My lines decry'd, and my Employment thought
> A useless folly, or presumptuous Fault.

But two of the ode's most important lines were probably overlooked by most of its readers:

> The Cause indeed is a defect in Sense;
> But still the Spleen's alleg'd, and still the dull pretence.

After Willis and Sydenham, this was the first unequivocal statement that melancholia was a mental disorder, that medical science had failed to discover its cause, but that surely the spleen had nothing to do with it.

Anne Finch recognized spleen as a disease to be feared and avoided. A contrary view was taken by Elizabeth Carter (1717–1806), who wrote under the pseudonym "Eliza." She was an early representative of the "graveyard school" with its tombs and yew trees, midnight moonshine and gloomy shade. In her *Ode to Melancholy* (1739) she apostrophizes melancholy as a "companion" and "ideal guest," a condition "to be cultivated and cherished, invoked and indulged in."[30] It is not difficult to believe she could so indulge herself because in fact she did not suffer from the malady. The charge of self-indulgence can be levelled at many writers who assumed a melancholy air because it was a fashionable posture.

The Countess of Winchilsea's *Spleen* was influential not only because of its subject, its author's social status, and the knowledge by the select reading public that her account was personal and real, but also because even as medical ideas had shaped her poem, the poem in turn had impact on medical thought. The Gulstonian lecture for 1722 was given before the Royal College of Physicians by William Stukeley (1687–1765), a man of broad cultural interests, a classical scholar and antiquarian, a Fellow of the Royal Society, and a respected London physician. When he published *Of the Spleen, its Description and History, Uses and Diseases, particularly the Vapors, with their Remedy* the following year, he appended the Countess's ode to it. Stukeley rejected both humoral and neural theories and found the anatomic seat of melancholy in its classical, antique locus, the spleen: "we may venture to call the vapors a relaxation of the tonic action of the spleen [which becomes] much swell'd and stuffed with thick unactive blood." Today's vocabulary might label this as passive splenic congestion. Stukeley also recognized a connection between emotional disturbance and genital status. He noted that the spleen was smaller in women than in men, an effect he attributed to menstrual flux. In women, splenic congestion led to uterine congestion, and menstruation restored "reasonable *aequilibrium* . . . between the containing vessels and the contained blood." When *aequilibrium* was not restored by cyclical menses, as in pregnancy, irregular cycles, or at menopause, symptoms of the vapors were likely to develop. In parallel fashion Stukeley accounted for male hypochondriasis: "I judge the corpora cavernosa of the penis exactly of the same fabric with the spleen, and the actions of both, their inflations and depletions seem perfectly analogous; and that of the internal part cannot be better and more sensibly explain'd than by the external." Histologic studies in the next century were to refute this analogy, but even in our own century the effects of penile congestion upon men's emotional states would not be denied. Stukeley also shared with Burton and the Countess a suspicion that a religious bent of mind favored the development of melancholy:

> Wisely therefore did our ancestors keep their jesters to entertain them at dinner, to make 'em laugh and digest well, the first topic in health, whence they begat an athletic and hardy race, that did such wonders in arms. Quite contrary to the practice in religious houses, colleges, where the scripture is preposterously read at mealtimes, and a superfluous demureness of countenance prepares them for all the diseases of an unactive spleen.[31]

He was not the first to claim that victims of the spleen had poor digestions and led sedentary, contemplative, unathletic lives. We know little of his personal character, but he was a formidable polymath who led a busy, extroverted life. Remedies such as a hearty appetite and healthy exercise were not original with him. Burton, Willis, Sydenham, and many writers before and after cited such common sense measures to counteract melancholy.

Bridging the gap between physicians and the literati, though not uncritically accepted by the latter (see *Peri-Bathous, or the Art of Sinking in Poetry* by "Martinus Scriblerus"), was the figure of Sir Richard Blackmore (1653–1729), who attested to the medical validity of spleen as a psychosomatic illness in his prolix, semi-heroic poem *The Creation* (1712):

> The spleen with sullen vapours clouds the brain,
> And binds the spirit with its heavy chain,
> Howe'er the cause fantastick may appear,
> Th' effect is real and the pain sincere.

At that time he seems to have accepted the old-fashioned humoral theory, but after he retired from practice he wrote essays on several medical subjects, among them *A Treatise of the Spleen and Vapours* in 1725. Here he was more a physician and less a poet. He was among those who subscribed to the idea that the spleen was a distinctively English

OF THE
SPLEEN,
ITS
DESCRIPTION
AND
HISTORY,
USES and *DISEASES*,
PARTICULARLY THE
VAPORS, *with their* REMEDY.

Being a LECTURE *read at the Royal College of Physicians*, London, 1722.

To which is Added

Some ANATOMICAL OBSERVATIONS in the Diffection of an ELEPHANT.

By *WILLIAM STUKELEY*, M.D. CML. & SRS.

Nihil temere credendum, nihilque negligendum.
Hippoc. 6. Epidem. §. 2.

LONDON:
Printed for the AUTHOR. MDCCXXIII.

THE
English Malady:
OR, A
TREATISE
OF

Nervous Diseases of all Kinds,

AS

Spleen, Vapours, Lowness of Spirits, Hypochondriacal, and Hysterical Distempers, &c.

In THREE PARTS.

PART I. Of the Nature and Cause of Nervous Distempers.
PART II. Of the Cure of Nervous Distempers.
PART III. Variety of Cases that illustrate and confirm the Method of Cure.

With the AUTHOR's *own* CASE *at large.*

───────Facilis descensus Averni,
*Sed revocare Gradum, superasque evadere ad Auras,
Hic* Labor, *hoc* Opus est. *Pauci quos Æquus amavit,*
Jupiter, *aut ardens evexit ad Æthera Virtus
Dis Geniti potuere*───────

By GEORGE CHEYNE, M.D.
Fellow of the College of Physicians at Edinburgh, and F.R.S.

LONDON:
Printed for G. STRAHAN and
J. LEAKE at Bath. MDCCXXXIII.

disease, a point made by previous writers and more effectively in the next decade by Cheyne, and he now wrote of the "Hypochondriacal Affections which in my judgment consist in the irregular and disturbed Motions of the Spirits, and the irritable Disposition of the Nerves; and this was the Opinion of Dr. Willis and Dr. Sydenham." He applied the new science's idea of fibers and vessels to bolster his concept of the spleen as the seat of melancholy:

> The Spleen is a System of membranaceous Fibers, Nerves, and Blood-Vessels, so closely connected that they leave only little Cells and narrow Apartments, but no Cavity capacious enough to be the receptacle of any Recrementious Liquors, supposed to be separated by occult strainers from the Blood: Nor can any secretory Vessels be discovered . . . designed for carrying off any superfluous or hurtful Humours lodged there.

But Blackmore did not appreciate dualities or psychological polarities. He could not perceive that mania could be the obverse of depression and wrote indignantly:

> It was an odd Fancy to make this Bowel [i.e. organ] the Cistern and Sink of the gross Lees . . . of the Blood, and at the same time to suppose it to be the Spring of pleasant Humour and Alacrity . . . to make it at once the Fountain of Mirth and Melancholy, that causes us by turns to laugh and cry. This extravagant Conceit may well make the Reader merry; but how the Impurities and foul Dregs in the Spleen should cause the Patient profuse Laughter is an unaccountable mystery.[32]

One may accuse Blackmore of insensitivity, even an inability to comprehend how the same hand could pen *L'Allegro* and *Il Penseroso*, but it was similar reasoning that later in the century led John Hunter to believe that an organ could suffer from only one disease at a time, thereby contracting both syphilis and gonorrhea when he had bargained for only the latter.

Shortly after Blackmore's treatise, another member of the Royal College of Physicians, Nicholas Robinson (1697?–1775) of Christ's Hospital, published *A New System of the Spleen*, a monograph that has not received the attention it merits. Many of his comments are perceptive, one including the patient's comprehension of his sense of plight: "in all Cases of Spleen, we ought to distinguish between the Perceptions and the Knowledge that accompanies those Perceptions." This may be read as a glimpse into the difference between conscious and unconscious knowledge, but at heart Robinson was an empiricist: "the Spleen, Vapours &c. are real Diseases, and no Ways depending on the imaginary whims of Fancy. Now, if they be real Diseases, they must have Symptoms," which he proceeds to enumerate with the skill of an experienced observer and articulate teacher. He classified mental disease much as we do today, taking into account the severity of symptoms and their chronicity. The "spleen or vapours" corresponds to mild early depression; "hypochondriack melancholy" is equated with "longer continuance . . . wherein all the symptoms are heighten'd to a surprizing degree"; true melancholia is the state of chronic depression from which the patient could "degenerate into the natural or religious Melancholy" or else into "Lunacy or Enthusiastick Madness." These latter terms fit easily into the modern concept of manic-depressive disease, and Robinson deserves credit as an early taxonomist of psychiatric entities.

Even more unusual was Robinson's attempt to develop a mechanical theory of mental disease based on anatomic principles, using the fiber as an anatomic unit:

> in all Cases, where those Machinulae of the Brain and Nerves, either recede too far from, or are brought too near each other, there will be either a Contraction or a Relaxation of the Fibres, which will be attended with the sensation of Pain in the Fibre, and the Perception of Uneasiness in the Mind. . . . In all cases of the Spleen, Vapours, and Hypochondriack Melancholy . . . the Fibres of the Muscles and other Vessels are so relax'd that they cannot assist the Mind in voluntary Motion.

His argument was based on the idea that mind without brain was inconceivable and therefore psychological processes were expressions of physical events within the nervous system. The question, unasked and unanswered in the eighteenth century, was whether mental illness was brain disease. In the nineteenth century this question led to a division into opposing schools, psychic *vs.* somatic. Robinson must be counted as a forerunner of the somatic school, and as such a descendant of Willis. To Willis's emphasis on the nervous system he added Newtonian ideas on gravity:

> Every Change of the Mind, therefore, indicates a Change in the bodily Organs; nor is it possible for the Wit of Man to conceive how

the Mind can, from a chearful, gay Disposition, fall into a sad and disconsolate State, without some Alterations in the Fibres, at the same Time; for the relative Gravity of the Body ... what we call Lowness of Spirits, is not otherwise increas'd upon these Changes, but as the Body weighs heavier to the Mind.

To the nerves Robinson applied a mechanical metaphor:

they are, by laws of Nature, made to exist to a Mind fitly dispos'd with proper Organs to receive their Impression: But if the Structure or Mechanism of these Organs happens to be disorder'd, and the Springs of the Machine out of Tune, no wonder the Mind perceives the Alteration, and is affected with the Change. ...[33]

Almost a century and a half separate Bright's "false stringed lute" from Robinson's "Springs ... out of Tune." The substance of the metaphors is much the same, but the stance and the choice of vocabulary reflect the distance between the Renaissance and the Modern. The springs of Robinson's machine suggest it is a shorter distance to Huxley's *Brave New World* and Fordean society than was the distance from More's *Utopia* to eighteenth-century England.

Contemporary with Blackmore's and Robinson's was another approach to melancholia. In 1724, George Cheyne (1671–1743), a Scottish physician who moved to London with an established reputation, published *An Essay of Health and Long Life* (1724), advocating moderation in food and drink, proper attention to sleep, exercise, and fresh air, and prudent management of the passions. The sensible advice and sound hygienic principles were addressed to lay readers, but Cheyne made no attempt to supply psychological insights. Cheyne was popular both socially and medically: among his friends were Swift, Pope, Gay, and Arbuthnot; among his patients were Samuel Richardson, Lord Hervey, and the Countess of Huntingdon. Though the *Essay of Health* did not deal with melancholia *per se*, its implication was clear, and John Arbuthnot (1667–1735) expanded the approach in his *Essay concerning the Nature of Aliments* (1731). Recognizing constitutional differences, Arbuthnot wrote *inter alias* of people with "lax and weak fibers" and others whose fibers were "too elastick and strong," prescribing diets he thought appropriate for each type. The stage was now set for the appearance of the most popular and influential book on melancholy in the eighteenth century, Cheyne's *The English Malady* (1733).

Cheyne included his own case history; he too suffered from low spirits on occasion, also accompanied by lethargy and easy fatigability. In addition, he was obese; a contemporary report states he weighed 32 stone, which is equivalent to 448 lbs., not a credible figure. He had taken the cure at Bath in 1725, perhaps with benefit, but *The English Malady* did not appear until he was 62 years old and assured of a readership. The text is not notable for any new ideas, but it was addressed to an educated lay audience and found its target. He stressed the British climate and diet as predisposing to melancholy, echoing ideas of previous writers:

> *The* Moisture *of our* Air, *the Variableness of our* Weather . . . *the* Richness *and* Heaviness *of our Food* . . . *the* Inactivity and sedetary *Occupations of the better Sort, (among whom this* Evil *mostly rages) and the Humour of living in great, populous, and consequently unhealthy Towns, have brought forth a* Class *and* Set *of Distempers . . . scarce known to our Ancestors. . . .* These nervous *Disorders . . . computed to make almost one* third *of the Complaints of the People of* Condition *in* England.[34]

Some decades earlier Sir William Temple had written that spleen arose from "the great uncertainty and many changes of our weather in all seasons," and John Arbuthnot had compared John Bull's moods as rising and falling with the weather-glass. John Purcell had emphasized gastrointestinal symptoms, as had many previous medical writers, phenomena that surely struck a responsive chord in Cheyne, who was given to overeating. Cheyne assigned the organic basis for melancholy to the nerves. His recommendations of a low diet, exercise, and fresh air were simple and proved popular; *The English Malady* had its sixth edition in 1739, and later ones followed. It is clear that in the decade between 1725 and 1735, due largely to Blackmore, Robinson, Arbuthnot, and Cheyne, the medical profession no longer attributed melancholy to humors or the spleen. One of the last efforts to revive the fallacy was by (Sir) John Hill (1716?–1775), an apothecary of dubious qualifications, a self-promoter and *Vielschreiber* whose *Hypochondriasis* of 1766 claimed that "To call Hypochondriasis a fanciful malady, is ignorant and cruel. It is a real and a sad disease: an obstruction of the spleen by thickened and distempered blood; extending itself often to the liver."[35] Few educated readers took Hill seriously, but one cannot gauge his impact on the naive.

By mid-century, medical ideas about melancholy centered on neural doctrines and gastrointestinal symptoms. Robert Whytt (1714–66),

Professor of Medicine at Edinburgh, one of the few experimental neurophysiologists of the century, published *Observations on . . . those Disorders which have been commonly called Nervous, Hypochondriac, or Hysteric* (1765) in which he reduced the predisposing causes to two: "I. A too great delicacy and sensibility of the nervous system, II. An uncommon weakness, or a depraved and unnatural feeling, in some organs of the body." Among the particular occasional causes he listed first wind, worms, or a tough phlegm in the stomach or bowels, then aliments improper in quantity or quality, and finally obstruction in the viscera of the lower belly—all gastrointestinal phenomena. Whytt's insistence that melancholy, regardless of the term applied, was a disease of nerves or organs put the seal on the idea of somatic etiology.[36]

It was Whytt's opposite number William Cullen (1710–90), Professor of Medicine at Glasgow, who coined the word *neurosis*. In his *First Lines in the Practice of Physic* (1777) Cullen's comments on hypochondriasis deal almost exclusively with dyspepsia and flatulence as prominent symptoms; low spirits or depressed affect are subordinate to the gastrointestinal complaints. Use of the word spleen persisted in literature long after it ceased to have its former medical meaning, and vapours, too, became a word used by nonmedical writers only. Hysteria and hypochondria maintain their place in the medical vocabulary, albeit with different meanings. "Spleen" was officially adopted into the French language in 1798 by the Académie française which defined it as "ennui de toutes choses, maladie hypochondriaque propre aux Anglais." It was not until 1880 when George Beard coined the term neurasthenia (literally, weak nerves) that a convenient new label was found for eighteenth-century spleen.[37]

Among the observed medical facts that genuinely troubled Cheyne was the high rate of suicide in England. Accurate vital statistics do not exist, but many writers of the period agreed that suicide was, as Thomas Gray put it, "epidemical." Moore[38] has summarized much of the evidence about suicide as a response to the emotional vicissitudes of life in eighteenth-century England. But by and large, victims of the spleen did not take their own lives; they learned to live unhappily and miserably with their affliction, as did their relatives and friends. To be sure, suicide can be considered as melancholia carried to its logical conclusion, but it is characteristic of neurosis that it need not follow the laws of logic or the rules of reason. Episodic depression was common among the major and minor literary figures of the period, but only a few developed a full-blown psychosis, and only a handful committed suicide. A simple survey will suffice.

Matthew Prior's dexterity at writing amusing light verse did not preserve him from periodic fits of despondency. Sir Samuel Garth, the physician-poet, often complained of the tedium of life and attempted suicide on one occasion. Jonathan Swift's irascibility was countered by periods of depression. Alexander Pope's physical ills were enough to account for his ill temper, but he, too, suffered from periods of low spirits and work inhibition. Thomas Parnell, a close friend to both Swift and Pope, the founder of the "graveyard school of poetry," was troubled by prolonged episodes of melancholia, described by Goldsmith as "fits of the spleen," and would retire to his native Ireland and drink heavily; there is some evidence that he died in a state of melancholia bordering on depressive psychosis. There is no doubt that William Collins suffered from depressive psychosis, first in its agitated form, then in a state of vegetative withdrawal, for several years before he died. Thomas Gray described his symptoms in a Latin manuscript that he did not publish. William Cowper attempted suicide three times and was confined; that he was able to live out his days and continue to function as a poet was because his family had the means to provide him with a sheltered and protected environment. One must exclude Christopher Smart from the list of melancholics; he was confined because of religious monomania, and there is no evidence he was depressed, usually somewhat the contrary. However, Thomas Chatterton did commit suicide, as did such lesser poets as Eustace Budgell, Thomas Carey, and Henry Needler. Samuel Johnson's "vile melancholy" is familiar to every reader, as is James Boswell as *The Hypochondriack* of the epoch. Laurence Sterne conformed to Arbuthnot's sally about the weather-glass; on rising, he would look at the weather-vane, and if it pointed to an east wind, would return to bed. Sterne's remedy was to write *Tristram Shandy*: "If 'tis wrote against anything, an' please your worships, ['tis] against the spleen."

Concern with both the prevalence of melancholia and the rising suicide rate led to proliferation of publications telling the public how to avoid the spleen. Best known among them are two poems, *The Spleen* (1737) by Matthew Green (1696–1737), published posthumously, and *The Art of Preserving Health* (1744) by John Armstrong (1709–79). Both poets had firsthand acquaintance with the disease. Green, an obscure customs clerk, described with wit and common sense his personal regimen to avoid bouts of depression. He believed the disease occurred "when nerves convulse" and wrote:

> When by its magic lantern spleen
> With frightful figures spreads life's scene,

an image that prefigures T. S. Eliot's "But as if a magic lantern threw the nerves in patterns on a screen." Yet there is still a residuum of old-fashioned humoral theory in Green. He advocated "the plainest food/ To mend viscidity of blood" so that:

> Through my veins my blood doth quicker shoot,
> And by swift current throws off clean
> Prolific particles of Spleen,

lines that suggest he was acquainted with both Harvey's ideas on circulation and Willis's explosive particles. In addition to a simple diet, Green recommended drink in moderation, exercise in open air, attendance at diverting plays and concerts, and avoidance of thinking about tragic or religious subjects as well as the enjoyment of female society. John Armstrong, whose M.D. degree from Edinburgh was not recognized in London, earned a precarious living as a writer and became one of Smollett's circle in the 1750s.[39] He lacked Green's light touch, but as expected, he too recommended a safe, sane, and sober regimen, moderation, avoidance of excitement, and such other guides as common sense might dictate.

In a different vein is the Latin poem *Neuropathia* (1740) by Malcolm Flemyng (1702–64), who had received his M. D. degree at Rheims and practiced at Hull. He grouped hysteria and hypochondria under the terms "Neuropathy" and ascribed them to the prevailing doctrine of tension and relaxation of nerve fibers, writing vaguely about the irritability of nerves: "Nempe irritatis nervis, liquor cerebri." Many lines are devoted to discussing whether nerves were hollow tubes carrying Willis's animal spirits or whether they were solid structures conducting vibrations. It was not until 1755 that J. Richardson[40] suggested that the neural impulse "is carried by the Nerves . . . by the quick motion of Electrick fire." Flemyng also suggested that "If we were clever enough to induce a tertian or quartan fever by a safe and certain method, we might go far in curing those diseases which depend on a weakness of the nerves or spirits." It was not until 1917 that Wagner-Jauregg introduced malaria therapy for central nervous system syphilis; Flemyng's "tertian or quartan fever" suggests he might have observed such benefits from endemic malaria or other fevers in the east coast Fens.

Lest twentieth-century readers think that English eighteenth-century writers overemphasized the weather as a cause of melancholy, we must recall that from November through March England was cold, dark, and damp: the only source of heat was the fireplace; five yards away from it one was cold. Even on sunny winter days the hours of daylight were short; candles and oil lamps cast only small circles of light to relieve the gloom. Few winter days were sunny, and London in particular was known for its smoke and fog. Southeast England from East Anglia down to Kent was exposed to the east wind sweeping in from the North Sea; even today a few consecutive days of that cold, damp, penetrating wind chills one to the bones and produces malaise.

By mid-century the spleen and its congeners were common coin in literature. Coeval with the Countess of Winchilsea's *Spleen* had been a skit by Steele in the *Tatler* (1708) in which he relates how he cured Tom Spindle, a poet, of a serious attack; both he and Addison wrote later comments on the topic. Fielding's *Amelia* (1751), often called the first English psychological novel, shows the heroine in a fit of spleen, "One of the worst disorders that can possibly attend a woman. . . . our physicians have not yet agreed upon its name. Some call it the fever of the spirits, some a nervous fever, some the vapours and some the hystericks." Post-Cheynean acceptance of the spleen's universality can be found in Goldsmith's *The Citizen of the World* (1762). Letter 90 tells us that when "the men of this country are once turned of thirty, they regularly retire every year at proper intervals to lie in of the *spleen*." In the same letter, he created "the man in black," a literary archetype of the disease. Among his fellow literati Goldsmith was reckoned as a "doctor," having had a brief, undocumented exposure to medical training, but in fact his medical background was almost nil, less even than James Joyce's, and his purely literary manner of dealing with melancholia testifies to the wisdom of his choice of career.

Sterne's *Sentimental Journey* (1768) was written as an antidote to Smollett's *Travels through France and Italy* (1766). The easy-going, pleasure-loving Anglican divine cast Smollett, who had been apprenticed to a Glasgow surgeon and had served as a naval surgeon but had not shed the dour Scottish skepticism of his youth, as Dr. Smelfungus, the stereotype of "the splenetic traveller." A passing comment by Smollett reveals the gulf between their outlooks. In a letter from Boulogne purportedly written at the outset of his trip, Smollett observes: "I know not whether I may be allowed to compare the Romish religion to comedy and Calvinism to tragedy. The first amuses the senses and excites ideas of mirth and good-humour; the other, like tragedy, deals in the passions of terror and pity" (*Travels*, Letter IV). Smollett could also be choleric, but he managed to insert a splenetic character into several of his novels—for example, Narcissa's aunt in *Roderick Random*, Celinda in *Ferdinand Count Fathom*, Cadwallader Crabtree in *Peregrine Pickle*, and Matthew Bramble in *Humphrey Clinker*, all written between 1748 and 1771. Crabtree might be taken as Smollett's caricature of himself, a mixture of spleen and choler, but Bramble is the leading character in a travelling outpatient clinic stocked with figures with both real and fancied diseases. Many of his letters are to his physician, Dr. Lewis, and the novel opens with one, beginning:

> The pills are good for nothing—I might as well swallow snow-balls to cool my reins—I have told you this over and over, how hard I am to move. . . .

In a later letter Bramble writes:

> Yet I cannot help thinking, I have some right to discharge the overflowings of my spleen upon you, whose province it is to remove those disorders that occasioned it.

A major theme in the novel is Bramble's gradual return to good health and mental equipoise by following a regimen of healthy exercise and moderation.

The spleen also made sporadic appearances in eighteenth-century theater. An early example is Colley Cibber's *The Double Gallant, or the Sick Lady's Cure* (1707), but George Colman's *The Spleen, or Islington Spa* (1776), derived from Molière's *Le Malade Imaginaire*, is more typical of the ability of playwrights of that period to assimilate topical material into a standard plot.

Intimate revelation of one's personal problems was not common in eighteenth-century literature, but in 1742 Thomas Gray, detached from the world and leading a donnish life, wrote to his friend Richard West about his own psyche:

> Mine, you are to know, is a white Melancholy, or rather *Leucocholy* ... which though it seldom laughs or dances, nor ever amounts to what one calls Joy or Pleasure, yet is a good easy sort of a state, and *ça ne laisse que de s'amuser*. The only fault of it is *insipidity*; which is apt now and then to give a sort of Ennui, which makes one form certain little wishes that signify nothing. But there is another sort, black indeed, which I have now and then felt, that has something in it like Tertullian's rule of faith, *Credo quia impossibile est*; for it believes, nay, is sure of everything that is unlikely, so it be but frightful; and on the other hand excludes and shuts its eyes to the most possible hopes, and everything that is pleasurable; from this the Lord deliver us![41]

Gray's felicitous informal style supplies evidence that he suffered from episodes of true depression. The coinage of the word *leucocholy* pays tribute to classical humoral theory, and one regrets the word did not receive wider usage. Gray was twenty-six when he wrote to West, yet his facility at playing with words seems a long-practiced, well-rehearsed defense to mask, or at least neutralize, his implicit psychopathology.

Though Gray admits to black moods, one must be wary about attaching self-reference to the line in his *Elegy*, "Melancholy marked him for her own." The phrase refers to the unknown youth buried in the country churchyard. Gray does not identify with the youth; his attitude is one of detachment, colored somewhat by his own lack of fulfillment. His posture is that of a painter unrolling a canvas on which he has painted his own version of the *Et in Arcadia ego* theme; depicting or contemplating the transitory nature of life, though one aspect of the melancholic tradition in literature, does not qualify as melancholia in a medical sense.

More typical of the mid-eighteenth-century poem on melancholy than Gray's *Elegy* is Thomas Warton's *The Pleasures of Melancholy* (1747). The shift in poetic attitude from the Countess of Winchilsea's ode and Matthew Green's hudibrastics is striking; the Countess displayed herself as victim, Green his efforts at self-therapy. Warton presented melancholy as a continuation of Milton's contemplative attitude in *Il Penseroso*. He knew the topography of Melancholy's landscape, and his ambit led him to

> solemn glooms
> Congenial with my soul; to cheerless shades,
> To ruin'd seats, to twilight cells and bow'rs,
> Where thoughtful Melancholy loves to muse,

and he decorated his lines with the paraphernalia and stock images of the melancholic stance—for instance, "yon ruin'd abbey's moss-grown piles," "the lone screech-owl's note," "the hollow charnel," and other Gothic furniture, telling his reader that

> Few know that elegance of soul refin'd
> Whose soft sensation feels a quicker joy
> From Melancholy's scenes. . . .

Perhaps it is unkind to fault Warton's iambs. Doubtless they struck a responsive chord in readers of his day and fitted the prevailing mode of poetic discourse. But his melancholy is far removed from spleen or "hypochondriack mania." Unlike his friend Collins, there is nothing in Warton to suggest he was in a stage of pre-psychotic depression. In neither *The Pleasures of Melancholy* nor *The Suicide* does Warton suggest his declamations refer to his own psyche or his own spleen.

In the penumbra of Gray and Warton is the "graveyard school" of poets who wrote with varying degrees of skill on themes associated with death and *pompes funèbres*. Sad and mournful as their favorite subjects were, lachrymose their tone, there is no evidence in their elegies or epitaphs that any of them suffered from a melancholic spleen himself or took notice of its medical points of reference. Their ideas lack originality of thought or expression, their images are conventional, they lack even the energy of the Babu poet over a century later whose lines on the death of Queen Victoria,

> Dust to dust, ashes to ashes;
> Into the tomb the great Queen dashes

have an idiom and perspective that is unique. Literary conventions of the time debarred them from profound personal involvement. They tended to divorce their literature from life.

Gray and Warton typify "academic poets" of the era, and in like fashion one can propose Edward Young to exemplify the mid-eighteenth-century poet motivated by religious impulses. He was in holy orders and an active clergyman. His *Night Thoughts* (1742–45) found a wide audience because he wrote of "wave to wave of fancied misery," and he was concerned with the vanities of earthly life and the promise of the soul's immortality. He was the Martin Tupper of his age, and like his academically sheltered brethren had a penchant for morbid introspection, though he did not—in fact, could not—wear his spleen upon his sleeve.

A notable exception to the canon of detachment was William Cowper, who revealed his own plight on occasion—for instance, in some lines written to his friend Robert Lloyd in 1754 shortly before his first major breakdown. Cowper told his friend that he composed light verse to escape from depressing thoughts,

> to divert a fierce banditti
> (Sworn foes to anything that's witty),
> That, with a black infernal train,
> Make cruel inroads in my brain,
> And daily threaten to drive thence
> My little garrison of sense:
>   The fierce banditti which I mean
>   Are gloomy thoughts led on by spleen.

The lines are doggerel, and writing light verse was inadequate psychotherapy for Cowper's deep-seated religious melancholia.[42] Having weathered three attempts at suicide, toward the close of his life he was able to rationalize his malady: "it pleased God that I should be born in a country where melancholy is the national characteristic; and of a house more than commonly subject to it. To say the truth, I have often wished myself a Frenchman."[43] An astonishing statement from a writer so quintessentially British, but nowhere in Cowper's poems or correspondence do we find he had much insight into his condition.

Both Gray and Cowper shared with Cheyne, Sterne, and many others a sense of ill omen about the east wind. Gray trembled "at an east wind,"[44] and Cowper wrote of "the unhealthful east, / That breathes the spleen" (*The Task*, IV, lines 363–364). There is even a comparable allusion in *Bleak House*: Mr. Jarndyce was always conscious of an uncomfortable sensation when the wind was blowing from the east.

We cannot fail to mention Johnson and Boswell, both of whom were chronic melancholics. Two of Johnson's episodes were severe, almost to the point of psychosis. Boswell's journals record many days of low spirits and hypochondriasis, but they often alternated with periods of good, even high, spirits. Johnson's definitions of the vocabulary of melancholia in his *Dictionary* (1755) revert to humoral concepts. Boswell's essays in *The Hypochondriack* (1777-83) are somewhat more up to date, though he gives almost no evidence of having read medical literature. But there is such a wealth of biographical information about Johnson and Boswell, thanks to the latter, and their psychological problems can be so closely related to the circumstances of their lives that they are better treated in detail elsewhere.[45]

Late eighteenth-century detachment was reversed by the heightened self-awareness and self-scrutiny of Romanticism, to say nothing of its rejection of controlled literary expression that led to the untrammeled morbid imagination of the Romantic Agony. The year 1802 is a convenient watershed; both Wordsworth's *Resolution and Independence* and Coleridge's *Dejection: An Ode* bear that date. We can dismiss as hyperbole Wordsworth's lines:

> We poets in our youth begin in gladness;
> But thereof come in the end despondency and madness.

As usual, Wordsworth states his case inaccurately. Many poets do not begin their careers in happiness; only a minority wind up despondent and mad. But had Coleridge's poem been written a century before, it would have been called *Spleen: An Ode:*

> A grief without a pang, void, dark, and drear,
> A stifled, drowsy, unimpassioned grief,
> Which finds no natural outlet, no relief,
> In word, sigh, or tear—

Like the Countess of Winchilsea, Coleridge leaves no doubt that he was writing from personal experience. The diction is of a later vintage, but the mood is the same.

Shelley's *Lines Written in Dejection, near Naples* (1818) are an example of a fit of spleen, even down to

> I could lie down like a tired child
> And weep away the life of care.

One is tempted to growl that Shelley was a spoiled, willful youth, the verses juvenile and jejune, and that weeping away life's cares is a self-indulgence that ill becomes a man. But, having chastised the lad and his verses, one must concede that the emotion is personal and real, quite common among adolescents, experienced even by wordly-wise adults. One recalls Burton's comment that "windy vapours . . . compel good, wise, honest, discreet men . . . to dote, speak and do that which becometh them not." It is uncontrolled, almost aleatory, self-indulgence that distinguishes romantic from eighteenth-century melancholy; romantic poets took no account of medical notions about the nature and seat of the disorder. Chiefly, they were preoccupied with their own reactions and responses coupled with simultaneous exposition and catharsis of their sufferings.

A post-Cheynean echo is found in Keats's letter to his friend Reynolds, written in 1818 just before he left London for a journey to the north country:

> The climate here weighs us down . . . Tom is quite low-spirited. It is impossible to live in a country which is continually under hatches. Who would live in a region of Mists . . . when there is such a place as Italy? It is said that England from its clime produces a Spleen. . . .[46]

Tom's low spirits were probably the effect of advancing tuberculosis, and as for Italy's sunny skies, Keats himself died there three years later. Keats had studied medicine and was licensed; he was certainly familiar with contemporary ideas of melancholia, yet writing to a friend, he chose to use the medically obsolete term, spleen. But in the letter the word is devoid of medical denotation.

The following year Keats wrote his *Ode to Melancholy,* a poem that owes no debt to his medical training. He recognized that mental depression, at times, can have a sudden onset:

> But when the melancholy fit shall fall
> Sudden from Heaven like a weeping cloud.

But his intention was not clinical. One asks: Why from Heaven rather than from one's own psyche? A medically influenced poem would have directed Keats's gaze inward rather than upward. He seems to equate melancholy's onset with enjoyment of the perishable, sensuous delights of Beauty, assigning the dubious pleasures of melancholy to the lot of him

> whose strenuous tongue
> Can burst Joy's grape against his palate fine;
> His soul shall taste the sadness of her might,
> And be among the cloudy trophies hung.

Fusing sensuous pleasure with subsequent melancholy and the idea that the successful hedonist will taste Melancholy's might is a masochistic posture far removed from the eighteenth century. Consciously or not, Keats helped create an atmosphere of *morbidezza* that prefigures the *Weltschmerz* of his successors. As with Shelley, his early death precludes our following his ideas to their mature development. But a glance at Baudelaire's *Spleen et Idéal* (1861) suggests what happens when eighteenth-century equipoise is rejected in favor of self-indulgence:

> Je sais que la douleur est la noblesse unique
> Ou ne mordront jamais la terre et les enfers....

NOTES

1. Timothy Bright, *A Treatise of Melancholie* (London, 1586), p. 38.
2. Bright, pp. 102–103.
3. See J. Banister, *The Historie of Man, suck'd from the Sappe of the most approved Anathomistes* (London, 1578), pp. 69–81.
4. Thomas Walkington, *Optick Glasse of Humors, or the Touchstone of a Golden Temperature: Or the Philosopher's Stone to make a Golden Temper* (London, 1607), p. 226.
5. L. Lemnius, *The Touchstone of Complexions*, trans. Thomas Newton (London, 1581), p. 137. The original Latin text was first published in 1561.
6. See John Dover Wilson, *What Happens in Hamlet* (Cambridge: Cambridge University Press, 1935), pp. 309–320.
7. Robert Burton, *Anatomy of Melancholy*, ed. H. Jackson (London: Dent, 1972), III, pp. 398–399.
8. See John F. Sena, "Melancholic Madness and the Puritans," *Harvard Theological Review*, 66 (1973), 293–309.
9. See *God's Plot, the Paradoxes of Puritan Piety, being the Autobiography & Journal of Thomas Shepard*, ed. Michael McGiffert (Boston: University of Massachusetts Press, 1972).
10. Burton, *Anatomy*, I, pp. 414–417.
11. Hansreudi Isler, *Thomas Willis, 1621–1675: Doctor and Scientist* (New York: Hafner, 1968).
12. See *Thomas Willis's Oxford Lectures* (Oxford: Sandford, 1980) and Willis's *Oxford Casebook: 1650-1652* (Oxford: Sandford, 1981), both edited by Kenneth Dewhurst.
13. See John P. Wright, "Hysteria and Mechanical Man," *Journal of the History of Ideas*, 41 (1980), 233–247; and E. T. Carlson and M. M. Simpson, "Models of the Nervous System in Eighteenth-Century Psychiatry," *Bulletin of the History of Medicine*, 43 (1969), 101–115.
14. Thomas Willis, *Two Discourses concerning The Soul of Brutes, Which is that of the Vital and Sensitive of Man*, trans. S. Pordage (London, 1683), pp. 188, 192–193. The original Latin version, *De anima brutorum*, appeared in 1672.
15. Willis, *Casebook*, pp. 126–127.
16. See L. F. Calmeil, *De la folie* (Paris, 1845), I, pp. 387ff.
17. See J. P. Falret, "De la folie circulaire," *Bulletin de l'Académie Impérial de Médicine*, 19 (1854), 382–416.
18. Thomas Sydenham, *Works*, trans. R. G. Latham (London, 1848–1850), II, p. 85.
19. Sydenham, *Works*, II, pp. 88–89.
20. Sir William Temple, "Of Health and Long Life," in the *Works* (London, 1814), III, pp. 297–298.
21. See Michel Foucault, *Madness and Civilization: A History of Insanity in the Age of Reason*, trans. Richard Howard (New York: Pantheon Books, 1965).
22. See James Carkesse, *Lucida Intervalla: Containing divers Miscellaneous Poems Written at Finsbury and Bethlem* (London, 1679), p. 31. This work has been made more recently available in Michael DePorte's Augustan Reprint Society edition (Los Angeles: Clark Memorial Library, 1979).
23. E. M. Sickles, *The Gloomy Egoist: Moods and Themes of Melancholy from Gray to Keats* (New York: Columbia University Press, 1932), p. 2.
24. See John F. Sena's "Belinda's Hysteria: The Medical Context of *The Rape of the Lock*" in this volume.

25. Jonathan Swift, *Gulliver's Travels*, ed. H. Davis (Oxford: Basil Blackwell, 1965), pp. 263–264.
26. C. A. Moore, "The English Malady," in *Backgrounds of English Literature: 1700–1760* (Minneapolis: University of Minnesota Press, 1953), Chapter V, pp. 179–235.
27. See John Purcell, *A Treatise of Vapours, or, Hysterick Fits* (London, 1702).
28. Bernard Mandeville, *A Treatise of the Hypochondriack and Hysterick Passions* (London, 1711).
29. See Anne Finch, Countess of Winchilsea, *The Spleen: a Pindarique Ode* (London, 1709).
30. See John F. Sena, "Melancholy in Anne Finch and Elizabeth Carter: The Ambivalence of an Idea," *Modern Language Review Yearbook*, 1 (1979), 108–119.
31. William Stukeley, *Of the Spleen, its Description and History, Uses and Diseases, particularly the Vapors, with their Remedy. To which is added some Anatomical Observations on the Dissection of an Elephant* (London, 1723), pp. 49–58, 64–82.
32. See Sir Richard Blackmore, *A Treatise of the Spleen and Vapours: or, Hypochondriacal and Hysterical Affections* (London, 1725), especially pp. 210–212.
33. Nicholas Robinson, *A New System of the Spleen, Vapours, and Hypochondriack Melancholy: Wherein all the Decays of the Nerves and Lowness of the Spirits are mechanically accounted for* (London, 1729), pp. 192, 199, 226, 234, 241.
34. George Cheyne, *The English Malady: or, a Treatise of Nervous Diseases of all Kinds, as Spleen, Vapours, Lowness of Spirits, Hypochondriacal, and Hysterical Distempers, &c.* (London, 1733), pp. i–ii.
35. John Hill, *Hypochondriasis: A Practical Treatise* (London, 1766; rpt. with an introduction by G. S. Rousseau, Los Angeles: Clark Memorial Library, 1969), p. 3.
36. Robert Whytt, *Observations on the Nature, Causes, and Cure of those Disorders which have been commonly called Nervous, Hypochondriac, or Hysteric, to which are prefixed some Remarks on the Sympathy of the Nerves*, 2nd ed., corrected (Edinburgh, 1765), pp. 94, 108–109.
37. See G. M. Beard, *A Practical Treatise on Nervous Exhaustion—Neurasthenia, Its Symptoms, Nature, Sequences, Treatment* (New York: W. Wood, 1880).
38. See Moore, "English Malady," note 26.
39. William B. Ober, "John Armstrong (1709–1779): A Scot in London," *New York State Journal of Medicine*, 65 (1965), 2711–2717.
40. See J. Richardson, *Thoughts upon Thinking, or a new Theory of the Human Mind, wherein the physical Rationale of the Formulation of our Ideas, the Passions, Dreaming, every Faculty of the Soul, is attempted upon Principles entirely new* (London, 1755).
41. Letter to Richard West, 27 May 1742, in *The Letters of Thomas Gray*, ed. D. C. Tovey (London: Bell, 1900), I, p. 102.
42. William B. Ober, "Madness and Poetry: A Note on Collins, Cowper, and Smart," *Bulletin of the New York Academy of Medicine*, 46 (1970), 203–266.
43. Letter to Mrs. King, 4 August 1791, in the *Correspondence of William Cowper*, ed. Thomas Wright (New York: Dodd Mead, 1904), IV, p. 104.
44. Letter to Thomas Warton, 24 May 1771, in *The Letters of Thomas Gray*, III, p. 320.
45. William B. Ober, "Johnson and Boswell: 'Vile Melancholy' and 'The Hypochondriack.'" *Bulletin of the New York Academy of Medicine*, 61 (1985): 657–678. For Boswell, also see Allen Ingram, *Boswell's Creative Gloom: A Study of Imagery and Melancholy in the Writings of James Boswell* (London: Macmillan, 1982).
46. Letter to John Hamilton Reynolds, 10 April 1818, in John Keats, *Complete Poetical Works and Letters* (Boston: Houghton-Mifflin, 1899), p. 297.

A useful guide to the literature on melancholy in the eighteenth century has been compiled by John F. Sena, *A Bibliography of Melancholy, 1600-1800* (London: Nether Press, 1970).

NEUROPATHIA:
SIVE,
De MORBIS
HYPOCHONDRIACIS,
ET
HYSTERICIS,
LIBRI TRES,
POEMA MEDICUM.
CUI PRAEMITTITUR
Dissertatio Epistolaris prosaica ejusdem Argumenti.

—— *Ego nunc, quoniam haec ratio plerumque videtur*
Tristior esse quibus non est tractata, retroque
Vulgus abhorret ab hac; volui tibi suaviloquenti
Carmine Pierio rationem exponere nostram;
Et quasi musaeo dulci contingere melle:
Si tibi forte animum tali ratione tenere
Versibus in nostris possem. ——   LUCRET.

Autore MALCOLUMBO FLEMYNG, M. D.

EBORACI:
Excudebant CÆSAR WARD, et RICARDUS CHANDLER,
Sumptibus Autoris.
MDCCXL.

Yorick and the "Eternal Fountain of our Feelings"

JOHN A. DUSSINGER

On his journey through the Bourbonnais after his emotional encounter with the deranged peasant girl, Maria, Yorick indulges in an apostrophe that may be taken as the crux of any reading of Laurence Sterne's *A Sentimental Journey:*

> —Dear sensibility! source inexhausted of all that's precious in our joys, or costly in our sorrows! thou chainest thy martyr down upon his bed of straw—and 'tis thou who lifts him up to HEAVEN—eternal fountain of our feelings!—'tis here I trace thee—and this is thy divinity which stirs within me—not, that in some sad and sickening moments, *"my soul shrinks back upon herself, and startles at destruction"*—mere pomp of words!—but that I feel some generous joys and generous cares beyond myself—all comes from thee, great—great SENSORIUM of the world! which vibrates, if a hair of our heads but falls upon the ground, in the remotest desert of thy creation.[1]

To judge from the reception of this work since the eighteenth century, interpretation will vary in accordance with how closely Sterne the writer is to be identified with Yorick the narrator; but in recent years, it seems to me, there has been a substantial consensus toward recognizing the double nature of the author as both satiric wit and Man of Feeling.[2] Just as phenomenological and post-structuralist criticism has uprooted traditional assumptions about the text's objective status, so the whole issue of authorial intention has grown too complex to be absorbed satisfactorily by the principles of classical rhetoric. The inherent indeterminacy of language and the uncertain boundary between fiction and nonfiction demand the reader's active role in constituting the text; and Sterne's narrative art, as Dr. John Eustace understood at once, quite consciously exploits this creative involvement.[3]

Whether stressing the verbal or the metaphysical aspects, previous commentary has engendered at least four basic interpretations of this apostrophe: (1) that it is Yorick's, not Sterne's, infatuation with a God who vibrates emotionally at the slightest event; (2) that it is distrustful of as well as celebratory toward Yorick's/Sterne's sensibility; (3) that the inflated language implies a disembodied ascent for the moment only to be collapsed in the final episode, "The Case of Delicacy"; and (4) that it is an exalted expression of feeling coming from within the individual but inextricably joined to the cosmic system.[4] Without for once denying the ambivalent playfulness of the narrative, which partly accounts for these diverse responses, I wish to consider why the last view, supported by a number of prominent historical scholars, may be closest to the author's original conception, even if it means having him appear much less modern than his twentieth-century ahistorical readers would wish.

While trying once again to place Yorick/Sterne in his intellectual milieu it may also be instructive to examine how our predilections against the ideological content of the apostrophe continually interfere with our reading. Paradoxically, this background cannot be ignored: when a neo-Aristotelian critic like Wayne Booth chooses to do so, for instance, he finds Sterne's novel "troublesome" because it fails to give adequate "warning" about its ironic intent. Yet collecting the information necessary to gloss the various allusions in the text falls within the same hermeneutic circle. Thus, contrary to other historical scholars, Arthur Cash prefers to divide the author and narrator categorically: "The infatuated Yorick is not to be taken as the spokesman for the Philosophy of Laurence Sterne."[5] But how do we decide this? Since the historical data fail to point ineluctably to this choice, perhaps Cash feels constrained to improve Sterne's reputation as a moralist by exalting him over his admittedly vulnerable protagonist. The trouble is that defining a background to a work already presupposes a critical stance of some kind. Take the central eighteenth-century mind/body dilemma, both "central" and "dilemma" by all accounts on the subject. In Cash's view, the most likely context for Yorick's apostrophe is the controversy between Leibniz and Clarke over Newton's explanation in the *Opticks* of space as God's sensorium. Against Leibniz's objection that God would therefore require sense organs and not be pure spirit, Clarke replied that Newton had intended the opposite meaning of the soul as a living, immaterial substance being present to the things themselves. Cash infers that Sterne is rendering Yorick as a caricature of the sensationalist that Leibniz had accused Newton of being.[6] But the decision to read the apostrophe in this way is not really more objective than Dilworth's New Critical interpretation. After all, if three intelligent contemporaries—Newton, Leibniz, and Clarke—had difficulty in understanding one another, at this distance from the original heat on the subject the modern reader is left with mere hypotheses about Sterne's connection, if any, to that controversy while composing the *Journey*.

A recent essay avoids this rigid dualism between author and character by emphasizing the blend of irony and feeling in the tone of the apostrophe: "The element in this passage that survives the satire is the direct link Yorick makes between sense and sentiment, his recognition of the human ability to endow objective phenomena with personal meaning."[7] A subsequent statement, however, reverses the priority of the experience: "A hair falling on the remotest desert is evidence of 'generous joys and generous cares beyond myself.'" Although elsewhere amply endowing objective phenomena with delusive intentions, here for once Yorick is finally testifying that his individual feelings are not self-rooted but inherently sympathetic with the Other like the "great SENSORIUM" of the godhead that is present to all phenomena. Instead of developing his important insight concerning the link between sense and sentiment, however, Chadwick takes cues from Mayoux and Braudy to welcome the text's indeterminacy as an outlet for unlimited inventiveness in the reader.

Another recent essay shows the very different problem of overdeterminacy by attempting to find a source for Sterne's associationism in David Hartley's theory of vibrations.[8] Happily, the tenuous juxtaposition of a radical determinism with Sterne's joyous physiology does prompt Lamb to concede at one point: "Although this account would not look out of place in Martinus Scriblerus's system of muscular morality, and although we might expect Sterne to see it as ridiculous as Swift and Arbuthnot saw similar mechanist theories, it seems to be the case that Sterne finds an intelligible account of human behavior in a doctrine like Hartley's."[9] Aside from the lack of any evidence that Sterne ever read Hartley, not only the Cartesian mechanism but the lackluster, quasi-scientific style of the *Observations on Man* would be anathema to Shandeism. Sterne, for instance, uses repeatedly the vibration theory of the nerves commonplace among Newton's followers to describe sensations, and he especially makes the feelings equivalent to musical sound. Thus while Tristram "felt the kindliest harmony vibrating within me, with every oscillation of the chaise alike" and all his perceptions "touch'd upon some secret spring either of sentiment or rapture," the moment is ripe for "the sweetest notes I ever heard" of Maria's vespers (IX. xxiv. 438). Yorick's paternalistic sentiments, in turn, "touch'd upon the string on which hung all her sorrows—she look'd with wistful disorder for some time in my face; and then, without saying any thing, took her pipe, and play'd her service to the Virgin—The string I had touch'd ceased to vibrate—in a moment or two Maria returned to herself—let her pipe fall—and rose up" (273-274). Likewise, in a jocular letter to Mrs. Vesey, probably written in 1761, Sterne surrenders himself to this neural/musical figure during some flirtatious innuendo:

> But that You are sensible, and gentle and tender—& from [one] end to the other of you full of the sweetest tones & modulations, requires a Connoisseur of more taste & feeling—in honest truth You are a System of harmonic Vibrations—You are the sweetest and best tuned of all Instruments—O Lord! I would give away my other Cassoc to touch you—but in giving this last rag of my Priesthood for this pleasure You perceive I should be left naked—‹nay› if not quite dis-*Orderd:*—so divine a hand as y^{rs} would presently get me into Order‹s› again—but if Yo[u] suppose, this would leave me, as You found me—believe me dear Lady, You are mistaken.[10]

As in Sterne, George Cheyne's medico-theology exploits this figure to suggest the close interaction between mind and body:

> the Intelligent Principle, or *Soul*, resides somewhere in the Brain, where all the Nerves, or Instruments of Sensation terminate, like a *Musician* in a finely fram'd and well-tun'd Organ-Case; that these

> Nerves are like Keys, which, being struck on or touch'd, convey the Sound and Harmony to this sentient Principle, or *Musician*.[11]

By contrast to Cheyne and Sterne, however, Hartley is unequivocal toward the metaphor: "For that the Nerves themselves should vibrate like musical Strings, is highly absurd; nor was it ever asserted by Sir *Isaac Newton,* or any of those who have embraced his Notion of the Performance of Sensation and Motion, by means of *Vibrations.*"[12]

Hartley's appeal to Newton's authority while rejecting the musical analogy raises a larger problem than attributing sources wrongly: the problem for the modern reader of grasping the way contemporaries in a given culture responded to each other. Unlike Sterne, for instance, Hartley seems to be impatient with the pervasive arbitrariness of discourse and is seeking a means to explain the tendency of language to change. As Michel Foucault observes:

> In the Classical age, to make use of signs is not, as it was in preceding centuries, to attempt to rediscover beneath them the primitive text of a discourse sustained, and retained, forever; it is an attempt to discover the arbitrary language that will authorize the deployment of nature within its space, the final terms of its analysis and the laws of its composition. It is no longer the task of knowledge to dig out the ancient Word from the unknown places where it may be hidden; its job now is to fabricate a language, and to fabricate it well—so that, as an instrument of analysis and combination, it will really be the language of calculation.[13]

Gabriel Josipovici's recognition of a "demonic analogy" in modern literature, "a world of infinite correspondences . . . without any stable reality underpinning them all," seems at first glance to be a consequence of the epistemic mutation that Foucault describes here; but just as Dante may represent an ordered metaphysics wholly unavailable to the present age, so Sterne belongs to a discourse which is arbitrary compared to the medieval culture but still far from the "private mythology" sometimes ascribed to him.[14] As Slawkenbergius reminds us: "It is the lot of few to trace out the true springs of this and such like revolutions—The vulgar look too high for them—Statesmen look too low—Truth (for once) lies in the middle" (IV. 271). Unlike the modern writer both Sterne and Hartley communicated in their "language of calculation," trusting that no matter how arbitrary the system worked.

Yorick's exuberant physicality in the *Journey* may owe something to the ideological shift from mechanism to materialism that affected the scientific climate between 1717, when the Leibniz-Clarke correspondence was published, and 1768, when Sterne wrote Yorick's narrative. As Robert Schofield has shown, the original impetus from the *Principia* and the *Opticks* in the late seventeenth and early eighteenth centuries was to explain all natural phenomena in terms of primary particles related by attraction and repulsion, and predictable in their motions by the Calculus. By the 1740s, however, in conjunction with other subjective tendencies in the culture—Richardson's novels, the meditational poems of Gray, Young, Collins, and Cowper, the Wesleyan Evangelical movement, the solipsism of Berkeley and Hume—a new generation of natural philosophers began seeking the causes of phenomena in unique substances having qualities in proportion to their quantity. Though often used interchangeably, "mechanism" and "materialism" denote for Schofield these two distinctly different tendencies, the latter, non-mathematical and anti-Newtonian in spirit, though attributing to the vague aether hypothesis in the *Opticks* a source for the new iatric interest in physiology and chemistry.[15]

Sterne's place in the mid-century intellectual revolution appears in his constant attack on the traditional mind/body dualism—whether in ancient philosophy, in medieval theology, or in Cartesian mechanism. What Yorick rejects in quoting the "mere pomp of words" from Addison's *Cato* is Plato's familiar argument in the *Phaedo* that the rational soul welcomes death as a release from the prison of the body.[16] Since this dualism applies equally to the Pauline/Augustinian doctrines of the world, flesh, and devil, Sterne's unorthodox invoking of current physiology to interpret the story of Job in a sermon is directed not only against Stoics like Seneca or Epictetus but against the ascetic tradition of Christianity as well: "one is led to doubt, whether the greatest part of their heroes, the most renowned for constancy, were not much more indebted to good nerves and spirits, or the natural happy frame of their tempers, for behaving well, than to any extraordinary helps, which they could be supposed to receive from their instructors."[17] As in the sermons, Tristram constantly stresses the close interdependence of mind and body: "A Man's body and his mind, with the utmost reverence to both I speak it, are exactly like a jerkin, and a jerkin's lining;—rumple the one—you rumple the other" (III. iv. 120).

If the conditions of this middle state are often laughable, however, so are the pretenders to a rationalistic ideal:

> I love the Pythagoreans (much more than ever I dare tell my dear Jenny) for their . . . "getting out of the body, in order to think well." No man thinks right whilst he is in it; blinded, as he must be, with his congenial humours, and drawn differently aside, as the bishop and myself have been, with too lax or too tense a fibre——Reason is, half of it, Sense; and the measure of heaven itself is but the measure of our present appetites and concoctions.
> (VII. xiii. 376)

No matter the particular context of the duality—in Platonism, Stoicism, Pythagoreanism, Cartesianism, or the new Methodism—Sterne remains contemptuous of any scheme to place mind firmly over the body. Implicit in his assault on the old binary metaphysics is a temporizing of orthodox theology with the enlightened humanism greatly influenced by the experimental philosophy. In this context his statement about his last work, notwithstanding its echoing Yorick's words, seems reliable: "my Sentimental Journey will, I dare say, convince you that my feelings are from the heart, and that that heart is not of the worst of molds—praised be God for my sensibility!"[18]

While fairly straightforward in opposing the traditional hierarchy of mind over body and of reason over the passions, Sterne's attitude toward the rival claims of mechanism and materialism, on the one hand, and of vitalism, on the other, is more complex. During the initial scene at Calais, after reaching a benevolistic high, aided of course by the wine, Yorick declares with apparent contradiction in view of his circumstances: "In doing this, I felt every vessel in my frame dilate—the arteries beat all chearily together, and every power which sustained life, perform'd it with so little friction, that 'twould have confounded the most *physical precieuse* in France: with all her materialism, she could scarce have called me a machine" (68-69). In a recent letter, Eric Rothstein, of the University of Wisconsin, suggested to me that Yorick's sense of his blood circulation proves that he is more than a machine because it was done without the usual means of producing heat: "Yorick's warmth and elevation of spirits occur without this friction, in fact with physical symptoms (dilation) which discourage friction, and thus which tend to disprove the Boerhaavean mechanism." But of course at this early stage of the *Journey* the occasion does not warrant the excitement aroused later for the apostrophe, and his automatic dismissal of the Franciscan immediately afterwards leaves no doubt that his behavior is often mechanical, despite himself, as he usually acknowledges after the fact.

Like many of his informed contemporaries, Yorick is curious, if not neurotically driven, to find out whether there is a ghost in the machine. His scene with Maria is qualitatively different from his solitary performance at Calais: despite the mechanical motions with the handkerchief to wipe away Maria's tears as well as his own, this time he seems to feel genuine sympathy with the Other; and the erotic motive reinforces rather than undermines the interaction:

> as I did it, I felt such undescribable emotions within me, as I am sure could not be accounted for from any combination of matter and motion.
>
> I am positive I have a soul; nor can all the books with which materialists have pester'd the world ever convince me of the contrary. (271)

Unless we assume that Sterne is ridiculing the feelings by showing their bodily symptoms, then Yorick's claim here to spirituality, it seems to me, hits at the older kinematic mechanics promulgated by the Cartesians in favor of the mid-century tendency toward vitalism, which emphasized a purposive "sentient principle" in the corporeal system.

More specifically, the fear of being no more than a machine may allude to La Mettrie's *L'Homme machine* (1747), as some scholars have believed; but if so, it is doubtful whether Sterne knew the book well enough to comprehend its remarkably Shandean attack on the outmoded matter-and-motion kinematics. Aram Vartanian defines La Mettrie's purpose:

> To understand the special filiation of mood and idea in that work *L'Homme machine*, we must first recall that at the time what was really felt to be deafening was the metaphysics of dualism, which, with the theology it supported, had ossified into a series of platitudes. By contrast, materialism came as a quickening and liberating current. Because it was possible to see in matter a source of spontaneous energy, the man-machine became associated in the moral sphere, somewhat paradoxically, with attitudes of freedom from restraint and *joie de vivre*.[19]

Unlike Descartes's *bête machine*, which Leibniz and others at the time scorned because it excluded consciousness, La Mettrie's *homme machine* incorporates Leibniz's idea of *force motrice*, the self-moving power of the organism. Taking a long neglected principle from Francis Glisson, who in the 1670s objected to the Cartesian clock analogy by pointing out the inherent movement in all the parts of the animal body, both La Mettrie and Haller advanced the concept of irritability on the findings of recent experiments with muscle tissue. Another important discovery of the 1740s, Trembley's polyp, with its astonishing ability to develop new zoophytes after being severed, complemented the principle of irritability: "The cosmic machine resembles the organism in that its moving and directing principle is to be found inside, not outside, its own structure."[20] Ironically, therefore, a *physical precieuse* in La Mettrie's camp could very well have called Yorick a machine and not at all be confounded by his spasmodic outbursts, which on the contrary reveal the very force of living matter from within.

While La Mettrie's machine hypothesis was an ingenious attempt to bridge the extremes of vitalism and mechanism, more conservative contemporaries like Jerome Gaub and Robert Whytt had a similar interest and may have been more readily available to Sterne. Gaub's objective was to apply physiological knowledge to the treatment of major mental disorders; trained by Boerhaave and also a professor of medicine at Leyden, he delivered his academic oration *De regimine mentis quod medicorum est* in 1747, with La Mettrie in the audience.[21] Although prudently maintaining a respectable mind/body dualism, Gaub's demonstration of the profound interaction between physical and mental states was neither far from the *homme machine* nor from Tristram's rumpled jerkin and its lining. Drawing upon Galen's and Hippocrates' psychosomatic doctrines to counter the Platonic incorporeal *psyché*, Gaub cautiously admits that "the power of the mind over the body is probably no greater than that of the body over the mind."[22] But what would have been most disturbing in the era of Locke and Newton is Gaub's theme that the irrational, often unconscious and involuntary, phenomena of emotions and unknown bodily processes predominate in the system for good or ill. In both mind and body he finds an agent of arousal, the *enormôn*, quite beyond the control of the rational faculties: "When it slumbers you might think it absent entirely, so little does it then do; when it is aroused it breaks forth with a most violent impulse hardly to be contained." He calls the corporeal *enormôn* the "neural man": "This structure of nerves is no less animated from within by its motive power than it itself stirs up the rest of the body's inert mass throughout which it extends. In this sense it represents a kind of man within a man."[23]

Much more polemically doctrinal than Gaub, Robert Whytt, professor of medicine at Edinburgh, also steered safely between vitalism and mechanism while showing the supreme importance of the nerves in the living organism. He criticizes Georg Stahl specifically for "extending the influence of the soul, as a rational agent, over the body a great deal too far"; and he dismisses the Cartesians for reducing all phenomena to mechanical principles. To refine his position further, he declaims against the "modern Materialists [who] have imagined the *anima* to be no other than a more subtle kind of matter lodged chiefly, in the brain and nerves, and circulating with the grosser fluids" and against "a few authors [who] have run even such lengths, as to suppose the very *animus,* or rational soul itself, material."[24] Nevertheless, if disturbed by the materialists, Whytt is quick to deny the scholastic opinion that the soul exists in an individual point and argues from physiological evidence that it "must be present at one and the same time, if not in all the parts of the body, yet, at least, where-ever the nerves have their origin; i.e. it must be, at least, diffused along a great part of the brain and spinal marrow." To support this psychosomatic thesis Whytt points out that "some of the greatest Philosophers of the last and present age, supposed the soul to be extended," naming Gassendi, Henry More, Isaac Newton, and Samuel Clarke.[25] Having established his orthodoxy in the tradition of the Anglican Church and the Royal Society, Whytt then describes the involuntary motions of the nerves as primary and of the blood as secondary, the "sensibility" or irritability of the heart deriving from the *sensorium commune* and all the feelings excited in the mind and nerves. With some diffidence in admitting the determinism of the involuntary motions in the body, he compensates by stressing the idea of "a general sympathy which prevails through the whole system" and the remarkable "*consent* between various parts of the body" to allay any fears of either old or new machine hypotheses.[26]

Surely nothing in Gaub, Whytt, or even in much of La Mettrie conflicts with Sterne's celebration of life as corporeal motion directed by some instinctive power in the organism; on the contrary, to the modern reader the eighteenth-century medical writer and fictional writer seem almost indistinguishable. Furthermore, any argument to prove a rationalistic theology as a norm in Sterne's sermons will need to skip deftly over the abundant concern with the involuntary, hidden dynamics of vibrations and fluids that not only mitigate the individual's moral accountability but on the positive side ally him to the whole system of Nature:

> in the present state we are in, we find such a strong sympathy and union between our souls and bodies, that the one cannot be touched or sensibly affected, without producing some corresponding emotion in the other,—Nature has assigned a different look, tone of voice, and gesture, peculiar to every passion and affection we are subject to; and, therefore, to argue against this strict correspondence which is held between our souls and bodies,—is disputing against the frame and mechanism of human nature.—We are not angels, but men cloathed with bodies, and, in some measure, governed by our imaginations, that we have need of all these external helps which nature has made the interpreters of our thoughts.

Tristram plays on the psychosomatic dilemma in the same language: "nor are we angels, I wish we were,—but men cloathed with bodies, and governed by our imaginations" (V. vii. 273); and doubtless because of our corporeal state, we are damned to syllogizing by our noses while angels and spirits do it by intuition.[27]

Like his contemporaries in physiology, Sterne understands the irrational element in man to exert an all-important function of survival. If the imagination, clothed with the body, thwarts our analytic ability, its illusory power, corresponding with the purposive motions of the body, is indispensable. In his sermon "Trust in God," rather than the usual emphasis from orthodox rationalism on the freedom to believe or not to believe, Sterne seems to identify religious faith with some unknown involuntary process of nature:

> though in fact it no way alters the nature of the cross accidents to which we lay open, or does at all pervert the course of them,—yet [it] imposes upon the sense of them, and like a secret spring in a well-contrived machine, though it cannot prevent, at least it counterbalances the pressure,—and so bears up this tottering, tender frame under many a violent shock and hard justling, which otherwise would unavoidably overwhelm it.—Without such an in-

> ward resource, from an inclination, which is natural to man, to trust and hope for redress in the most deplorable conditions,—his state in this life would be, of all creatures, the most miserable.[28]

Just as Gaub prefers to avoid giving a name to the "certain something both in the body and in the mind" to underscore its mysterious presence, and just as Whytt repeatedly acknowledges his perplexity at how the mind affects the body, so Sterne adopts the indefinite pronoun for the heuristic idea of this "inward resource" to prolong life against all odds.

But in *Tristram Shandy*, when the idea recurs with much of the same language, the conversation between Walter and Toby implies ironically the hobby-horse penchant for assigning a name to the ineffable powers manifest in daily life:

> Though man is of all others the most curious vehicle, said my father, yet at the same time 'tis of so slight a frame and so totteringly put together, that the sudden jerks and hard jostlings it unavoidably meets with in this rugged journey, would overset and tear it to pieces a dozen times a day—was it not, brother *Toby*, that there is a secret spring within us—Which spring, said my uncle *Toby*, I take to be Religion. . . . Figuratively speaking, dear *Toby*, it may, for aught I know, said my father; but the spring I am speaking of, is that great and elastic power within us of counterbalancing evil, which like a secret spring in a well-ordered machine, though it can't prevent the shock—at least it imposes upon our sense of it.

While charitably indulging his brother's figurative use of "Religion," Walter, as a natural philosopher, quixotically believes that his own mechanistic nomenclature ("elastic power") somehow denotes the thing signified exactly (IV. viii. 209).[29]

Sterne's insight into the ultimate mystery of the natural processes and above all into the arbitrary analogical discourse of his time brings us back to the problem of reading the *Journey*. Unlike Toby or Walter, Yorick is self-conscious about the inadequacy of language to enclose and communicate his perceptions; and perhaps for this reason alone his apostrophe to "Dear sensibility" and his constant theme of universal benevolence may seem too conventional to represent the implied author, who elsewhere appears eerily at the margins of classical discourse. Aesthetically a lot is at stake here, but rather than bisect author and narrator into discrete entities to preserve what is essentially modern in the *Journey* it is more relevant to the historical scholar to understand Sterne's originality in proffering an unusually complex Man of Feeling, one who often finds himself trapped in mechanical behavior and knows it after the fact, but also one who in the right situation experiences emotional peaks that dissolve the self with the Other. A major rhetorical strategy, after showing repeated failures in Yorick to get beyond the mechanical reflexes, is to suggest that "settled principle of humanity and goodness" of purposive emotion against the many delusions, freely admitted by the narrator, of a permissive imagination; it may be that this strategy worked far better for the eighteenth-century reader than for us.

Neither formalist analyses nor historical glosses suffice for our immersion in Yorick's quest of the heart, and the fact that Sterne did not live to finish the work is hardly at issue. As Hans-Georg Gadamer has argued, the historical text is to some extent beyond recovery and the most earnest pursuit of objective knowledge about the past will be encircled by the thought-structures of the present.[30] A main obstacle in the *Journey*, of course, is its subject-matter: the sensiblity, with all its neural threads, musical vibrations, pulse of blood, and erotic arousal. No amount of affirmation ("mere pomp of words"), Yorick well knew, will communicate the actual epiphany of oneness attested to in the apostrophe; but the following vignettes, "The Supper" and "The Grace," achieve a rare moment of imaginative feeling before the relapse in the final scene of the novel:

> —In a word, I thought I beheld *Religion* mixing in the dance—but as I had never seen her so engaged, I should have look'd upon it now, as one of the illusions of an imagination which is eternally misleading me, had not the old man, as soon as the dance ended, said, that this was their constant way; and that all his life long he had made it a rule, after supper was over, to call out his family to dance and rejoice; believing, he said, that a chearful and contented mind was the best sort of thanks to heaven that an illiterate peasant could pay—
>
> —Or a learned prelate either, said I. (284)

The context here reminds us of the pastoral motif in Sterne's sermons as well as in Tristram's joyful encounter with the peasants of Languedic.[31] But Yorick's tone, it should be noted, lacks uncle Toby's naïve trust in figurative language; and most importantly, the experience, like the speaker's in Keats's "Ode to a Nightingale," appears to be originating from without—from the vertiginous phenomenon of the group dancing which momentarily draws the sickly prelate in the black frock coat into its movements. Remembering past solipsistic illusions, Yorick hesitates before losing himself in the scene; and in doing so he gains our assurance.

Eighteenth-century pietism is no longer in fashion (the "illiterate peasant" is a cliché of the sentimentalists), but Sterne's art in rendering emotion is not dated like the subject matter. What can be astonishingly effective in the reading is the rhythm of verbal ejaculation and carefully timed silences: hence the usual straining of syntax and punctuation as well as of typography to capture the spoken language of the moment. In the passage above a single-sentence paragraph moves from the immediate apotheosis of the dance and Yorick's incredulous response to the later verification given in indirect discourse from the old man's testimony concerning the family's ritual of thanksgiving. By sleight of hand, the syntax brushes the peasantry with the divine inflatus; and at the same time the "I" and "thou" of social and ontological difference become fused at the period. But the pause in reading enforced by the typographical spacing and the measured dashes has the expressive power of the carefully timed silence within a musical score, and it is characteristic of Sterne's resistance to the deadening conventions of the printed word and of the artistic risks he dared in engaging the reader in the margins of discourse. Perhaps among all the eighteenth-century writers of fiction he understood best that mysterious phenomenon of spontaneous energy—call it the *force motrice*, the *enormôn*, "secret spring," or "*Religion* mixing in the dance"—and wrote the only autobiographical novel in the period to give this energy a temporal form in language. For Sterne, writing, like the sensibility itself, seemed to depend on a kind of "contagion" with the reader, if it were to work at all.[32] Whatever we decide about Yorick's apostrophe to sensibility, in particular, the style of the *Journey* demands a reader with a similar responsiveness to the body's equality with the mind, against traditional prejudices to the contrary; but perhaps most important for Sterne's aesthetics, it demands a reader willing to confront its intentional indeterminacy.

NOTES

1. *A Sentimental Journey*, ed. Gardner D. Stout, Jr. (Berkeley and Los Angeles: University of California Press, 1967), pp. 277–278. All further references are to this edition and in parentheses in the text. References to *Tristram Shandy* are to the Riverside Edition by Ian Watt (Boston, Mass.: Houghton Mifflin, 1965), the volume, chapter, and page numbers included in parentheses in the text.

2. Alan Dugald McKillop, for instance, may have defined the prototype of most interpretations since the 1950s, in *The Early Masters of English Fiction* (Lawrence and London: University of Kansas Press, 1956), pp. 182–219. It may be an indication of McKillop's originality that so careful an historical scholar as Martin Battestin should overlook this study when reaching similar conclusions about the profoundly important "body language" in Sterne; see "'A Sentimental Journey' and the Syntax of Things," *Augustan Worlds*, ed. J. C. Hilson, M. M. B. Jones, and J. R. Watson (New York: Barnes & Noble, 1978), pp. 223–239.

3. Probably every reader knows the story, but I'll repeat it anyway: "Your walking stick is in no sense more *shandaic* than in that of its having *more handles than one*—The parallel breaks only in this, that in using the stick, every one will take the handle which suits his convenience. In *Tristram Shandy*, the handle is taken which suits their passions, their ignorance or sensibility. There is so little true feeling in the *herd* of the *world*, that I wish I could have got an act of parliament, when the books first appear'd, 'that none but wise men should look into them.'" See the *Letters of Laurence Sterne*, ed. Lewis Perry Curtis (Oxford: Clarendon Press, 1935), p. 411. [To Dr. John Eustace, London, 9 February 1768].

4. For most recent examples of these four interpretations see the following: (1) Arthur Hill Cash, *Sterne's Comedy of Moral Sentiments: The Ethical Dimensions of the Journey* (Pittsburgh, Penn.: Duquesne University Press, 1966), pp. 89–101; (2) Joseph Chadwick, "Infinite Jest: Interpretation in Sterne's *A Sentimental Journey*," *ECS*, 12 (1978–79), 190–205; (3) Jonathan Lamb, "Language and Hartleian Associationism in *A Sentimental Journey*," *ECS*, 13 (1979–80), 285–312; and (4) Gardner Stout, Introduction to his edition of the *Journey*, p. 35, a position well taken by such scholars as McKillop, Traugott, Tuveson, Brady, Battestin, and others. Although Chadwick cites my chapter on the *Journey* in my *The Discourse of the Mind in Eighteenth-Century Fiction* (The Hague: Mouton, 1974) as the opposite extreme of Stout's view and thus of my argument here, it is only superficially so. The abundant evidence of Yorick's paranoiac failure to communicate with others (my previous argument) increases all the more the significant moments of real sympathy toward his belief in the proximity of the sensorium to the godhead.

5. See Wayne C. Booth, *The Rhetoric of Fiction* (Chicago, Ill.: University of Chicago Press, 1961), p. 316; and Cash, *Sterne's Comedy*, p. 95.

6. Cash, p. 95.

7. Chadwick, "Infinite Jest," 198.

8. Lamb, "Language and Hartleian Associationism," esp. 299–312.

9. Lamb, 303.

10. *Letters of Laurence Sterne*, p. 138.

11. George Cheyne, *The English Malady: Or, A Treatise of Nervous Diseases of all Kinds* (London, 1733), pp. 4–5. Among the some fifty items on natural philosophy and

medicine in the Todd and Sotheran sale catalogue of Sterne's library, the three works by Cheyne listed are as follows: *Essay on Health and Long Life* (1725), *English Malady* (1733), and *Essay on Regimen* (1740). Bibliographical scholars have pointed out the unreliability of this catalogue as indication of Sterne's actual reading, but nevertheless the possibility remains that he read these and other works mentioned in the context of eighteenth-century medicine.

12. David Hartley, *Observations on Man, His Frame, His Duty, and His Expectations* (London: Printed by Samuel Richardson, 1749), Part I, pp. 11–12.
13. Michel Foucault, *The Order of Things* (New York: Random House, 1970), pp. 62–63.
14. Quoted from Mark Loveridge, *Laurence Sterne and the Argument about Design* (London and Basingstoke: Macmillan, 1982), pp. 38–39. Though Loveridge's study is among the freshest in recent years, his reading of the *Journey* is not far from the old Putney, Dilworth, and Cash division between author and narrator.
15. Robert E. Schofield, *Mechanism and Materialism: British Natural Philosophy in An Age of Reason* (Princeton, N.J.: Princeton University Press, 1970), pp. 91–114. In view of Sterne's obvious stylistic parallels with Cheyne's physiology, Schofield's point that the latter's Newtonianism moved gradually from the early corpuscular theory to the materialistic, vitalistic, and mystical universe (pp. 58–59) is suggestive of Tristram's conclusion that "we live amongst riddles and mysteries" (IV. xvii. 219).
16. Dougald MacMillan and Howard Mumford Jones, the editors of *Plays of the Restoration and Eighteenth Century* (New York: Henry Holt, 1931), identified Plato's *Phaedo* as the source for Cato's soliloquy in Act V, scene one (footnote 1 on p. 544).
17. Sermon XV, "Job's Expostulation with His Wife," *The Sermons of Mr. Yorick* (Oxford: Shakespeare Head, 1927), I, 175. Further references to the sermons indicate volume and page numbers of this edition.
18. *Letters*, pp. 395–396. [To William Stanhope, 27 September 1767].
19. Aram Vartanian, *La Mettrie's "L'Homme Machine": A Study in the Origins of an Idea* (Princeton, N.J.: Princeton University Press, 1960), p. 31.
20. Vartanian, p. 26.
21. Vartanian, pp. 90–91. See L. J. Rather's Introduction to his translation of Gaub's work, *Mind and Body in Eighteenth Century Medicine* (Berkeley and Los Angeles: University of California Press, 1965), esp. pp. 1–16. References to Gaub are to this translation.
22. Gaub, p. 38.
23. Gaub, pp. 60 and 64. Gaub borrowed the term *enormôn* from Hippocrates.
24. Robert Whytt, *An Essay on the Vital and involuntary Motions of Animals* (Edinburgh, 1751), pp. 276–277, and 280.
25. Whytt, p. 380. Cf. "*Objects* are perceiv'd by our *Senses* to move, insomuch as different parts of the *Object* striking on the same, or different Extremities of Nerves, successively cause different *Refluxes* of the *Spirits* to the *Commune Sensorium*, one after another. All *Perception* is caused in the *Soul*, by the Motion which is excited in the *Nerves* and *Organs*; as likewise the *Reflux* of *Spirits* to the Brain," Mat[thew] Beare, M.D., *The Sensorium: A Philosophical Discourse of the SENSES* (Exon, 1710), p. 9. Malcolm Flemyng, a contemporary of Whytt's, trusts Providence with the ulti-

mate mystery of the mind/body relationship: "concerning the manner of the operation of our will upon the fluids and solids of our body, it is common to, and equal in all possible explications of animal sensation and motion. And as it may, I think, be rightly referred to the positive laws of union, between our corporeal and incorporeal parts, that is, between mind and body, established by our all wise and all powerful creator; it only affects these minute philosophers called materialists," *The Nature of the Nervous Fluid, or Animal Spirits, Demonstrated* (London, 1751), pp. 39-40.

26. Robert Whytt, *Observations on the Nature, Causes, and Cure of those disorders which have been commonly called Nervous, Hypochondriac, or Hysteric: to which are prefixed some remarks on the sympathy of the nerves*, 2nd ed. (Edinburgh, 1765), p. vi. Like Yorick, Whytt attributes the life principle to this power of sympathy, which derives from the nerves: "Could we suppose the circulation of the blood were to remain, after a total abolition of the sentient powers of the brain and nerves, there would be no more *sympathy* between those of any hydraulic machine. As in this case, the motion of the fluids would be merely mechanical, so every change made in any of its parts, must be the result of mechanism alone, and consequently, wholly different from *consent*, which, as it depends upon feeling, cannot be explained upon mechanical principles," p. 32.

27. Sermon XVI, "The Worship of God," II, 239–240.

28. Sermon VII, "Trust in God," II, 148.

29. A similar quandary arises over the "solutions of noses" when Toby opposes his final cause to Walter's material cause: "—There is no cause but one, replied my uncle *Toby*,—why one man's nose is longer than another's, but because that God pleases to have it so.—That is *Grangousier's* solution, said my father. —'Tis he, continued my uncle *Toby*, looking up, and not regarding my father's interruption, who makes us all, and frames and puts us together in such forms and proportions, and for such ends, as is agreeable to his infinite wisdom.———'Tis a pious account, cried my father, but not philosophical—there is more religion in it than sound science. 'Twas no inconsistent part of my uncle *Toby's* character,—that he feared God, and reverenced religion" (III. xli. 179). While discussing Hartley's scheme for a philosophical language for "real essences" that would be as precise in meaning as mathematical symbols, Lamb includes Walter with Comenius, Wilkins, Leibniz, and Condillac in this search for a universal nomenclature; and he makes the important point about the nominalism of the *Journey*: "To be fair to Yorick the resort to literal language is a sign of uncertainty rather than in any faith in the power of the name; yet there is an aspect of his journey that shows language being purified by sheer happiness" (p. 309). He then proceeds to argue, wrongly, I believe, that the apostrophe and the subsequent language pertaining to the Bourbonnais experience becomes too disembodied to be convincing. Unlike Toby, who is content to look heavenward rather than agonize over "solutions," Yorick, though a clergyman by profession, is radically empirical throughout his journey; and at moments he can be just as deliberate about words as he is skeptical about things.

30. Gadamer, *Truth and Method* (New York: Seabury Press, 1975), esp. pp. 235–274: "The elevation of the historicality of understanding to the status of hermeneutical principle."

31. See Stout's note on this passage in his edition of the *Journey*, p. 284; also pp. 28–31 and Appendix E, pp. 338–342.
32. Also see Edmund Burke: "by the contagion of our passions, we catch a fire already kindled in another, which probably might never have been struck out by the object described," *A Philosophical Enquiry into the Origin of our Ideas of the Sublime and Beautiful*, ed. James T. Boulton (London: Routledge and Kegan Paul, 1958), pp. 175–176; and Loveridge: "To read is to lay oneself open, like the Abderites, to 'contagion.' The sympathy of reading is like the sympathy of sentiment," *Laurence Sterne and the Argument about Design*, p. 208. Loveridge quotes the above passage from Burke and also one from Coleridge in 1825: "Sensibility . . . is for the greater part a quality of the nerves, and a result of individual bodily temperament . . . in its mere self . . . it proves little more than the coincidence or contagion of pleasurable or painful sensations in different persons."

The New Rhetoricians:
Psychology, Semiotics, and Critical Theory

JAMES ENGELL

The subject of rhetoric seems from the beginning to have flourished under what Johnson calls "the shelter of academick bowers," and those studying it have come largely from schools and pulpits. Most poets learn rhetoric from other poets. This is the short cut Longinus recommends when he says that Plato shows us a way to attain the sublime without paying attention to figures of speech:

> And what, and what manner of way, may that be? It is the imitation and emulation of previous great poets and writers. . . . For many men are carried away by the spirit of others as if inspired . . . from the great natures of the men of old there are borne in upon the souls of them who emulate them . . . what we may describe as effluences. . . .[1]

In *The Minstrel* (I. St. 43) James Beattie pictures his young genius seduced by the art of an aged, female bard, not by university lectures:

> Then, as instructed by tradition hoar,
>   Her legend when the Beldame 'gan impart,
>   Or chant the old heroic ditty o'er,
>   Wonder and joy ran thrilling to his heart;
> Much he the tale admired, but more the tuneful art.

Yet from 1750 through the 1780s a group of professors and divines—many of them Scottish and none of them particularly good poets, with the possible exception of Beattie himself—completely renovated the study of rhetoric and applied it to contemporary English literature. These critics, whom we might call the New Rhetoricians to distinguish them from their more classical formalist counterparts in the Renaissance and earlier eighteenth century, altered the course of English letters and provided a basis for the romantic veneration of the expressive and emotional power of figurative, natural language. The New Rhetoricians are properly considered as a unified movement. They are, prior to our own century, the most important and cohesive group of critics in English. The appeal of their lectures and volumes, often used as texts on both sides of the Atlantic, lasted into Queen Victoria's reign.

Depending how large a net is cast, the New Rhetoricians encompass anywhere from a half dozen to scores of lecturers, ministers, and educators—anyone who jumped on the bandwagon to write an essay on syntax or a how-to book on style and elocution. But the important names are few (some transcend the group through their other activities): Adam Smith, George Campbell, Joseph Priestley, Hugh Blair, James Beattie, and—if we stretch our scope a bit—Thomas Gibbons, Lord Kames, Thomas Sheridan, and Robert Lowth.[2] It was a great day for Scotland. Not until the mid twentieth century would a group of English-speaking critics study, in such a thorough and systematic fashion, the psychological, semiotic, and linguistic foundations of literature.

Considering language as a series of signs and significations, time-honored terms they use with frequency and care, the New Rhetoricians became the first British critics to mount a collective effort explaining literature and literary forms in light of the structure of language. Specifically championing the idea of "theory," they develop, to borrow the title of George Campbell's important work of 1776, a "philosophy of rhetoric." (I. A. Richards would consciously revive this phrase for the title of his 1936 volume, part of a larger attempt to resurrect principles of the New Rhetoric as a basis for modern critical study.) The last major rhetorics of the old stock appeared in the late 1750s, John Lawson's *Lectures Concerning Oratory* (1758) and John Ward's *System of Oratory* (1759).[3] The New Rhetoricians deserve their epithet, if only because their books are no longer handbooks, and they consistently refute Samuel Butler's charge of jargon and mere classification (*Hudibras* I. i. 89-90):

>For all a rhetorician's rules
>Teach nothing but to name his tools.

And although they draw on classical rhetoricians, they subordinate formal divisions, long lists of terms, and rote strategies, in favor of a robust psychological approach, natural style, and a firm linguistic and grammatological foundation. Adam Smith, in his *Lectures on Rhetoric and Belles Lettres* (1762–63, but delivered as early as 1748) sets the fresh tone when he asserts that it was from "Figures, and divisions and subdivisions of them, that so many systems of rhetoric, both ancient and modern, have been formed. They are generally a very silly set of books and not at all instructive."[4] The new rhetorics—beginning with Smith's *Lectures* and including principally George Campbell's *Philosophy of Rhetoric* (1776), Hugh Blair's *Lectures on Rhetoric and Belles Lettres* (1783), Joseph Priestley's *Lectures on Oratory and Criticism* (1777, but delivered first in 1762), James Beattie's *Essays on Poetry and Music As They Affect the Mind* (1778), and, to a lesser degree, Lowth's *Poesi Sacra Hebraeorum* (1753), Kames's *Elements of Criticism* (1762), Thomas Sheridan's *Elocution* (1762), and Thomas Gibbons's *Rhetoric* (1767)—remain useful explorations in the theory and practice of literature.

In its wider sense rhetoric means the power of language, and the art of rhetoric analyzes the means by which that power may be obtained. But the New Rhetoric was intended as both a complete system of criticism and a guide to improving style and taste. The New Rhetoricians invoke Aristotle, Dionysus of Halicarnassus, Longinus, Cicero, and Quintilian, but they wish primarily to establish the "radical principles" of language and literature;[5] the literature they examined was, by and large, not ancient but emphatically contemporary. Rhetoric, they decided, derives from close reading, observation, and the study of the actual practice of writers. It goes beyond analysis and interpretation—it shows how good habits may be reinforced, how faults may be shunned. The final goal is improved understanding and improved praxis. Rhetoric begins with practice, proceeds through theory, and returns to the original acts of speaking and writing. Its procedure shifts between the descriptive and prescriptive.

Blair, in his *Lectures on Rhetoric and Belles Lettres* (1783), claims that criticism, taste, and rhetoric are nearly synonymous.[6] In academic papers we may indulge the luxury of separating them. As intelligent readers living in the world at large, we cannot. This fundamental message, which stands behind the best eighteenth-century criticism, attracted Saintsbury so much that he based his history of criticism on the stance taken by the New Rhetoricians. For "the Criticism or modified Rhetoric," of which Saintsbury's book "attempts to give a history, is pretty much the same thing as the reasoned exercise of Literary Taste." If Rhetoric avoids "the disease of technical jargon," which severs it from the generally educated public, then it can become "the Literary Criticism that it ought to be."[7] This is the ideal of the New Rhetoricians—to identify taste with criticism, not to separate the two. Blair "is to be very particularly commended," says Saintsbury, "for accepting to the full the important truth that 'Rhetoric' in modern times really means 'Criticism.'" The New Rhetoric is nothing less than "the Art of Literature, or in other words Criticism."[8]

The revival of rhetoric flourished in just those places, the Scottish universities and learned societies, where the most interesting philosophical debates were contested. Philosophy and rhetoric, philosophy and poetry, have always been hot and cold lovers. The special or essential purpose of rhetoric is not to instruct or to convey truth (though Bacon and others thought it should),[9] but to please, to persuade, and to do so in the most irresistible way. But if philosophy suspects the artfulness of rhetoric, it can hardly resist embracing it. One could, along with Quintilian, insist that the ideal orator and rhetorician be moral and honest "such as to have a genuine title to the name of philosopher,"[10] but there could be no guarantees. The best orator in *Paradise Lost* is Satan. Seen in a larger framework, rhetoric cleaves to the essential worth of inventive language and, more broadly, the value of imaginative art. Rhetoric—so conceived—places literature in the context of our most pressing questions of learning, faith, and action. In an "information" culture devoted increasingly to the visual image and to quantification, and at a time when the approaches to literary study are scattered, it is salutary to return to this basic concept of rhetoric.[11]

II

Even while pursuing elaborate systems and theory, the New Rhetoricians profess an empirical bias. Their theories derive from wide reading and return to specific, formative examples. At the outset of his *Lectures on Rhetoric and Belles Lettres,* Blair expresses the group spirit: "The rules of Criticism are not formed by any induction, *a priori* . . . that is, they are not formed by a train of abstract reasoning, independent of facts and observations. Criticism is an art founded wholly on experience. . . ." Hume, in *The Standard of Taste* (1757), likewise remarked that the basis for "rules" of art "is the same with that of all the practical sciences, experience." This "humble *a posteriori* method" is the one Saintsbury claims for his *History.*

Later in his *Lectures* Blair affirms that "All science"—and by this he includes systematic criticism—"arises from observations on practice."[13] The method, then, is indeed "scientific," but Blair, Johnson, and others also consider criticism an "art." Can it be both art and science? The answer apparently is yes, and the implication is that we waste a lot of breath in trying to decide the difference. As with many human affairs subject to general principles, criticism—like politics—is at once a science and an art. It is a science but not an exact one.[14] It is an art, but not a fictive one. Aristotle begins his "art" of rhetoric by saying that his topic deals with matters of general interest "not confined to any *special* science," but that rhetoric is more than a knack and "can be reduced to a system . . . and such an examination admits it to be the function of an art."[15] George Campbell, like Northrop Frye, compares criticism to mathematics, but confesses that critical principles never attain the clarity and perfection of mathematical axioms. Some leeway, which is the essence of critical judgment, always persists.[16]

"Pure logic," says Campbell, cannot govern criticism, because logic "regards only the subject" or work at hand, "which is examined solely for the sake of information." Criticism must mediate. It is concerned with broader communication and considers not only the subject, but "the speaker and the hearers, and both the subject and the speaker for the sake of the hearers, or rather for the sake of the effect intended to be produced in them."[17] Though some terms the New Rhetoricians employ are not now current, they pay considerable attention to what we style "reader response."

Any critic who understands both a text and responses to it must possess two kinds of knowledge: (1) a command of interpretation and the possible significance of a text; and, (2) in order to gauge the purpose and success of that text in rousing its audience and communicating with it, a psychological acuity—the critic must be a student of the mind and the passions, of intellect and emotion as they are expressed not just in literature but in experience at large.

The New Rhetoricians are some of the most perceptive psychologists of their time. If close reading was one leg of the stiff twin compass they used to measure literature, then the other leg was nothing less than knowledge of human nature. One psychologist has recently remarked that any of his colleagues working on anything other than language "is just wasting his time."[18] The critic becomes a psychologist in order to help the student of rhetoric become one too. In this sense, at least, the rhetorician is a humanist and a moralist—not a preceptor of moral rules, but one who studies *mores*. Quintilian made this connection centuries ago.[19] Its fundamental truth resurfaces in the university title of several New Rhetoricians: they are professors of moral philosophy. To emulate great poetry requires an open approach to *mores*—to "life and manners," that key phrase which informs so many pieces of criticism from Dryden through Hazlitt, and is repeated by Johnson in his *Preface to Shakespeare*. This openness to experience is part of the reason Johnson readily forgives Shakespeare's mingled drama as "a practice contrary to the rules of criticism," for "there is always an appeal open from criticism to nature." We approach nearer "to the appearance of life." While Priestley confirms that a person must be "in some sense, a *logician* before he be an orator," he qualifies this immediately: "More especially is it of consequence . . . to be well acquainted with *human nature*," with the "passions, prejudices, interests and views" of the audience—in short, with "plain principles of human actions."[20]

As schoolboys, most New Rhetoricians were whipped into mastering difficult Greek and Latin texts. They took careful reading as a matter of course. What they then add is an insistence on the means by which passions, emotions, and human motives are portrayed. Riding the crest of the Scottish Common Sense School and the associationists' approach, Lord Kames begins his *Elements of Criticism* (1762) with a rough introduction to psychology. Campbell's *Philosophy of Rhetoric*, first delivered to "a private literary society" in 1757, commences with "a tolerable sketch of the human mind," for only with this in hand, says Campbell, can we "ascertain, with greater precision, the radical principles of that art, whose object it is, by the use of language, to operate on the soul of the hearer." The origin of poetry and of those imitative arts aimed at "internal tastes," and the "springs" by which these arts "can be regulated, must be sought for in the nature of the human mind, and more especially in the principles of the imagination."[21] This is a profound connection, a critical view that, perhaps more than any other single one, has shaped European and American literature of the last two hundred years: the principles of criticism become nothing less than the principles of imagination itself. As Coleridge would say in the *Biographia*, "The *rules* of the IMAGINATION are themselves the very powers of growth and production."[22]

While we now recognize this as the main critical stance developing in the mid and late century, Campbell goes further and claims that not only is criticism based on psychology, particularly on the imagination, but the converse: psychology may best be understood through criticism. "In this view," rhetoric "is perhaps the surest and the shortest, as well as the pleasantest way of arriving at the science of the human mind."[23] Hans Aarsleff explains Condillac's importance for linguistics in a similar vein. Condillac realizes that "with the use of artificial signs, language puts thought in control of itself."[24] Grasped and followed to its source, the taxonomy of rhetoric does more than name or reflect; it analyzes states of consciousness and psychological phenomena. Linguistic tools belong to the workshop of the mind. The bond between states of mind and figures of speech, between psychology and stylistics, was suggested as early as John Hoskins's *Directions for Speech and Style* (composed 1599-1600), where Hoskins admits that "though all metaphors go beyond the signification of things, yet they are requisite to match the compassing sweetness of men's minds, that are not content to fix themselves upon one thing but they must wander."[25] The mind will be delighted with its own activity exercised through metaphor and invention.

The emphasis on psychology, rudimentary at first, rapidly matured. Above all it meant, as Thomas Gibbons phrased it, that ". . . Rhetoric is by no means restrained to the truth and precision of Logic."[26] It is not strictly logical because we are not. The passions are involved, and they are essential. "So far therefore it is from being an unfair method of persuasion to move the passions," says Campbell, "that there is no persuasion without moving them."[27] Hazlitt, who studied under Priestley, imbibed this principle thoroughly, and John Mahoney has called Hazlitt's criticism *The Logic of Passion*. Its godparents are the New Rhetoricians. Unless wild and unruly, passion strengthens all acts of the psyche. "When in such a degree as to rouse and kindle the mind, without throwing it out of the possession of itself," claims Blair, passion "is universally found to exalt all the human powers. It renders the mind infinitely more enlightened, more penetrating, more vigorous and masterly, than it is in its calm moments."[28] The notion of passion as the enemy of reason had been generally debunked by this time. Campbell desires that the orator engage "all . . . powers of the mind, the imagination, the memory, and the passions. These are not the supplanters of reason, or even rivals in her sway; they are her handmaids. . . ."[29] From here it is a short step to Wordsworth's concept of imagination as "Reason in her most exalted mood."

Every trope and figure may be grasped as the specific "sign" or "vehicle" of a feeling or passion. Word play is mind play—or a play of passions—and at its best it associates all our sensibilities. A particular trope or figure does not always represent the same feeling, but certain passions may be more closely linked with certain figures. A simple metaphor may show love or hate; asyndeton may express the excitement of anger or joy . What is crucial is that the mind is thrown into emotional activity and, guided by the meanings of individual words, will interpret the figure in a way that heightens all feeling and perception. Blair sees the key to metaphor as abridged resemblance: "The mind . . . is exercised without being fatigued; and is gratified with the consciousness of its own ingenuity." All figures are "prompted either by the imagination or by the passions."[30]

This attitude struggled toward a science of psychology, and critics like Thomas Sheridan, father of the playwright and politician, decried the wide difference in "principles" and "definition or descriptions" contained in the "variety of treatises which have lately been published on the passions."[31] But Sheridan and others also saw that in as much as rhetorical language was based on passion, it was foolish to expect it to communicate precisely, or to transmit exactly what an author intended. It is a "common delusion," says Sheridan, "that by the help of words alone," we can "communicate all that passes" in our minds. We need to recall that "the passion and the fancy have a language of their own, utterly independent of words, by which only their *exertions* can be manifested and communicated."[32] No human language operates like a binary computer language, a series of ones and zeroes, on or off. Language, despite its flexible variety and richness, cannot delineate a pure passion as it is itself.

With the new psychological interest, perceptions of both nature and what it meant to imitate nature through the medium of language changed. "Truth to nature" became something of a stale injunction. Nature may be external to us, but once we perceive it, and especially once we express it in words, it is twined with the psyche.[33] We give it human reference—we humanize it. Nature is an endless text we read with all our senses. Art ceases simply to imitate or describe nature and begins instead to imitate our experience of nature. Nature is unemotional. We bring to it our passion, and we express our feelings to others; we imitate states of consciousness not only by portraying human action directly or meditatively, but through the text of nature as we imitate nature in a psychologically attuned language. The New Rhetoricians establish a critical theory that becomes the backbone of Romantic poetry and criticism.[34] In many ways, the New Rhetoricians have more in common with Hazlitt, Coleridge, and Wordsworth than they do with Johnson, Goldsmith, or Reynolds, though the changing emphasis of *The Discourses* (1769–91) derives in part from Reynolds's acquaintance with the new rhetorics.

The stance of the New Rhetoricians produced immediate repercussions. As rhetorical language is used by the poet to animate nature—to express the peculiar interaction of Psyche and Pan—we find ourselves "humanizing nature," a gift Coleridge claimed for Shakespeare. The New Rhetoricians anticipate, too, Hazlitt's concept of "gusto," and what Keats called the "greeting of the spirit." In poetic language, the ideal of sympathy or sympathetic identification of poet with subject depends on similitudes, on figures of speech, if only simple metaphors. As Beattie tersely put it, "The philosophy of Sympathy ought always to form a part of the science of Criticism."[35] Naturally enough character criticism, such as Morgann's *Essay on Falstaff*, grew in interest and acuity.

III

In conjunction with the psychological approach to rhetoric and nature, at least three other critical ideas emerged. Personification or prosopopeia was analyzed so that it hinged on the verb rather than on an adjective or noun. The more a human motive or feeling acts through a natural form or—better yet—through a natural action itself, the more effective. Blair marks three levels of personification. The "obscure degree" is buried in common adjectives: "a raging storm, a deceitful disease." A higher level tends to personify substantive nouns (Johnson's Wolsey with "Law in his voice, and fortune in his hand") or natural objects as they act in sympathy with us. Blair praises Homer, Shakespeare, and Milton for this excellence, as when Eve:

> So saying, her rash hand in evil hour
> Forth reaching to the fruit, she pluck'd, she eat;
> Earth felt the wound; and nature, from her seat
> Sighing through all her works gave signs of woe,
> That all was lost.
> *(Paradise Lost* IX, lines 780-784)

But the highest personification occurs when objective nature and subjective humankind act as one. The forms of nature "are introduced, not only as feeling and acting, but as speaking to us, or hearing and listening when we address ourselves to them." This boldest use "is the style of strong passion only." So Eve, on quitting Eden:

> Must I thus leave thee, Paradise? thus leave
> Thee, native soil, these happy walks, and shades,
> Fit haunt of Gods? where I had hope to spend
> Quiet, though sad, the respite of that day,
> Which must be mortal to us both. O flowers!
> That never will in other climate grow . . . .
> (XI, lines 269-274)

In sum, personification works effectively when it avoids abstractions, substantives, stasis, and description; it succeeds when it involves the actions and passions of nature and soul to break down the barrier between them until nature becomes a human cosmos.[36] Thomas Gibbons gives a similar example, the "case when Milton tells us, that *nature sighed*, and *the sky wept some sad drops* upon our first parents eating the forbidden fruit."[37]

Secondly, the New Rhetoricans re-examined the relation of poetry and truth (or "reality") under the headings of Kames's "ideal presence" or "waking dream," Blair's "pleasing illusion," Trapp's "wide difference between falsehood and fiction," and Campbell's "fiction of the mind" or "of the imagination."[38] All these—however interpreted—look ahead to Coleridge's "willing suspension of disbelief" or "negative faith," or farther ahead to Oscar Wilde's "lying" and farther back to Sidney's "feigning," where the poet neither lies nor tells the truth.

What is the upshot of this concept of illusion or presence, this fiction or dream? Do the New Rhetoricians have anything in common on the subject, and do they add to its presentation by Dryden, Johnson, and Hume? (The topic is often slanted toward illusion created in the theater.) Carried to its extreme, their position leads to a remarkable conclusion: the pleasure or delight caused by the arousal and chemical-like mixing of our passions is produced by style, by a mysterious power or impression (*stylus*) of words as they cohere and create; all truth in literature is symbolic because words are relational and symbolic. Language can make contradictions to experience consistent, "disagreeables" can "evaporate," for a new mode (an imitation, not a copy) of experience is created.

The New Rhetoricians became aestheticians by defining aesthetic values in terms of emotionally charged figures of speech that imitate nature or, more importantly, figures of speech that imitate perceived nature and the percipient mind in interplay. The pathetic, the marvellous, the sublime, and especially the beautiful are, to a large degree, constructs of words and symbols. Metaphoric language brings the sensuous within the bounds of intellectual communication most effectively and completely. Without such language, without rhetoric, the aesthetic sense would not only be mute; it would be undeveloped. The dream of Kames or Keats awakes in "the fine spell of words," in poerty which "alone can save / Imagination from the sable charm / And dumb enchantment." Aesthetics and rhetoric are intimate allies, actually interdependent, a point stressed by Beattie's *Essays on Poetry and Music As They Affect the Mind* (1778).

The present discussion does not deal primarily with aesthetic theory, but we should note that the Rhetoricians looked with acuity at the verbal definitions and embodiments of aesthetic values. There were great obstacles to overcome: "no word in the language is used in a more vague signification than Beauty," remarks Blair. The word was never adequately defined and, by the late nineteenth century, began to lose currency. Moreover, nature or experience, as much as language, may be the source of aesthetic feelings, but language is the only possible means of naming and analyzing those feelings and, as such, *any* science of aesthetics becomes bound up, by necessity, in significations of words.[39]

As long as rhetoric flourished, the beneficial effects of what we call the New Criticism flourished also. The New Critic is a species of rhetorician. As Leopold Damrosch notes, the character in Addison's *Tatler* 163, Ned Softly, is actually "a New Critic striving to be born."[40] It is dangerous to equate "close reading" (whatever we mean by that term) with New Criticism, but the two overlap. Critical examples and passages given by the New Rhetoricians are often exercises in close reading. Blair's last five *Lectures* (XX–XXIV) examine, paper by paper—even sentence by sentence—the *Spectator* series (Nos. 411–414) on the pleasures of the imagination and Swift's letter to the Earl of Oxford. Blair's close reading can gauge rhetoric and stylistics with a micrometric vengeance. In one instance he devotes almost a full page to the fact that Addison does not repeat the article *the* when he writes, "Our sight is the most perfect, and most delightful of all our senses."[41]

Many examples given by the New Rhetoricians we later find in the practical criticism and commentary of Romantic poets. Wordsworth, in his note to *The Thorn*, cites the song of Deborah to show that "repetition and apparent tautology are frequently beauties of the highest kind." Coleridge, at the end of chapter seventeen of the *Biographia*, cites Wordsworth in turn, to show that "Such repetitions I admit to be a beauty of the highest kind." When Thomas Gibbons analyzes the passionate repetition of a word or phrase as *Epanaphora*, from the Greek meaning *I repeat*, he quotes as one example: Deborah's "triumphal ode, where she describes the death of Sisera by Jael, *Judg.* v. 27. 'At her feet he bowed, he fell, he lay down; at her feet he bowed, he fell: where he bowed, there he fell down dead.'"[42] And when Wordsworth, in his 1815 Preface, commends Milton for describing Satan as "*hanging in the clouds* like a fleet far off at sea," he echoes Beattie's praise that "Satan flying among the stars is said by Milton to '*Sail* between worlds and worlds': which has an elegance and force far superior to the proper word *Fly*."⁴³

As Beattie makes clear, rhetoric should bend language—especially the language of poetry—toward the *less* artificial. This principle informs his claim that "the utility of figurative expression" is "in making language more *pleasing* and more *natural*"; or, "that by tropes and figures language may be made more natural and more pleasing, than it could be without them. It follows that tropes and figures are more necessary to poetry, than to any other mode of writing...." The poet, in quest of "sympathies he would communicate to others," speaks a natural language and "addresses himself to the passions and sympathies of mankind."⁴⁴ Wordsworth's 1800 Preface—in which the poet is a man prompted by the spontaneous overflow of powerful feelings, speaking the real language of men to men—is a short critical distance away. Almost forty—perhaps as much as fifty—years earlier, Adam Smith told his students that "the perfection of style consists in express[ing] in the most concise, proper, and precise manner the thought of the author, and that in a manner which best conveys the sentiment, passion, or affection with which it affects—or he pretends it does affect—him, and which he designs to communicate to his reader."⁴⁵ Smith was not specifically discussing poetry, but that is also to the point, for Smith, like Wordsworth, saw no essential difference between the language of prose and verse. Smith is already supporting a natural rhetoric based on sympathy and affect: "When the sentiment of the speaker is expressed in a neat, clear, plain, and clever manner, and the passion or affection he is possessed of and intends, *by sympathy,* to communicate to his hearer, is plainly and cleverly hit off, then and then only the expression has all the force and beauty that language can give it. It matters not the least whether the figures of speech are introduced or not." They work "only so far as they happen to be the just and natural forms of expressing that sentiment."⁴⁶

IV

Jacques Derrida begins a short essay that connects Rousseau with recent linguistic theory by stating, "Linguistics are becoming more and more interested in the genealogy of linguistics."⁴⁷ Several of his other points recapitulate what André Joly said ten years earlier (1972) in his

Foreword to a reprint of the 1796 French translation of James Harris's *Hermes* (1751). Joly begins, "La linguistique, lentement, découvre son passé." And this discovery is not a retooling of literary history but a realization that critical theory has sometimes been narrower in context and background, more historically and philosophically naive than it might. Critics will increasingly find similarities and connections between twentieth-century theory and studies from the mid 1600s through the early 1800s.

The justified appeal and seeming novelty of semiotics results in part from a collective shift (or amnesia) in linguistic study beginning in the early 1800s and extending as far as the middle 1900s. The ascendent historical and comparative methods did not emphasize the study of language as psychological. Jonathan Culler notes that, "Rejecting the link between language and mind, the nineteenth century lost interest in the word as a sign or representation."[48] In a longer summary, which Culler cites, Hans Aarsleff puts an open-and-shut case:

> It is universally agreed that the decisive turn in language study occurred when the philosophical, a priori method of the eighteenth century was abandoned in favor of the historical a posteriori method of the nineteenth. The former began with mental categories and sought their exemplification in language, as in universal grammar, and based etymologies on conjectures about the origin of language. The latter sought only facts, evidence, demonstration; it divorced the study of language from the study of mind.[49]

In other words, when the pioneer Saussure "came to take issue with his immediate predecessors, he returned," says Culler, "albeit at a different level of sophistication and in a different way, to the concerns of the eighteenth century."[50] While the New Rhetoricians claimed *a posteriori* methods for rhetoric and taste, their attitude to language was *a priori*, and their richest exploration remains Campbell's *Philosophy of Rhetoric*.[51] The New Rhetoricians took the perennial concepts of sign, thing signified, and signification and—with great flexibility—applied psychological and semiotic analyses to modern literature with an eye to teaching effective and creative composition, all supported by a theoretically sophisticated view of the intrinsic bonds between mind and language.

Aarsleff maintains the importance of French linguistics, particularly of Condillac, in the eighteenth century. One of several corroborating evidences provided by the New Rhetoricians comes from Hugh Blair's remark that, "While the French Tongue has long been an object of attention to many able and ingenious writers of that nation . . . the Genius and Grammar of the English . . . have not been studied with equal care, or ascertained with the same precision."[52]

Of course, many early adventures into the science of language proved ludicrous, dull, or impractical. Swift makes fun of them in Gulliver's third voyage. Rather than speak or write, and in the belief that things are truer than the inevitable deception of words, philosophers hand each other objects instead (a ready supply of which they burden themselves with by means of backpacks). Gulliver encounters a word machine, a giant mechanical frame or billboard with small cubes that rotate individually and at random to produce messages or signs. Far-fetched? The study of language relies on analysis and system, which can produce self-complicating Ptolemaic universes that lose touch, however interestingly or stupidly, with the larger world. It turns out that Swift's story was not exaggerated. The pain of good satire is to realize that folly and cruelty are, in fact, as bad as imagined. George Campbell avers that Swift's account "is not excessive, as I once thought it. The boasts of the academists on the prodigies performed by his frame, are far less extravagant" than Raimund Lully's magical circles of logic or Athanasius Kircher's coffer of arts, "which in truth they very much resemble."[53]

The New Rhetoricians examined the fundamental nature of literature as symbolic communication. This rich and problematic study grasped the old chestnut of words and things.[54] The mode of discourse adopted by the New Rhetoricians sounds "modern" and refers specifically to ideas, signs, signification, thing signified, and language as the vehicle. There is no *naturalité de signe* for the New Rhetoricians. Unanimously they reject it and, except for onomatopoetic words, declare our correspondence between sound and meaning to be "arbitrary." Campbell best sums up the position:

> Language is purely a species of fashion . . . in which, by the general, but tacit consent of the people of a particular state or country, certain sounds come to be appropriated to certain things, as their signs, and certain ways of inflecting and combining those sounds come to be established, as denoting the relations which subsist among the things signified.

In other words, "every smatterer in philosophy will tell us, that there can be no natural connexion between the sounds of any language, and the things signified."[55]

Combining the theoretical and practical, the New Rhetoricians concluded that communication by words must be imperfect; words and things enjoy no intrinsic relation, as Byron laments in *Childe Harold* (3. 114):

> I do believe,
> Though I have found them not, that there may be
> Words which are things, hopes which will not deceive . . .
>
> I would also deem
> O'er others' griefs that some sincerely grieve;
> That two, or one, are almost what they seem,
> That goodness is no name, and happiness no dream.

So while the New Rhetoricians agreed that "In matters of criticism, as in the abstract sciences, it is of the utmost consequence to ascertain, with precision, the meanings of words, and . . . to make them correspond to the boundaries assigned by Nature to the things signified," they also realized that words signify not only things imperfectly, they do no better job with ideas. This is what Wordsworth refers to as the "sad incompetence of human speech," and perhaps what Shelley meant when he has Demogorgon say, "the deep truth is imageless." Each phrase or sentence, even each definition of a word—let alone a long text—becomes a complex interplay of variously imperfect signs.[56] All language thus proceeds by a kind of relational metalepsis (a point we shall take up in a moment). But however faulty, linguistic communication does operate within a range of meanings and saves itself from collapsing into "nonsense." Metalepsis may be all we have, but it is clearer than obfuscation or total suspicion of language. Perfect clarity or "true" communication is a mirage, a collective delusion perhaps, but at least it keeps us walking ahead.

Shelley briefly expresses the collective social and self-referential nature of language at the outset of the *Defence*. If our "social sympathies" develop and we use language to communicate what we see each do as "a social being," then "even in the infancy of society" we will "observe a certain order in . . . [our] words and actions, distinct from that of the objects and the impressions represented by them, all expression being subject to the laws of that from which it proceeds."

Metalepsis abridges the self-referential nature of language and provides a model by which words, as arbitrary signs, relate to each other in order to salvage sense from chaos. In metalepsis, as John Ward's *Oratory* defines it,

> two or more Tropes, and those of a different kind are contained under one word, so that gradations or intervening senses come between the word that is expressed, and the thing designed by it. The contests . . . between Sylla and Marius proved very fatal to the *Roman* state. Julius Caesar was then a young man. But Sylla, observing his aspiring genius, said of him, In one Caesar there are many Mariuses . . . Now in this expression there is a *Metalepsis*, for the word *Marius*, by a Synecdoche or Antonomasia, is put for any ambitious or turbulent person; and this again by a Metonymy of the cause for the ill effects of such a temper to the Public. So that Sylla's meaning, divested of these Tropes, was, that Caesar would prove the most dangerous person to the *Roman* state that ever was bred in it: which afterwards proved true in the event.[57]

In as much as each word in a sentence or a text, side by side or in proximity with other words, signifies not only one thing or idea but part of the confluence of many other words or tropes, we might extend Ward's analysis and say that all language and all texts (from *teks* meaning, among other things, to weave) proceed by a kind of metalepsis. All language is arbitrary; meaning inheres in its inner relations and transitive identities. We must communicate with imperfect, self-referring signifiers or else, like Gulliver's dumb philosophers, hand each other objects. (Naturally enough, many important acts in life still use ritualistic objects: water, bread, wine, rings, dust, ashes, candles, and eggs.)

The New Rhetoricians saw that the processes of thought and understanding proceed only by means of language of some sort, and then only by the relational or metaleptic processes of the signs and images provided by language. We cannot think other than by signs. The mind not only communicates by images, it cannot even think without them. As Campbell asks pointedly, "what hath given rise to the distinction between ratiocination and imagery?"[58] Coleridge later proposed an essay on the impossibility of thinking without images! Rhetoric, which creates and employs images, not only is a vehicle, it may be viewed as part of thought itself. Words used habitually become icons or signs of such power that they are "greater" than the nature and the ideas they imitate. Campbell admits the connection "between words and things is, in its origin, arbitrary." Yet, he goes on, "the difference in the effect is not so considerable as one would be apt to imagine. In neither case is it the matter . . . but the power of the sign that is regarded by the mind."[59] As for words that are things, Childe Harold "found them not," yet Byron in *Don Juan* (3.88) protests

> But words are things, and a small drop of ink,
>   Falling like dew, upon a thought, produces
> That which makes thousands, perhaps millions, think. . . .

Language is the vehicle of thought, and without it thought remains inert, not only incommunicable but perhaps unthinkable. The mind is an analogical organ and thinks by signs. Purely direct experience is signless, but it is thoughtless too. If the performance of language as a vehicle seems problematic, this is true with any medium. We do not encounter light as a particulate phenomenon also manifesting properties of a wave; it is simply a medium permitting us to see because our eyes react to it. Photons strike the retina, but it is not photons we consciously perceive. Yet, our cones and rods do react to light and not the actual objects that reflect the light. So it is with words; they become the photons of thought. Language as a "vehicle" is a premise of the new rhetoric. Emerson, brought up on the New Rhetoricians, remarks in "The Poet" that "all language is vehicular and transitive, and is good, as ferries and horses are, for conveyance, not as farms and houses are, for homestead."[60] I have not found "tenor," but "vehicle" appears abundantly in the New Rhetoricians, whom I. A. Richards was reading when, discussing Kames, he (and not Ransom) introduced tenor and vehicle in his own *Philosophy of Rhetoric* (1936).

Much of the new rhetoric depends, in fact, on the realization that words are imperfect and slippery signifiers. This helps explain the neoclassical and late-eighteenth-century obsession with clarity—not that writers and critics trusted words, but that they distrusted them so much. Priestley urges, "A regard to *perspicuity* would direct us (if we would be understood) to explain distinctly the meaning of every word we use, that is of the least doubtful signification."[61] Language is a cutting edge blunted by use; it must be sharpened constantly. So Eliot grieves that

> Words strain,
> Crack and sometimes break, under the burden,
> Under the tension, slip, slide, perish,
> Decay with imprecision, will not stay in place,
> Will not stay still.[62]

But the language of the tribe must be purified, and for us there is only the trying. As Campbell puts it succinctly, we try "to convey our sentiments into the minds of others.... Language is the only vehicle by which this conveyance can be made."

The New Rhetoricians glean fresh perspective on style from the general imperfection of language. It is the very lack of ultimate precision and accuracy in language that permits individual style. With perfect communication, style would be impossible. As Priestley shows, it is by substituting and employing "other words of similar signification" in different orders and degrees of precision that we arrive at a particular emphasis, rhythm, and sense. It is in the awareness and command of the very elusive qualities of signifiers and significations that "the accuracy and excellency of style doth greatly consist."[63] Recently, Jonathan Culler has applied this principle to genres and figurative language:

> Indeed, one might say that debates about rhetoric and the appropriateness of particular expressions in specific genres are possible only because there are various ways of saying the same thing: the figure is an ornament which does not trouble the representational function of language.[64]

V

A certain remissness will at times seize the most attentive reader; whereas an author of discernment is supposed to have carefully digested all that he writes. It is reported of Lopez de Vega, a famous Spanish poet, that the Bishop of Beller, being in Spain, asked him to explain one of his sonnets, which he said he had often read, but never understood. Lopez took up the sonnet, and after reading it over and over several times, frankly acknowledged that he did not understand it himself; a discovery which the poet probably never made before.

But though the general fact hath been frequently observed, I do not find that any attempt hath been yet made to account for it.[65]

This sounds like Browning's confession that when he wrote one of his poems only he and God knew what it meant, and now only God. Campbell relates the anecdote of Lope de Vega near the beginning of the best discussion of language as sign and signification in the New Rhetoricians, "The nature and power of signs, both in speaking and in thinking."[66] Campbell's whole treatment merits an extended study, but here we may use his major points to summarize our discussion. He establishes three connections: "First, that which subsisteth among things; secondly, that which subsisteth between words and things; thirdly, that which subsisteth among words, or the different terms used in the same language."[67] The background is Lockean, and Campbell relies on association in his analysis. In brief, the point is that we use language so habitually and immediately, that words—like living creatures—develop their own connections and associations; they form, as it were, a second nature. This nature is not identical, but analogous to our direct experience: "Now, as by the habitual use of a language . . . the signs would insensibly become connected in the imagination, wherever the things signified are connected in nature; so by the regular structure of a language, this connection among the signs is conceived as analogous to that which subsisteth among their archetypes." As a result of this habitual (metaleptic) activity, we do not always exercise the "leisure to give that attention to the signs which is necessary in order to form a just conception of the things signified."[68] Of couse we can be led down the dead end of nonsense, as was Lope in his sonnet, but the same "insensibility" of the inner structural associations of language also permits it to carry powerful meaning and feeling. Signs develop this power not because they are tyrannical or because we suppress our intentions, but because the mind, by constant association, seeks its own shortest route of communication and understanding, and that route admits language in its most symbolic or significatory mode. It is a question of psychological habit and efficiency.

The New Rhetoricians established a psychological basis for a figurative, natural language expressing the action of the mind in a state of excitement or strong emotion. More than any other group or critic, the New Rhetoricians also link our classical heritage of rhetoric, from Aristotle through the Renaissance, with semiology and linguistics.

(The work of Campbell especially demands more study.) The New Rhetoric presents no one synthesis. Ironically, its insights prove inimical to systematic logic, for these critics realized that literature—as rhetoric—derives its greatest power from passionate expression. As Blair states, the poetry and eloquence "which gains the admiration of mankind . . . is never found without warmth, or passion. Passion, when in such a degree as to rouse and kindle the mind, without throwing it out of the possession of itself, is universally found to exalt all the human powers. It renders the mind infinitely more enlightened, more penetrating, more vigorous and masterly, than it is in its calm moments."[69]

Some of the dullest books written are those purporting to explain the methods and mysteries of great literature. The New Rhetoricians are dull at times; there are *longueurs*. But they are rarely opaque. They avoid what Arnold later called the "jargon of modern criticism." Many of them were academics, but they addressed the generally educated public. They asserted that the *telos* of critical study is the powerful use of language as it incites us to think, feel, and act, not as it scrutinizes only our critical faculties and systems. They realized that literature *qua* literature, as a separate discipline, is an ornament of society and can be thought of as a necessity only if it furthers or is associated with other goals, cultural values, or larger concerns of human conduct. If we view critical tradition as a river flowing newly forward even as it follows its previous course as well, then the New Rhetoricians form part of the permanent navigable channel.

As with all literary or critical movements that perceive literary values and styles not simply as ends in themselves but having at least the possibility of serving larger human ends and needs, the New Rhetoricians neither subverted nor supported prevailing literary taste. They proved "conservative" and "liberal." They were at once scientific—that is, systematic and empirical—and intuitive; they trusted the perceptions of developed taste and a trained ear.[70] Their major aim was to improve the practice of religion and education in general; they hardly set out to form a school of criticism, at least not self-consciously. Any one of them would first consider himself a theologian, economist, educator, moral philosopher, or public servant. One remarkable feature of their criticism taken in the gross is that we rarely encounter an explicit distinction between fiction and exposition such as sermons, essays, and speeches. (We see this as early as Smith's *Lectures* of 1748–51.)[71] Literature for them is one body, at least as conceived from the standpoint of rhetoric. Many New Rhetoricians were doctors of divinity who wanted their students to write and deliver good sermons and to read and appreciate not only the message of the Bible, but its beauty and poetry as well. We could say, without exaggeration, that one impetus for the new criticism of the late eighteenth century was religion, and this is not said for dramatic effect.

The art of rhetoric brings the idea of *mimesis* full circle. As imitation may depict what Priestley (and later Hazlitt) calls the "principles of human actions," the end of rhetoric is to move readers and hearers to appreciate, to decide, and to act.[72] Literature so conceived is bound up with our every choice and experience. The motives of writing and of criticism become the motives of human action at large.

NOTES

1. Longinus, *On the Sublime*, trans. W. Rhys Roberts (Cambridge: Cambridge University Press, 1899), p. 81.
2. For general studies see Wilbur Samuel Howell, *Eighteenth-Century British Logic and Rhetoric* (Princeton, N.J.: Princeton University Press, 1971), pp. 441–691, esp. pp. 536–691; George A. Kennedy, *Classical Rhetoric and Its Christian Secular Tradition from Ancient to Modern Times* (Chapel Hill: University of North Carolina Press, 1980), pp. 220–241, esp. pp. 227–241.
3. For "theory," see for example George Campbell, *The Philosophy of Rhetoric* (London: W. Strahan, 1776), I, 25–83. On p. 83 Campbell refers to "the theory now laid down and explained." Howell (pp. 616–633) treats Lawson "as much . . . for the new rhetoric as for the old" (p. 630). For Ward and Lawson see Kennedy, pp. 228–229. Vincent M. Bevilacqua and Richard Murphy, editing Joseph Priestley, *A Course of Lectures on Oratory and Criticism* (Carbondale: Southern Illinois University Press, 1965 [rpt. 1777 ed]), refer to Ward and Lawson as "the culmination of classical rhetoric in the eighteenth century" (p. xxii).
4. Adam Smith, *Lectures on Rhetoric and Belles Lettres . . . Reported by a Student in 1762–63*, ed. John M. Lothian (London: Thomas Nelson and Sons, 1963), p. 23. The manuscript is not in Smith's hand; some lectures may have been recorded partly from memory. On the persistent view of rhetoric as mere terminology, see Wayne C. Booth, "The Scope of Rhetoric Today: A Polemical Excursion," *The Prospect of Rhetoric*, ed. Lloyd F. Bitzer and Edwin Black (Englewood Cliffs, N.J.: Prentice-Hall, 1971), p. 94. Jonathan Culler, *Structuralist Poetics: Structuralism, Linguistics, and the Study of Literature* (Ithaca, N.Y.: Cornell University Press, 1975), sees the labels of rhetoric as "a sterile and ancillary activity. . . . But a semiological or

structuralist theory of reading enables us simply to reverse the perspective and to think of training in rhetoric as a way of providing the student with a set of formal models which he can use in interpreting literary works" (p. 179). This almost summarizes the program of the New Rhetoricians.

5. Campbell, I, p. 95.
6. Hugh Blair, *Lectures on Rhetoric and Belles Lettres* (London: W. Strahan, 1783), I, pp. 8–9.
7. George Saintsbury, *A History of Criticism and Literary Taste in Europe* (New York: Dodd, Mead, 1900–04), I, pp. 4, 72.
8. Saintsbury, II, pp. 463, 470–471.
9. Karl Richards Wallace, *Francis Bacon on Communication & Rhetoric* (Chapel Hill: University of North Carolina Press, 1943), pp. 32–33, 217–218, 222–223.
10. Quintilian, *Institutio Oratoria*, trans. H. E. Butler (Cambridge, Mass.: Harvard University Press, Loeb Classical Library, 1958), I, Bk. I, Pref. 18 (p. 15; see also pp. 9–14).
11. See J. Hillis Miller, "The Function of Rhetorical Study at the Present Time," *The State of the Discipline 1970s–1980s, ADE Bulletin*, 62 (Sept.–Nov. 1979), 10–18, esp. 12–13.
12. Saintsbury, I, pp. 36–37, 4.
13. Blair, I, p. 276.
14. Johnson defines *critick* as "A man skilled in the art of judging literature," but the second definition under *critick* (critique) is "Science of criticism." See Harry Levin, "Why Literary Criticism is Not an Exact Science," *Grounds for Comparison* (Cambridge, Mass.: Harvard University Press, 1972), pp. 40–56.
15. Artistotle, *The "Art" of Rhetoric*, trans. John Henry Freese (Cambridge, Mass.: Harvard University Press, Loeb Classical Library, 1975), Bk. I, i, 1 (p. 3).
16. See for instance Campbell, I, pp. vii–x, 155–159, 367–370. Quintilian, I, Bk. II, xiv, 1–38 (pp. 299–319) contains a classical summary of "what is rhetoric?" For discussion on the leeway of interpretation, see Paul B. Armstrong, "The Conflict of Interpretations and the Limits of Pluralism," *PMLA*, 98 (1983), 341–352.
17. Campbell, I, p. 96.
18. O. Hobart Mowrer, "The Psychologist Looks at Language," *The American Psychologist*, 9 (November, 1954), 660, as quoted by Marie Hochmuth Nichols, *Rhetoric and Criticism* (Baton Rouge: Louisiana State University Press, 1963), p. 28. Nichols's first chapter, "Rhetoric and Public Address as Humane Study," pp. 3–18, is illuminating.
19. Quintilian, II, Bk. VI, ii, 8–9 (pp. 421–423).
20. Priestley, ed. Bevilacqua and Murphy, pp. 3–4.
21. Campbell, I, pp. vii, 12. The modern reprint of Campbell's *Philosophy* is edited by Lloyd F. Bitzer (Carbondale: Southern Illinois University Press, 1963), who reprints the London edition of 1850. By 1912 the *Philosophy* had entered eleven editions. In New York it was reprinted nineteen times between 1845 and 1887 (see Bitzer, pp. xxx–xxxi). The edition quoted here throughout is the first (1776).
22. Samuel Taylor Coleridge, *Biographia Literaria*, ed. James Engell and W. Jackson Bate (Princeton, N.J.: Princeton University Press, Bollingen Series LXXV,

1983), II, p. 84.
23. Campbell, I, p. 16; see Karl R. Wallace, "The Fundamentals of Rhetoric," in Bitzer and Black, p. 11.
24. Hans Aarsleff, *The Study of Language in England 1780–1860* (Princeton, N.J.: Princeton University Press, 1967), p. 23; cf. also pp. 20–25. Aarsleff states (p. 53) that Horne Tooke conceived of language *as* thought, not just as that which makes thought possible.
25. John Hoskins, *Directions for Speech and Style*, ed. Hoyt H. Hudson (Princeton, N.J.: Princeton University Press, 1935), p. 8.
26. Thomas Gibbons, *Rhetoric* (London: J. and W. Oliver, 1767), p. 448.
27. Campbell, I, p. 200. Does this concern what Susan Sontag calls an erotics of art?
28. Blair, II, p. 6.
29. Campbell, I, p. 187.
30. Blair, I, pp. 296, 275.
31. Thomas Sheridan, *A Course of Lectures on Elocution* (London: J. Dodsley, 1787 [first edition, 1762]), p. xii.
32. Sheridan, p. xii, italics added. We might recall T. S. Eliot's remark that communication alone does not explain poetry; or Coleridge's, that poetry is most enjoyed when understood imperfectly.
33. See, for example, Blair, I, pp. 94–95, on the difference between imitating and describing nature; also Samuel Johnson, in *Rambler* 36, where he says the effects of nature on the ear and eye are "incapable of much variety of description."
34. For another view see M. H. Abrams, *The Mirror and the Lamp: Romantic Theory and the Critical Tradition* (New York: Norton, 1958 [rpt. of 1953 Oxford University Press edition]), pp. 53–54.
35. See Gibbons, p. 392; Campbell, I, pp. 242–248. James Beattie, *Essays on Poetry and Music as They Affect the Mind* (Edinburgh: William Creech, 1778), p. 194; also see *Dissertations Moral and Critical* (London: W. Strahan, 1783), pp. 166–190.
36. Blair, I, pp. 327, 330, 332–334, 335.
37. Gibbons, p. 394. See Morton W. Bloomfield, "Personification-Metaphors," *The Chaucer Review*, 14 (1980), 287–297, and Earl R. Wasserman, "The Inherent Values of Eighteenth-Century Personification," *PMLA*, 65 (1950), 435–463.
38. Gibbons, pp. 95–96; Campbell, I, pp. 306–309, 314–338; Kames, Henry Home, Lord, *Elements of Criticism* (Edinburgh: A. Millar, 1762), I, 104–127; see also Abrams, pp. 270–271, 324–325.
39. Blair, I, pp. 81, 75; Campbell (I, 207) offers an interesting defense and definition of the "rather modern" term, "the *sentimental*."
40. Damrosch, "The Significance of Addison's Criticism," *SEL,* 19 (1979), 430.
41. Blair, I, p. 410.
42. Wordsworth, *Wordsworth's Poetical Works*, ed. E. de Selincourt and Helen Darbishire (Oxford: Clarendon Press, 1940–49), II, p. 513; Coleridge, *Biographia*, ed. Engell and Bate, II, p. 57; Gibbons, pp. 207–208, 210.
43. Beattie, *Essays*, p. 263.
44. Beattie, *Essays*, pp. 285, 285–286, 287. For another view of the stress on natural

language, see Abrams, pp. 16, 288.
45. Smith, *Lectures,* ed. Lothian, p. 51.
46. Smith, *Lectures,* pp. 22–23, original italics.
47. Derrida, "The Linguistic Circle of Geneva," trans. Alan Bass, *Critical Inquiry,* 8 (1982), 675.
48. Culler, *Ferdinand de Saussure* (New York: Penguin, 1976), p. 57.
49. Aarsleff, p. 127.
50. Culler, *Saussure,* p. 58.
51. Kennedy (p. 233) assesses Campbell as "innovative and challenging," and sees him departing "radically" from traditional terms and presentations.
52. Blair, I, p. 138.
53. Campbell, II, pp. 125–129 and 127–129n.
54. See, for example, anon., *The Way to Things by Words, and to Words by Things* (London: Davies and Reymers, 1766); Thomas Gunter Browne, *Hermes Unmasked; or, The Art of Speech Founded on the Association of Words and Ideas* (London: T. Payne, 1795).
55. Campbell, I, p. 340; see also II, p. 112; I, p. 342; Blair, I, p. 105; Culler, *Saussure,* pp. 10–15.
56. Campbell, I, pp. 38–39. Wordsworth's phrase appears not only in *The Prelude,* but in the 1815 Preface to *Lyrical Ballads* as well.
57. As quoted by Gibbons, p. 69, from John Ward, *A System of Oratory* (London: printed for John Ward, 1759), II, p. 25–26.
58. Campbell, I, p. 192; cf. Aarsleff, pp. 53, 20–25.
59. Campbell, II, pp. 112–113. For Addison's treatment of nature (things), description (signs), and the activity of the mind involved with them, see *Spectator* 416.
60. *Rambler* 202 uses "vehicle" similarly, as does Blair, I, pp. 98, 289. In Johnson's *Dictionary,* the second definition of *tenour* is "sense contained; general course or drift," and the illustration is from Locke: "Reading it must be repeated again and again with a close attention to the *tenor* of the discourse, and a perfect neglect of the divisions into chapters and verses." Under the third definition of *vehicle,* Johnson quotes L'Estrange: "The gaiety of a diverting word, serves as a *vehicle* to convey the force and meaning of a thing."
61. Priestley, *Lectures,* p. 47; cf. Campbell, I, p. 39.
62. *Burnt Norton,* 11. 149–153; see also *East Coker,* 11. 172–189.
63. Priestley, *A Course of Lectures on the Theory of Language, and Universal Grammar* (Warrington: W. Eyres, 1762), pp. 163, 164.
64. Culler, *Structuralist Poetics,* p. 135.
65. Campbell, II, p. 93.
66. The chapter is Vol. II, Bk. II, Ch. VII (pp. 92–129).
67. Campbell, II, pp. 96–97.
68. Campbell, II, pp. 101,102.
69. Blair, II, p. 6.
70. For theoretical discussion, see Campbell, "Of the different sources of Evidence, and the different subjects to which they are respectively adapted," I, pp. 103–163.

71. Howell (p. 547) says Smith "made rhetoric the general theory of all branches of literature—the historical, the poetical, the didactic or scientific, and oratorical."
72. Wallace, "The Fundamentals of Rhetoric," in Bitzer and Black, p. 19, n. 7, cites Everett Hunt in *The Rhetorical Idiom*, ed. Donald Bryant (Ithaca, N.Y.: Cornell University Press, 1958), p. 4: "If we can keep as basic our conception that the humanities embrace whatever contributes to the making of free and enlightened choices, whether it be knowledge scientific, sociological, or poetic, and that in addition to adequate knowledge of all the alternatives there must be imagination to envision all the possibilities and sympathy to make some of the options appeal to the emotions and powers of the will, we can see that rhetoric is an essential instrument for the enterprises of the human spirit."

Selected Bibliography of Primary Materials

DAVID G. SCHAPPERT

To prepare a bibliography on a specific topic would seem to imply a knowledge of the extent of that topic. When one compiles a bibliography of the works of an individual author, for example, what to include or not to include is usually clear.

When preparing a bibliography which relates to even a short period of time in the history of a discipline, however, the situation is less clear. Furthermore, such a selection might encourage the reader to perceive the topic from the perspective of the bibliographer, a perspective that may be narrow or wrong-headed. The listing of books may seem to be prescriptive, and imply that every meaningful document on the topic is listed.

This is a working bibliography, and I refuse to make such an all-inclusive claim. William James, it is said, "wished, by treating Psychology *like* a natural science, to help her become one." The goal of this bibliography is not to make psychology become something, or seem to be something, but, rather, to provide scholars with a tool for further exploration. In the introduction, Christopher Fox suggests that to explore eighteenth-century psychology we need to look at a wide range of contexts. This bibliography reflects that belief.

There are other bibliographies which scholars may also wish to consult. Those on more specific topics include John F. Sena's *A Bibliography of Melancholy* (London: Nether Press, 1970) and Morris N. Young's *Bibliography of Memory* (Philadelphia, Penn.: Chilton, 1961). Heinrich Laehr's *Die Literatur der Psychiatrie, Neurologie und Psychologie von 1459–1799* (Berlin: Reimer, 1895) is an indispensable source of information. Other valuable works include R. I. Watson's *Eminent Contributors to Psychology* (New York: Springer, 1974–76), Oskar Diethelm's *Medical Dissertations of Psychiatric Interest, printed before 1750* (New York: Karger, 1971), Wayne Viney, et al., *The History of Psychology: A Guide to Information Sources* (Detroit, Mich.: Gale Research, 1979), and Leonard Zusne's *Biographical Dictionary of Psychology* (Westport, Conn.: Greenwood, 1984).

The present bibliography is largely, though not exclusively, limited to books. Scholars, however, may also wish to examine the wide range of materials which appeared in periodicals during the eighteenth century. Sources which they would want to consult might include *Philosophical Transactions of the Royal Society* (London, 1665–); *Acta Eruditorum* (Leipzig, 1682–1731); *Nouvelle de la Republique des Lettres* (Amsterdam, 1684–1718); *Bibliotheque Universelle et Historique*, and its successors, *Bibliotheque choisie, Bibliotheque Ancienne et Moderne*, and *Bibliotheque raisonné des ouvrages des savans de l'Europe* (Amsterdam, 1686–1753); *Present state of the republick of letters* (London, 1728–36), superseded by *History of the Works of the Learned* (London, 1737–43); *The Annual Register: or, A View of the History, Politics, and Literature for the Year* (London, 1758–); *Magazin zur Erfahrungsseelenkunde* (Berlin, 1783–93); *Beiträge zur philosophischen Anthropologie und der damit verwandten Wissenschaften* (Vienna, 1794–96); *Allegemeines Repertorium für empirische Psychologie* (Nürnberg, 1796–99); *Psychologisches Magazin* (Jena, 1796–98); *Psychologisches Magazin* (Altenberg, 1796–97); *Neue Beiträge zur Bereicherung der Menschenkunde uberhaupt und der Erfahrungsseelenkunde inbesondere* (Leipzig, 1798); *The Spectator; The Tatler;* and *The Rambler*, among others.

Abbadie, Jacques. *L'art de se connoître soi-mesme, ou La recherche des sources de la morale.* The Hague: 1692.

An account of the Progress of an Epidemical madness, in a letter to the President and Fellows of the College of Physicians. London, 1735.

Adair, James Makittrick. *Essays on fashionable diseases.* London, [1790?].

———. *Medical Cautions; chiefly for the consideration of invalids. Containing essays on fashion-*

able diseases. Bath, 1786.

———. *A philosophical and medical sketch of the natural history of the human body and mind. To which is subjoined, An essay on the difficulties of attaining medical knowledge, intended for the information and amusement of those who are, and are not, of the medical profession.* London, 1787.

Adams, George. *An essay on electricity . . . to which is added a letter to the author from Mr. John Birch, surgeon on the subject of medical electricity.* London, 1784.

Adams, Joseph. *Observations on morbid poisons, phagedaena, and cancer, . . . on the laws of venereal virus and also some preliminary remarks on the language and mode of reasoning adopted by medical writers.* London, 1795.

Adams, Thomas. *Mystical Bedlam, or the World of Mad-Men.* London, 1615.

[Agnostos.] *Remarks upon the notion of extraordinary impulses and impressions on the imagination, indulged by many professors of religion: contained in a letter to a friend.* London, 1800.

Aikin, John. *Thoughts on hospitals.* London, 1771.

Akenside, Mark. *The pleasures of imagination. A poem. In three books.* 4th edn. London, 1744.

Alberti, M. and C. Sussenbach. *Dissertatio inauguralis medica de therapi imaginaria.* Halle, 1721.

Albinus, Bernhardus. *De catalepsi.* Leyden, 1676.

Alison, Archibald. *Essays on the nature and principles of taste.* Edinburgh, 1790; rpt. Hildesheim: G. Olms, 1968.

Andree, John, the Elder. *Cases of the epilepsy, hysteric fits, and St. Vitus Dance, with the process of cure: interspersed with practical observations. To which are added cases of the bite of mad creatures, . . .* London, 1746.

Anthropologie Abstracted, or the idea of humane nature reflected in briefe philosophicall, and anatomicall collections. London, 1655.

Apinus, M. Sigism. Jacobus. *Dissertatio de variis discendi methodis memoriae causa inventis, eorumque usu, et abusu, recognita, et aucta.* Leipzig, 1725.

Applegarth, Robert. *A Theological Survey of the Human Understanding; Intended as an Antidote against Modern Deism.* Salisbury, 1776.

Arbuthnot, John. *An essay concerning the effect of Air on Human Bodies.* London, 1733.

———. *An essay concerning the nature of aliments.* London, 1731.

———, et al. *Memoirs of the extraordinary life, works, and discoveries of Martinus Scriblerus.* Dublin, 1741; rpt. [edited by Charles Kerby-Miller] New Haven, Conn.: Yale University Press, 1950.

Archer, John. "Cure of melancholy and distraction." In *Every man his own doctor.* London, 1673.

Argens, Jean-Baptiste de Boyer, Marquis d'. *Lettres juives, ou correspondance philosophique, historique et critique . . .* 6 vols. The Hague, 1736–38.

———. *La philosophie du bon sens, ou réflexions philosophiques sur l'incertitude des connoissances humaines . . .* London, 1737; rpt. [of 1768 edn.] Farnborough, Mass.: Gregg, 1972.

Armstrong, John. *The art of preserving health: a poem. In four books. I. Air. II. Diet. III. Exercise. IV. The passions.* London, 1744; rpt. New York: Arno, 1979.

———. *The oeconomy of love.* London, 1736.

Arnauld, Antoine. *Des vraies et des fausses idées, contre ce qu'enseigne l'auteur De la recherche de la Verité* [N. Malebranche]. Cologne, 1683.

———, et al. *La logique où l'art de penser: contenant, outre les regles communes, plusieurs observations nouvelles, propres à former le jugement.* Paris, 1662; rpt. Hildesheim: G. Olms, 1970. *The Art of Thinking; Port Royal Logic.* Trans. James Dickoff and Patricia

James. Indianapolis: Bobbs-Merrill, 1964.

Arnold, Thomas. *A case of hydrophobia, commonly called canine madness, from the bite of a mad dog, successfully treated.* London, 1793.

———. *Observations on the nature, kinds, causes, and prevention of insanity, lunacy, or madness.* 2 vols. Leicester, 1782–86; rpt. New York: Arno, 1976.

Astruc, Jean. "De phantasia sive imaginatione," [1723] and ". . . sympathia partium a certa nervorum positura in interno sensorio?" [1736]. In *Disputationum analomicarum selectarum.* 8 vols. Göttingen, 1746–52.

———. *Traité des maladies des femmes.* 6 vols. Paris, 1743.

Atkins, John. *A compendious treatise on the contents, virtues, and uses of cold and hot mineral springs in general: . . . to which are annexed the opinions of Sir John Floyer and Dr. Baynard on the great use and effect of bathing in the sea.* London, n.d.

Aubrey, John. *Miscellanies.* London, 1696.

Auenbrugger, Leopold. *Inventum novum.* London, 1761; rpt. Vienna: J. Safar, 1922.

Austin, Gilbert. *Chironomia; or, A Treatise on Rhetorical Delivery.* London, 1805; rpt. Carbondale: Southern Illinois University Press, 1966.

Bacmeister, Joannes. *Propositiones sequentes de melancholia.* Rostock, 1593.

Bacon, Francis. *The Works.* Ed. J. Spedding et al. London, 1857–74.

Baillie, Joanna. *A series of plays: in which it is attempted to delineate the stronger passions of the mind. Each passion being the subject of a tragedy and a comedy.* London, 1789; rpt. New York: Garland, 1977.

Baillie, John. *An essay on the sublime.* London, 1747; rpt. [with an introduction by Samuel Holt Monk] Los Angeles, Calif.: William Andrews Clark Memorial Library, 1953.

Baillie, Matthew. *The morbid anatomy of some of the most important parts of the human body.* London, 1793; rpt. [of 1808 ed.] Oceanside, N.Y.: Dabor Science, 1977.

Bairer, Joh. Guil. *Diss. de memoria.* Amsterdam, 1708.

Baker, G. *De affectibus animi et morbis inde oriundis.* Cambridge, 1755.

Balfour, James. *A Delineation of the nature and obligation of morality.* 2nd edn. Edinburgh, 1763.

Balguy, John. *Collection of Tracts moral and theological.* London, 1734.

Banister, J. *The Historie of Man, suck'd from the Sappe of the most approved Anathomistes.* London, 1578; rpt. New York: Da Capo, 1969.

Bankhead, Charles. *Dissertatio medica inauguralis, de hysteria, . . .* Edinburgh, 1790.

Barbieri, Lodovico, Viscount. *Nuovo sistema intorno l'anima delle bestie, con la rigezione degli altri sistemi sin'ora proposti.* Vicenza, 1750.

Barrow, Isaac. *The Usefulness of Mathematical Learning Explained and Demonstrated: Being Mathematical Lectures Read in the Publick Schools at the University of Cambridge.* London 1734; rpt. London: Cass, 1970.

———. *The Theological Works of Isaac Barrow.* Ed. Alexander Napier. 9 vols. Cambridge, 1859.

Barthez, Paul Joseph. *Nouveaux élémens de la Science de l'Homme.* 2 vols. Montpellier, 1778.

Bartholinus, Erasmus. *De naturae mirabilis quaestiones academicae.* Copenhagen, 1674.

Battie, William. *De principiis animalibus exercitationes viginti quatuor in Theatro colegii medicorum Londinensium.* London, 1757.

———. *Treatise on madness.* London, 1758; rpt. New York: Brunner/Mazel, 1969.

Battus, Conr. *De melancholia hypochondriaca.* Rostock, 1605.

Baumgarten, Alexander. *Aesthetica.* 3rd edn. Frankfurt, 1758; rpt. [of selections] Hamburg: F. Meiner, 1983.

Baxter, Andrew. *An appendix to the first part of The enquiry into the nature of the human soul, wherein the principles laid down there, are cleared from some objections.* London, 1750.

———. *An Enquiry into the Nature of the Human Soul; Wherein the Immateriality of the Soul is Evinced from the Principles of Reason and Philosophy.* London, c. 1733; rpt. [of 1737 ed.] New York: Arno, 1981.

Baxter, Richard. *The certainty of the worlds of spirits.* London, 1681.

———. *The cure of melancholy and over much sorrow by faith and physick.* London, 1682.

———. *The immortality of a mans soul, and the nature of it, and of the spirits.* London, 1682.

———. *The signs and causes of melancholy. With directions suited to the case of those who are afflicted with it. Collected out of the works of Mr. Richard Baxter, for the sake of those, who are wounded in spirit. By Samuel Clifford.* London, 1716.

Bayfield, Robert. *Exercitationes anatomica, in varias regiones humani corporis.* London, 1668.

Bayle, Pierre. *The Dictionary Historical and Critical of Mr. Peter Bayle, translated and edited by Pierre Des Maizeaux.* 2nd edn. 5 vols. London, 1734–38; rpt. [of selections, trans. and ed. Richard H. Popkin with Craig Brush] Indianapolis: Bobbs-Merrill, 1965.

———. *Dictionnaire historique et critique.* 4 vols. Rotterdam, 1697.

[Baynard, Edward.] *Health, a poem. Shewing how to procure, preserve, and restore it. To which is annex'd The doctor's decade.* 2nd edn. London, [1719?].

Bayne, D. *A new essay on the nerves and the doctrine of the animal spirits rationally considered; shewing the great benefit of and true use of bathing, and drinking the Bath waters, in all nervous disorders and instructions; with two dissertations on the gout and on digestion, with the distempers of the stomach and intestines.* London, 1738.

Baynes, Stanhope. *Disputatio medica, inauguralis, de hypochondriasi.* Edinburgh, 1777.

[Beare, Matthew.] *The sensorium: a philosophical discourse of the senses: wherein their anatomy, and their several sensations, functions, and offices, are succinctly [sic] and accurately describ'd.* Oxford, 1710.

Beattie, James. *Dissertations, moral and critical, on memory and imagination, on dreaming; on the theory of languages; on fable and romance; on the attachment of kindred; and illustrations of sublimity.* London, 1783; rpt. New York: Garland, 1971.

———. *Elements of Moral Science.* 2 vols. Dublin, 1790-93; rpt. Delmar, N.Y.: Scholars' Facsimiles and Reprints, 1976.

Beauchêne, E.-P. Ch. de. *De L'influence des affections de l'ame sur les maladies des femmes.* Paris, 1781.

Beausobre, Louis de. *Essai sur le bonheur.* Berlin, 1758.

Beddoes, Thomas. *A guide for self-preservation, and parental affection; or plain directions for enabling people to keep themselves and their children free from several common disorders.* London, [1793?].

———. *Hygëia; or essays moral and medical, on the causes affecting the personal state of our middling and affluent classes.* 3 vols. Bristol, 1802–03.

Behrens, Conrad Barthold. *De suffocatione hysterica.* Helmstadt, 1684.

Behrens, R. A. *Considerationem animae rationalis medicam . . . examini submittit.* Leipzig, 1720.

Belcher, William. *Disputatio medica inauguralis, de hysteria . . .* Edinburgh, 1793.

Bell, Charles. *Idea of a new anatomy of the brain.* [London, 1802?]; rpt. London: Dawsons of Pall Mall, 1966.

Bell, J. *The general and particular principles of animal electricity and magnetism. Showing how to magnetise and cure different diseases, to produce crises, as well as somnambulism, or sleep-walking.* London, 1792.

Bellet, Isaac. *Lettres sur le pouvoir de l'imagination des femmes enceintes où l'on combat le préjugé qui attribue à l'imagination des mères le pouvoir d'imprimer sur les corps des enfants.* Paris, 1745.
Belot, Jean. *L'oeuvre des oeuvres; ou le plus parfait des sciences steganographiques Paulines, Armadelles et Lullistes, par lesquelles facilement se comprend . . . et l'on cognoist son genie, et par ici uy la perfection de toutes les sciences, que l'on peut acquerir par neuf leçons, contenues en ce livre.* Paris, 1622.
Belsham, William. *Essays philosophic, historical, and literary.* London, 1789.
Bentham, Edward. *An Introduction to Logick, Scholastick and Rational.* Oxford, 1773; rpt. Menston, York: Scolar Press, 1969.
Bentley, Richard. *Matter and motion cannot think: or, a confutation of atheism from the faculties of the soul.* London, 1692.
Bercke, Johann. *Passionem hystericam.* Erfurt, 1672.
Berger, Christian Gottlieb. *De melancholia hypochondriaca.* Frankfurt an der Oder, 1715.
Bergier, Nicolas-Sylvestre. *Esamen de matérialisme: ou Réfatation du Système de la nature.* 2 vols. Paris, 1771.
Berkeley, George. *Alciphron: or the minute philosopher.* London, 1732.
_____. *Essay Towards a New Theory of Vision.* Dublin, 1709.
_____. *Siris.* London, 1744.
_____. *Three dialogues between Hylas and Philonous. The design of which is plainly to demonstrate the reality and perfection of humane knowledge, the incorporeal nature of the soul, and the immediate providence of a deity.* London, 1713.
_____. *The Works of George Berkeley, Bishop of Cloyne.* Ed. A. A. Luce and T. E. Jessop. 9 vols. Edinburgh: Nelson, 1948–75.
Berkenhout, John. *A treatise on hysterical and hypochondriacal diseases.* London, 1777.
Bernoulli, Jacques. *Jacobi Bernoulli . . . Ars conjectandi, opus posthumum.* Basel, 1713.
Bethum, John. *A short view of the human faculties and passions. With remarks and directions respecting their nature, improvement, and government.* 2nd edn. Edinburgh, 1770.
Beutel, Joh. C. *De mania.* Jena, 1648.
Bichat, Xavier. *Recherches physiologiques sur la vie et la mort.* Paris, 1800; rpt. [in English: *Physiological researches on life and death.*] New York: Arno, 1977.
Bienville, J. D. T. de. *La nymphomanie, ou, Traité de la fureur utérine.* Amsterdam, 1771. *Nymphomania.* Trans. Edwin Sloane Wilmot, M.D. London, 1775.
Billings, Peter. *Folly predominant . . . to which is added a dissertation on the impossibility of curing lunatics in Bedlam.* London, 1755.
Billy, J. B. M. de. *Nouveau traite de la mémoire, où l'on explique d'une manière nette & mecanique ses effects les plus suprenans.* Paris, 1708.
Blackmore, Richard. *A discourse upon the plague, with a prefatory account of malignant fever.* London, 1721.
_____. "An essay upon the spleen." In *Essays upon several subjects.* London, 1717; rpt. Hildesheim: G. Olms, 1976.
_____. *Natural theology, or moral duties considered apart from positive.* London, 1728.
_____. *The Nature of Man: a poem.* London, 1711.
_____. *A treatise of the spleen and vapours: or hypochondriacal and hysterical affections.* London, 1725; rpt. Surrey: Unwin Brothers, 1979.
Blair, Hugh. *Lectures on Rhetoric and Belles Lettres.* London, 1783; rpt. [of 1785 ed.] New York: Garland, 1970.
Blair, Patrick. *Botanick Essays. In two parts. The first containing, the structures of the flowers and the fructification of plants, with their various distributions into method : and the second, the*

generation of plants, with the sexes and manner of impregnating the seed: also containing the animacula in semine masculino. London, 1720.

Blakeway, Robert. *An essay towards the cure of religious melancholy.* London, 1717.

Bleker, Georgius Fridericus. *De melancholia hypochondriaca.* Kiel, 1673.

Blochmann, Johannes Gottlieb. *De morbis ex atonia cerebri nervorumque nascentibus.* Halle, 1708.

Blondel, James Augustus. *The power of the mother's imagination over the foetus examin'd. In answer to Dr. Daniel Turner's book, intitled A defence of the XIIth chapter of the first part of a treatise, De morbis cutaneis.* London, 1729.

_____. *The strength of imagination in pregnant women examin'd: and the opinion that marks and deformities in children arise from thence, demonstrated to be a vulgar error.* London, 1727.

Blount, Charles. *Anima mundi; or, An historical narration of the opinions of the ancients concerning man's soul after this life; according to unenlightened nature.* London, 1679.

_____. *Oracles of reason.* London, 1693.

Blount, Thomas Pope. *Essays on Several subjects.* London, 1691.

Blum, Emanuel. *De dolore hypochondriaco, vulgo sed falso putato splenetico.* Leipzig, 1683.

Boenneken, J. *Sistans melancholia vulgo. Die Schwermütigkeit.* Erfurt,1728.

Boerhaave, Herman. *Aphorismi de cognoscendi et curandis morbis, in usum doctrinae domesticae digesti.* Leyden, 1709.

_____. *Dr. Boerhaave's Academical Lectures on the Theory of Physic, Being a Genuine Translation of his Institutes, and Explanatory Commentary.* 6 vols. London, 1757.

_____. *Institutiones medicae in usus annuae exercitationes domesticos.* Paris, 1722.

_____. "De usu ratiocinii mechanici in medicina." London, 1703. In *Opuscula selecta neerlandicorum in arte medica.* Rpt. Amsterdam, 1907.

Bolten, J. Ch. *Gedanken von psychologischen Kuren.* Halle, 1751.

Bond, John. *An essay on the incubus, or night-mare.* London, 1753.

Bonnet, Charles. *Essai analytique sur les facultés de l'ame.* Copenhagen, 1760; rpt. Hildesheim: G. Olms, 1973.

_____. *Essai de psychologie; ou, Considerations sur les operations de l'ame, sur l'habitude et sur l'education.* Leyden, 1754; rpt. Hildesheim: G. Olms, 1978.

_____. *La Palingénésie philosophique, ou Idées sur l'état passé et sur l'état futur des êtres vivans.* Geneva, 1770.

Bontekoe, Cornelius. *Nouveau elemens de medecine.* Paris, 1718.

Booker, Moore. *The true gratification of the sensual appetites recommended, in a sermon.* Dublin, 1756.

[Bordenave, Toussaint.] *Essai sur la physiologie.* Amsterdam, 1756.

Bordeu, Theophile de. *Recherches anatomique sur la position des glands et sur leur action.* Paris, 1751.

Borelli, Giovanni Alfonso. *De motu animalium.* Rome, 1680–81.

[Bougeant, Guillaume Hyacinthe.] *Amusement philosophique sur le langage des bêtes.* La Haye, 1739; rpt. Geneva: Droz, 1954.

Bouguer, Pierre. *Essai d'optique sur la gradation de la lumière.* Paris, 1729.

Boullier, David Renaud. *Essai phiosophique sur l'ame des bêtes, où l'on traite de son existence et de sa nature, et où l'on mêle par occasion diverses réflexions sur la nature de la liberté, sur celle de nos sensations, sur l'union de l'ame et du corps, sur l'immortalité de l'ame et où l'on réfute plusieurs objections de Mr. Bayle.* Amsterdam, 1728.

Boush, William. *Dissertatio medica inauguralis, de hysteria.* Edinburgh, 1778.

[Bowen, Thomas.] *An historical account of the origin, progress, and present state of Bethlem hospital.* London, 1783.

Bradberry, Robert. *The power of imagination, or the senses deceived*. London, 1791.
Bragge, Francis. *A practical treatise of the regulation of the passions*. London, 1708.
Brancacci, Giovanni. *Ars memoriae vindicata, auctore d. Joanne Brancaccio . . . Accessit artificium poeticum ad scripturas divinas in promptu habendas, memoriterque ediscendas accommodatum*. Palermo, 1702.
Branch, T. *Thoughts on dreaming. Wherein the notion of the sensory, and the opinion that it is shut up from the inspection of the soul in sleep, and that spirits supply us with all our dreams, are examined by revelation and reason*. London, 1737.
Brathwait, Richard. *Essaies upon the five senses, with a pithie one upon retraction*. London, 1620.
Brocklesby, Richard. *Reflections on antient and modern musick, with the application to the cure of diseases*. London, 1749.
Brookes, R. *The general practice of physic*. 2 vols. London, 1751.
Broughton, John. *Psychologia; or, An account of the nature of the rational soul. In two parts. The first, being an essay towards establishing the received doctrine of an immaterial and . . . immortal substance, united to human body. The second, a vindication of that doctrine, against a late book, called Second thoughts &c* [by William Coward]. London, 1703.
Brown, John. *Essays on the Characteristics*. London, 1751; rpt. New York: Garland, 1970.
Browne, Peter. *The procedure, extent, and limits of human understanding*. London, 1728; rpt. [of 1729, 2nd edn.] New York: Garland, 1976.
Browne, Richard. *Medicina musica, or a mechanical essay on the effects of singing, musick, and dancing on the human bodies, to which is annexed a new essay on the nature and cure of the spleen and vapours*. London, 1674.
Browne, Thomas Gunter. *Hermes unmasked; or, The art of speech, founded on the association of words and ideas*. London, 1795–96; rpt. Menston, York: Scolar Press, 1969.
Bruckshaw, Samuel. *One More Proof of the Iniquitous Abuse of Private Madhouses*. London, 1774.
Brydall, John. *Non compos mentis*. London, 1700.
Buffon, George Louis, Comte de. *Barr's Buffon. Buffon's natural history, containing a theory of the earth, a general history of man, of the brute creation and of vegetables, minerals, &c*. 10 vols. London, 1792.
Bulwer, John. *Anthropometamorphosis: man transformed: or the artificial changeling historically presented*. London, 1650.
Burgh, James. *The art of speaking. Containing, I. An essay; in which are given rules for expressing properly the principal passions and humors, . . . and II. Lessons taken from ancients and moderns . . .* London, 1761.
Burke, Edmund. *A Philosophical Enquiry into the Origin of Our Ideas of the Sublime and Beautiful*. London, 1757; rpt. [of 1759 edn.] Menston, York: Scolar Press, 1970. Also see James T. Boulton's edition, London: Routledge and Kegan Paul, 1958.
Burrows, George Man. *Commentaries on the causes, forms, symptoms, and treatments, moral and medical, of insanity*. London 1828; rpt. New York: Arno, 1976.
Burthogge, Richard. *An essay upon reason, and the nature of spirits*. London, 1694; New York: Garland, 1976.
——— . *Organum vetus and novum. Or, a discourse of reason and truth. Wherein the natural logick common to Mankinde is briefly and plainly described*. London, 1678; rpt. Chicago, Ill.: University of Chicago Press, 1921.
Burton, Robert. *The Anatomy of melancholy. What it is, with all the kindes, causes, symptoms, prognostickes, & several cures of it. By Democritus Iunior*. Oxford, 1621; rpt. New York: E. P. Dutton, 1932.

Butler, Joseph. *The analogy of religion, natural and revealed, to the constitution and course of nature. To which are added two brief dissertations: I. Of personal identity. II. Of the nature of virtue.* 2nd edn. London, 1736.

―――. *Fifteen sermons, &c.* London, 1726.

―――. *Works.* Ed. W. E. Gladstone. 2 vols. Oxford: Clarendon Press, 1896.

Buxton, Jedidiah. *Jedidiah Buxton, a poor labourer; born at Elmton in Derbyshire: who without being able to write or cast accounts in the ordinary method; perform'd the longest calculations and solv'd the most difficult problems in arithmetic by the strength of his memory . . .* Piccadilly, 1781.

Cabanis, Pierre-Jean-Georges. *Rapports du physique et du moral de l'homme.* Paris, 1802; rpt. [in English: *On the relations between the physical and moral aspects of man.* Trans. Margaret Duggan Saidi]Baltimore, Md.: Johns Hopkins University Press, 1981.

Cadogan, William. *A dissertation on the gout, and all chronic diseases, jointly considered.* London, 1771.

―――. *An essay upon nursing, and the management of children, . . . In a letter to one of the governors of the Foundling hospital.* London, 1748.

[Campbell, Archibald.] *Enquiry into the Original of Moral Virtue.* Westminster, 1728.

Campbell, George. *Philosophy of Rhetoric.* 2 vols. London, 1776; rpt. Carbondale: Southern Illinois University Press, 1963.

Cannac, P. *Dissertatio physica de memoria.* Geneva, 1723.

Carkesse, James. *Lucida Intervalla.* London, 1679; rpt. [with an introduction by Michael V. DePorte] Los Angeles, Calif.: William Andrews Clark Memorial Library, 1979.

Carrere, Joseph. *Dissertatio medica de vitali corporis et animae foedere.* Perpignan, 1758.

Casaubon, Meric. *A treatise concerning enthusiasme, as it is an effect of nature: but is mistaken by many for either divine inspiration, or diabolical possession.* London, 1655; rpt. Gainesville, Fla.: Scholars' Facsimiles and Reprints, 1970.

Castelli, Bartolomeo. *Lexicon Medicum.* Padua, 1713.

Chambers, Ephraim. *Cyclopedia; or, An Universal Dictionary of Arts and Sciences.* 2 vols. London, 1728.

Chandler, G. *An inquiry into the various Theories and Methods of Cure in Apoplexie and Palsies.* London, 1785.

Chanet, Pierre. *De l'instinct et de la connoissance des amimaux avec l'examen de ce que M. de La Chambre a escrit sur cette matière.* La Rochelle, 1646.

―――. *Eclaircissement de quelques difficultez touchant la connoissance de l'imagination.* La Rochelle, 1648.

Chanler, Isaac. *Disputatio medica inauguralis, de hysteria.* Edinburgh, 1768.

Charleton, Walter. *The Darkness of Atheism Dispelled by the Light of Nature.* London, 1652.

―――. *Enquiries into Human Nature.* London, 1697.

[―――.] *The Immortality of the Human Soul, Demonstrated by the Light of Nature.* London, 1657.

[―――.]*Natural History of the Passions.* London, 1674. [Often attributed to J. F. Senault, though incorrectly.]

―――. *Two Discourses. I. Concerning the different wits of men: II. Of the mysterie of vintners.* London, 1669.

Chauvin. *Lexicon philosophicum.* Leovardiae, 1713.

―――. *Lexicon, rationale sive thesaurus philosophicus ordine alphabetico digestus.* Rotterdam, 1692.

Cheselden, William. *Anatomy of the Human Body.* 4th edn. London, 1730.

Cheyne, George. *An Essay concerning the Improvements of the Theory of Medicine*. Edinburgh, 1702.

———. *An Essay of Health and Long Life*. London, 1724; rpt. New York: Arno Press, 1979.

———. *The English Malady*. London, 1733.

———. *An Essay on Regimen. Together with five Discourses, Medical, Moral and Philosophical: Serving to Illustrate the Principles and Theories of Philosophical Medicin, and Point out Some of its Moral Consequences*. London, 1740.

———. *The Natural Method of Cureing the Diseases of the Body, and the Disorders of the Mind Depending on the Body. In Three Parts. Part I. General Reflections on the Oeconomy of Nature in Animal Life. Part II. The Means and Methods for Preserving Life and Faculties. and also concerning the Nature and Cure of Acute, Contagious, and Cephalic Disorders. Part III. Reflections on the Nature and Cure of Particular Distempers*. London, 1742.

———. *Philosophical Principles of Religion. In Two Parts. Part I. Containing the Elements of Natural Philosophy, and the Proofs of Natural Religion Arising from Them. The Second Edition, Corrected and Enlarged. Part II. Containing the Nature and Kinds of Infinities, Their Arithmetik and Uses; together with the Philosophick Principles of Reveal'd Religion*. London, 1705.

Chiarugi, V. *Della pazzia in genere e in specie: trattoto medico analitico con una centuria di osservazioni*. 3 vols. Florence, 1793–94.

———. *La fisica dell'uomo, ossia corso completo di medicina ad uso degli ufficiali di sanita'*. 2 vols. Florence, 1811–12.

———. *Saggio teoricopratico sulle malatie cutanee sordide osservate nel R. Spedale Bonifacio di Firenze*. Florence, 1799.

Chubb, Thomas. *A Discourse concerning Reason*. London, 1731.

Clark, William. *A Medical Dissertation concerning the Effects of the Passions on Human Bodies*. London, 1727.

Clark, John. *Foundation of Morality, in theory and practice considered*. York, [172-?].

Clarke, John. *An Examination of the Notion of Moral Good and Evil, Advanced in a late Book, Entitled, The Religion of Nature Delineated* [by William Wollaston]. London, 1725.

Clarke, Samuel. *A Collection of Papers, Which Passed between the Late Learned Mr. Leibnitz and Dr. Clarke, in the Years 1715 and 1716; Relating to the Principles of Natural Philosophy and Religion. With an Appendix. To which are added, Letters to Dr. Clarke concerning Liberty and Necessity, from a Gentleman of the University of Cambridge* [Richard Bulkekey]*: with the Doctor's Answers to Them. Also, Remarks upon a Book, Entituled, A Philosophical Enquiry concerning Human Liberty* [by Anthony Collins]. London, 1717.

———. *A Letter to Mr. Dodwell, Wherein All the Arguments in his Epistolary Discourse against the Immortality of the Soul are Particularly Answered, and the Judgement of the Fathers concerning That Matter are Truly Represented*. London, 1706.

———. *A Defence of an argument made use of in a letter to Mr. Dodwel, to prove the immateriality and natural immortality of the soul*. London 1707.

———. *A Second Defence of an Argument Made Use of in a letter to Mr. Dodwel, to prove the immateriality and natural immortality of the soul*. London, 1707.

———. *A Third Defence of an Argument Made Use of in a letter to Mr. Dodwel, to prove the immateriality and natural immortality of the soul*. London, 1708.

———. *A Fourth Defence of an Argument Made Use of in a Letter to Mr. Dodwel, to prove the immateriality and natural immortality of the soul*. London, 1708. [The Clarke-Collins controversy is reprinted in full in vol. III of Clarke's *Works*, London, 1738.]

———. *A Demonstration of the Being and Attributes of God; More Particularly in Answer to Mr.*

Hobbs, Spinoza, and Their Followers. Wherein the Notion of Liberty is Stated, and the Possibility and Certainty of it Proved, in Opposition to Necessity and Fate. London, 1705.
———. *The Government of Passion,* London, 1711.
Clarke, Samuel, b. 1721. *A Short Relation, concerning a Dream, which the Author had on the Eighteenth Day of September, in the Year One Thousand Seven Hundred and Sixty Nine. With some Remarks on the Late Comet.* Boston, 1774.
Clauberg, Johann. *De cognitione Dei et nostri, quaetenus naturali rationis lumine, secundum veram philosophiam, potest comparari exercitationes centum, duisburgi ad rhenum.* Amsterdam, 1656; rpt. [in *Opera omnia philosophica.* 2 vols.] Hildesheim: G. Olms, 1968.
———. *Opera physica, id est, physica contracta, disputationes physicae, theoria viventium, & conjunctionis animae cum corpore descriptio.* Amsterdam, 1691.
[Clayton, Robert.] *An Essay on Spirit.* Dublin, 1750.
Clubbe, John. *Physiognomy; being a sketch only of a larger work upon the same plan; wherein the different tempers, passions, and manners of men, will be particularly considered.* London, 1763.
Coffeteau, Nicolas. *A Table of Humane Passions. With Their Causes and Effects.* Trans. E. Grimeston. London, 1621.
[Colliber, Samuel.] *Free thoughts concerning Souls: In Four Essays. I. Of the Humane Soul consider'd in its own Nature. II. Of the Human Soul compared with the Souls of Brutes. III. Of the supposed Prae-existent State of Souls. To which is added, An Essay on Creation.* London, 1734.
Collier, Arthur. *Clavis Universalis: or, a New Inquiry after Truth. Being a Demonstration of the Non-Existence, or Impossibility, of an External World.* London, 1713; rpt. New York: Garland, 1978.
Collier, Jeremy. "Of the Spleen" in *Essays Upon Several Moral Subjects.* London, 1697; rpt. Hildesheim: G. Olms, 1969.
Collier, John. *Human Passions Delineated in above 120 Figures droll, satyrical, and humourous; design'd in the Hogarthian style.* Manchester, 1773.
Collins, Anthony. *A Dissertation on Liberty and Necessity. wherein the process of ideas, from their first entrance into the soul, until their production of action, is delineated.* London, 1729.
———. *An essay concerning the use of reason in propositions, the evidence wherof depends upon human testimony.* London, 1707.
[———.] *A letter to the learned Mr. Henry Dodwell; containing some remarks on a (pretended) demonstration of the immortality of the soul.* London, 1707.
[———.] *A reply to Mr. Clark's Defence of his letter to Mr. Dodwell. With a postscript relating to Mr. Milles's answer to Mr. Dodwell's epistolary discourse.* London, 1707.
[———.] *Reflections on Mr. Clark's Second defence of his letter to Mr. Dodwell.* London, 1708.
[———.] *An answer to Mr. Clark's Third defence to his Letter to Mr. Dodwell.* London, 1708.
———. *A Philosophical Enquiry concerning human Liberty and Necessity.* London, 1715.
Colman, George. *The Spleen; or, Islington Spa. A comick piece, of two acts.* London, 1776.
Colombier, J. *Instruction sur la maniere de gouverner les insensés, et de travailler a leur guerison dan les asyles qui leur son destinés.* Paris, 1785; rpt. Nedeln, Liechtenstein: Kraus Reprints, 1978.
Comenius, Johann Amos. *Orbis sensualium pictus, hoc est omnium fundamentalium in mundo rerum & in vita actionum pictura & nomenclatura.* Copenhagen, 1672.
Condillac, Etienne Bonnot de. *Essai sur l'origine des conaissances humaines.* Amsterdam, 1746; rpt. [of 1756 edn., in English. Trans. T. Nugent] Gainesville, Fla.: Scholars' Facsimiles and Reprints, 1971.
———. *Traité des animaux.* Paris, 1755.
———. *Traité des sensations.* Paris, 1745.

———. *Traité des sistèmes*. The Hague, 1749.

Condorcet, Antoine Nicolas, marquis de. *Esquisse d'un tableau historique des progrès de l'esprit humain*. Paris, 1745; rpt. [in English. Trans. Jane Barraclough] London, Weidenfield and Nicolson, 1955.

[Cooke, Thomas.] *Some Observations on Taste, and on the Present State of Poetry in England*. Prefixed to *An Ode on Beauty*. London, 1749.

Cooper, Thomas. *Tracts on Medical Jurisprudence. Including Farr's Elements of Medical Jurisprudence, Dease's Remarks on Medical Jurisprudence, Male's Epitome of Juridical or Forensic Medicine, and Haslam's Treatise on Insanity*. Philadelphia, 1819.

Cordemoy, Geraud de. *De la parole*. Paris, 1668; rpt. in *Philosophical Discourse Concerning Speech (1668) & a Discourse Written to a Learned Frier (1670)* [Introduction by Barbara Ross] Gainesville, Fla.: Scholars' Facsimiles and Reprints, 1972.

———. *Les oeuvres du feu M. de Cordemoy*. Paris, 1704.

Coronier, et al. *Rapport de M. M. Cornier, Maloet, Darcet . . . sur les avantages reconnus de la nouvelle methode d'administrer l'electricité dans les maladies nerveuses*. Paris, 1783.

Corp, Doctor. *An Essay on the Changes Produced in the Body by the Operations of the Mind, by the late Dr. Corp of Bath*. London, 1791.

[Coward, William.] *Farther thoughts concerning human soul, in defence of Second thoughts; wherein the weak efforts of the Reverend Mr. Turner, and other less significant writers are occasionally answer'd*. London, 1703.

[———.] *The Grand Essay: Or, a Vindication of Reason, and Religion, Against Impostures of Philosophy. Proving according to those Ideas and Conceptions of Things Human Understanding is capable of forming to it self. I. That the Existence of any Immaterial Substance is a Philosophic Imposture, and impossible to be conceived. 2. That all matter has Originally created in it, a principle of Internal, or Self Motion. 3. That matter & Motion must be the foundation of Thought in Men and Brutes. To which is Added, A Brief Answer to Mr. Broughton's Psycholo. &c.* London, 1704.

[———.] *The Just Scrutiny: Or, a Serious Enquiry into the Modern Notions of the Soul . . . With a Comparative Disquisition Between the Scriptural and Philosophic State of the Dead*. London [1705?].

[———.] *Second thoughts concerning human soul. Demonstrating the notion of the human soul . . . to be an invention of the heathens, and not consonant with the principles of philosophy, reason, or religion*. 2nd edn. London, 1702.

Cowper, William. *Myotomia reformata; Or, A New Administration of All the Muscles of Human Bodies; Wherein the True Uses of the Muscles Are Explained, the Errors of Former anatomists concerning Them Confuted, and Several Muscles Not Hitherto Taken Notice of Described*. London, 1694.

Cowper, William, 1731–1800. *Memoir of the Early Life of William Cowper, Esq*. London, 1816.

Cox, Joseph Mason. *Practical observations on Insanity, in which some suggestions are offered towards an improved mode of treating diseases of the mind . . . to which are subjoined remarks on medical jurisprudence*. London, 1806.

———. *Querdam de mania*. London, 1787.

Crawford, Charles. *A dissertation on the Phaedon of Plato: or dialogue of the immortality of the soul . . . To which is annexed, a psychology; or, an abstract investigation of the nature of the soul*. London, 1773.

Crellius, Johannes Fridericus. *De melancholia hysterica*. Leipzig, 1732.

Crichton, Alexander. *An inquiry into the nature and origin of mental derangement. Comprehending a concise system of the physiology and pathology of the human mind and a history of the

passions and effects. 2 vols. London, 1798; rpt. New York: AMS Press, 1976.
Croft, Herbert. *Love and madness. A Story too true: in a series of letters between parties, whose names would perhaps be mentioned, were they less known, or less lamented.* 3rd edn. London, 1780.
Crooke, Helkiah. Μικροκοσμογραφία. *A Description of the Body of Man.* London, 1615.
Croone, W. *De ratione motus musculorum.* Amsterdam, 1664.
Crouch, Nathaniel. *Unparallel'd varieties; or, the matchless actions and passions of mankind, displayed in near four hundred notable instances and examples.* 4th edn. London, 1728.
Crousaz, Jean Pierre de. *De mente humana substantia a corpore distincta et immortali, dissertatio philosophico-theologica.* Groningae, 1726.
──────. *La Logique, où Système de reflexions qui peuvent contribuer à la netteté à l'éntendue de nos connoissances.* 4 vols. Amsterdam, 1725.
Cruden, Alexander. *The London-Citizen Exceedingly Injured; Or, a British Inquisition Display'd, in an Account of the Unparallel'd Case of a Citizen of London, Bookseller to the late Queen, Who Was in a Most Unjust and Arbitrary Manner Sent on the 23rd of March Last, 1738, by One Robert Wrightman, a Mere Stranger, to a Private Madhouse.* London, 1739.
──────. *Mr. Cruden Greatly Injured: An Account of a Trial between Mr. Alexander Cruden Bookseller to the Late Queen, Plaintif, and Dr. Monro, Matthew Wright, John Oswald, and John Davis, Defendants; in the Court of the Common-Pleas in Westminster Hall July 17, 1739, on an Action of Trespass, Assault and Imprisonment: the said Mr. Cruden, Tho' in His Right Senses, Having Been Unjustly Fined and Barbarously Used in the Said Matthew Wright's Private Madhouse at Bethnal-Green for Nine Weeks and Six Days, till He Made His Wonderful Escape May 31, 1738. To which is Added a Surprising Account of Several Other Persons, Who Have Been Most Unjustly Confined in Madhouses.* London, 1740.
Cudworth, Ralph. *A Treatise concerning Eternal and Immutable Morality.* London, 1731; rpt. New York: Garland, 1976.
──────. *A Treatise of Free-will.* London, 1838.
──────. *The true Intellectual System of the Universe.* London, 1678; rpt. New York: Garland, 1978.
Cullen, William. *Apparatus ad nosologiam methodicam. Seu synopsis nosologiae methodicae in usum stodiosorum.* Amsterdam, 1775.
──────. *First lines of the practice of physic, for the use of the students in the University of Edinburgh.* 4 vols. Dublin, 1777–84.
──────. *Institutions of Medicine.* 3rd edn. Edinburgh, 1785.
──────. *Nosology; or, a Systematic Arrangement of Diseases.* Edinburgh, 1772.
──────. *A Treatise of the Materia Medica.* 3rd American edn. Philadelphia, 1789.
Culverwell, Nathaniel. *An Elegant and Learned Discourse of the Light of Nature, with several other treatises.* London, 1652; rpt. Toronto: University of Toronto Press, 1971.
Cumberland, Richard. *De Legibus Naturae Disquisito Philosophica, in qua earum Forma, Summa Capita, Ordo, Promulgatio & Obligatio e Rerum Naturae Investigantur; quinetiam Elementa Philosophiae Hobbianae cum Moralis tum Civilis Considerantur & Refutantur.* London, 1672.
──────. *A Treatise on the Laws of Nature. Made English from the Latin by John Maxwell . . . To which is prefix'd, An Introduction concerning the Mistaken Notions Which the Heathens had of the Deity, and the Defects in Their Morality, Whence the Usefulness of Revelation May Appear. At the end is subjoin'd, An Appendix, containing Two Discourses, 1. Concerning the Immateriality of Thinking Substance. 2. Concerning the Obligation, Promulgation, and Observance of the Law of Nature, by the Translator.* London, [1727].

Currie, James. "Two letters on the establishment of a lunatic asylum at Liverpool." In *Medical Reports on the effects of water, cold, and warm as a remedy in fever and febrile cases.* London, 1804.
D'Alembert, Jean. *Oeuvres philosophiques, historiques et littéraires de d'Alembert.* 18 vols. Paris, 1805.
Dambésieux, abbé. *Reflexions sur la physique moderne; ou, la philosophie newtonienne comparée avec celle de Descartes.* Paris, 1757.
Daquin, Joseph. *Philosopie de la folie, ou Essai philosophique sur le traitement des personnes attaquées de folie.* Paris, 1792; rpt. Nedeln, Liechtenstein: Kraus Reprints, 1978.
Darwin, Erasmus. *Zoonomia. Or the laws of organic life.* 2 vols. London, 1794–96; rpt. New York: AMS Press, 1974.
D'Assigny, Marius. *The art of memory.* London, 1697; rpt. [ed. Michael V. DePorte] New York: AMS Press, 1985.
[Defoe, Daniel.] *An Essay on the History and Reality of Apparitions.* London, 1727.
Deleboë, Sylvius. *Opera medica.* Amsterdam, 1680.
Descartes, René. *Oeuvres.* Ed. Charles Adam and Paul Tannery. 13 vols. Paris, 1897–1910; rpt. Paris: J. Vrin, 1964–75.
———. *The Philosophical Works of Descartes.* Trans. E. S. Haldane and G. R. T. Ross. 2 vols. Cambridge: Cambridge University Press, 1911. See, among others, *The Passions of the Soul, Rules for the Direction of the Mind, Meditations on First Philosophy,* and *Discourse on Method.*
———. *Treatise of Man.* French text with English trans. by T. S. Hall. Cambridge, Mass: Harvard Monographs in the History of Science, 1972.
A Description of Bedlam with an Account of its Present Inhabitants both Male and Female. To which is subjoined an essay upon the nature causes and cure of madness. London, 1772.
[Desgabets, Robert.] *Critique de la Critique de la Recherche de la verité; où, l' on découvre le chemin qui conduit aux connoissances solides. Pour servir de reponse à la lettre d' un academicien* [S. Foucher]. Paris, 1675.
Destutt de Tracy, Antoine Louis Claude, comte. *Elémens d'idéologie.* Paris, 1803; rpt. Detroit, Mich: Center for Public Health, 1973.
Diderot, Denis. *The Early Philosophical Works.* Trans. M. Jourdain. New York: Burt Franklin, 1916.
———, [et al.] *Encyclopédie, ou dictionnaire raisonné des sciences des arts et des métiers, par une société des gens de lettres.* 35 vols. Paris, 1751–80.
———. *Oeuvres de Denis Diderot.* Paris, 1800; rpt. Paris: Hermann, 1975– . See, among others, *Lettre sur les aveugles, Lettres sur les sourds et les meuts,* and *Réflexions sur le livre de l'esprit, par M. Helvetius.*
Digby, Kenelm, Sir. *Of Bodies, and of Man's Soul. To Discover the Immortality of Reasonable Souls.* London, 1669.
———. *Two Treatises, in the One of Which the Nature of Bodies, in the Other the Nature of Mans Soule; Is Looked into: in the Way of Discovery, of the Immortality of Reasonable Soules.* Paris, 1644; rpt. New York: Garland, 1977.
Dilly, Antoine. *Traitté de l'ame et de la connoissance des bêtes, ou après avoir demontré la spiritualité de l'ame de l'homme, l'on explique par la seule machine, les actions les plus surprenantes des animaux, suivant les principes de Descartes.* Amsterdam, 1691.
Dionis, Pierre. *Nouvelle anatomie de l'homme, suivant la circulation du sang, & les dernieres découvertes.* 3rd edn. Paris, 1695.
A Dissertation upon the nervous system to show its influence upon the soul. [London?], 1780.

Ditton, Humphrey. *A Discourse concerning the Resurrection of Jesus Christ. In Three Parts . . . Together with an Appendix containing the Impossible Production of Thought, from Matter and Motion; the Nature of Humane Souls, and of Brutes: the Anima Mundi, and the hypothesis of the* τόπᾶν; *as also, concerning Divine Providence, the Origin of Evil, and the Universe in General*. London, 1712.

Doddridge, Philip. *A Course of Lectures on the Principle Subjects in Pneumatology, Ethics, and Divinity; with References to the Most Considerable Authors of Each Subject*. London, 1763.

Dodwell, Henry, the Elder. *An epistolary discourse, proving, from the Scriptures and the first fathers, that the soul is a principle naturally mortal*. London, 1706.

Downes, John. *De Affectione Hypochondriaca*. Leyden, 1660.

Drage, William. *A Physical Nosonomy*. London, 1665.

Dreams and Moles With their Interpretation and Signification. London, c. 1750.

Dubos, Jean Baptiste. *Critical Reflections on Poetry, Painting, and Music*. London, 1719; rpt. New York: AMS Press, 1978.

Duff, William. *An essay on original genius*. London, 1767; rpt. New York: Garland, 1970.

Dufour, Abbe. *L'Ame ou le sisteme des Matérialistes, soumis aux seules lumières de la raison*. Avignon, 1759.

_____. *Essai sur les functions et les maladies de l'entendement humain et sur les maladies qui les dérangent*. Amsterdam, 1770; rpt. Nedeln, Liechtenstein: Kraus Reprints, 1978.

Du Laurens, Andre. *A Discourse of the preservation of the sight; of melancholike diseases, of rheumes, and of old age*. London, 1599; rpt. Oxford: Oxford University Press, 1938.

Dumas, Jean. *Traité du Suicide*. Amsterdam, 1733.

Du Mond, Jan. *De Hypochondriacorum morbosis affectibus*. Utrecht, 1705.

Earle, John. *Micro-cosmographie, or a piece of the world discovered in essayes and characters*. London, 1628; rpt. West Orange: Albert Saifer, 1980.

Edwards, Jonathan. *A careful and strict enquiry into the notion of that freedom and will which is supposed to be essential to moral agency*. Boston, 1754.

_____. *A treatise concerning religious affections*. Boston, 1746.

Elliot, J. *Philosophical Observations on the Senses of Vision and Hearing*. London, 1780.

Elliott, John. *The Medical Pocket-Book*. Philadelphia, 1784.

Encyclopaedia Britannica; or, A Dictionary of Arts and Sciences. Compiled upon a New Plan . . . By a Society of Gentlemen in Scotland. 3 vols. Edinburgh, 1771.

An Enquiry into Dr. Ward's Practice of Physick . . . With An Examination into the Origin, and Meaning of the Words Empiricism, Empirick, Quack-Doctor, and Quack. And, An Exact Account of the Present State of Physick. London, 1749.

An Enquiry into the Nature of the Human Soul, Its Origin, Properties, and Faculties; Considered Both in Regard to Itself, and Its Union with the Body. In Which Several Received Opinions Are Confuted concerning Both. London, 1750.

Erbery, William. *The Mad Mans Plea*. London, 1653.

Erhard, J. B. "Über die Melancholie" in *Beitr. zur phil. Anthro*. Vienna, 1794-96.

Erhardt, Thomas Aquinas. *Ars memoriae, sive clara & perspicua methodus excerpendi nucleum rerum ex omnium scientarum monumentis. Expedita quoque ratio per apertas rhetorices vias excerptis utendi. Opus in tres partes divisum, litteratis sedulis cultoribus, novellis praecipue verdi Divini praeconibus, ac vitae religiosae tyronibus utile*. Augusta Vindelicorum, 1715.

Esprit, Jacques. *La fausseté des Vertus humaines*. Paris, 1691.

Esquirol, Jean Etienne Dominique. *Medicine légale relative aux aliénés et aux sourds-muets: ou les lois appliquées aux desordres de l'intelligence*. Paris, 1827.

―――――. *Les passions considérées comme cause, symptomes, et moyens curatifs de l'aliénation mentale.* Paris, 1805.
An essay on personal identity. London, 1769.
An essay on the force of the imagination. With an ode to charity. London, 1774.
An essay on the force of the imagination in pregnant women. London, 1772.
An essay on the soul of man. London, 1744.
An Essay towards Demonstrating the Immateriality and Free-Agency of the Soul, in Answer to Two Pamphlets: one intitled, A Philosophical Enquiry into the Physical Spring of Human Actions, &c., Supposed to Have Been Wrote by Mr. Samuel Strutt; and the Other, Intitled, A Philosophical Enquiry concerning Human Liberty, Supposed to Have Been Wrote by Anthony Collins, Esq. London, 1760.
An essay upon the two distinct powers or properties of the human soul, viz. the will and the understanding. London, 1757.
Fabri, Honoré. *Tractatus duo.* Nuremburg, 1677.
Falconer, William. *Dissertation on the Influence of the Passions upon the Disorders of the Body.* London, 1788.
―――――. *Remarks on the influence of climate, situation, nature of country, population, nature of food, and way of life, on the disposition and temper, manner and behavior, intellects, laws and customs, form of government, and religion, of mankind.* London, 1781.
Fallowes, T. *The Best Method for the Cure of Lunatics, with some Accounts of the Incomparable Oleum Cephalicum used in the same, prepared and administered.* London, 1705.
Farmer, Hugh. *A dissertation on miracles; designed to shew, that they are arguments of a divine interposition.* London, 1771.
―――――. *An essay on the demoniacs of the New Testament.* London, 1775.
―――――. *Letters to the Reverend Dr. Worthington: in answer to his late publication intitled, An impartial enquiry into the case of the Gospel demoniacks.* London, 1778.
Faucett. *Über Melancholie.* Leipzig, 1785.
Faulkner, B. *Observations on the general and improper Treatment of Insanity with a plan for the more speedy and effectual recovery of Insane Persons.* London, 1789.
Fawcet, Benjamin. *Observations on the Causes and Cure of Melancholy, especially of that which is called Religious Melancholy.* Shrewsbury, 1780.
Fearn, John. *An Essay on Consciousness, or a Series of Evidences of a distinct Mind.* 2nd edn. London, 1812.
―――――. *A manual of physiology of mind, comprehending the first principles of physical theology: with which are laid out the crucial objections to the Reideian theory.* London, 1829.
Felltham, Owen. *Resolves: Divine, Moral, Political.* 12th edn. London, 1709.
Felton, Henry. *A discourse concerning the universality and order of the resurrection: being a sequel to that, wherein the personal identity is asserted.* London, 1733.
Fenner, William. *The Souls Looking-glasse, Lively Representing Its Estate before God: With a Treatise of Conscience.* Cambridge, 1640.
Ferguson, Adam. *Institutes of Moral Philosophy.* Edinburgh, 1772; rpt. [of 1773 edn.] New York: Garland, 1978.
―――――. *Principles of Moral and Political Science.* 2 vols. Edinburgh, 1792; rpt. New York: Garland, 1978.
Ferrand, James. 'Ερωτομανια, *or A Treatise Discoursing of the Essence, Causes, Symptoms, Prognosticks, and Cure of Love, or Erotique Melancholy.* Oxford, 1640.
Ferriar, John. *Medical Histories and Reflections.* London, 1792.
Fichte, Johann Gottlieb. *Sämmtliche Werke.* Ed. I. H. Fichte. 8 vols. Berlin, 1845-46. See, among others, *Über den Begriff der Wissenschaftslehre* (1794) and *Grundlage der*

gesamtem Wissenschaftslehre (1794).
Fiddes, Richard. *A general treatise of Morality formed upon the principles of Natural Reason only. With a preface in answer to two essays lately published in the fable of bees.* London, 1724.
Finxius, David. *De melancholia.* Helmstadt, 1607.
Fischer, Jo. Conrad. *Explanatio adfectus maniaci levioris rarissimo sensuum quorundam augmento stipati.* Halle, 1734.
Fitzgerald, Thomas. *Bedlam: A Poem.* London, 1776.
Flacht, Friedrich. *De melancholia et idiopathica et sympathica.* Basel, 1620.
Flavell, John. Πηευματολογίας *A treatise of the soul of man.* London, 1685.
Fleming, C. *A Survey of the Search after Souls.* London, 1758.
Fleming, C. A. *Lehrbruch der Allgemeinen Empirischen Psychologie.* 1796.
Flemyng, Malcolm. *An introduction to physiology.* London, 1759.
———. *The Nature of the Nervous Fluid; or, Animal Spirits Demonstrated.* London, 1751.
———. *Neuropathia: sive, de morbis. Hypochondriacis et hystericis, libri tres, poema medicum.* Eboraci, 1740.
———. *A New Critical Examination of an Important Passage in Mr. Locke's Essay on Human Understanding.* London, 1751.
Foote, Samuel. *A Treatise on the passions, so far as they regard the stage.* London, 1747.
Fordyce, David. "The elements of moral philosophy," in *The Perceptor*, ed. R. Dodsley. London, 1748.
Formey, Jean Henri Samuel. *L'Anti-Sans-Soucy, ou la Folie des nouveaux philosophes.* 2 vols. Bouillon, 1761.
———. *Le bonheur, où nouveau système de jurisprudence naturelle.* Berlin, 1754.
———. *Principes de morale, déduits de l'usage des facultés de l'entendement humain.* Leyden, 1762.
Forrester, James. *Dialogues on the passions, habits, and affections peculiar to children; wherein the infant state of the soul is fully displayed.* London, 1748.
Forster, W. *A treatise on the Causes of Most Diseases Incident to Human Bodies.* Leeds, 1745.
Fortesque, James. *A View of Life in Its Several Passions.* London, 1749; rpt. New York, Garland, 1971.
Fowler, Dr. *An enquiry into the nature and origin of mental derangement.* London, 1799.
Freeman, S. *A Letter to Hypochondriac and Nervous Patients.* London, 1789.
Freke, John. *An essay to show the cause of electricity and why some things are nonelectricable, in which is also considered its influence in the blasts on human bodies.* London, 1746.
———. *A treatise on the nature and property of fire.* London, 1752.
Freke, William. *The divine grammar: or select rules leading to the more nice syntax and articulate construction of dreams, visions and apparitions.* London, 1703.
———. *The Fountain of Monition and Intercommunication Divine.* London, 1703.
———. *Lingua Tersancta.* London, 1703.
Friderich, Joa. Arnold. *Dissertatio de memoriae laesione.* Jena, 1668.
Frings, P. *A Treatise of Phrensy.* London, 1746.
Fuchs, Johannes Conradus. *De melancholia.* Jena, 1671.
Fuller, Francis. *Medicina Gymnastica.* London, 1705.
Fuller, Thomas. *Introductio ad sapientiam: or, the art of right thinking.* London, 1731.
Gall, Francois Josef. *On the organ of the moral qualities and intellectual faculties & the plurality of the cerebral organs.* 2 vols. in 1. London, n.d.
———.*Untersuchungen ueber die Anatomie des Nervensystems ueberhaupt, und des Gehirns insbesondere.* Paris, 1809.

Galvani, Luigi. *De viribus electricitatis in motu musculari. Commentarius.* [Bologna, 1791.]
Ganne, A. *L'homme physique et morale.* Paris, 1771.
Garth, Samuel. *The Dispensary.* London, 1699; rpt. Delmar, N.Y.: Scholars' Facsimiles and Reprints, 1975.
Gassendi, Pierre. *Opera Omnia.* Lyon, 1658; rpt. Stuttgart-Bad Cannstatt: F. Frommann, 1964.
―――. *De vita et moribus Epicuri.* Paris, 1647; rpt. Amsterdam: Rodopi, 1968.
Gaubius, Hieronymous David. *Adversariorum varii argumenti.* Leyden, 1771.
―――. *Commentaris in institutiones pathologiae medicinalis.* 3 vols. in 4. Vienna, 1792.
―――. *Institutiones pathologiae medicinalis.* Leipzig, 1759.
―――. *Sermo academicus de regimine mentis.* Leyden, 1747. Trans. L. J. Rather, in *Mind and Body in eighteenth century medicine; a study based on Jerome Gaub's De regimine mentis.* London: Wellcome Historical Medical Library, 1965.
Gautier d'Agoty, J. *Exposition anatomique des organes des sens jointe à la neurologie entière du corps humain et conjectures sur l'electricité animale et le siège de l'ame.* Paris, 1775.
Gay, John. *Dissertation concerning the Fundamental principle of Virtue or Morality* [prefixed to Edmund Law's translation of Archbishop King's "Essay on the Origin of Evil"]. London, 1731; rpt. [in *The English Philosophers from Bacon to Mill,* ed. E. A. Burt, pp. 767–785] New York: Modern Library, 1939.
Genius, Michael. *De melancholis hypochondriaca.* Leyden, 1669.
Gerard, Alexander. *An essay on genius.* London, 1774; rpt. New York: Garland, 1970.
―――. *An essay on taste.* London, 1759; rpt. New York: Garland, 1970.
Gerber, Christian Gottlob. *De melancholia hypochondriaca.* Erfurt, 1715.
Gerdil, Giacinto Sigismondo. *Defense du Sentiment du P. Malebranche sur la nature & l'origine des idees, contre l'examen de M. Locke.* Turin, 1748.
―――. *L'Immaterialité de l'ame demontrée contre M. Locke, par les mêmes Principes, par lesquels ce Philosophe démontre l'Existence & l'Immaterialité de Dieu, avec des nouvelles preuves de l'Immaterialité de Dieu, et de l'ame, Tirées de l'Ecriture des Peres & de la raison.* Turin, 1747.
―――. *Recueil de Dissertations sur quelques principes de philosophie & de religion.* Paris, 1760.
Gibbons, Thomas. *Rhetoric.* London, 1767; rpt. Menston, York: Scolar Press, 1969.
Gibbs, James. *Observations of various eminent cures of scrophulous distempers, commonly called the king's evil, . . . To which is added, An essay, concerning the animal spirits, and the cure of convulsions.* London, 1712.
Gifford, Richard. *Outlines of an Answer to Dr. Priestley's Disquisitions relating to Matter and Spirit.* London, 1781.
Gildon, Charles. *The Post-boy rob'd of his mail: or, the Pacquet Broke Open.* London, 1692; rpt. New York, Garland, 1972.
[Gilpin, William.] *An essay upon Prints; Containing Remarks upon the Principles of Picturesque Beauty, the Different Kinds of Prints, and the Characters of the Most Noted Masters.* London, 1768.
[Girard, J. Fr.] *Mesmer blessé, où Response à lettre du R. P. Hervier, sur le magnestisme animal.* Paris, 1784.
Glanvill, Joseph. *Essays on Several Important Subjects in Philosophy and Religion.* London, 1676; rpt. New York: Johnson Reprint Company, 1970.
―――. *Saducismus Triumphatus.* London, 1681; rpt. Gainesville, Fla.: Scholars' Facsimiles and Reprints, 1960.
―――. *Scepsis scientifica: or, Confest Ignorance, the way to Science; in an Essay on the Vanity of Dogmatizing, and Confident Opinion.* London, 1665; rpt. New York: Garland, 1978.

Glisson, Francis. *De naturae substantia energetica.* Paris, 1672.
Glock, Johannes Georgius. *De catalepsi-epilepsi.* Tübingen, 1690.
Glück Fridericus Gothofredus. *De mania.* Leipzig. 1685.
Godwin, William. *An Enquiry concerning Political Justice.* London, 1793; rpt. [ed. F. E. L. Priestley] Toronto: University of Toronto Press, 1946.
Goethe, Johann Wolfgang von. *Zur Farbenlehre. Theory of Colours.* Trans. Lock Eastlake. **Cambridge, Mass.: MIT Press, 1970.**
Gohl, Johann Daniel. *Insufficientia Cerebri ad Sensum et Motum Animalis Expenditur.* Colberg, 1732.
Goodwin, Philip. *The mystery of dreames, historically discoursed.* London, 1658.
Gordon, Thomas. *The Humourist.* London, 1720-25; rpt. New York: Garland, 1970.
Gott, Samuel. *The Divine History of the Genesis of the World.* London, 1670.
Gotter, Johann Jacobus. *De suffocatione uterina.* Erfurt, 1672.
Gottsched. *Disputationum anatomicarum selectarum.* Göttingen, 1748.
Gottwaldt, Christopher. *De melancholia hypochondriaca.* Leyden, 1662.
Greding, Johann Ernst. *Vermischte medicinische und chirurgische Schriften.* Altenburg, 1781.
[Gregory, John.] *A comparative view of the state and faculties of man with those of the animal world.* London, 1765.
Grey, Richard. *Memoria technica: or, a new method of artifical memory.* London, 1730.
Griffith, Thomas. *De affectu hypochondriaco.* Leyden, 1725.
Groat, Robert. *Dissertatio medica, inauguralis, de hysteria.* Edinburgh, 1783.
A Groatsworth of Wit for a Penny; or, The Interpretation of Dreams. London, c. 1750.
Grove, Henry. *An essay towards a Demonstration of the Soul's Immateriality.* **London, 1718.**
Guer, Jean Antoine. *Histoire critique de l'ame des bêtes.* 2 vols. Amsterdam, 1749.
Guerbois, D. F. N. *Essai sur la nostalgie.* Paris, 1803.
Haghen, Cornelius Van Der. *De melancholia hypochondriaca.* Leyden, 1715.
Hahn, Jo. Fr. *De maniacis hydropathes.* Leipzig, 1748.
Haizmann, Christoph. *Schizophrenia 1667: A Psychiatric Study of an Illustrated Autobiographical Record of Demoniacal Possession.* Trans. Ida McAlpine and Richard Hunter. London: William Dawson and Sons, 1956.
Hales, Stephen. *Statical Essays: containing Haemastaticks.* London, 1733; rpt. New York: Hafner, 1964.
Hall, M. *Essay on Disorders of the Digestive Organs and General Health.* Keene, N.H., 1823.
Haller, Albrecht von. *De partibus corporis humani sensibilibus et irritabilibus.* Göttingen, 1752–53; rpt. [in English: *A Dissertation of the Sensible and Irritable Parts of Animals*] Baltimore, Md.: Johns Hopkins University Press, 1936.
———, praeses. *Dissertatio . . . sistens experimenta quaedam circa corpus callosum, cerebellum duram meningem, in vivis animalibus instituta.* Göttingen, [1749?].
———. *Elementa physiologiae corporis humani.* 8 vols. Lausanne, 1757–66.
———. *Mémoires sur la nature sensible et irritable des parties du corps animal.* 4 vols. Lausanne, 1756–60.
———. *Primae lineae Physiologiae.* Göttingen, 1751; rpt. [in English: *First Lines of Physiology*] New York: Johnson Reprint, 1966.
Hamel, Jean Baptiste. *De consensu veteris et nova philosophiae.* 2 vols. Paris, 1763.
———. *De corpore animato, libri quatuor, seu promotae per experimenta philosophiae, specimen alterum.* Paris, 1673.
Hamilton, Robert. "History of a remarkable case of nostalgia affecting a native of Wales, and occurring in Britain." In *Medical Commentaries, of the year MDCCLXXXVI.* Edinburgh, 1787. Vol. I, pp. 343–348.

Hampton, Benjamin. *The Existence of the Human Soul after Death Proved from Scripture, Reason and Philosophy. Wherein Mr. Lock's Notion that Understanding May be Given to Matter, Mr. Hobbs's Assertion That There is no Such Thing as an Immaterial Substance . . . Dr. Coward's Book of Second and Further Thoughts . . . are . . . confuted . . . With an Appendix, Shewing That the Above Mentioned Principles Are the Occasion of Civil Wars.* London, 1711.

Hanniel, Statius Ioachim. *De melancholia hypochondriaca.* Leyden, 1677.

Hargrave, Francis. *Brief deductions relative to the aid and supply of the executive power, according to the law of England, in cases of infancy, delirium, or other incapacity of the King.* London, 1788.

Harper, Andrew. *A treatise on the real cause and cure of insanity, in which the nature and distinctions of the disease are fully explained, and the treatment established on new principles.* London, 1789.

H[arris], J[ames]. *Hermes, or a Philosophical Inquiry Concerning Universal Grammar.* London, 1751; rpt. New York: AMS Press, 1975.

Harris, John. *The divine physician: prescribing rules for the prevention and cure of most diseases as well of the body, as the soul. . . . In two parts.* 2nd edn. London, 1709.

———. *Lexicon technicum: or, an Universal English Dictionary of Arts and Sciences.* 2 vols. London, 1704–10; rpt. London, Cass, 1971.

Hartcliffe; John. *A Treatise of Moral and Intellectual Virtues; Wherein their Nature is fully explained, and their Usefulness proved, as being the best Rules of Life.* London, 1691.

[Hartley, David.] *An Enquiry into the Origin of the Human Appetites and Affections, Shewing How Each Arises from Association. With an Account of the Entrance of Moral Evil into the World. To which are added, Some Remarks on the Independent Scheme Which Deduces All Obligation on God's Part and Mans from Certain Abstract Relations, Truth, &c.* London, 1747. [Attribution by Stephen Ferg.]

———. *An introduction towards an essay on the origin of the passions; in which is . . . shewn how they are all acquir'd and that they are no other than association of ideas of our own making, or what we learn of others.* London, 1741. [Attribution by Stephen Ferg.]

———. *Observations on Man, His Frame, His Duty, and His Expectations. In Two Parts.* London, 1749; rpt. New York: AMS Press, 1973.

———. *Hartley's Theory of the Human Mind, on the Principle of the Association of Ideas; with Essays relating to the Subject of It. By Joseph Priestley.* London, 1775.

Hartmann, Georg Volkmar. *Epistola de bruto ex homine ad . . . Georgium Ernestium Stahlium.* Erfurt, 1733.

[Harvey, Gideon?] *The accomplisht physician, the honest apothecary, and the skilful chyrugeon detecting their necessary connection on each other; Withall a discovery of the frauds of the quacking empirick, the praescribing surgeon, and the practicing apothecary.* London, 1670.

———. *Archelogia philosophica nova.* London, 1663.

———. *The Art of curing disease by expectation.* London, 1689.

———. *The Conclave of physicians, detecting their intrigues, frauds, and plots, against their patients.* London, 1683.

———. *Morbus Anglicus; or, the Anatomy of Consumption . . . To which are added, some Brief Discourses on Melancholy, Madness, and Distraction occasioned by Love.* London, 1666.

Harvey, William. *Exercitationes de Generatione Animalium.* London, 1651; rpt. [in English. Trans. Gweneth Whitteridge] Oxford: Blackwell Scientific, 1981.

Haslam, John. *Medical jurisprudence as it relates to insanity.* London, 1817; rpt. New York: Garland, 1979.

———. *Observations on madness and melancholy.* 2nd edn. London, 1809; rpt. New York:

Arno, 1976.
Hawkins, John. *Discursus de Melancholia Hypochondriaca Potissimum.* Heidelberg, 1633.
H[aworth], S[amuel]. 'Ανθρωπολογία, *or, A Philosophic Discourse Concerning Man. Being the Anatomy Both of his Soul and Body. Wherein the Nature, Origin, Union, Immateriality, Immortality, Extension, and Faculties of the one, and The Parts, Humours, Temperaments, Complexions, Functions, Sexes, and Ages, respecting the other, are concisely delineated.* London, 1680.
Hay, William. *Deformity, an essay.* 2nd edn. London, 1754.
Haygarth, John. *Of the imagination, as a cause and as a cure of disorders of the body; exemplified by fictitious tractors, and epidemical convulsions.* Bath, 1800.
Heberden, William. *Commentaries on the History and Cure of Diseases.* London, 1803; rpt. New York: Hafner, 1962.
Hecquet, Philippe. *Le Nuralisme des convulsions dans les maladies de l'epidemie convulsionnaire.* Soleure, 1733.
Hegel, Georg Wilhelm Friedrich. *Phänomenologie des Geistes.* Würzburg, 1807. *Phenomenology of Spirit.* Trans. A. V. Miller with analysis and foreword by J. N. Findlay. Oxford: Clarendon Press, 1977.
Heibergii, Thom. Severin. *Diss. de memoriae debilitate.* Copenhagen, 1766.
Heister, Lorena. *Compendium anatomicum.* Amsterdam, 1748.
Helmont, Franciscus Mercurius van. *The spirit of disease; or, diseases from the spirit: laid open in some observations concerning man, and his diseases. Wherein is shewed how much the mind influenceth the body in causing and curing diseases.* London, 1694.
Helmont, Johann B. van. *Opuscula medica inaudita. I. De lithiasi. II. De febribus. III. De humoribus galeni. IV. De peste.* Amsterdam, 1644.
———. *Ortus medicinae.* Amsterdam, 1648.
———. *Oriatrike, or physic refined.* London, 1662.
Helvetius, Claude Adrien. *De l'esprit.* Amsterdam, 1758. *De l'esprit: or, essays on the mind, and its several faculties.* London, 1759; rpt. New York: Burt Franklin, 1970.
———. *De l' homme, de ses facultes intellectueles et de son education.* London, 1773.
Herfelt, H. G. *De affectione hypochondriaca.* Duisburg on Rhine, 1678.
Herwig, Henning Michael. *The art of curing sympathetically, or magnetically, proved to be most true both by its theory and practice . . . With a discourse concerning the cure of madness, and an appendix to prove the reality of sympathy.* London, [1700].
Herz, Marcus. *Versuch über den Schwindel.* Berlin, 1791.
Heydenreich, Justus Rudolph. *Proponens juvenem melancholia laborantem (Jüngling mit Melancholie).* Jena, 1675.
Hiffernan, Paul. *Reflections on the structure, and passions, of man, under the following heads, viz. I. On the structure of man. II. On the passions, . . . III. The transitoriness of life.* London, 1748.
Highmore, Nathaniel. *De hysterica & hypochondriaca passione, responsio epistolaris ad Doctorem Willis medicum Londiniensem celeberrimum.* London, 1670.
———. *Exercitationes duae quarum prior de passione hysterica; altera de affectione hypochondriaca.* Oxford, 1660.
Hill, Aaron. *An essay on the art of acting; in which, the dramatic passions are properly defined and described, with applications of the cures peculiar to each, and selected passages for practice. . . . Now first revised and separately published.* London, [1779].
Hill, George Nesse. *An essay on the Prevention and Cure of the Insanity.* London, 1814.
Hill, John, Sir. *The Construction of the Nerves and Causes of Nervous Disorders.* London, 1758.
———. *Hypochondriasis. A practical treatise on the nature and cure of that disorder; commonly*

called the hyp and hypo. London, 1766; rpt. [with an introduction by G. S. Rousseau] Los Angeles, Calif.: William Andrews Clark Memorial Library, 1969.

———. *Valerian, or the Virtues of the Root in Nervous Disorders.* 3rd edn. London, 1758.

Hill, Philippina. *A novel and genuine display of the leading disposition of the human mind. With a sketch of modern life. In* [w]*hich the following passions and effects are characterized: ambition-disappointment-revenge.* [London, 1785?].

Hill, Thomas. *The Moste Pleasaunte Arts of the Interpretation of Dreames.* London, 1576.

Hobbes, Thomas. *Elements of Philosophy, the first section concerning Body.* London, 1656.

———. *English Works of Thomas Hobbes.* 11 vols. And *Opera Philosophica* [Latin Works], 5 vols. Ed. Sir William Molesworth. London, 1839–45; rpt. Aalen, Scientia, 1961 [English Works] and 1966 [Latin Works].

———. *Humane Nature: Or, the Fundamental Elements of Policie, Being A Discoverie of the Faculties, Acts and Passions of the Soul of Man, from Their Original Causes: According to Such Philosophical Principles as Are Commonly Known or Asserted.* London, 1650.

———. *Leviathan, or the Matter, Form, and Power of a Commonwealth.* London, 1650.

———. *Tripos, in three discourses.* London, 1684.

Hofer, J. *Dissertation de Nostalgia.* Basel, 1678.

———. *De religiosorum morbis.* Basel, 1716.

Hoffman, Friedrich. *Fundamenta Medicinae.* Halle im Magdeburgischen, 1695; rpt. New York: American Elsevier, 1971.

———. *Opera omnia physico-medica.* Geneva, 1740.

———. *Operum omnium physico-medicorum supplementum.* Geneva, 1749.

Hofstetter, Johannes Christophorus. *De somnambulatione.* Halle, 1695.

Hogarth, William. *The Analysis of Beauty.* London, 1753; rpt. [ed. Joseph Burke] Oxford: Clarendon Press, 1955.

Holbach, Paul Heinrich Dietrich, Baron d'. *Système de la nature, ou des Loix du monde Physique & du monde moral.* Amsterdam, 1770; rpt. [of the London, 1820 edn.] New York: Garland, 1984.

Holland, Philip. *Dissertatio medica inauguralis, pauca de mente in corpus effectibus.* Edinburgh, 1782.

Hooke, Robert. *Philosophical experiments and observations.* London, 1726; rpt. London: Cass, 1967.

———. *The posthumous works of Robert Hooke.* London, 1705; rpt. Hildesheim: G. Olms, 1971. See, among others, *The nature, motion and effects of light* and *An Hypothetical explication of memory.*

Hornstein, P. Joa. Bapt. *Dialecta analogicis imaginibus illustrate in phantasiae et localis memoriae auxilium, ad faciliorem rerum logicarum perceptionem, et mentis oculorum acil subjecta.* Frib. Brisgojae, 1771.

Horst, Gregor. *De mania.* Giessen, 1677.

Hoskins, John. *Directions for Speech and Style.* Princeton, 1935.

Huarte de San Juan, Juan. *Examen de ingenios para las sciencias: Donde se muestra la differencia de habilidades que ay en los hombres, y el genero de letras que a cada uno responde en particular.* Valencia, 1580; rpt. [of 1594 trans.] New York: Da Capo, 1969.

Hugo. *Tractatus de memoria.* London, 1717.

Huhn, Georg. *De mania.* Helmstadt, 1644.

Hume, David. *Dialogues concerning Natural Religion.* London, 1779.

———. *Enquiries concerning Human Understanding, and concerning the Principles of Morals.* London, 1777; [ed. L. A. Selby-Bigge, 3rd edn. rev. P. H. Nidditch] Oxford: Clarendon Press, 1975.

———. *Essays Moral and Political.* Edinburgh, 1741; rpt. New York: Garland, 1970.
———. *Four dissertations. I. The natural history of religion. II. Of the passions. III. Of tragedy. IV. Of the standard of taste.* London, 1757.
———. *Philosophical Essays concerning Human Understanding.* London, 1748; rpt. Westport, Conn.: Greenwood, 1980.
———. *A Treatise of Human Nature; Being an Attempt to Introduce the Experimental Method of Reasoning into Moral Subjects.* 2 vols. London, 1739–40; rpt. [ed. L. A. Selby Bigge, 2nd edn. rev. P. H. Nidditch] Oxford: Clarendon Press, 1978.
Hunter, John. *Essays and observations on natural history, anatomy, physiology, psychology, and geology.* 2 vols. London, 1861.
———. *Observations on certain parts of the animal oeconomy.* London, 1786.
[Hutcheson, Francis.] *An Essay on the Nature and Conduct of the Passions and Affections.* London, 1725; rpt. New York: Garland, 1971.
———. *Inquiry into the original of our Ideas of Beauty and Virtue.* London, 1725; rpt. New York: Garland, 1971.
———. *A short Introduction to Moral Philosophy.* Glasgow, 1747.
Hutchinson, John. *An attempt to explain the oeconomy of the human frame, upon the principles of the new philosophy.* London, 1749.
Hutton, James. *Dissertations on different subjects in natural philosophy.* Edinburgh, 1792.
Hutton, Timothy. *An investigation of the principles of knowledge, and of the progress of reason from sense to science and philosophy.* Edinburgh, 1794.
The Hyp, a burlesque poem in five canto's. Including the adventures of Sir Valetude Whim, and his retinue. London, 1731.
Irish, David. *Levamen infirmi: or, cordial counsel to the sick and diseased. Containing I. Advice concerning physick . . . with an account of the author's remedies, and how to take them. II. Concerning melancholy, frensie, and madness . . . III. A miscellany of pious discourses.* London, 1700.
———. *Transcript of an agreement between 'Dr.' Irish and Joseph Chitty, husband of a prospective patient suffering from 'Hipocondriack melancholy Madness' to cure her for the sum of 10* [pounds sterling]. 1702. [Ms. in Guildford Muniment Room]
Itard, Jean Marc Gaspard. *De l'éducation d'un homme sauvage; où, Des premiers développemens physiques et moraux de jeune sauvage de l'Aveyron.* Paris, 1801.
Jackson, John. *A Defence of Human Liberty; In Answer to the Principal Arguments Which Have Been Alledged against It; and Particularly to Cato's Letters on that Subject. In Which Defence the Opinion of the Antients, concerning Fate, Is Also Distinctly and Largely considered.* London, 1725.
———. *A dissertation on Matter and Spirit. With Some Remarks on a Book, Entitled, An Enquiry into the Nature of the Humane Soul* [by Andrew Baxter]. London, 1735.
———. *The Existence and Unity of God; Proved from his Nature and Attributes. Being a Vindication of Dr. Clarke's Demonstration of the Being and Attributes of God. To which is added, An Appendix, Wherein is Considered, the Ground and Obligation of Morality.* London, 1734.
Jacob, Hildebrand. *Bedlam, a poem.* London, [1723].
[James VI (and I).] *Daemonologie.* Edinburgh, 1597.
James, Robert. *A Medicinal Dictionary.* 3 vols. London, 1743–45.
———. *A new method of preventing and curing the madness caused by the bite of a mad dog.* London, 1741.
———. *A treatise on canine madness.* London, 1760.
Jennings, Henry Constantine. *A Physical Enquiry into the powers and properties of spirit, and,*

how far by analogical inferences resulting from experimental and natural phanomena, the human intellect may be enabled to attain to any rational conception of omnipotence. Chelmsford, 1787.

Joannet, Abbé Jean-Baptiste-Claude. *Les Bêtes mieux connues, ou le pour et contre l' ame des bêtes.* 2 vols. Nancy, 1770.

Jöcher, C. G. *Affectus musicae in hominem.* Leipzig, 1714.

Johnson, J. *A treatise on Derangements of the Liver, Internal Organs and Nervous System.* London, 1816.

Johnstone, J. *Essay on the Use of the Ganglions of the Nerves.* Shrewsbury, 1771.

———. *Medical Essays and Observations, with Disquisitions relative to the Nervous System.* London, 1795.

———. *Medical jurisprudence. On madness.* Birmingham, 1800.

Jones, John. *The mysteries of opium reveal'd.* London, 1700.

Jones, William. *The nature, uses, dangers, sufferings, and preservatives, of the human imagination.* London, 1796.

Jorden, E. *A briefe discourse of a disease called the suffocation of the mother. Written upon the occasion which hath been of late taken thereby, to suspect possession of an evill spirit, or some such like supernaturall power. Wherein is declared that divers strange actions and passions of the body of man, which in the common opinion, are imputed to the Divell, have their true natural causes, and do accompany this disease.* London, 1603; rpt. New York: Da Capo, 1971.

A Journey through the head of a modern poet, being the substance of a dream occasioned by reading the sixth book of Virgil. London, 1750.

Kames, Henry Home, Lord. *Elements of criticism.* Edinburgh, 1762.

———. *Essays on the principles of Morality and Natural Religion.* Edinburgh, 1751; rpt. [of 1758 edn.] Hildesheim: G. Olms, 1976.

———. *Introduction to the art of thinking. Second edition, enlarged with additional maxims and illustrations.* Edinburgh, 1764.

Kant, Immanuel. *Allegemeine Naturgeschichte und Theorie des Himmels.* Leipzig, 1755.

———. *Gesammelte Schriften.* 23 vols. Berlin, 1902–55.

———. *Kritik der praktischen Vernunft.* Riga, 1788; rpt. [in English: *Critique of Practical Reason.* Trans. Lewis White Beck] Indianapolis: Bobbs-Merrill, 1956.

———. *Kritik der reinen Vernunft.* Riga, 1781; rpt. [in English: *Critique of Pure Reason.* Trans. Norman Kemp Smith] London, 1929.

———. *Metaphyisiche Anfangsgründe der Naturwissenchaft.* Leipzig, 1786.

———. *Träume eines Geistersehers, erläuert durch Träume der Metaphysik.* Leipzig, 1766.

Kaulizius, Michael. *De oblivione.* Jena, 1690.

Keble, Joseph. *An essay of human actions.* London, 1710.

Keill, James. *The anatomy of the human body, abridged.* London, 1698.

———. *Tentamina medico-physica, ad quasdam quaestiones, quae oeconomiam animalem spectant, accomodata.* London, 1718.

Khonn, Alphonsus. *De catalepsi.* Strasbourg, 1662.

Kiaer, Mich. *Diss. de justa memoriae cultura.* Copenhagen, 1766.

King, William. *The Dreamer.* London, 1754.

———. *De origine mali.* Dublin, 1702–04.

———. *An Essay concerning the Origin of Evil. Translated from the Latin, with large Notes; Tending to Explain and Vindicate Some of the Author's Principles against the Objections of Bayle, Leibnitz, the Author of a Philosophical Enquiry concerning Human Liberty* [Anthony Collins]; *and Others. To which is prefix'd, A Dissertation concerning the Fundamental Principle and Immediate Criterion of Virtue. As also, The Obligation to and Approbation of it. With Some Account of the Origin of the Passions and Affections.* London, 1731. [Diss. by

John Gay, translation and notes by Edmund Law.]

Kinneir, David. *A new essay on the nerves, and the doctrine of animal spirits rationally considered; . . . with two dissertations on the gout and on digestion, with the distempers of the stomach and intestines.* London, 1738.

Kirkland, T. *A Treatise on Child-bed Fevers, and on the methods of preventing them, being a supplement to the books lately written on the subject. To which are prefixed two dissertations. The one on the brain and nerves; the other on the sympathy of the nerves and on the different kinds of irritability.* London, 1774.

Knight, Richard Payne. *An analytical inquiry into the principles of taste.* London, 1805; rpt. [of the 1808 edn.] Westmead: Gregg International, 1972.

———. *A Dialogue on the distinct characters of the picturesque and the beautiful.* London, 1801.

Knight, Thomas. *Transmutation of the Blood.* London, 1725.

Knittel, S. J. *Via regia ad omnes scientias et artes, hoc est ars universalis scientarium omnium atriumque arcana facilius penetrandi.* Prague, 1687.

Kornmesser, Jacob. *De affectione hypochondriaca.* Rostock, 1665.

Kruger, J. G. *Versuch einer experimentalen Seelenlehre.* 1756.

La Caze, L. *Idée de l'homme physique et moral pour servir d'introduction à un traité de médicine.* Paris, 1755.

La Chambre, Marin Cureau de [Louis de]. *L'art de connoistre les hommes.* Paris, 1659. *The Art how to know men.* London, 1665.

———. *Les caracteres des passions.* 3 vols. Paris, 1640–59.

———. *La lumière.* Paris, 1657.

———. *Le système de l'ame.* Paris, 1665.

———. *Traité de la connoissance des animaux.* Paris, 1647.

La Forge, Louis de. *Traitté de l'esprit de l'homme, de ses facultés et fonctions, et de son union avec les Corps.* Paris, 1666.

Lahme, Christoph. *De memoria.* Hannoviae, 1693.

Lambert. *Anlage zur Architektonik oder Theorie des Einfachen und Ersten in der philosophischen und mathematischen Erkenntnis.* Riga, 1771.

La Mettrie, Julien Offray de. *Abrége de la théorie Chymique . . . Auquel on a joint le Traité du Vertige.* Paris, 1741.

———. *Histoire naturelle de l'âme, nouvelle edition . . . augmentée de la Lettre Critique à Madame la Marquise du Chattelet.* Oxford, 1747.

———. *L'homme-machine.* Leyden, 1748; rpt. [ed. by Aram Vartanian] Princeton, N.J.: Princeton University Press, 1960. For a French and English text, see *Man A Machine.* La Salle, Ill.: Open Court, 1912.

———. *Oeuvres philosophiques.* 3 vols. *Traité de l'âme. L'abrége des systemes. L'homme plants. Les animaux plus que machines. Anti-Sénèque, ou Discours sur le bonheur. Système d'Epicure.* Amsterdam, 1774; rpt. Hildesheim: G. Olms, 1970.

Lamy, Dom Francois. *De la connoissance de soi-mesme.* 4 vols. Paris, 1694–98.

Lamy, Guillaume. *Explication méchanique et physique des fonctions de l'âme sensitive, ou des sens, des passions et du mouvement volontaire.* Paris, 1678.

Langermann, Johann Gottfried. *De methodo cognoscendi curandique animi morbos stabilienda.* Jena, [1797].

Langhorne, John. *Letters on Religious Retirement, Melancholy, and Enthusiasm.* London, 1761.

Langrish, Browne. *The Croonian Lectures on Muscular Motion.* London, 1747.

———. *A New Essay on Muscular Motion. Founded on Experiments, Observations, and the*

Newtonian Philosophy. London, 1733.
Langton, Zachary. *An essay concerning the human rational soul. In three parts. Shewing I. The origin. II. The Nature. III. The excellency of this soul upon the natural as well as revealed principles.* Liverpool, 1755.
Lannoy, Arnold. *De mania.* Leyden, 1674.
Laroque, Raimund. *De l'influence des passions sur l'économie animale, considérée dans les quatre ages de la vie.* Montpellier, l'an VI.
Lavater, Johann Caspar. *Physiognomy; or the corresponding analogy between the conformation of the features, and the ruling passions of the mind.* London, 1800.
[Law, Edmund.] *A defence of Mr. Locke's opinion concerning personal identity; in answer to the first part of a late essay on that subject.* Cambridge, 1769.
Law, William. *Remarks upon a book, intituled The Fable of the bees.* 3rd edn. London 1762.
Lawrence, Herbert. *The passions personify'd, in familiar fables.* London, [1773].
[Layton, Henry.] *Observations upon a treatise intitl'd Psychologia: Or, An Account of the Nature of the Rational Soul* [by John Broughton]. London, [1703].
_____. *A Search after Souls, and Spiritual Operations in Man.* 2 vols. London, [1693?].
Leake, J. *Medical instructions towards the prevention, and care of chronic or slow diseases peculiar to women, especially those proceeding from over delicacy of habit called nervous or hysterical; from female obstructions, weakness, and inward decay; a diseased state of the womb, or critical change of constitution at particular periods of life.* London, 1777.
Lebrun, Charles. *A method to learn to design the passions.* London, 1734; rpt. [with an introduction by Alan T. McKenzie] Los Angeles, Calif.: William Andrews Clark Memorial Library, 1980.
Le Camus, Antoine. *Médecine de l'esprit: Où l'on traite des dispositions & des causes physiques qui, en consequence de l'union de l'âme avec les corps, influent sur les operations de l'esprit: & des moyens de maintenir ces opérations dans un bon état, ou de les corriger lorsqu'elles sont viciées.* Paris, 1753.
Le Cat, Claude Nicolas. *Traité des sensations et des passions.* 2 vols. Paris, 1767.
_____. *Traité du Fluide des Nerfs.* Berlin, 1765.
_____. *Traité de l'existence, de la nature et des propriétés du fluide des nerfs et principalement de son action dans le mouvement musculaire; suivi des Dissertations sur la sensibilité des méninges, des tendons, l'insensibilité du cerveau, la structure des nerfs, l'irritabilité hallerienne.* Berlin, 1765.
Le Clerc, Daniel. *Histoire de la Médecine.* La Haye, 1729.
_____. *Logica, Ontologia, et Pneumatologia.* Cambridge, 1704.
Lee, Henry. *Anti-Scepticism: or, Notes Upon each Chapter of Mr. Lock's Essay.* London, 1702; rpt. New York: Garland, 1978.
Le Grand, Père Antoine. *Dissertatio de carentia sensus et cognitionis in brutis.* London, 1675.
_____. *An Entire Body of Philosophy, according to the Principles of the Famous Renate des Cartes.* London, 1694; rpt. New York: Johnson Reprint Company, 1972.
Leibniz, Gottfried Wilhelm. *Opera Omnia.* 6 vols. Geneva: 1768. See, among others, *Nouveau Essais sur l'entendement humain* (1765), *Monadologie* (1714), and *Essais de Theodicée sur la bonté de Dieu* (1710).
_____. *Opuscules et fragments inedits de Leibniz.* Paris: 1803; rpt. Hildesheim: G. Olms, 1961.
Lemnius, Levinus. *De miraculis occultis naturae.* 3 vols. Antwerp, 1581.
_____. *De habitu et constitutione corporis.* London, 1561.
Le Roy, Charles Georges. *Lettres sur les animaux.* Nuremberg, 1768.

Lessing, Gotthold Ephraim. *Laokoon.* Berlin, 1766; rpt. Stuttgart; Reclam, 1967.
———. *Laocoön.* Trans. Edward Allen McCormick. Baltimore, Md.: Johns Hopkins University Press, 1974.
———. *A Letter to the Author of a Book Entituled An Enquiry into the Nature of the Human Soul.* London, 1741.
Levesque de Pouilly, Louis Jean. *The theory of agreeable sensations. In which after the laws observed by Nature in the distribution of pleasure are discovered, the principles of natural theology, and moral philosophy are established.* London, 1749.
[Lichtenberg, Georg Christoph.] *Ueber physiognomik; wider die physiognomen.* 2nd edn. Göttingen, 1778.
Liddel, Duncan. *De melancholia.* Helmstadt, 1596.
Lieutaud, Joseph. *Anatomie historique et practique.* Paris, 1776.
———. *Essais anatomiques.* Paris, 1766.
———. *Précis de la matiere medicale.* Paris, 1770.
Linné, Carl von. *Genera Morborum.* Upsala, 1759.
———, praeses. *Oeconomia naturae, eller Skaparens allvisa inrattning pa var jord, i agttagen vid de skapade tingens betraktande i de tre naturens riken.* [Stockholm], 1750.
Locher, Maximilian. *Observationes practicas circa Luem Veneream, Epilipsium et Maniam.* Vienna, 1762.
Lock Asylum. *An account of the institution of the Lock Asylum, for the reception of penitent female patients, when discharged cured from the Lock Hospital.* [London], 1796.
Locke, John. *Works.* 10 vols. London: Tegg, 1823.
———. *The Educational Writings.* Ed. James L. Axtell. Cambridge: Cambridge University Press, 1968.
———. *An Essay concerning Human Understanding.* Ed. Peter H. Nidditch. Oxford: Clarendon Press, 1975.
Lorry, Anne Charles. *De melancholia et morbis melancholicis.* Paris, 1765.
Lossius. *Physische Ursachen des Wahren.* Gotha, 1775.
Louis, Antoine. *Essay sur la nature de l'âme, où l'on tâche d'expliquer son union avec le Corps, & les loix de cette union.* Paris, 1747.
———. *Observations sur l'electricité où l'on tache expliquer son méchanisme & ses effects sur l'effets sur l'oeconomie animale avec remarques sur son usage.* Paris, 1747.
Louyer-Villermay, J. B. *Recherches Historiques et Médicales sur l'Hypocondrie.* Paris, 1802.
Lowde, James. *Discourse concerning the Nature of Man.* London, 1694; rpt. New York: Garland, 1979.
———. *Moral Essays; wherein some of Mr. Lock's and Mons. Malbranch's opinions are briefly examined.* London, 1699.
Lowe, Solomon. *Arithmetic in two parts; containing I. A system of the art, in memorial verses, and dictionary-wise; . . . II. A collection of exercises . . .* London, 1749.
———. *Mnemonics delineated; in a small compass and easy method, for the better enabling to remember what is most frequently wanted, and most difficultly retained or recollected.* London, 1737.
Lubber, Henr. Aph. *Artificium memoriae.* Hamburg, 1713.
Ludwig, Ch. G. *Institutiones medicinae clinicae.* Leipzig, 1758.
Macbride, David. *A Methodical Introduction to the Theory and Practice of Physic.* London, 1772.
Madness: a poem. Written by a gentleman when under confinement for lunacy. London, 1728.
Maine de Biran, Pierre. *Influence de l'habitude sur la faculté de penser.* Paris, [1803]; rpt.

Paris: Presses Universitaires de France, 1954.
[Malebranche, Nicolas.] *De la Recherche de la Verité. Ou l'on traitte de la Nature de l'esprit de l'homme, & de l'usage qu'il en doit faire pour éviter l'erreur dans les Sciences.* 3 vols. Paris, 1674-78; rpt. [in English: *The Search after Truth*. Trans. Thomas Lennon and Paul Olscamp] Columbus: Ohio State University Press, 1980.
Malphigi, Marcello. *Opera omnia*. London, 1686.
Mandeville, Bernard. *The Fable of the Bees, or Private vices publick benefits. Containing several discourses to demonstrate that human frailities . . . may be turned to the advantage of the civil society*. London, 1714; rpt. Hildesheim: G. Olms, 1981. See also Oxford, 1924, ed. F. B. Kaye. 2 vols.
———. *A treatise of the hypochondriack and hysterick passions, vulgarly call'd hypo in men and vapours in women. In three dialogues*. London, 1711; rpt. [of 1730 edn.] New York: Arno Press, 1976.
Manningham, R. *The Symptoms, Nature, Causes and Cure of the Febricula, or Nervous or Hysteric Fever, Vapours, Hypo, or Spleen*. London, 1746.
Marat, J. P. *De l'homme où des principles des lois de l'influence de l'âme sur le corps et le* [word missing?] *du corps sur l'âme*. Paris, 1773.
Martin, Benjamin. *The Philosophical Grammar: Being a View of the Present State of Experimental Physiology, or Natural Philosophy . . . In Four Parts: I. Somatology. II. Cosmology. III. Aerology. IV. Geology*. London, 1735.
Mason, John. *Self-knowledge*. Glasgow, 1745.
Mason, S. *Practical Observations in Physic, wherein is exhibited the aetiology, or the rise and nature, of the most prevalent distempers, with a plain, rational and concise method of treating them. With a new hypothesis concerning the cure of apoplexies, palsies and many nervous complaints, as also of the gout. To which are added rules and directions now to preserve good health and long life*. Birmingham, 1747.
Mathis, Johannes Conradus. *De mania*. Strasbourg, 1669.
Mauclerc, John Henry. *The power of imagination in pregnant women discussed; with an address to the ladies, on the occasion*. London, 1740.
Maupertius, Pierre Louis Moreau De. "Du Droit sur les betes" and "Sur l'Ame des betes," in *Oeuvres de M. de Maupertius*. Dresden, 1752; rpt. Hildesheim: G. Olms, 1960.
Mauricheau-Beauchamp, R.-P. "Modifications que l'éducation et les habitudes ont apportées dans la développement de la nostalgie," in *Memoires de la Société Médicale d'Emulation*. 2nd edn. Paris, 1802.
Mayerne, Theodore Turquet de. *A treatise of the gout, written originally in the French tongue . . . whereunto is added advice about hypochondriacal fits by the same author*. London, 1676.
Maynwaring, Everard. *Tutela Sanitatis*. London, 1664.
Mayow, John. *Tractatus quinque medico-physici*. Oxford, 1674; rpt. [in English: *Medico-physical Works*] Edinburgh: Alembic Club, 1907.
Mead, Richard. *A Mechanical Account of Poisons; in Several Essays*. London, 1702.
———. *Medical Precepts and Cautions*. London, 1751.
———. *Of the Power and Influence of the Sun and Moon on Humane Bodies*. London, 1712.
Meckel, J. F. *Dissertatio inauguralis medica anatomico physiologicae de quinto parte nervorum cerebri*. Göttingen, 1748.
Meikle, James. *Metaphysical Maxims; Or, Thoughts on the Nature of the Soul, Free Will, and the Divine Prescience*. Edinburgh, 1797.

Mendelssohn, Moses. *Letters on the Sensations*. London, 1755.
———. *Phaedon oder Über die unsterblichkeit [über] der seele in drey gesprächen*. Berlin, 1767.
Phaedon [rpt. of 1782 translation] New York: Garland, 1973.
———. *Morgenstunden, oder Vorlesungen das Dasein Gottes*. Berlin, 1786.
Mentzelius, Johann Christian. *De aegro melancholia hypochondriaca laborante*. Frankfurt an der Oder, 1684.
Mesmer, Friedrich Anton. *Mémoire sur la découverte du magnétisme animal*. Geneva, 1779.
———. *Précis historique des faits relatifs au magnétisme animal jusques an Avril 1781*. London, 1781.
Mesmer guéri ou lettre d'un provincial au r. p. N***, en reponse a sa lettre intitulee, Mesmer blessé. Paris, 1784.
Mesnardière. H. *Raisonnemens sur la nature des esprits qui servent aux sentimens*. Paris, 1635.
———. *Traité de la Melancholie*. La Fleche, 1635.
Midriff, John. *Observations on the Spleen and Vapours; Containing Remarkable Cases of Persons of both Sexes, and all Ranks, from the aspiring Directors to the Humble Bubbler, who have been miserably afflicted with these Melancholy Disorders since the Fall of South-sea, and other publick Stocks; with the proper Method for their Recovery, according to the new and uncommon Circumstances of each Case*. London, 1721.
Mirabaud, J.B. *Systeme de la Nature*. London, 1770.
The mirror of human nature. Wherein are exhibited analytical definitions of the natural and moral faculties, affections, and passions. London, 1775.
Molyneux, William. *Dioptrica Nova. A Treatise of Dioptricks, In Two Parts*. London, 1692.
Monboddo, James Burnett, Lord. *Of the Origin and Progress of Language*. 6 vols. London, 1773-92.
Monro, Alexander, 1697-1767. *The Anatomy of the Human Bones and Nerves and lateal sac and ducts*. 7th edn. Edinburgh, 1763.
———. *A System of Anatomy and Physiology*. 2nd edn. 3 vols. London, 1787.
Monro, Alexander, 1733-1817. *Experiments on the nervous system, with opium and metalline substances; made chiefly with a view of determining the nature and effects of animal electricity*. Edinburgh, 1793.
Monro, John. *Remarks on Dr. Battie's treatise on madness*. London, 1758; rpt. London: Dawsons of Pall Mall, 1962.
Montenari, Antonio. *Trattenimento metafisico interno ai principali sistemi dell' anima delle bestie* . . . Verona, 1761.
Montesquieu, Charles-Louis de Secondat, Baron de. *De l'esprit des lois*. Geneva, 1748. *Spirit of Laws*. Trans. David Wallace Carrithers. Berkeley: University of California, 1977.
Moor, Bartholomeus De. *Dissertatio de suffocatione hupochondriaca et hysterica*. Leyden, 1699.
Moore, Charles. *A Full Inquiry into the Subject of Suicide*. London, 1790.
Moore, John. *Of Religious Melancholy*. London, 1692.
More, Henry. *A Collection of Several Philosophical Writings*. 2nd edn. London, 1662; rpt. New York: Garland, 1978.
———. *Enthusiasmus triumphatus, or a discourse of the nature, causes, kinds, and cure, of enthusiasme*. London 1656: rpt. [with an introduction by Michael V. DePorte] Los Angeles, Calif.: William Andrews Clark Library, 1966.
———. *The Theological Works of the most Pious and Learned Henry More*. London, 1707.
Morfouace de Beaumont, Gilles. *Apologie des bestes, ou leurs connoissances et raisonnement*

prouvés contre le système des philosophes cartésiens, qui pretendent que les brutes ne sont que des machines automates. Neufchatel, 1732.

Morgagni, Giovanni Battista. *De sedibus et causis morborum per anatomen indagatis*. Venice, 1761. *The seats and causes of diseases, investigated by anatomy; in five books, containing a great variety of dissections*. London, 1769; rpt. Mount Kisco, N. Y.: Futura Publishing Co., 1980.

Morgan, Thomas. *The mechanical practice of physick; in which the specifick method is examin'd and exploded; and the Bellinian hypothesis of animal secretion and muscular motion, consider'd and refuted. With some occasional remarks and scholia on Dr. Lobb's Treatise of the small pox, Dr. Robinson on the animal oeconomy, and Professor Boerhaave's Account of the animal spirits and muscular motion*. London, 1735.

———. *Philosophical Principles, in Three Parts*. London, 1725.

———. *Physico-Theology; Or, A Philosophical-Moral Disquisition concerning Human Nature, Free Agency, Moral Government, and Divine Providence*. London, 1741.

Mortimer, Cromwell. *An address to the publick: containing narratives of the effects of certain chemical remedies in most diseases*. London, 1714.

Morton, Richard. *Opera medica*. 2 vols. London, 1737.

Muhle, Fieni Thorulfi. *Examen facultatis cognoscitivae inferioris et superioris*. Copenhagen, 1722.

Munro, A. *Microscopical inquiries into the nerves and brain*. Edinburgh, 1780.

———. *Observations on the structure and functions of the nervous system*. Edinburgh, 1783.

Muratori, Lodovico Antonio. *Della forza della fantasia umana*. Venice, 1740.

Muys, Wyerus Wilhelmus. *De catalepsi*. Utrecht, 1701.

Neale, H. J. *Practical Dissertations on Nervous Complaints and other Diseases*. London, 1788.

[Nedham, Marchmont.] *Medela medicinae. A plea for the profession, and a renovation of the art of physik, out of the noblest and most authentick writers*. London, 1665.

Neuse, Johann Georg. *De melancholia*. Jena, 1685.

Nevett, Thomas. *The rational oeconomy of humane bodies, wherein the nature of the chyle, blood, lymph, and other juices, is discover'd*. London, 1704.

Newton, Isaac. *Opticks or a treatise of the reflections, refractions, inflections and colours of light*. London, 1704; rpt. New York: Dover, 1979.

———. *Philosophiae naturalis principia*. London, 1686. *Mathematical Principles of Natural Philosophy and His System of the World*, Trans. Andrew Motte in 1729; rev. Florian Cajori. 2 vols. Berkeley: University of California Press, 1934.

Nicholls, F. *De Anima Medica*. London, 1773.

Nicolai, E. A. *Gedanken von der Wirkung der Eingildungskraft im menschlichen Körper*. Halle, 1751.

Nietzki, A. *Elements of Universal Pathology*. London, 1766.

Norris, John. *An Essay Towards the Theory of the Ideal or Intelligible World. Designed for Two Parts. The First considering it Absolutely in it self, and the Second in Relation to Human Understanding*. 2 vols. London, 1701-04; rpt. New York: Garland, 1978.

———. *A letter to Mr. Dodwell, concerning the immortality of the soul of man. In answer to one from him, relating to the same matter. Being a farther pursuance of the Philosophical discourse*. London, 1709.

———. "On Solitude," in *Miscellanies*. London. 1687.

[Nourse, Timothy.] *A Discourse of Natural and Reveal'd Religion*. London, 1691.

Observations on the bad effects which are to be dreaded from the establishment of a foundling hospital at Edinburgh; and on the benefit which may be expected from a proper lunatic asylum.

Edinburgh, 1800.
Ogilvie, John. *Philosophical and Critical Observations on the Nature, Character, and Various Species of Composition*. 2 vols. London, 1774; rpt. New York: Garland, 1970.
Oliver, William. *A relation of a very extraordinary sleeper, at Tinsbury, near Bath. With a dissertation on the doctrine of sensation*. London, 1707.
Onomatologia Medica. London, 1755.
Owen, John. *Pneumatology: or, a discourse concerning the Holy Spirit*. London, 1792.
Pardies, Père Ignace Gaston, S. J. *Discours de la connoissance des bestes*. Paris, 1672; rpt. New York: Johnson Reprint Company, 1972.
Pargeter, William. *Observations on maniacal disorders*. Reading, 1792.
Parker, Samuel. *An account of the nature and extent of the divine dominion and goodnesse, especially as they refer to the Origenian hypothesis concerning the preexistence of souls*. Oxford, 1666.
_____. *Essays on Divers Weighty and Curious Subjects*. London, 1702.
_____. *A free and impartial censure of the Platonick philosophie; with an account of the Origenian hypothesis, concerning the preexistence of souls*. 2nd edn. Oxford, 1667.
_____. *Six Philosophical Essays*. London, 1700.
Paulet, J. J. *L'antimagnetisme, ou origine progrès, desudence renouvellement et refutation du magnétisme animal*. Paris, 1784; rpt. Geneva: Slatkine Reprints, 1980.
[_____.] *Mesmer justifié*. Paris, 1784.
Pauli, Henricus. *Propositiones sequentes de melancholia, curatio*. Rostock, 1593.
Pauli, Johann. *Disputatio medica inauguralis de animi commotionum vi medica*. Leipzig, 1700.
Paxton, Peter. *Essay concerning the Body of Man, wherein its changes or diseases are considered and the operation of medicines observed*. London, 1701.
_____. *Specimen physico-medicum, de corpore humano, & ejus morbis, or An essay concerning the knowledge and cure of most diseases afflicting man*. London, 1711.
Peart, E. *Physiology or an attempt to explain the functions and laws of the nervous system, the contraction of muscular fibres*. London, 1798.
Pechlin, J. N. *Observationum physico-medicarum libri tres*. Hamburg, 1691.
Percival, T. *Essays Medical and Experimental*. London, 1767.
Percy, Ch. *A mechanical account of the hysterical passions*. London, 1755.
Perfect, William. *Annals of Insanity, Comprising a Selection of Curious and Interesting Cases in the Different Species of Lunacy, Melancholy, or Madness, with the Modes of Practice in the Medical and Moral Treatment as Adopted in the Cure of Each*. London, 1794; rpt. New York: Arno Press, 1976.
_____. *Cases of Insanity, the Epilepsy, Hypochondriacal Affection, Hysteric Passion, and Nervous. Disorders successfully treated*. London, 1781.
_____. *Methods of cure, in some particular cases of insanity: the epilepsy, hypochondriacal affection, hysteric passion, and nervous disorders. Prefixed with some account of each of those complaints*. London, [1778?].
_____. *Select Cases in Different Species of Insanity or Madness*. London, 1787.
Perrault, Claude. *De la mécanique des animaux*. Paris, 1721.
_____. *Essais de Physique*. Paris, 1680.
_____. *Oeuvres diverses de physique et de méchanique*. Paris, 1721.
Perronet, Vincent. *A Second Vindication of Mr. Locke, Wherein his Sentiments relating to Personal Identity Are clear'd from some Mistakes of The Rev. Dr. Butler, in his Dissertation on that Subject. And the various Objections rais'd against Mr. Locke, by the late learned Author [i.e. Andrew Baxter] of An Enquiry into the Nature of the Human Soul, are consider'd. To which are added Reflections on some passages of Dr. Watt's Philosophical Essays*. London,

1738.

———. *Some enquiries, chiefly relating to spiritual beings; in which the opinions of Mr. Hobbes, with regard to sensation, . . . are taken notice of . . . In four dialogues.* London, 1740.

———. *A Vindication of Mr. Locke, from the Charge of giving encouragement to Scepticism and Infidelity, and from several other Mistakes and Objections of the Learned Author of the Procedure, Extent, and Limits of Human Understanding* [i.e. Peter Browne]. *In Six Dialogues. Wherein is likewise Enquired, Whether Mr. Locke's True Opinion of the Soul's Immateriality was not mistaken by the late learned Mons. Leibniz.* London, 1736.

Perry, Charles. *A mechanical account and explication of the hysteric passion, under all its various symptoms and appearances. And likewise of all such other diseases as are peculiarly incident to the sex. . . . To which is added, an appendix. Being a dissertation on cancers in general; but more especially such as happen in the breasts of women.* London, 1755.

———. *On the Causes and Nature of Madness. As also the natures and properties of opium and volatiles considered in a remonstrance to Dr. Herrm. Lafnau, on his behaviour touching a late case. To which is added a postscript.* London, 1723.

[Pestalozzi, Johann Heinrich.] *Meine nachforschungen über den gang der natur in der entwiklung des menschengeschlechts, von dem verfasser Lienhard und Gertrud.* Zurich, 1797; rpt. Bad Heilbrunn: J. Klinklardt, 1968.

Petit, Antoine. *Deux consultations medico-légales, la première tendante à prouver qu'un briquetier de la ville de Liège . . .* Paris, 1767.

———. *Traité des maladies des femmes enceintes, des femmes en couche, et des enfants nouveaux nés.* 2 vols. Paris, [1799].

A Philosophical Dissertation upon the Inlets to Human Knowledge. London, 1739.

The philosophy of the passions; demonstrating their nature, properties, effects, use and abuse. In two volumes. London, 1772.

Pinel, Philippe. *Nosographie philosophique ou la méthode de l'analyse appliqué à la médecine.* Paris, 1798.

———. *Observations sur une espèce particulière de melancolie qui conduit au suicide, La médecine éclairée par les sciences physiques.* Paris, 1791.

———. *Traité Medico-philosophique sur l'alienation mentale.* Paris, 1809; rpt. New York: Arno Press, 1976.

Pistorius, Hermann Andrew. *Notes and additions to Dr. Hartley's Observations on Man; tr. from the German original.* Leipzig, 1772.

Pitcairne, Archibald. *The Philosophical and Mathematical Elements of Physick.* London, 1718.

———. *The whole works of Dr. Archibald Pitcairn, published by himself. Wherein are discovered the true foundation and principles of art and physic. With cases and observations upon most distempers and medicines.* London, 1715.

Playford, John. *An Antidote Against Melancholy: Made up in Pills.* London, 1661.

Poetical frenzy, or a venture in rhyme. London, 1776.

Poisson P. *Commentaire ou remarques sur la methode de R. Descartes.* Vandosme, 1670.

Pomme, Pierre. *Traité des affections vaporeuses de deux sexes, ou maladies nerveuses vulgairement appelées maux de nerfs.* Paris, 1760.

Porterfield, William. *A Treatise on the Eye, the Manner and Phaenomena of Vision.* 2 vols. Edinburgh, 1759.

[Pownall, Paul.] *Intellectual physics, an essay in the nature of being.* Bath, 1795.

Pressavin, Jean-Baptiste. *Nouveau traité des vapeurs.* Lyons, 1770.

———. *Traité des maladies des nerfs dans lequel on développe les vrais principes des vapeurs.* Lyons, 1769.
Price, Richard. *The Nature and Dignity of the Human Soul.* London, 1766.
Price, Uvedale. *A dialogue on the distinct characters of the picturesque and the beautiful. In answer to the objections of Mr. Knight.* London, 1801.
———. *An essay on the picturesque, as compared with the sublime and the beautiful; and, on the use of studying pictures, for the purposes of improving real landscape.* London, 1794.
Priestley, Joseph. *A Course of Lectures on Oratory and Criticism.* London, 1777; rpt. Carbondale: Southern Illinois University Press, 1965.
———. *Disquisitions relating to Matter and Spirit; To which is added, The History of the Philosophical Doctrine concerning the Origin of the Soul, and the Nature of Matter; with its Influence on Christianity, especially with Respect to the Doctrine of the Preexistence of Christ.* 2 vols. London, 1777; rpt. New York: Arno Press, 1975.
———. *The Doctrine of Philosophical Necessity Illustrated; Being an Appendix to the Disquisitions relating to Matter and Spirit. To which is added, An Answer to the Letters on Materialism, and on Hartley's Theory of the Mind.* London, 1777; rpt. New York: Garland, 1976.
———. *An Examination of Dr. Reid's Inquiry into the Human Mind, on the Principles of Common Sense; Dr. Beattie's Essay on the Nature and Immutability of Truth; and Dr. Oswald's Appeal to Common Sense in Behalf of Religion.* London, 1774.
———. *A Free Discussion of the Doctrines of Materialism, and Philosophical Necessity, in a Correspondence between Dr. Price and Dr. Priestley. To which are added, by Dr. Priestley, An Introduction, Explaining the Nature of the Controversy, and Letters to Several Writers who have Animadverted on his Disquisitions relating to Matter and Spirit, or his Treatise on Necessity.* London, 1778.
Printz, Caelestinus Amandus. *De mania.* Jena, 1708.
Prohaska, G. "De functionibus systematis nervosi Commentatio," in *Adnotationum academicorum fasciculus tertius.* Prague, 1784.
———. *Physiologie; oder, Lehre von der Natur des Menschen.* Vienna, 1820.
Purcell, John. *A treatise of vapours, or, hysterick fits. Containing an analytical proof of its causes, . . . together with its cure at large.* London, 1702.
Quincy, John. *Lexicon Physico-Medicum: or, A New Medicinal Dictionary.* London, 1719.
Raulin, Joseph. *Traité des affections vaporeuses du sexe avec l'exposition de leurs symptômes, de leurs différentes causes et la methode de les guérir.* Paris, 1758.
———. *Traité des maladies des femmes en couche avec la methode des les guérir.* Paris, 1777.
Recherches curieuses de philosophie, ou dissertation sur les principes des choses naturelles, dans laquelle, par le secours d'une méthode nouvelle, on traite de la generation des hommes, des animaux, des arbres, des plantes, de la formation du monde et de sa durée, des causes des vents, du tonerre, de la foudre, de l'esprit, du raisonnement. par T. S. J. F. 1713. MS Bibliotheque nationale, fond francais, 9107.
Reeve, Thomas. *A cure for the epidemical madness of drinking tar water, lately imported from Ireland by a certain R-t R-D Doctor. In a letter to his L-p.* London, 1744.
Reflections on ancient and modern music with the application to the cure of diseases; to which is subjoined an essay to solve the question wherein consisted the difference of ancient musik from that of modern times. London, 1749.
Regis, Pierre Sylvain. *Systeme de philosophie.* 7 vols. Paris, 1690.
Reid, John. *De Insania.* Edinburgh, 1798.

———. *Essays on Insanity, Hypochondriasis and Other Nervous Affections*. London, 1816.
Reid, Thomas. *Essays on the Active Powers of Man*. Edinburgh, 1788; rpt. Cambridge, Mass.: MIT Press, 1969.
———. *Essays on the intellectual powers of man*. Edinburgh, 1785; rpt. Cambridge, Mass.: MIT Press, 1969.
———. *An inquiry into the human mind*. Edinburgh, 1764; rpt. Chicago, Ill.: University of Chicago Press, 1960.
———. *Works*. 2 vols. Edinburgh, 1846-63.
Reil, Johann Christian. *Rhapsodieen über die Anwendung der psychischen Curmethode auf Geisteszerrüttungen*. Halle, 1803.
———. *De Structura Nervorum*. Halle, 1796.
———. *Ueber die Erkenntniss und Cur der Fieber. Besondere Fieberlehre*. Halle, 1805.
Rentzius, George. *De melancholia hypochondriaca*. Tübingen, 1595.
Revillon, Claude. *Recherches sur la Cause des Affections Hypocondriaques*. Paris, 1779.
Reynolds, Edward. *A Treatise of the Passions and Faculties of the Soul of Man. With severall Dignities and Corruptions thereunto belonging*. London, 1650; rpt. Gainesville, Fla.: Scholars' Facsimiles and Reprints, 1971.
[Reynolds, Frances.] *An Enquiry Concerning the Principles of Taste, and of the Origin of Our Ideas of Beauty*. London, 1785; rpt. [with an introduction by James Clifford] Los Angeles, Calif.: William Andrews Clark Memorial Library, 1951.
Rhenanus, Johann. *De melancholia*. Marburg, 1615.
Ribow, Georg Heinrich. *Dissertatione historico philosophica de anima brutorum*. Helmstadt, 1728.
Richardson, Charles. *Dissertatio medica inauguralis de male hysterico*. Edinburgh, 1763.
Richardson, J., of Newent. *Thoughts upon thinking, or a new theory of the human mind; wherein a physical rationale of the formation of our ideas, . . . is attempted upon principles entirely new*. 2nd edn. London, 1773; rpt. New York: Garland, 1972.
Ridley, Humphrey. *The Anatomy of the Brain*. London, 1695.
Rivière, Lazare. *Institutiones medicae in quinque semiotice libros distinctae quibus totidem medicinae partes, physiologia, pathologia, et therapeutice dilueide explicantur*. London, 1656.
———. *Praxix medica integre morborum theoria & quamplurismus selectissimus locupletata*. 7th edn. London, 1653.
Robinet, Jean Baptiste René. *Vue philosophique de la gradation naturelle des formes de l'etre; ou, Les essais de la nature qui apprend à faire l' homme*. Amsterdam, 1768.
Robinson, Bryan. *A Treatise of the Animal Oeconomy*. Dublin, 1732.
Robinson, Nicholas. *An essay on the gout, and all gouty affections incident to affect mankind. Comprizing the various natures, symptoms, and causes, thro' every branch and stage of the disease*. London, [1755?].
———. *A new system of the spleen, vapours, and hypochondriack melancholy: wherein all the decays of the nerves, and lowness of spirits are mechanically accounted for*. London, 1729.
———. *A new theory of physick and diseases, founded on the Newtonian philosophy*. London, 1725.
Roche, Abbé Antoine Martin. *Traité de la nature de l'ame et de l'origine de ses connoissances, contre le systême de M. Locke et de ses partisans*. 2 vols. Paris, 1759.
Roche, D. de la. *Analyse des functions du systeme nerveaux*. 2 vols. Geneva, 1770.
Rogers, Samuel. *The Pleasures of Memory*. London, 1792.
Rogers, Timothy. *A discourse concerning trouble of mind, and the disease of melancholly . . . By

Timothy Rogers, M.A. who was long afflicted with both. London, 1691.
Rohault, Jacques. *Tractatus physicus. Latine vertit, recensuit & adnotationibus, ex Isaaci Newtoni Philosophia maximan partem haustis, amplicavit Samuel Clarke. Cum animadiversionibus integris Antonii Le Grand.* Amsterdam, 1708.
Rorario, Girolano. *Hieronymi Rorarii exlegati pontificii, quod animalia bruta ratione utantur melius homme, libri duo.* Sylvae-Ducis, 1702.
Röser, Johannes. *De Admirando illo Affectu Catalepsi.* Rinteln, 1692.
Rotheram, John. *An Essay in the Distinction between the Soul and Body of Man.* Newcastle upon Tyne, 1781.
Rousseau, Jean Jacques. *Discours sur l' origine et les fondemens de l'inegalité parmi les hommes.* Amsterdam, 1755.
──────. *Du contrat social; or Principes du droit politique.* Amsterdam, 1762.
──────. *Émile, ou, De l'education.* Amsterdam, 1762.
──────. *Oeuvres complètes.* Ed. Bernard Guyon et al. 5 vols. Paris: Editions Gallimard, 1959.
Rowley, W. *A Treatise on Female, Nervous, Hysterical, Hypochondriacal, Bilious, Convulsive Diseases; Apoplexy and Palsy; with thoughts on Madness, Suicide, etc. In which the principal disorders are explained from anatomical facts, and the treatment formed on several new principles.* London, 1788.
──────. *Truth Vindicated or the Specific Differences of Mental Diseases.* London, 1789.
Rush, Benjamin. *An enquiry into the influence of physical causes upon the moral faculties.* Philadelphia, 1786.
──────. *Medical Inquiries and Observations.* 3rd edn. Philadelphia, 1809; rpt. New York: Arno Press, 1972.
Rymer, J. A. *A Tract upon Indigestion, and the Hypochondriac Disease, and upon the Atonic or Flying Gout; with the methods and cure by means of a new remedy of medecine; and direction for taking it in a variety of cases of nervous affections, muscular and vascular relaxation, broken constitutions, in malignant and putrid fevers. With above fifty-six select cases, chiefly anomalous, of dyspepsy, hysteria, hypochondriasis, the inflammatory and atonic gout, vertigo, apoplexy, palsy.* London, 1789.
S., M. *A Philsophical Discourse of the Nature of Rational and Irrational Souls.* London, 1695.
Saint-Hyacinthe, Thémiseul de. *Recherches philosophiques, sur la nécessité de s'assurer par soi-meme de la verité; sur la certitude de nos connoissances; et sur la nature des etres.* London, 1743.
Salmon, William. *Ars anatomica; or, the anatomy of humane bodies. In 7 books. Representing to the mind a true and compleat idea of the whole humane frame.* London, 1714.
──────. *A New Practice of Physic.* London, 1726.
Saunders, Richard. *Physiognomie . . . with the Subject of Dreams Made Plain.* London, 1653.
Sauvages de la Croix, Francois Boissier de. *Nosologia methodica sistens morborum classes.* Amsterdam, 1763.
──────. *Etude sur Sauvages, ses Oeuvres et sa doctrine.* Montpellier, 1780.
Sbaragli, Joannes Hieronymus. *Entelechia, seu anima sensitiva brutorum, demonstrata contra Cartesium.* Bononiae, 1716.
Scheffer, Sebastian. *De melancholia desipientia.* Helmstadt, 1652.
Scheidemantel. *Von den Leidenschaften als Heilmittel betrachtet.* Frankfurt an der Oder, 1787.
Schlapperitius, Johann Ludwig. *De mania.* Jena, 1673.

Schleiermacher, Georg Ludwig. *De catalepsi, rarissimo affectuum*. Giessen, 1695.
Schmid, E. G. E. *Empirische Psychologie*. 1791.
Schmidius, Justus Andreas. *De suffocatione uterino*. Jena, 1681.
Schmidt, Christopherus Philippus. *De animi morbis*. Halle, 1708.
Schroder, Joh. Frid. *Aegrum affectu maniaco laboratem sistens*. Erfurt, 1695.
Schultz, Gothofredus. *De melancholia ex utero, in puerpera observata & curata*. Frankfurt an der Oder. 1705.
Scott, John. *A fine picture of enthusiasm, chiefly drawn by Dr. John Scott, . . . Wherein the danger of the passions leading in religion is strongly described. To which is added, an application of the subject to the modern Methodists, . . . With a word or two concerning . . . Deists*. London, 1744.

———. *Histories of gouty, bilious and nervous cases, with the safe and easy means by which they were remedied, related by the patients themselves in sundry letters*. London, 1780.
Scrubb, Tim. *A Rod for the Hyp-Doctor*. London, 1731.
Senault, Jean Francois. *De l'usage des passions*. Leyden, 1644.
Sennert, D. *Duo tractatus de dignotione et curatione scorbuti et reliquorum ab eo dependentium affectum hypochondriacorum: I. De scorbuto & hypochondriacis affectibus*. Jena, 1624.

———. *The Institutions . . . of . . . Physick and Chirugery*. London, 1656.
Sennert, Michael. *De affectione hypochondriaca*. Wittenberg, 1628.
Sergeant, John. *Solid Philosophy Asserted, against the Fancies of the Ideists*. London, 1697; rpt. New York: Garland, 1984.
Shaftesbury, Anthony Ashley Cooper, 3rd Earl of. *Characteristicks of men*. 3 vols. London, 1711. Also see the edition of London, 1900. Ed. John M. Robertson; rpt. Gloucester, Mass: Peter Smith, 1963. 2 vols.
Sharpe, William. *A dissertation upon genius*. London, 1755; rpt. Delmar, N.Y.: Scholars' Facsimiles and Reprints, 1973.
Shaw, Peter. *A New Practice of Physick*. London, 1726.

———. *The reflector: representing human affairs, as they are; and may be improved*. London, 1750.
Sheridan, Thomas. *A discourse being introductory to his course of lectures on elocution and the English language*. London, 1759; rpt. [with an Introduction by G. P. Mohrmann] Los Angeles, Calif.: William Andrews Clark Memorial Library, 1969.
A short treatise on canine madness, particularly the bite of mad dogs; some cautions to prevent the danger, and remedies for injuries received thereby: together with those of other enraged animals. London, [1795?].
Shower, John. *The Mourner's Companion and Funeral Discourses on Several Texts*. London, 1692.
Silhon, Jean de. *De l'immortalité de l'ame*. Billaine, 1634.
Sims, R. C. *As essay on the nature and constitution of man; comprehending an answer to the following question, proposed by a learned society: "Are there any satisfactory proofs of the immateriality of the soul? . . . "* London, 1793.
Simson, Thomas. *An inquiry how far the vital and animal actions of the more perfect animals can be accounted for independent of the brain*. Edinburgh, 1752.
Smith, Adam. *Works. With an account of his life by Dugald Stewart*. 5 vols. London, 1811–12; rpt. Aalen, Germany: Zeller, 1963.

———. *Theory of Moral Sentiments*. London, 1759; rpt. New York: Garland, 1971.
Smith, Daniel. *A Treatise on Hysterical and Nervous Disorders*. London, 1778.
Smith, H. *An Essay on the Nerves*. London, 1794.
Smith, John, 1630–79. Γερονομία Βασιλική. *King Solomon's portraiture of old age. Wherein*

Selected Bibliography of Primary Materials 339

is contained a sacred anatomy both of soul and body. And a perfect account of the infirmities of age, incident to them both. London, 1666.

Smith, John, 1618–52. *Select Discourses, Treating, I. Of the True Way or Method of Attaining a Divine Knowledge. 2. Of Superstition. 3. Of Atheism. 4. Of the immortality of the Soul. 5. Of the Existence and Nature of God. 6. Of prophecy. 7. Of the Difference between the Legal and the Evangelical Righteousness, the Old and the New Covenant, &c. 8. Of the Shortness and Vanity of a Pharisaick Righteousness. 9. Of the Excellency and Nobleness of True Religion. 10. Of a Christians Conflicts with, and Conquests over, Satan.*[Compiled by John Worthington.] *As also, A Sermon preached by Simon Patrick at the Author's Funeral. With a Brief Account of his Life and Death.* London, 1660.

Smith, W. *A Dissertation on the Nerves, containing an account, I. of the nature of man, 2. of the nature of brutes, 3. of the nature and the connection of soul and body, 4. of the threefold life of man, 5. of the symptoms, causes and cure of all nervous diseases.* London, 1768.

Smyth, James Carmichael. *A description of the jail distemper, as it appeared among the Spanish prisoners at Winchester, in the year 1780.* London, 1795.

Society of the Court of Comus. *Tales to kill time or, a new method to cast off care, and to cure melancholy, vapours, and all hypochondriacal complaints.* London, 1757.

Soemmering, G. *Über das Organ der Seele.* Köningsberg, 1796.

———. *Vom Bau des menschlichen Körpers.* Frankfurt am Main, 1791–96.

Soldini, Francesco Maria. *De anima brutorum commentaria.* Florence, 1776.

———. *Delle origini della pazzia d'un filosofo fiorentino.* Florence, 1770.

Somerville, William. *The Hyp: A Burlesque Poem in Five Cantos.* London, 1731.

Southcomb, Lewis. *Peace of Mind and Health of Body.* London, 1750; rpt. New York: Garland, 1970.

Spinoza, Benedict. *Spinoza Opera.* 4 vols. Heidelberg, 1924. See, among others, *Renati Descartes Principorum Philosophiae, Pars I et II* (1663), *Ethics* (1677), and *Tractatus de Intellectus Emendatione* (1677).

———. *On the Improvement of the Understanding, The Ethics, and Correspondence,* Trans. R. H. M. Elwes. New York: Dover, 1955.

———. *A Theologico-Political Treatise and A Political Treatise.* Trans. R. H. M. Elwes. New York: Dover, 1951.

Stahl, G. E. *Considerations sur la dycrasie veineuse.* Paris, 1860.

———. *De Medicina Medicinae Necessaria.* Halle, 1702.

———. *Negotium otiosum seu skiamachia.* Halle, 1720.

———. *Neu-verbesserte Lehre von den Temperamenten, welche bey dieser neuen Auflage mit dem zweyten Theil, der von Veränderung der Temperamenten, handelt.* 2 vols. in 1. Leipzig, 1723.

———. *Ueber den mannigfaltigen Einfluss von Gemüthsbewegungen auf den menschlichen Körper.* Halle, 1695; rpt. Leipzig: Barth, 1961.

Stark, John *Dissertatio medica, inauguralis, de malo hypochondriaco.* Edinburgh, 1783.

Stearns, J. *A History of Animal Magnetism, revealed to the world, containing philosophical reflections on the publication of a pamphlet, entitled: A true and genuine discovery of animal electricity and magnetism; also an exhibition of the advantages and disadvantages that may arise in consequence of said publication; and many other curious observations never before published.* London, 1791.

Steno, Nicolaus. *Discours sur l'anatomie du cerveau.* Paris, 1669; rpt. Copenhagen: Nyt nordisk forlag, 1965.

———. *Elementorum myologiae specimen.* Florence, 1667.

Stephani, Joh. Jac. *De somnambulis.* Basel, 1701.
Stewart, Dugald. *Elements of the philosophy of the human mind.* London, 1792; rpt. New York: Garland, 1971.
_____. *Some account of a boy born blind and deaf collected from authentic sources of information.* Edinburgh, 1815.
_____. *The Works.* Ed. Sir William Hamilton. 11 vols. Edinburgh, 1854–60.
Stochius, Antonius. *De affectione hypochondriaca.* Utrecht, 1730.
Stockmann, Jo. Car. *De variae therapiae necessitate in hypochondriaco quam hysterico malo.* Halle, 1747.
Storie, George Henry. *Dissertatio medica inauguralis de hysteria.* Glasgow, 1786.
Ströhlin, J. F. *Philosophische Rede über die Associationsgesetze unserer Begriffe.* Stuttgart, 1788.
Strother, Edward. *An Essay on Sickness and Health, In which Dr. Cheyne's Mistaken Opinions in his late Essay, are occasionally taken Notice of.* London, 1725.
[Strutt, Samuel.] *A Defense of the late learned Dr. Clarke's Notion of Natural Liberty: in Answer to Three Letters Wrote to Him by a Gentleman at the University of Cambridge, on the Side of Necessity. Together with Some Remarks on Mr. Locke's Chapter of Power.* London, 1730.
[_____.] *A Philosophical Enquiry into the Physical Spring of Human Actions, and the Immediate Cause of Thinking.* London, 1732.
Stuart, Alexander. *Three Lectures on Muscular Motion.* London, 1739.
Stuart, David. *Disputatio medica, inauguralis, de mania.* Edinburgh, 1777.
[Stubbes, George.] *A Dialogue on Beauty. In the manner of Plato.* London, 1731; rpt. New York: Garland, 1970.
Stukeley, William. *Of the spleen, its description and history, uses and diseases, particularly the vapors, with their remedy.* London, 1722.
Sulzer, Johann Georg. *Allgemeine Theorie der Schönen Künste.* 4 vols. Leipzig, 1771–74.
_____. *Unterredungen über die Schönheit der Natur.* Berlin, 1770; rpt. Frankfurt am Main: Athenäum, 1971.
_____. "Zergliederung des Begriffs der Vernunft," in *Vermischte philosophische Schriften.* 1758; rpt. Hildesheim: G. Olms, 1974.
Süssenbach, Christophorus. *De therapia imaginaria. Von Menschen die aus Einbildung gesund werden.* Halle, 1721.
Swedenbourg, Emanuel. *The Soul, or Rational Psychology.* Regium Animale, 1744.
_____. *A theosophic lucubration on the nature of influx, as it respects the communication and operations of soul and body.* London, 1770.
Swieten, Gerhard van. *Commentaria in Hermanni Boerhaavi Aphorismos de cognoscendis et curandis morbis.* 5 vols. Leyden, 1745–72.
Sydenham, Thomas. *Dissertatio epistolaris ad Gulielmum Cole, . . . de affectione hysterica.* London, 1682.
_____. *The Whole Works of . . . Thomas Sydenham.* London, 1696; rpt. [of 1852 edn.] London: Sydenham Society, 1979.
Synge, Edward. *The Cure of Melancholy.* London, 1742.
_____. *Sober Thoughts for the Cure of Melancholy; especially that which is Religious.* Dublin, 1738.
Tackius, Eberhard. *De nostalgia.* Giessen, 1707.
Taylor, Jeremy. *Ductor dubitantium, or the rule of conscience.* London, 1660.
Taylor, John. *Examination of the Scheme of Morality advanced by Dr. Hutcheson.* London,

1759.
Tenon, Jacques René. *Memoire sur les hopitaux de Paris.* Paris, 1788.
Terrasson, Jean. *La Philosophie applicable a tous les objets de l'esprit et de la raison.* Paris, 1754.
Tetens, Johan Nicolai. *Philosophicle Versuche über die menschliche Natur und ihre Entwicklung.* Riga, 1777; rpt. Hildesheim: G. Olms, 1979.
Thetzell, Georgius C. *Dissertatio philosophica, quod, Deus memoriae sit expers, paucis ostendens.* London, 1795.
Thompson, T. *An Historical and Critical Treatise of the Gout.* London, 1742.
Thomson, A. *An Inquiry into the Nature, Causes and Method of Cure of Nervous Disorders. In a letter to a friend.* London, 1781.
Thomson, George. 'Ορθομεθοδος ἰατροχυμικη, *or the direct method of curing chymically.* London, 1675.
Thoner, Aug. *De melancholia.* Basel, 1590.
Tiedemann, Dietrich. *Dietrich Tiedemanns Beobachtungen über die entwickelung der seelenfahigkeiten bei kindern. Mit einleitung, sowie mit einem litteraturverzeichnis zur kinderpsychologie.* Altengurg, 1897.
———. *Handbuch der psychologie, zum gebrauche bei vorlesungen und zur selbstbelehrungbestimmt.* Leipzig, 1804; rpt. Bruxelles: Culture et Civilisation, 1970.
Tissot, S. A. A. D. *De la santé des gens de lettres.* Paris, 1770.
———. *De l'influence des passions de l'ame dans les maladies, et des moyens d'en corriger les mauvais effets.* Paris, 1798.
———. *Essai sur les maladies des gens du monde.* 2nd edn. Lausanne, 1770.
———. *Memoire de Haller.* 4 vols. Lausanne, 1756–60.
———. *L'onanisme.* Lausanne, 1760. See *Onanism: or a treatise upon the disorders produced by masturbation: or the dangerous effects of secret and excessive venery.* London, 1781.
———. *Traité des nerfs et de leurs maladies.* Paris, 1778.
Toulmin, George Hoggart. *The eternity of the universe.* London, 1789.
A treatise of diseases of the head, brain, and nerves. More especially of the palsy, apoplexy, . . . To which is subjoin'd, A discourse of the nature, real cause and certain cure of melancholy in men, and vapours in women. 4th edn., corrected. London, 1721.
A treatise on the Dismal Effects of Low-Spiritedness. London, 1750.
Trenchard, John. *The Natural History of Superstition.* London, 1709.
Trosse, George. *The Life of the Reverend Mr. George Trosse: Written by Himself, and Published Posthumously According to His Order.* London, 1714; rpt. Montreal: McGill-Queen's University Press, 1974.
Trotter, Thomas. *An essay, medical, philosophical, and chemical, on drunkenness, and its effects on the human body.* London, 1804.
———. *A View of the Nervous Temperament.* London, 1807.
Trusler, John. *On the passions.* [London, 1796.]
Tryon, Thomas. *The Knowledge of a Man's Self.* London, 1703–04.
———. *A Treatise of Dreams and Visions.* London, 1689.
Tucker, Abraham. *The Light of Nature Pursued.* 7 vols. London, 1778; rpt. [of 1805 edn.] New York: Garland, 1977.
Tuke, Richard. *The souls warfare comically digested into scenes acted between soul and her enemies; wherein she cometh off victrix with an angelical plaudit.* London, 1672.
Tuke, Samuel. *Description of the retreat, an institution near York, for insane persons of the Society of Friends.* York, 1813; rpt. London: Dawsons of Pall Mall, 1964.

———. *Practical hints on the construction and economy of pauper lunatic asylums; including instructions to the architects who offered plans for the Wakefield Asylum, and a sketch of the most approved design.* York, 1815.

Turnbull, George. *Principles of moral philosophy.* 2 vols. London, 1739–40; rpt. Hildesheim: G. Olms, 1976.

Turner, Daniel. *An Answer to a Pamphlet on the Power of Imagination in Pregnant Women.* London, 1729.

———. *A discourse concerning gleets. Their cause and cure. With a prefatory account of Professor Boerhaave's new comments on the venereal disease; . . . To which is added, a defence of the 12th chapter of the first part of a treatise De morbis cutaneis, . . . containing some remarks upon a discourse lately printed and entituled, The strength of imagination in pregnant women examin'd & c.* London, 1729.

———. *The force of the mother's imagination upon her foetus in utero, still farther considered: in the way of a reply to Dr. Blondel's last book, entitled, The power of the imagination over the foetus examined. To which is added, the twelfth chapter of the first part of a treatise De Morbis Cutaneis . . .* London, 1730.

Turner, John. *Vindication of the separate existence of the soul.* London, 1707.

Turner, William. *A Compleat History of the Most Remarkable Providences.* London, 1697.

———. *The history of all religions in the world.* London, 1695.

Two Dissertations concerning Sense and the Imagination. With an Essay on Consciousness. London, 1728; rpt. New York: Garland, 1976. This work has been attributed to Zachary Mayne and, more recently, to Charles Mayne. The editor finds both of these attributions doubtful.

Tyson, Edward. *Orang-outang, sive homo sylvestris; or, The anatomy of a pygmie compared with that of a monkey, an ape and a man.* London, 1699.

Unverzagt, Henningus. *De melancholia.* Helmstadt, 1614.

Unzer, Johann August. *Erste Gründe einer Physiologie der eigentlichen thierischen Natur thierischer Körper.* Leipzig, 1771.

Usher, James. *Clio: or a discourse on taste.* London, 1767; rpt. New York: Garland, 1970.

Uvedale, C. *The Construction of the Nerves and the Causes of Nervous Disorders practically explained.* London, 1758.

Valangin, Francois Joseph Pahud de. *A treatise on diet, or the managemnt of human life; by physicians called the six non-naturals, viz. I. The air. II. Food. III. Excretions and retentions. IV. Motion and rest. V. Sleep and watching. VI. The affections of the mind.* London, 1768.

Valerius, Henricus. *Diss. de memoria.* 1703.

Van Diik, C. *De suffocatione hypochondriaca.* Leyden, 1665.

Van Eems, J. *Hermanni Boerhaave Praelectiones Academicae De Morbis Nervorum.* 2 vols. Leyden, 1761.

Vater, Christian. *De melancholia seu delirio tristi.* Wittenberg, 1680.

———. *De memoria et capitis laesione gravissima, a colica spasmodica male curate.* Wittenberg, 1722.

Vauvenargues de la Clapiers, marquis de. *Introduction à la connaissance de l'esprit humain.* Paris, 1746.

Vere, James. *A physical and moral enquiry into the causes of that internal restlessness and disorder in man, which has been the complaint of all ages.* London, 1778.

Vermeiren, Nicolaus. *De suffocatione hypochondriaca.* Leyden, 1668.

Vieussens, R. *Neurographia Universalis.* Lyons, 1685.

Vogel, Rudolf Augustin, praeses. *De insania longa dissertatio solemnis.* Göttingen, [1763].

Vogler, Tob. *Mnemosynologia, sive de memoria libellus theorico-practicus.* Jena, 1676.
Voight, Joannes Casparus Ignatius. *De passione seu affectione hypochondriaca.* Prague, 1678.
Vulson, Marc de, Sieur de la Colombiere. *The Court of Curiosity.* 3rd edn. London, 1681.
Wainewright, Jeremiah. *A Mechanical Account of the Non-Naturals.* London, 1707.
Walch, Johann Georg. *Philosophisches Lexicon.* Leipzig, 1740; rpt. Hildesheim: G. Olms, 1968.
Walker, Sayer. *A treatise on nervous diseases . . . and . . . of the symptoms and causes of these diseases as may lead to a rational and successful method of cure.* London, 1796.
Walkington, Thomas. *Optick Glasse of Humors, or the Touchstone of a Golden Temperature: Or the Philosopher's Stone to make a Golden Temper.* London, 1607; rpt. [of 1631 ed.] Delmar, N.Y.: Scholars' Facsimiles and Reprints.
Wall, Martin. *Bite of a mad dog. Directions to prevent canine madness by ablution.* [Oxford, 1791.]
Wallich, Simon. *De melancholia hypochondriaca.* Leyden, 1678.
Wallis, George, and G. Motherby. *A New Medicinal Dictionary.* 4th edn. 1795.
Walterus, Godofredus. *De suffocatione hypochondriaca in vivo.* Leyden, 1688.
Waterhouse, Benjamin. *The Botanist, together with a discourse on the principle of vitality.* Boston, 1811.
Watts, Isaac. *Discourses of the love of God, and its influence on all the passions: with a discovery of the right use and abuse of them in matters of religion. A devout meditation is annexed to each discourse.* London, 1729.
——. *The doctrine of the passions explain'd and improv'd: or, a brief and comprehensive scheme of the natural affections . . . to which is added a defence against the temptation to self-murther. Together with some reflections on excess in strong liquors, duelling, and other practices.* Dublin, 1737.
——. *Logick: Or, The Right Use of Reason in the Enquiry after Truth, With a Variety of Rules to guard against Error, in the Affairs of Religion and Human Life, as well as in the Sciences.* 2nd edn. London, 1726; rpt. New York: Garland, 1984.
[——.] *Philosophical Essays on Various Subjects, viz. Space, Substance, Body, Spirit, The Operations of the Soul, the Resurrection of the Body, the Production and Operations of Plants and Animals; with some Remark's on Mr. Locke's Essay on the Human Understanding. To which is subjoined a Brief Scheme of Ontology, Or The Science of Being in general with its Affections.* London, 1733.
The Way to Things by Words, and to Words by Things. London, 1766; rpt. Menston, York: Scolar Press. 1968.
Webster, John. *The displaying of supposed Witchcraft; wherein it is affirmed that there are many sorts of deceivers and impostors, and divers persons under a passive delusion of melancholy and fancy.* London, 1677.
——. *Practical Observation on the Preservation of Health.* London, 1804.
Wegener, Georg Ferd. *De natura labe et praesidiis memoriae humanae.* Göttingen, 1752.
Weikard, Melchior Adam. *Der philosophische Artz.* 3 vols. Frankfurt am Main, 1799.
Wendius, Joh. Christian. *De catalepsi.* Erfurt, 1689.
Wesley, John. *Primitive Physick.* London, 1747; rpt. Beverly Hills, Calif.: Woodbridge Press, 1973.
Westhoff, R. *De affectu hypochondriae.* Argentorati, 1668.
Whichcote, Benjamin. *Select Sermons of Dr. Whichcot[e]. In Two Parts.* London, 1698.
Whitehead, John. *Materialism philosophically examined, or, the immateriality of the soul assert-*

ed and proved, on philosophical principle; in answer to Dr. Priestley's Disquisitions on matter and spirit. London, 1778.
Whitfield, Theodosia. *The soul display'd. Being an essay on the passions.* London, 1727.
Whytt, Robert. *An account of some experiments made with opium on living and dying animals.* Edinburgh, 1756.
———. *An Essay on the Vital and involuntary Motions of Animals.* Edinburgh, 1751.
———. *Observations on the dropsy in the brain, by Robert Whytt, . . . To which are added his other treatises never hitherto published by themselves.* Edinburgh, 1768.
———. *Physiological Essays: Containing, I. An Inquiry into the Causes which Promote the Circulation of the Fluids in the Very Small Vessels of Animals, II. Observations on the Sensibility and Irritability of the Parts of Men and Other Animals; occasioned by Dr. Haller's later Treatise on These Subjects.* Edinburgh, 1755.
———. *Observations On the Nature, Causes, and Cure of those disorders which have commonly been called Nervous.* 3rd edn. Edinburgh, 1767.
———. *Works.* Edinburgh, 1768.
Willis, John. *Mnemonica, or, the Art of Memory . . . also a Physical Treatise of Cherishing Natural Memory.* London, 1661; rpt. New York: Da Capo, 1973.
Willis, Thomas. *Affectionum quae dicuntur hystericae et hypochondriacae, vindicata contra responsionem epistolarum Nathanielis Highmore.* London, 1670.
———. *Cerebri anatome, cui accessit nervorum descriptio et usus.* London, 1664; rpt. [in English: *The Anatomy of the Brain and Nerves*] 2 vols. Montreal: McGill University Press, 1965.
———. *Pathologiae cerebri et nervosi generis in quo agitur de morbis convulsivis.* Oxford, 1667.
———. *Two Discourses Concerning the Soul of Brutes.* Gainesville, Fla.: Scholars' Facsimiles and Reprints, 1971.
Wilson, Andrew. *Medical Researches: being an enquiry into the nature and origin of hysterics in the female constitution and into the distinction between that disease and hypochondriac or nervous disorders.* London, 1777.
———. *Nature and origin of hysteria.* London, 1776.
[Wimpey, Joseph.] *Remarks on a Book, intitled, An Enquiry into the Nature of the Human Soul* [by Andrew Baxter]. *Wherein the Immateriality of the Soul is Evinced from the Principles of Reason and Philosophy.* London, 1741.
Wincklemann, Abbe Johann Joachim. *Gedanken über die Nachamung der griechischen Werke in der Mahleray und Bildhaver-Kunst.* Friedrichstadt, 1755. *Reflections on the Painting and Sculpture of the Greeks, with Instructions for the Connoisseur, and An Essay on Grace in Works on Art.* 2nd edn. London, 1767.
Windle, William. *An enquiry into the Immateriality of Thinking Substances, Human Liberty, and the Original of Motion, Particularly in Answer to a late Pamphlet, intitled, A Philosophical Enquiry into the Physical Spring of Human Actions and Immediate Cause of Thinking* [by Samuel Strutt]. London, 1738.
Winter, Fridericus. *De mania.* Erfurt, 1710.
Withers, Thomas. *Observations on the abuse of medicine.* London, 1775.
Witty, John. *The First Principles of Modern Deism confuted.* London, 1707.
Wolff, Christian, Freiherr von. *Psychologia Empirica.* Frankfurt am Main, 1732; rpt. Hildesheim: G. Olms, 1968.
———. *Psychologia Rationalis.* Verona, 1737; rpt. Hildesheim: G. Olms, 1968.
Wolfhaed, Leo. *De melancholia.* Basel, 1577.
Wollaston, William. *The Religion of Nature Delineated.* 2nd edn. London, 1724; rpt. New

York: Garland, 1978.

Woodward, John. *An Idea of the Nature and Mechanism of Man.* London, 1718.

──────. *Select cases, and consultations, in physick. By the late eminent John Woodward . . . Now first published by Dr. Peter Templeman.* London, 1757.

──────. *The state of physick: and of diseases; with an inquiry into the causes of the late increase of them.* London, 1718.

Wright, Thomas. *The passions of the minde in general.* London, 1601.

Young, Edward. *Conjectures on Original Composition.* London, 1759; rpt. Manchester: Manchester University Press, 1918.

──────. *The Universal Passion. In seven Characteristical satyrs.* London, 1750.

──────. *A vindication of providence: or, a true estimate of human life. In which the passions are consider'd in a new light. Preach'd in St. George's church . . .* London, 1728.

──────. *The Works of the Author of Night-Thoughts.* 4 vols. London, 1757.

Young, George. *A Treatise on Opium, founded upon practical observations.* London, 1753.

Zückert, J. F. *Von den Leidenschaften.* 2nd edn. Berlin, 1768.

Zwinger, Theodor. *Compendium medicinae universae . . . institutiones chymiam, pharmiciam, et praxim medicam succincte tradens.* Basel, 1724.

Zyl, D. van. *De memoria, ejusque vitiis.* London, 1694.

INDEX

Aaron, Richard: 103, 104, 107, 122n.
Aarsleff, Hans: 283, 290 (quoted), 300n, 301n.
Abrams, M. H.: 222n, 300n, 301n.
absolute beauty: 156, 157, 165n. See also: beauty, relative beauty.
Académie française: 245.
accountability: see personal identity and moral accountability, dreams and accountability.
action theory: 16. See also: animal spirits, body, motion, nervous system, physiology.
Adair, James: 20n.
Addison, Joseph: 149–64, 164n, 165n–166n, 171–172, 179–180, 187, 193n, 195n, 236, 248, 264, 288, 301n; and beauty, 149–163; and deformity, 154; and faculties of mind, 151, 152, 153, 165n; and imagination, 149–154, 155, 165n, 166n, 180; and matter, 154; and nature, 151; and the senses, 152, Works: *Cato*, 264; "The Pleasures of the Imagination," 149, 152, 159. See also: *The Spectator, Tatler*.
aesthetic relativism: 165n.
aesthetics: see beauty, psychology and aesthetic response.
affections: 206. See also: passion.
affectivity: 201, 202, 205.
Aikins, Janet E.: 15.
Albrecht, W. P.: 165n.
Allen, Dr. Thomas: 75, 76, 77, 78, 79.
ambition, pleasures of: 199, 201, 211, 220n. See also:
intellectual pleasures.
Amyraldus, Moses: 170–171, 177, 181, 192n, 194n, 195n. Works: *A Discourse Concerning the Divine Dreams Mention'd in Scripture*, 170–171, 181.
anatomy: 5, 6, 18n, 242. See also: body, motion, physiology.
animal dreams: 173, 193n. See also: celestial dreams, dreams, natural dreams.
animal spirits: 6, 7, 15, 112, 113, 125n, 131, 132, 136, 141, 144n, 227, 230, 231, 232, 241, 247, 248; and brain, 6, 113, 131; and delusion, 132; in dreaming, 15; and "explosive particles," 231; and "hypochondriacal affections," 241; and hysteria, 131, 132, 136; and imagination, 113, 136; and insanity, 141, 144n; and melancholy, 144n, 232; and motion, 6, 112; and nervous system, 6, 144n, 230, 231, 247; and perception, 15; and senses, 131, 132, 144n; and spleen, 248. See also: "brain-traces."
Anne, Queen (of England): 236.
anthropology: 18n.
Anthropologie Abstracted: 6, 8–9.
antonomasia: 293. See also: figurative language.
apparitions: 171, 178. See also: delusion, dreams, phantasms.
Appleyard, J. A.: 220n.
Arbuthnot, John: 7, 19n, 243, 244, 262. Works: *An Essay concerning the*

INDEX

Nature of Aliments, 7, 243; *Memoirs of Scriblerus*, 7.
architecture: 58, 59, 60, 67n, 149, 153; baroque, 58; classical, 149; Gothic, 149, 153; and mental states, 58, 59, 60, 67n; Palladian, 58; Roman, 149.
Aristotle: 3, 12, 33, 150, 155, 162, 168, 204, 227, 233, 237, 279, 281, 296, 299n. Works: *The Art of Rhetoric*, 12; *Memory and Reminiscence*, 3; *On the Soul*, 3; *Parva Naturalia*, 3; *Sense and its Objects*, 3.
Armstrong, John: 246, 247. Works: *The Art of Preserving Health*, 246.
Armstrong, Paul: 299n.
Arnold, Matthew: 297.
Arnold, Dr. Thomas: 10.
Artaud, Antonin: 62, 67n.
Artemidorus: 167 (quoted), 171, 172, 181, 182, 187, 191, 192n, 193n, 194n 195n, 197n.
Arthos, John: 27, 47n.
assent: 107, 108, 116, 118.
association: 6, 15, 21n, 55, 56, 85n–86n, 103–122, 122n, 123n, 158, 159, 165n, 174, 175, 199–219, 220n, 221n, 222n, 223n, 261, 282, 296; and aesthetic response, 159; and custom, 111, 112, 117, 120, 121, 158, 204; and dreams, 174, 175; and education, 119–120, 158; and error, 106, 107, 109, 111, 123n; and faculties of mind, 112; and Hartley, 199–219, 220n, 221n, 222n, 223n; and Hume, 116–122; and Hutcheson, 158, 159; and imagination, 296; and language, 85n–86n, 106, 205, 208, 210; and Locke, 103–122, 122n; and matter, 158; and mechanism, 120, 121, 219, 221n; and reason, 112, 114, 120, 204; and senses, 165n; and Sterne, 261; and the unconscious, 15; and vibrations, 202, 205, 210, 219. See also: coalescence.
assurance: 117.
astrology: see spleen and astrology.

asyndeton: 284.
Aubrey, John: 171, 174, 192n, 195n. Works: *Miscellanies*, 174.
Auden, W. H.: 234.
Augustine: 4; influence of, 27, 264.
Austen, Jane: 27, 36, 42, 44–46, 46n, 186. Works: *Emma*, 44; *Mansfield Park*, 44, 45; *Northanger Abbey*, 24, 45; *Sense and Sensibility*, 46.
Austin, Gilbert: 12. Works: *Chironomia*, 12.
authorial intention, problem of: 260.
"automatical man": 7. See also: body as machine, mechanical man, mechanism.

Babb, Lawrence: 145n.
Backscheider, Paula R.: 196n.
Bacon, Francis: 87, 280, Works: *New Organon*, 87.
Bailey, Nathan: 47n.
Baine, Rodney M.: 193n.
Bakhtin, Mikhail: 67n.
Balguy, John: 5.
Ball, John: 132. Works: *The Modern Practice of Physic*, 132.
ballads: and Addison, 149, 159.
Balthus, Jean François: 174, 194n.
Balz, Albert G. A.: 17n.
Banister, J.: 226, 256n.
Barrow, Isaac: 95, 96, 97, 101n.
Barthes, Roland: 67n.
Bate, Walter Jackson: 42.
Battestin, Martin: 273n.
Battie, William: 10, 13, 20n, 21n.
Baxter, Andrew: 168, 171, 174, 176, 178, 179, 185, 187, 191n, 192n, 194n, 195n, 196n. Works: *An Enquiry into the Nature of the Human Soul*, 171.
Baxter, Richard: 145n, 193n, 195n, 197n.
Baudelaire, Charles: 255. Works: *Spleen et Idéal*, 255 (quoted).
Beard, George: 245, 257n.
Beare, Dr. Matthew: 274n.
Beattie, James: 5, 18n, 277, 278, 279,

INDEX 349

285, 287, 288–289, 300n–301n.
Works: *Elements of Moral Science*, 5;
Essays on Poetry and Music As They Affect the Mind, 279, 287; *The Minstrel*, 277 (quoted).
Beauchamp, Tom L.: 127n.
Beaumont, John: 194n, 195n.
beauty: 149–164, 205, 206, 211, 213, 254, 287, 288; and Addison, 149–164; artificial, 211, 213; and custom, 158, 159; definition of, 159; and education, 158, 159; and Hartley, 205, 206, 211, 213; and Hutcheson, 154–164; and Keats, 254; and matter, 154; natural, 211, 213; personal, 206; and rhetoric, 287, 299. See also: absolute beauty, psychology and aesthetic response, relative beauty.
Bedlam: see Bethlehem Hospital.
Bedlamite poems: 70–71.
Behan, David P.: 21n, 48n, 49n, 74, 85n.
benevolence: 46, 161, 163, 200, 201, 207, 211, 213–214, 265, 270.
Berkeley, Bishop George: 5, 10, 41, 264.
bestiality: 93; and insanity, 55.
bête machine: 267. See also: body as machine, **Cartesianism, Descartes, mechanism.**
Bethlehem Hospital (Bedlam): 70, 74, 76, 79, 80, 81, 106, 141, 234.
Bevilacqua, Vincent M.: 298n.
Bible: 32, 33, 194n, 288, 298; and prophetic dreams, 194n.
Bishop of Beller: 295.
Blackmore, Sir Richard: 10, 20n, 132, 137, 144n, 145n, 240–241, 243, 244, 257n. Works: *The Creation*, 240 (quoted); *A Treatise of the Spleen and Vapours*, 137, 240, 241, (quoted).
Blair, Hugh: 278, 279, 280, 281, 284, 286, 287, 288, 291, 297, 299n, 300n, 301n. Works: *Lectures on Rhetoric and Belles Lettres*, 279, 280, 281, 288.
Blake, William: 31–32, 33, 36, 37, 45, 48n. Works: "Mary," 32 (quoted).
Bloomfield, Morton W.: 300n.
Blount, Thomas: 47n.
blushing: 24, 35–36, 37, 46. See also: body, gesture.
Boccaccio: 46n.
body: 5, 6, 7, 112, 113, 114, 115, 131, 132, 144n, 173, 199, 200, 201, 202, 203, 210, 218, 219, 230, 242, 243, 261, 262–263, 264, 265, 266, 267, 268, 269, 270, 272, 274n–275n; as machine, 6, 7, 230, 242, 243, 261, 262, 265, 266; and mind, 6, 7, 112, 113, 114, 115, 131, 132, 144n, 173, 199, 200, 201, 202, 203, 210, 218, 219, 243, 261, 262–63, 264, 265, 267, 269, 270, 272, 274n–275n; and motion, 5, 6; and soul, 203, 264, 268, 269. See also: convulsions, gesture, mechanism, nervous system, physiology.
Boerhaave, Herman: 7, 19n, 267; influence of, 265.
Boileau-Despréaux, Nicolas: 164n.
Bond, William: 193n.
Booker, John: 192n.
Booth, Wayne C.: 260, 273n, 298n.
Boswell, James: 246, 252–253. Works: *The Hypochondriack*, 246, 253.
Boulton, James T.: 65n.
Boyer, A.: 125n.
Bradstreet, Anne: 228–229. Works: *Of the Four Humours in Man's Constitution*, 228–229 (quoted).
Brady, Frank: 273n.
brain: 6, 7, 113, 130, 131, 132, 141, 202, 203, 207, 210, 213, 220n, 226, 228, 230, 231–232, 242, 262, 268, 275n; and animal spirits, 6, 113, 131; and Hartley, 202, 203, 207, 210, 213, 220n; and hysteria, 130, 131; and imagination, 113; and insanity, 141; and language, 210; and logic, 210; and melancholy, 228, 231–232; and mental disorder, 242; and mind, 242; and

motion, 6; and nervous system, 6, 130, 131, 210, 230, 262, 275n; and pleasure, 207, 213; and sensation, 203; and senses, 131, 132; and soul, 230, 262; and spleen, 226. See also: "brain-traces".
"brain-traces": 15, 113–114, 141, 219.
Branch, Thomas:171, 174–175, 192n, 196n.
Braudy, Leo: 261.
Bright, Timothy: 194n, 195n 225–226, 227, 243, 256n. Works: *A Treatise on Melancholie*, 225–226 (quoted), 227.
Brissenden, R. F.: 191n.
Brody, Baruch A.: 85n.
Bromhall, Thomas: 195n.
Brooks, Cleanth: 164n.
Broome, William: 48n.
Broughton, John: 4. Works: *Psychologia; Or, An Account of the Nature of the Rational Soul*, 4.
Brown, Marshall: 47n.
Brown, Theodore: 18n.
Browne, Sir Thomas: 173, 176, 177, 193n, 194n.
Browne, Thomas Gunter: 301n.
Browning, Robert: 296.
Brydall, John: 2. Works: *Non Compos Mentis*, 2.
Buckingham, George Villiers, 2nd Duke of: 79.
Budgell, Eustace: 246.
Buickerood, James G.: 16, 18n, 22n, 124n.
Burke, Edmund: 276n.
Burtt, E. A.: 17n.
Burthogge, Richard: 178, 187, 194n.
Burton, Robert: 54, 126n, 131, 134, 135, 143n, 144n, 145n, 171, 173, 192n, 193n, 195n, 226–228, 229, 232, 235, 240, 254, 256n. Works: *The Anatomy of Melancholy*, 131, 226–228 (quoted).
Butler, Joseph: 5, 10, 40, 48n, 49n.
Butler, Samuel: 279. Works: *Hudibras*, 279 (quoted).
Byrd, Max: 66n.

Byron, George Gordon, Lord: 292, 294. Works: *Childe Harold's Pilgrimage*, 292 (quoted), 294; *Don Juan*, 294 (quoted).

Caesar, Julius: 74, 293.
Calmeil, L. F.: 232, 256n.
Calvinism: 228, 249.
Cambridge Platonists: 15.
Campbell, Duncan: 171–172, 180, 193n.
Campbell, George: 3, 5, 6, 11, 17n, 20n, 278, 279, 282–283, 284, 287, 290, 291–292, 293, 294, 295–296, 297, 298n, 299n, 300n, 301n. Works: *The Philosophy of Rhetoric*, 3, 278, 279, 282–283, 290, 291–292 (quoted), 295–296 (quoted).
Cardan: 171, 192n.
Carey, Thomas: 246.
Carkesse, James: 70–84, 84n, 234, 256n. Works: *Lucida Intervalla*, 70–84 (quoted passim), 234 (quoted).
Carlson, E. T.: 19n, 256n.
Carter, Elizabeth ("Eliza"): 239. Works: *Ode to Melancholy*, 239.
Cartesianism: 4, 107, 193n, 262, 264, 265, 266, 267, 268; and critique of Augustine, 4; and ideas of space and body, 107; reaction against, 267. See also: Descartes.
Cash, Arthur Hill: 260–261, 273n.
Casmann, Otto: 18n.
Castle, Terry: 168, 169, 188, 189, 191n.
Cato: 173.
Caton, Hiram: 124n.
causality: 65, 112, 116, 117, 118, 119, 120, 121, 122, 182, 189, 201, 202, 203, 204, 212, 214, 216, 218. See also: mechanism and causality, nature and causality.
celestial dreams: 173, 174, 179, 180, 193n. See also: animal dreams, dreams, natural dreams.
celibacy: see hysteria and sexual abstinence, melancholy and sexual

INDEX

abstinence, mental disorder and sexual abstinence.
Cervantes [Saavedra], Miguel de: 64. Works: *Don Quixote*, 54, 64, 74.
Chadwick, Joseph: 261, 273n.
chagrin d'amour: 227.
Chambers, Ephraim: 18n, 122n, 173. Works: *Cyclopaedia*, 173.
Chambre, Marin Cureau de la: 89, 90, 100n. Works: *The Character of the Passions*, 89.
chapbooks: and dreams, 171, 193n.
Charcot, Jean Martin: 230, 231.
Chatterton, Thomas: 246.
chemistry: 264.
Cheyne, George: 5, 13, 21n, 172, 173, 193n, 229, 241, 243–244, 245, 248, 252, 254, 257n, 262–263, 273n–274n. Works: *The English Malady*, 243–244 (quoted), 262–263 (quoted); *An Essay of Health and Long Life*, 243.
Christensen, Jerome: 220n.
Christ's Hospital: 241.
Church Fathers: 4, 17n.
Church of England: 71, 78–79, 268.
Cibber, Colley: 249. Works: *The Double Gallant, or the Sick Lady's Cure*, 249.
Cicero: 74, 174, 181, 279.
Clark, John: 10.
Clarke, Samuel: 14, 16, 21n, 121, 261, 264, 268; controversy with Leibniz, 261, 264.
Clarkson, Thomas: 49n.
classical rhetoric: 260, 270, 279, 296, 298n. See also: rhetoric.
classical styles of art: 153. See also: architecture.
coalescence: 14, 199–219, 222n. See also: Hartley, language and coalescence, religion and coalescence, vibrations and coalescence.
Coleridge, Samuel Taylor: 40, 41, 43–44, 49n–50n, 221n 253, 276n, 283, 285, 287, 288, 393, 299n–300n. Works: *Biographia Literaria*, 283, 288; *Dejection: An Ode*, 253 (quoted).
Collins, Anthony: 81.
Collins, William: 246, 251, 264.
Colman, George: 249. Works: *The Spleen, or Islington Spa*, 249.
Colombière, March de Vulson Sieur de la: 195n.
Comenius: 275n.
common sense: 125n.
commune sensorium: see sensorium.
compassion: 93, 160, 162. See also: sympathy.
Condillac, Etienne Bonnot de: 12, 20n, 275n, 283, 290.
conjecture: 55.
conscia virtus: 30, 32, 33, 44–45, 47n.
conscience: 26, 27, 29, 33, 37, 38, 48n.
conscious: 14, 15, 23–46, 242; and conscience, 26, 27; and guilt, 24, 27; and innocence, 24, 30; problem of defining, 23–28; and sexual sin, 28; as shared knowledge and solitary knowledge, 24.
consciousness: 13, 14, 15, 16, 21n, 29, 31–33, 34, 35, 39–41, 43, 44, 45, 47n, 48n, 49n, 50n, 64, 69, 71, 72, 74, 75, 76, 79, 81, 82, 84, 86n, 163, 175, 177, 200, 217–218, 267, 283, 285; and actions, 217; in Austen, 44, 45; and Blake, 32, 33; and confusion of terms, 13, 14; and delusion, 72; and Descartes' *bête machine*, 267; and dreams, 15, 40, 74; and guilt, 29, 32, 44; and Hartley, 200, 217–218; human and divine, 200, 218; and Hutcheson, 163; and imagination, 40, 79; and insanity, 74, 76, 79, 82; and Kant, 41; and language, 64; and Locke, 49n, 69, 71, 74, 76; and memory, 40, 47n, 49n; and personal identity, 21n, 39–41, 48n, 49n, 64, 69, 71, 72, 74, 75, 76, 79, 81, 82, 84, 86n, 177; and rhetoric, 283, 285; and sensation, 13, 40; and sensibility, 34; and sentimentality, 35; and soul, 15; and spirituality,

352 INDEX

43; and Steele, 31–33, 50n; and thought, 217. See also: personal identity.
contemplation: 160, 178.
convulsions: 131, 132, 231, 236; and hysteria, 131, 236.
corpuscular theory: 274n.
Cowper, William: 24, 28–29, 34, 46n, 246, 252 (quoted), 264. Works: *The Task*, 28–29 (quoted), 34, 252.
Cranston, Maurice: 123n.
Crawford, Charles: 4, 18n. Works: *Dissertation On The Phaedon of Plato*, 4.
Crichton, Dr. Alexander: 10, 11, 13, 20n, 21n. Works: *An Inquiry Into the Nature and Origin of Mental Derangement*, 10.
Crombie, A. C.: 19n.
Cudworth, Ralph: 14, 18n, 49n, 87, 95, 100n, 101n, 175, 176, 194n, 196n. Works: *A Treatise Concerning Eternal and Immutable Morality*, 175 (quoted); *The True Intellectual System of the Universe*, 14, 95 (quoted).
Cullen, William: 14, 21n, 143n, 145n, 245. Works: *First Lines of the Practice of Physic*, 14, 245.
Culler, Jonathan: 290, 295 (quoted), 298n–299n, 301n.
curiosity: 60.
custom: 110–111, 112, 116, 117, 118, 120, 121, 125n, 152, 158, 159, 204; and association, 111, 112, 117, 120, 121, 158, 204; and beauty, 158, 159; and belief, 120; and enthusiasm, 110; and error, 110–111, 112, 125n; and Hume, 116, 117, 118, 120, 121; and Hutcheson, 158, 159; and Locke, 110, 111, 112 116, 125n; and prejudice, 112, 116; and probability, 117, 118, 121; and reason, 116, 118; and taste, 152. See also: education.

Damrosch, Leopold: 288, 300n.

Dante: 99, 263.
D'Assigny, Marius: 12. Works: *The Art of Memory*, 12.
deadly sins: as modern psychological disorders, 21n.
Defoe, Daniel: 174, 176, 177, 178, 179, 193n, 194n, 195n. Works: *An Essay on the History and Reality of Apparitions*, 176, 177.
deformity: 154, 157, 158, 160. See also: matter and deformity.
delight: 150.
Delkeskamp, Corinna: 220n–221n.
delusion: 10, 51, 69–84, 84n–85n, 105–106, 114, 115, 131, 132–133, 136–37, 173, 179, 180–81, 182, 197n, 216, 237, 271, 292; and animal spirits, 132; and communication, 292; and dreaming, 173, 180–181, 182, 197n; and faculties of mind, 71, 72, 115; and finite and infinite beings, 216; in Godwin, 51; in Hartley, 216; and humoral tradition, 75; and hysteria, 131, 132–133, 136–137; and identity, 10, 72–76, 78, 81, 82, 83, 84, 84n–85n, 137; and imagination, 51, 72 114, 115, 132, 136–137, 179, 271; and Locke, 71, 81, 82, 115; and melancholy, 237; and physiology, 182; and reason, 105–106, 114, 115; of religious fanatics, 105; in Swift, 69, 80–84; in Tom o'Bedlam songs, 70–71. See also: enthusiasm, insanity, personal identity.
dementia: 226. See also: insanity.
Denham, John: 34. Works: *Cooper's Hill*, 34.
Deporte, Michael V.: 11, 17, 66n, 84n, 122n, 123n, 124n, 125n, 126n, 256n.
Derrida, Jacques: 289, 301n.
Descartes, René: 4, 5, 6–7, 17n, 19n, 108, 124n, 125n, 126n, 150, 176, 267; and cross-eyed women, 6; and Galen, 19n; influence of, 4, 7, 17n, 108, 124n; on mind and

body, 6; and sense perception, 176; and the workings of the eye, 19n; Works: *The Passions of the Soul*, 6; *Principles of Philosophy*, 108 (quoted); *Treatise of Man*. 6. See also: Cartesianism.
desire: 43, 163.
determinism: 107, 202, 210, 261, 268.
Dewhurst, Kenneth: 84n, 123n, 230, 256n.
dialogic novel: 64, 67n.
Dickens, Charles: 35–36. Works: *Bleak House*, 252; *Our Mutual Friend*, 35–36 (quoted).
Diderot, Denis: 11–12, 20n.
diet: and dreams, 173, 174; and vapors, 143n.
Dilworth, Ernest Nevin: 261.
Dionysus of Halicarnassus: 279.
distraction: 55.
Ditton, Humphrey: 5.
Doddridge, Philip: 5–6, 7–10, 18n. Works: *A Course of Lectures on the Principal Subjects in Pneumatology, Ethics, and Divinity*, 5, 7.
Donne, John: 92, 96, 100n.
Doody, Margaret Anne: 191n, 196n.
double personality: 74, 84n.
Drage, William: 85n.
dramatic poetry: Hutcheson on, 160, 161.
dreams: 15, 40, 55, 74, 167–191, 193n, 194n, 196n, 197n, 238; and accountability, 176–177; and age, 173; and animal spirits, 15; and association, 174, 175; causes of, 173–174, 194n; and consciousness, 15, 40, 74; definition of, 172–173; and delusion, 173, 180–181, 182, 197n; and diet, 173, 174; and eighteenth-century chapbooks, 171, 193n; and enthusiasm, 180, 181, 182; and faculties of mind, 178, 179; in Godwin, 55; and hypochondriasis, 181; and identity, 176–177; and imagination, 172, 175, 176, 177, 178, 179, 180, 182, 185, 187, 188, 191; and insanity, 177, 178, 188; interpretation of, 167–91 (passim); and melancholy, 173, 238; and memory, 178; and mental disorder, 55; and nature, 175, 176; and physiology, 15, 173, 180–181, 182; and probability, 176, 180, 182, 188–190; prophetic, 169, 180, 181, 182, 188, 194n; and reality, 74, 176–177, 187, 196n; in Richardson, 167–191; and sensation, 176; and the senses, 176, 193n; and soul, 171, 172, 176, 178, 179, 182, 193n; structure of, 174–175, 181, 185; and the supernatural, 169, 173–174, 179, 180, 181, 182, 193n, 194n; threefold division of, 193n; types of, 180–181. See also: animal dreams, celestial dreams, natural dreams, nightmares, oneirocriticism.
drugs: 12, 20n–21n. See also: pharmacology.
Dryden, John: 24, 25, 28, 30, 32–33 (quoted), 34, 37, 39, 42, 46n, 47n, 49n, 79, 82–83, 86n, 282, 287. Works: *Aeneid* (translation), 25 (quoted); *Astraea Redux*, 34; *Aureng-Zebe*, 30, 37; "Canace to Macareus" (translation), 28; "Helen to Paris" (translation), 28; *The Hind and the Panther*, 30; *The Spanish Friar*, 82–83 (quoted).
du Laurens, André: 115.
Dumas, Gilbert D.: 65n.
Duncan, William: 5.
Dussinger, John: 7, 273n.
Dutch Reformed Church: 228.
Dyche, Thomas: 47n.

Eagleton, Terry: 169–170 (quoted), 191n.
education: 110, 111, 112, 119–120, 152, 158, 159, 297; and association, 119–120, 158; and beauty, 158, 159; and enthusiasm, 110; and error, 110, 111, 112; and Hume, 119–120; and Hutcheson,

158, 159; and Locke, 110, 111, 112; and the New Rhetoricians, 297; and prejudice, 112; and taste, 152. See also: custom.
Eighteenth-Century Short Title Catalogue: 4.
electricity: and nerves, 231, 247.
elements: 229. See also: humoral tradition.
Elioseff, Lee Andrew: 164n.
Eliot, T. S.: 247, 294–295, 300n. Works: *Burnt Norton*, 294–295, (quoted).
Eliza: see Carter, Elizabeth.
Elizabeth, Queen (of England): 74.
Elizabethans: and supernatural, 85n.
Ellmann, Richard: 74, 85n.
Elyot, Sir Thomas: 227. Works: *Castel of Helth*, 227.
Emerson, Ralph Waldo: 294. Works: "The Poet," 294.
emotion: 12, 26, 226, 282, 296. See also: feeling, hysteria, passions, and sensibility.
Empson, William: 38, 49n.
enargeia: 161.
Engell, James: 3, 11, 42, 49n, 220n.
enormôn: 267–68, 272, 274n. See also: nervous system.
enthusiasm: 55, 56, 79, 82, 86n, 105, 109–110, 112, 115, 124n, 126n, 170, 173, 180, 181, 182, 228, 242; and custom, 110; and delusion, 105; and dreams, 180, 181, 182; and education, 110; and faculties of mind, 115; and imagination, 126n, 173; and insanity, 79, 82, 115, 126n, 242; and Locke, 56, 86n, 105, 109–110, 112, 115, 124n; and melancholia, 228, 242; and reason, 115. See also: melancholy, religion.
epic poetry: Addison on, 149, 159, 164n; Hutcheson on, 160, 161, 163.
Epictetus: 264.
epilepsy: and melancholia, 227.
epistemology: 16, 118, 120, 123n, 124n, 220n. See also: Hume, Locke, logic.
error: 55, 100n, 105, 106, 107, 108, 109, 110, 111, 113, 114, 115, 116, 122, 123n, 125n. See also: custom and error, education and error, imagination and error, language and error.
Essay on Consciousness, An: 14, 40, 74, 79, 175 (quoted).
Eustace, Dr. John: 260, 273n.

faculties on mind: 4, 5, 16, 53, 56, 71, 72, 80, 88, 105, 106, 107, 111, 112, 115, 116, 120, 123n, 126n, 150, 151, 152, 153, 165n, 178, 179, 213, 226, 267; in Addison, 151, 152, 153, 165n; and association, 112; and delusion, 71, 72, 115; and dreams, 178, 179; eighteenth-century study of, 4, 5, 16; and *enormôn*, 267;and enthusiasm, 115; and error, 107, 111; and Hartley, 213; and Hume, 116, 120; and insanity, 105, 106, 123n, 126n; in Locke, 5, 105, 106, 107, 111, 112; and melancholy, 226; and pleasure, 152, 153; and reader response, 150; and soul, 151. See also: faculty psychology, imagination, judgment, logic, memory, mind, reason, reflection, soul, understanding.
faculty psychology: 150.
Fairchild, Hoxie N.: 221n.
Falret, J. P.: 232, 256n.
family: in eighteenth century, 13.
fancy: 29, 39, 42, 43, 55, 71, 72, 153, 172, 175, 188, 212, 242; and aesthetic response, 153; and the creative process, 39, 42; and dreams, 172, 188; and Dryden, 39, 42; in Godwin, 55; and insanity, 71, 72; and Hartley, 212; and memory, 71, 72; and phantasms, 175; pleasures of, 43; in Richardson, 188; and spleen, 242. See also: imagination.
fantasies: see phantasms.

INDEX 355

Farquhar, George: 237. Works: *The Beaux' Stratagem*, 237.
fatuitas: 123n.
Feder, Lillian: 66n, 85n.
feeling: 37, 163, 200–201, 259, 284; defined in Hartley, 200–201. See also: hysteria and emotional instability, mechanism and feeling, passions, sensibility.
Felltham, Owen: 177, 179, 180, 194n, 195n.
Ferg, Stephen: 221n, 223n.
Ferrier, James Frederick: 16. Works: *Institutes of Metaphysic*, 16.
Ficino, Marsilio: 227.
Figlio, Karl M.: 19n.
Fielding, Henry: 64, 133, 145, 183, 196n, 248. Works: *Amelia*, 133 (quoted), 248; "An Essay on the Knowledge of the Characters of Men," 183.
figurative language: 154, 157, 208–209, 210, 277, 278, 283, 284, 286, 287, 293, 296, 300n–301n. See also: imagination and figurative language, language, rhetoric.
Finch, Anne, Countess of Winchilsea: 146n, 237–238, 239, 240, 248, 250, 253, 257n. Works: *The Spleen: A Pindarique Ode*, 237–238 (quoted), 239, 248.
Finsbury Madhouse: 70, 76, 77.
Fischer-Homberger, Esther: 15, 21n.
fixed ideas: 106, 114.
Flemyng, Malcolm: 247–248, 274n–275n. Works: *Neuropathia*, 247.
Flynn, Carol Houlihan: 191n.
folk medicine: 12, 21n.
folly: 123n.
Fontenelle, Bernard de: 195n.
force motrice: 267, 272.
Ford, Stephen: 14.
Foucault, Michel: 13, 66n, 234, 256n, 263 (quoted), 274n.
Fox, Christopher: 48n, 49n, 69–70, 84n, 85n.
Freke, William: 180, 181, 195n.

French, Roger Kenneth: 19n.
frenzy: 55, 227, 232. See also: delusion, insanity.
Freud, Sigmund: 6, 15, 38–39, 42, 44, 49n, 169, 170, 186, 230; on hysteria in men, 230.
Frye, Northrop: 281.
"fusing": 221n. See also: coalescence.

Gadamer, Hans-Georg: 271, 275n.
Galen: 19n, 114, 125n, 130, 131, 143n, 225, 267. See also: humoral tradition.
Galvani, Luigi: 231.
Garth, Sir Samuel: 246.
Gassendi, Pierre: 89, 268.
Gaub, Jerome: 7, 19n, 267–268, 270, 274n. Works: *De regimine mentis quod medicorum est*, 267. See also: "neural man".
Gay, John: 243. Works: *The Beggar's Opera*, 139.
Genette, Gérard: 197n.
gesture: 11–12, 269, 273. See also: blushing, body.
ghosts: 178. See also: apparitions.
Gibbons, Thomas: 278, 279, 283, 286, 288, 300n, 301n. Works: *Rhetoric*, 279.
Gibson, James: 103, (quoted), 104, 107, 108, 109, 122n, 124n.
Gildon, Charles: 194n.
Gingerich, S. F.: 221n.
Giuntini, Chiara: 221n.
Glanvill, Joseph: 171, 173–174, 179, 182, 194n, 195n, 197n.
Glisson, Francis: 267. See also: irritability.
Godwin: 51–65, 66n, 67n; and delusion, 51; and dreams, 55; and fancy, 55; and identity, 57, 58, 60, 64; and insanity, 51–52, 55, 58, 62; and language, 57, 60, 63; and mechanism, 65; and reason, 55. Works: *Caleb Williams*, 11, 51–65, (quoted passim); *Political Justice*, 53, 59, 64–65, (quoted).
Gold, Alex, Jr.: 65n, 66n, 67n.

Goldsmith, Oliver: 246, 248, 285. Works: *The Citizen of the World*, 248.
Goodwin, Philip: 170, 177, 179, 181, 182, 186, 191n, 193n, 194n, 195n. Works: *The Mystery of Dreams. Historically Discoursed*, 181.
Gothic conventions: 251; in architecture, 149; in poetry, 153, 251. See also: Graveyard School of Poetry.
Gott, Samuel: 88, 89, 100n. Works: *The Divine History of the Genesis of the World*, 88, 89 (quoted).
Gower, John: 232.
Grange, Kathleen M.: 11, 20n.
Graveyard School of Poetry: 239, 246, 251. See also: melancholy and Graveyard School of Poets.
Gray, Thomas: 28, 34, 245, 246, 250 (quoted), 251, 252, 264. Works: *Elegy Written in a Country Church-Yard*, 34, 250.
Gregory, Dr. John: 21n.
Green, Matthew: 246–47, 250. Works: *The Spleen*, 246–47 (quoted).
Greene, Donald: 21n, 27, 47n.
Greuze, Jean-Baptiste: 36.
grief: and melancholy, 153.
Gross, Harvey: 65n.
guilt: 27, 29 36, 37, 60, 65. See also: conscience, consciousness and guilt, sexuality and guilt.

habit: see custom.
Hagstrum, Jean H.: 13, 14–15, 47n, 48n, 50n.
Hall, T. S.: 19n.
Haller, Albrecht von: 7, 19n, 267.
hallucinations: 131, 133, 140, 238; and hysteria, 131, 133. See also: delusion, phantasms.
Hamilton, Sir William: 3, 4, 17n, 18n. Works: *Lectures on Metaphysics and Logic*, 3.
harmony: 155, 157, 158.
Harris, James: 290. Works: *Hermes*, 290.
Harth, Phillip: 126n.
Hartley, David: 3–4, 11, 17n, 66n, 199–219, 220n, 221n, 222n, 223n, 261, 262, 263, 274n, 275n; on animals, 220n; and association, 199–219 (passim), 220n, 221n, 222n, 223n; and beauty, 205, 206, 211, 213; chiliastic views of, 222n; and coalescence, 199–219; and consciousness, 200, 217–218; and delusion, 216; and faculties of mind, 213; and imagination, 199, 201, 211, 212, 213; and language, 199, 205, 208–210, 214, 221n; and mechanism, 201, 203, 219, 220n, 221n; moral and theological holism of, 220n; and passion, 206; physiology of, 199, 200, 202, 203, 205, 210, 212, 213, 222n; and reason, 204, 210; and religion, 100, 206, 211, 213, 214, 220n; and the senses, 222n; and sensation, 199–218 (passim); on vibrations, 202, 203, 204, 205, 210, 217, 219, 220n, 222n, 223n, 261. Works: *Observations on Man, His Frame, His Duty and His Expectations*, 199–219 (quoted passim), 262.
Harvey, William: 230, 247.
Hatch, Ronald B.: 221n.
Hathaway, Baxter: 165n.
Haven, Richard: 221n.
Hawkins, John: 48n.
Hayley, William: 48n.
Haywood, Eliza ("Justicia"): 174, 193n, 194n.
Hazlitt, William: 282, 284, 285, 298; and "gusto," 285.
headache and side pains: as psychosomatic disorders, 235.
heartbreak: 10.
hemp: 20n–21n. See also: pharmacology.
Hervey, John, Baron: 243.
Hill, [Sir] John: 244, 257n. Works: *Hypochondriasis: A Practical Treatise*, 244.
Hill, Thomas: 170, 173, 178, 182,

187, 192n, 194n, 197n.
Hippocrates: 130, 131, 134, 143n, 267, 274n.
Hirschman, A. O.: 12.
Hobbes, Thomas: 12, 18n, 55, 66n, 88, 100n, 140–141, 150, 163, 171, 172, 173, 176–177, 178, 179, 193n–194n, 195n. Works: *Leviathan*, 140.
Hofer, Johannes: 21n.
Hogg, James: 84n.
Hogle, Jerrold E.: 65n, 66n.
Howell, Wilbur Samuel: 298n, 302n.
Homer: 35, 36, 176, 286. Works: *Iliad*, 36 (quoted); *Odyssey*, 35 (quoted).
l'homme machine: 266, 267. See also: body as machine, mechanism.
honor: 161, 205, 211, 220n; pleasures of, 211, 220n; sense of, 161. See also: *conscia virtus*.
Hooke, Robert: 12, 20n–21n.
Horace: 30, 57.
Hoskins, John: 283, 300n. Works: *Directions for Speech and Style*, 283.
Howell, James: 99, 101n.
Hughes, John: 194n.
Hughes, M. W.: 86n.
Hume, David: 4, 7, 10–11, 16, 17n, 19n, 20n, 30, 40, 47n–48n, 49n, 104, 109, 116–122, 126n, 127n, 162, 164, 165n, 189, 197n, 264, 281, 287; and association, 116–122; and custom, 116, 117, 118, 120, 121; and education, 119–120; and faculties of mind, 116, 120; and personal identity, 40; and nature, 119; and passion, 11; physiology of, 19n; and reason, 116, 120; and the senses, 119. Works: *Abstract of . . . A Treatise of Human Nature*, 116 (quoted); *Dialogues Concerning Natural Religion*, 121; *Enquiries Concerning Human Understanding*, 7; *An Enquiry Concerning the Principles of Morals*, 30 (quoted); *Of the Standard of Taste and Other Essays*, 281; *A Treatise of Human Nature*, 10–11,

116–122 (quoted passim).
humoral tradition: 21n, 55, 75, 82, 130, 131, 134, 143n, 225–229, 230–231, 236, 239, 240, 241, 244, 247, 250, 253; and animal spirits, 231; and delusion, 75; in Godwin, 55; and hysteria, 130, 131, 134, 143n; and insanity, 82; in Johnson, 253; and melancholy, 225–29, 230, 236, 239, 240, 241, 244, 250; and nervous system, 230–231; rejection of, 230, 239, 244; and spleen, 225–229, 230, 236, 239, 240, 241, 244, 247; in Swift, 82; waning of, 21n. See also: Galen, spleen, vapors.
Hunt, Everett: 302n.
Hunter, John: 241.
Huntingdon, Countess of: 243.
Hutcheson, Francis: 4, 5, 10, 11, 13, 20n, 21n, 149, 154–164, 165n; and association, 158, 159; and beauty, 154–164; and custom, 158, 159; and education, 158, 159; and nature, 156; and passion, 5, 160, 162; and reason, 161, 163; and sensation, 155, 156–157, 163; and the senses, 155, 158, 159–160, 161; and sensibility, 156, 161. Works: *An Essay on the Nature and Conduct of the Passions and Affections*, 13, 161; *An Inquiry Concerning Moral Good and Evil*, 160–161 (quoted); *An Inquiry into the Original of Our Ideas of Beauty and Virtue*, 154–164 (quoted passim).
Huxley, Aldous: 243. Works: *Brave New World*, 243.
hydrophobia: 227.
hypochondriasis: 14, 21n, 181, 230, 232–233, 239–240, 241, 244, 245, 247; case studies of patients suffering from, 233; causes of, 245; definition of, 14, 21n; and dreams, 181; and hysteria, 230, 232–233, 247; in males, 239–240; and melancholy, 227, 242; and nervous system, 241, 245, 247; and physiology, 239–240; and spleen,

244; symptoms of, 245. See also: hysteria, melancholia, melancholy, spleen, vapors.

hysteria: 13, 129–142, 143n, 144n, 145n, 230, 232, 233, 235, 247; and affectation, 139–140, 142; and brain, 130, 131; case studies of patients suffering from, 233; causes of, 130–132, 134–135, 144n; and class structure, 130, 134, 139, 235; and confusion of terms, 13; cures for, 131, 138–139; and delusion, 131, 132–133, 136–137; difficulty in defining nature of, 130; and eighteenth-century women, 129–130, 132, 134, 135, 142, 145n, 235; and emotional instability, 132, 135–136, 139, 140, 142; in Fielding, 133; and humoral tradition, 130, 131, 134, 143n; and hypochondriasis, 230, 232–233, 247; and imagination, 132; and insanity, 132, 136, 140, 142; marriage as a cure for, 131, 228; **and melancholy, 144n, 231–232; and nervous system, 130, 131, 230,** 245, 247; and physiology, 131; in Pope, 10, 129–142; and reason, 140; and self-love, 140–141; and sexual abstinence, 130, 131, 134, 145n; in Swift, 235; symptoms of, 131, 132–133, 135, 136, 142, 144n. See also: spleen, uterus.

"hysteroepilepsy": 231.

iatrophysical medicine: 134. See also: body, mechanism.

identity: see personal identity.

imaginary identities: 69–84, 92, 137, 145n. See also: delusion, personal identity.

imagination: 14, 40, 42, 43, 51, 53, 55, 71, 72, 79, 80, 83, 84, 84n, 87, 88, 89–95, 97, 99, 100n, 106, 113, 114–115, 125n, 126n, 132, 136–137, 141, 149–154, 155, 165n, 166n, 172, 173–174, 175, 176, 177, 178, 179, 180, 182, 185, 187, 188, 191, 199, 201, 211, 212, 213, 269, 271, 283, 284, 287, 296; in Addison, 149–154, 155, 165n, 166n, 180; and animal spirits, 113, 136; and association, 296; and brain, 113; and Coleridge, 43, 283; and confusion of terms, 14; and consciousness, 40, 79; and criticism, 283; and delusion, 51, 72, 114, 115, 132, 136–137, 179, 271; in Descartes, 126n; distinction between primary and secondary, 152; divine, 87, 99; in dreaming, 172, 175, 176, 177, 178, 179, 180, 182, 185, 187, 188, 191; and enthusiasm, 126n, 173; and error, 100n, 106; and figurative language, 284; in Hartley, 199, 201, 211, 212, 213; and hysteria, 132; and identity, 79, 84; and insanity, 71, 72, 84, 84n, 106, 113, 114, 115, 126n, 141, 188; in Johnson, 42; and language, 296; in Locke, 72, 106, 126n; and melancholia, 136–137; and melancholy, 114–115, 126n, 153; and memory, 71, 72, 83, 84n, 88, 99, 152, 178; and nature, 175; Neostoic view of, 100n; in Otway, 87–100; and perception, 87, 88, 90, 92, 93, 99; and phantasms, 89, 175; pleasures of, 149–154, 199, 201, 211, 212, 213; and reality, 72, 90, 187, 287; and reason, 53, 115, 126n, 284; and rhetoric, 284; Scholastic view of, 100n; and self-love, 55, 141; and sensation, 84n; and the senses, 72, 152; and soul, 151, 178; and spiritual good, 89–95, 97, 99; in Sterne, 269, 271; and supernatural influence, 173–174; in Swift, 80, 83, 84; and unconscious, 42; and understanding, 89, 150. See also: faculties of mind, fancy, logic, senses and primary and secondary imagination.

imitation: 156, 157. See also:

INDEX

mimesis.
impressions: 57, 179, 205, 210; defined, 210. See also: "imprints".
"imprints": 113.
incubus: 173. See also: delusion, dreams, phantasms.
infatuation: 55.
Ingram, Allen: 257n.
innate ideas: 56, 81, 105, 123n, 165n, 202.
insanity: 2, 13, 51–52, 54, 55, 58, 62, 69–84, 84n–85n, 98, 105–106, 113, 114–115, 116, 123n, 126n, 132, 136, 140–141, 142, 144n, 146n, 177, 178, 188, 227, 232, 233, 234, 242; and animal spirits, 141, 144n; and brain, 141; and consciousness, 74, 76, 79, 82; and dreams, 177, 178, 188; in Dryden, 82–83; and enthusiasm, 79, 82, 115, 126n, 242; and faculties of mind, 105, 106, 123n, 126n; in Godwin, 51–52, 55, 58, 62; and humors, 82; and hysteria, 132, 136, 140, 142; and identity, 69, 71–84, 84n–85n; and imagination, 71, 72, 84, 84n, 106, 113, 114, 115, 126n, 141, 188; and institutionalization, 13, 234; and law, 2, 72–74; and literature, 51, 54, 69–84, 98, 136; and Locke, 69, 71–74, 79, 81, 82, 83, 105–106, 114–115, 116, 123n; and melancholia, 227, 242; and melancholy, 114–115, 140, 144n, 232, 233; and memory, 71, 72, 84n; in Otway, 98; and passions, 82, 140; and physiology, 141; and poetry, 70–71, 75, 79; in Pope, 136, 140, 141; and prejudice, 116; and reason, 72, 105–106, 114, 115, 116, 123n, 126n; and religion, 71, 76–78, 115; in Richardson, 188; and ruling passions, 55; and self-love, 55, 80, 83, 84, 140–141, 146n; and sensation, 84n; and soul, 177, 178; and spleen, 234; in Swift, 69, 79–84, 146n; symptoms of, 85n; and Tom o'Bedlam songs, 70–71; treatment of, 75, 234. See also: Bethlehem Hospital, Carkesse, delusion, enthusiasm, Finsbury Hospital, mental disorder.
insomnia: 7, 238.
instinct: 154, 202.
intellectual pains: classes of, 199.
intellectual physics: 3.
intellectual pleasures: 199–201, 207; classes of, 199.
internal sense: 158, 165n.
intuitive knowledge: 107, 219.
irritability: 7, 241, 247, 267, 268. See also: body as machine, conscious, Glisson, mechanism, nervous system, physiology, sensation and sensibility.
Isler, Hansreudi: 230, 256n.

Jackson, John; 192n.
Jackson, Stanley W.: 18n, 19n.
James I, King (of England): 197n.
James II, King (of England): 238.
James, Robert: 10, 134, 143n, 144n, 145n. Works: *A Medicinal Dictionary*, 10.
Johnson, Samuel: 1–2, 5, 10, 11, 16, 18n, 26, 27, 29, 30, 33, 39, 42–44, 45, 47n, 49n, 60, 246, 252–253, 277, 281, 282, 285, 286, 287, 299n, 300n, 301n. Works: *Dictionary*, 2, 5, 29, 253; *Preface to Shakespeare*, 1, 282; *Rambler*, 43 (quoted); *Rasselas*, 11, 39, 51, 60.
Joly, André: 289–290.
Josipovici, Gabriel: 263.
Joyce, James: 248.
judgment: 42, 117, 118, 124n, 178, 185, 216, 226; and delusion, 216; Descartes's theory of, 124n.
Justicia: see Haywood, Eliza.

Kallich, Martin: 122n, 221n.
Kames, Henry Home, Lord: 11, 278, 279, 282, 287, 294, 300n. Works: *Elements of Criticism*, 279, 282.
Kant, Immanuel: 41, 49n.

360 INDEX

Keats, John: 254, (quoted), 255, 272, 285, 287. Works: "Ode to Melancholy," 254–255 (quoted); "Ode to a Nightingale," 272.
Keele, Kenneth David: 19n.
Keener, Frederick M.: 17.
Keill, James: 5. Works: *The anatomy of the human body, abridged*, 5.
Kelly, Gary: 65n.
Kennedy, George: 298n, 301n.
Killigrew, Sir William: 229. Works: *Pandora*, 229.
King, William: 192n.
King, Mrs. (née Margaret Deveille): 257n.
Kircher, Athanasius: 291.
Kivy, Peter: 165n.
Korshin, Paul: 183, 185, 196n.
Korsmeyer, Caroline Wilkes: 165n.
Kraepelin, Emil: 232. Works: *Lehrbuch*, 232.
Krieger, Murray: 146n.

Lamb, Jonathan: 221n, 261, 273n, 275n.
La Mettrie, Julien Offray de: 266, 267, 268. Works: *L'homme machine*, 266. See also: *l'homme machine*.
language: 11, 57, 60, 63, 64, 67n, 85n–86n, 106–107, 123n, 152, 199, 205, 208–210, 214, 221n, 260, 263, 270, 277–298, 300n; as arbitrary, 152, 263, 291, 293; and association, 85n–86n, 106, 205, 208, 210; and brain, 210; and coalescence, 205, 208–210; and consciousness, 64; and error, 123n; and fashion, 291; formation of, 208; and God, 209; in Godwin, 57, 60, 63; in Hartley, 199, 205, 208–210, 214, 221n; and identity, 57, 60, 63, 67n; and imagination, 296; and imitation, 285; inadequacies of, 270, 292, 294–295; indeterminacy of, 85n–86n, 106–107, 123n, 260; of liberty, 221n; and Locke, 85n–86n, 106–107, 123n; and logic, 199, 210; and mind, 11, 287, 290, 291, 293; and nature, 286, 287, 292, 296; of necessity, 221n; and the New Rhetoricians, 277–298; and passion, 284–285; and physiology, 210; and psychology, 57, 63, 208–210, 282, 283, 285, 296; and social happiness, 214; in Sterne, 221n, 270; in Swift, 291; and thought, 294, 300n. See also: figurative language, gesture, New Rhetoricians, rhetoric, terms in eighteenth century.
Lapointe, François: 2–3, 17n.
laughter: 229, 232, 241; and malice, 229; and melancholy, 232; and tears, 241.
Lawson, John: 278, 298n. Works: *Lectures Concerning Oratory*, 278.
Lebrun, Charles: 12. Works: *A Method to Learn the Design of the Passions*, 12.
Lee, Nathaniel: 74.
Leibniz, Gottfried Wilhelm: 15, 261, 264, 267, 275n; controversy with Clarke, 261, 264; and *force motrice*, 267.
Lemnius, Levinus: 227, 256n. Works: *The Touchstone of Complexions*, 227 (quoted).
Leslie, Margaret: 221n–222n.
L'Estrange, Sir Roger: 301n.
"leucocholy": 250.
Levi, Anthony, S. J.: 100n.
Levin, Harry: 299n.
Lewis, C. S.: 26, 29.
libertarianism: 221n.
Lilly, William: 171, 192n, 193n.
linguistics: 39, 41, 278, 283, 289, 290, 296.
literature: and medicine, 10, 129–142, 225–255, 262, 265, 269, 273n–274n; and moral philosophy, 10; and physiology, 10; and psychology, 7, 10, 11, 12, 54, 278. See also: insanity and literature.
Lloyd, Robert: 252.
Locke, John: 2, 4, 5, 6, 7, 11, 12, 13, 14, 16, 18n, 19n, 21n, 37, 40, 48n,

INDEX 361

49n, 53, 56, 66n, 67n, 69–84, 84n, 85n–86n, 103–122, 122n, 123n, 124n, 125n, 126n, 150, 154, 163, 164n, 176, 177, 193n, 195n, 202, 220n, 267, 296, 301n; and association, 103–122, 122n; and consciousness, 49n, 69, 71, 74, 76; and custom, 110, 111, 112, 116, 125n; and education, 110, 111, 112; and enthusiasm, 56, 86n, 105, 109–110, 112, 115, 124n; and faculties of mind, 5, 105, 106, 107, 111, 112; and imagination, 72, 106, 126n; and insanity 69, 71–74, 79, 81, 82, 83, 105–106, 114–115, 116, 123n; and language, 85n–86n, 106–107, 123n; and mechanism, 7; and memory, 49n, 71; and personal identity, 2, 37, 40, 48n, 49n, 69, 71, 72–74, 76, 79, 81, 82, 83, 85n, 86n, 177; and physiology, 19n, 112–113; and reason, 53, 72, 105, 106, 108, 110, 112, 114, 116; and the senses, 72; and sensibility, 48n; and soul, 71. Works: *Conduct of the Understanding*, 111; *An Essay concerning Human Understanding*, 2, 4, 5, 13, 14, 16, 40, 56, 59, 103–122 (quoted passim); *Journals*, 105; *Some Thoughts Concerning Education*, 111.
locomotion: 144n. See also: motion.
logic: 5, 12, 16, 124n, 174, 199, 201, 204, 210–211, 281, 283, 291, 297. See also: brain and logic, faculties of mind, language and logic, psychology and logic.
Long, James: 221n.
Longinus: 277, 279, 298n. Works: *On the Sublime*, 277 (quoted).
Loveridge, Mark: 274n, 276n.
Lowde, James: 170.
Lowth, Robert: 278, 279. Works: *Poesi Sacra Hebraeorum*, 279.
Lully, Raimund: 291.
Luther, Martin: 74.
lycanthropy: 227.

MacDonald, Michael: 85n.
machina nervosa: 7, 19n. See also: body as machine, mechanism, nervous system, neural man, physiology.
Mack, Maynard: 20n, 36.
madness: see insanity.
Mahoney, John: 284.
Malebranche, Nicolas: 5, 7, 112, 113, 115, 125n, 193n. Works: *Recherche de la Vérité*, 113–114 (quoted).
Malphigi, Marcello: 7, 19n.
Mandelbaum, Maurice: 122n.
Mandeville, Bernard: 10, 13, 20n, 21n, 163, 237, 257n. Works: *The Fable of the Bees*, 237; *Treatise of the Hypochondriack and Hysterick Passions*, 237.
marijuana: psychological and physiological effects of, 20n–21n. See also: pharmacology.
marriage: 13; as cure for mental disorders in women, 131, 228.
Marsh, Robert: 221n, 222n.
Martinus Scriblerus: see *Memoirs of the Extraordinary Life, Works, And Discoveries of Martinus Scriblerus.*
Mary of Modena: 238.
materialism: 202, 203, 223n, 264, 265, 266, 268, 274n. See also: mechanism and materialism.
mathematics: 201, 204, 219, 222n, 264, 281; and criticism, 281; as explanatory model for analysis of mind, 204; as metaphor for distortion in dreams, 174; and natural philosophy, 264.
matter: 4, 17n–18n, 39, 121, 154, 158, 203, 264, 266, 267; in Addison, 154; and association, 158; and beauty, 154; concepts of, 266, 267; definition of, 4, 264; and deformity, 154; in Hutcheson, 158; and mechanism, 266, 267; and mind, 4, 17n–18n, 39, 121, 203, 264; and motion, 266; and sensation, 39, 203; and soul, 180.
Mayoux, Jean-Jacques: 261.

McCracken, David: 53, 65n, 66n.
McFarland, Thomas: 220n.
McKillop, Alan Dugald: 273n.
Mead, Richard: 144n.
"mechanical man": 230. See also: body as machine, mechanism, nervous system, physiology.
mechanism: 6, 7, 65, 120, 121, 201, 202, 203, 219, 220n, 221n, 243, 262, 264, 265, 266, 267, 268, 269, 270, 271, 275n; and association, 120, 121, 219, 221n; and body, 203; Boerhaavean, 265; Cartesian, 6, 262, 266, 267, 268; and causality, 202; and feeling, 275n; and Godwin, 65; and Hartley, 201, 203, 219, 220n, 221n; and human actions, 201; and Locke, 7; and materialism, 264, 265; and matter, 266, 267; and mind, 7, 65, 243; in Sterne, 262, 264, 265, 266, 269, 270, 271; and vibrations, 219; and vitalism, 266, 267, 268. See also: body as machine.
medicine: 3, 12; and causality, 218; and literature, 10, 129–142, 225–255, 262, 265, 269, 273n–274n.
melancholia: 129, 131, 134, 136, 137, 138, 225, 226, 232, 238, 242, 243, 246, 253, 254. See also: enthusiasm and melancholia, hypochondriasis, hysteria, imagination and melancholia, insanity and melancholia, melancholy, spleen.
melancholy: 55, 114–115, 126n, 140, 143n, 144n, 153, 173, 225–255; and animal spirits, 144n, 232; and brain, 228, 231–232; causes of, 231–232; and celibacy, 228; and confusion of terms, 143n, 230; cures for, 153; and delusion, 237; and dreams, 173, 238; an English malady, 229, 244, 248, 252; and faculties of mind, 226; and fashion, 229; and genius, 233; and the Graveyard School of Poets, 250–251; and grief, 153; and humoral tradition, 225–229, 230, 236, 240, 241, 244, 250; and hypochondriasis, 227, 242; and hysteria, 144n, 231–232; and imagination, 114–115, 126n, 153; and insanity, 114–115, 140, 144n; and laughter, 232; and men of letters, 227; and nervous system, 244–245; and religion, 115, 136, 226, 227, 240, 244, 242, 252; and sexual abstinence, 228; and sexual guilt, 229; and spleen, 229, 230, 232, 233, 237–238, 241, 244; symptomatology of, 227, 237, 244–245; types of, 226–227. See also: melancholia, spleen.
Memoirs of the Extraordinary Life, Works, And Discoveries of Martinus Scriblerus: 7, 69–70, 240, 261–262. See also individual contributors to the *Memoirs*: Arbuthnot, Gay, Oxford, Parnell, Pope, Swift.
memory: 5, 40, 41, 47n, 49n, 71, 72, 80, 83, 84n, 99, 125n, 152, 178, 284; and consciousness, 40, 47n, 49n; definition of, 5; and dreams, 178; and identity, 40, 41, 49n; and imagination, 71, 72, 83, 84n, 88, 99, 152, 178; and insanity, 71, 72, 84n; and Locke, 49n, 71; and oratory, 284; and reason, 284; and sensation, 84n; in Swift, 80, 83. See also: faculties of mind.
mental disorders (general): and class structure, 244; and fashion, 233; and fitful dreams, 55; and physiology, 7, 242, 267; and self-love, 141; and sexual abstinence, 130, 131, 132, 134, 145n, 228; treatment of, 12–13. See also specific disorders: hypochondriasis, hysteria, insanity, melancholy, spleen.
mental faculties: see faculties of mind.
meridies noctis: 96.
metalepsis: 292, 293, 296.
metaphor: and mind, 208, 283, 284,

287. See also: figurative language.
Metaphysics: and psychology, 4, 5, 12.
Methodism: 264, 265.
Migliorini, Ermanno: 165n.
Miles, Josephine: 29.
Miller, J. Hillis: 49n, 299n.
Miller, Jacqueline T.: 65n–66n.
Milton, John: 27–28, 32, 36, 37, 154, 177, 229, 250–251, 286, 288–289. Works: *Il Penseroso*, 229, 241, 251; *In Quintum Novembris*, 27; *L'Allegro*, 241; *Paradise Lost*, 32 (quoted), 37, 149, 154, 159, 177, 280, 286 (quoted).
mimesis: 151, 153, 154, 156, 164, 165n, 298. See also: imitation, nature and mimesis.
mind: definition of, 4; Hartley's analysis of, 201, 218; human and divine, 218; and self-knowledge, 177. See also: body and mind, faculties of mind, language and mind, matter and mind, mechanism and mind, nervous system and mind, sensibility and mind.
Mirandola, Gian Francesco Pico della: 92–93, 101n. Works: *On the Imagination*, 92–93 (quoted).
mirrors: and self-knowledge, 177–178.
moderation: and maintenance of psychic health, 243, 249.
Molière [Jean-Baptiste Poquelin]: 249. Works: *Le Malade Imaginaire*, 249.
Molyneux, William: 111, 112.
Montagu, Lady Mary Wortley: 130.
Montaigne, Michel de: 87, 88, 94, 100n, 101n. Works: "We taste nothing pure," 88.
Montesquieu, Charles-Louis de Secondat, Baron de: 12.
Montgomery, Robert L.: 11.
Moore, C. A.: 236, 245, 257n.
moral philosophy: 4, 5, 12; and criticism, 282; and literature, 10; and psychology, 4-5, 12, 206.

moral sense: 81, 154–155, 160, 161, 162, 163, 199, 211, 213, 214, 222n.
Moravia, Sergio: 19n–20n.
More, Henry: 5, 15, 79, 114, 115, 126n, 145n, 178, 179, 192n, 194n, 195n, 197n, 268. Works: *Enthusiasmus Triumphatus*, 79, 114 (quoted), 115.
More Thomas: 243.
Morgann, Maurice: 285. Works: *Essay on Falstaff*, 285.
motion: 6, 112, 204, 263, 264, 266, 267; involuntary, 231, 268–269; and mind, 6; voluntary, 231, 242. See also: body and motion, brain and motion, matter and motion.
Mowrer, O. Hobart: 299n.
Mozart, Wolfgang Amadeus: 36.
Mullan, John: 20n.
Murphy, Richard: 298n.
"muscular morality": 261–262.

Nabokov, Vladimir: 86n. Works: *Pale Fire*, 83.
Napier, Richard: 85n.
Nashe, Thomas: 172, 173, 192n, 193n, 194n.
natural dreams: 173, 193n. See also: animal dreams, celestial dreams, dreams.
natural language: see figurative language, gesture.
natural philosophy, 3, 4, 12, 171, 201, 204, 214, 273n.
natural theology: 3, 5, 121.
nature: 116, 118, 119, 151, 156, 165n, 175, 176, 269, 285, 286, 287, 292, 296, 300n; in Addison, 151; and aesthetic response, 151; and causality, 116, 118, 119; and description, 300n; and dreams, 175, 176; and gesture, 269; and Hume, 119; and Hutcheson, 156; and imagination, 175; and language, 286, 287, 292, 296; and mimesis, 156, 165n, 285, 287, 300n; and passion, 269; and

perception, 285, 287; and personification, 286; and probability, 116, 118, 119; and the senses, 285; and vibrations, 269.
necessity: 67n, 201, 202, 210, 219, 221n. See also: determinism, physiology and logical necessity.
Needler, Henry: 246.
nervous fever: see hysteria.
"nervous impression": 13, 210. See also: "brain-traces," impressions, "imprints," nervous system.
nervous system: 5, 6, 7, 13, 19n, 20n, 130, 131, 144n, 202, 203, 204, 205, 207, 210, 211, 213, 217, 230, 231, 241, 242, 244, 245, 247–248, 262, 263, 268, 274n, 275n, 276n; and animal spirits, 6, 144n, 230, 231, 247; and brain, 6, 130, 131, 210, 230, 262, 275n; and confusion of terms, 13; disorders of, 13, 20n, 217, 230, 244, 247–248; and electricity, 231, 247; and enôrmon, 268; and fashion, 20n; and hypochondriasis, 241, 245, 247; and hysteria, 130, 131, 230, 245, 247; and "impressions," 13, 210; and irritability, 241, 247; and melancholy, 244–245; and mind, 7, 19n, 203, 242; and perception, 7, 274n; and physiology, 7, 202, 207, 231, 242; and sensation, 7, 13, 202, 205, 262; and sensibility, 276n; and soul, 268, 274n; and spleen, 247, 248; and sympathy, 275n; and vibrations, 202, 203, 204, 205, 217, 262, 263. See also: animal spirits, "brain-traces," *machina nervosa*, "neural man," neurasthenia, neurologie, "neuropathy," neurosis, *sensorium commune*, vibrations.
"neural man": 7, 19n, 268.
neurasthenia: 245.
neurologie: 230.
"neuropathy": 247.
neurosis: 14, 21n, 245.
New Critics: 261, 288.

New Rhetoricians: 11, 278–298, 299n.
Newton, Sir Isaac: 121, 242, 261, 262, 263, 264, 267, 268, 274n; influence of, 262, 263, 274n. Works: *Opticks*, 261, 264; *Principia*, 264.
Newton, Thomas: 174.
Nichols, Marie Hochmuth: 299n.
Nidditch, P. H.: 126n.
nightmares: 173. See also: dreams.
Norris, John: 16.
nostalgia: 14, 21n.
Nourse, Timothy: 173, 179, 193n, 194n.
Novak, Maximillian E.: 20n, 196n.

Ober, William B.: 10, 257n.
Oberg, Barbara Bowen: 221n, 222n.
obsession: 55, 57, 58, 62, 106. See also: ruling passion.
oneirocriticism: 169, 170, 171, 172, 180, 188, 195n; defined, 169. See also: dreams.
onomatopoeia: 291. See also: sound and sense.
opinion: 104, 105, 122.
Orrery, Roger, Earl of: 49n.
Osler, Margaret J.: 196n.
Otway, Thomas: 11, 36, 87–100. Works: *Venice Preserved*, 11, 87–100 (quoted passim).
Ovid: 34, 138, 176.
Oxford, Robert Harley, 2nd Earl of: 288.

Palladianism: 58. See also: architecture.
Palmer, William J.: 197n.
Pardon, William: 47n.
Parker, Samuel: 179, 193n, 194n.
Parnell, Thomas: 246.
passion: 1, 5, 11, 12, 26, 43, 82, 110, 132, 135, 140–141, 142, 160, 162, 206, 226, 231–232, 242, 243, 249, 265, 269, 273n, 276n, 282,

283–285, 286, 289, 297; and aesthetic response, 160, 162; and Aristotle, 12; and association, 206; and Calvinism, 242; contagion of, 276n; and criticism, 282; and Descartes, 5; and Hartley, 206; of the heart, 231–232; and Hume, 11; and Hutcheson, 5, 160, 162; and hysteria, 132, 135, 140–141, 142; and insanity, 82, 140; and Johnson, 43; and language, 284–285; and melancholia, 243; and melancholy, 226, 231–232; moderation of, 243; and moral sense, 160; and nature, 269; and oratory, 284; and Pope, 11; and probability, 110; and psychology, 1; and reason, 26, 226, 265, 284; and rhetoric, 283–285, 286, 289, 297; in Smollett, 249; and spleen, 226; in Sterne, 265, 273n; and style, 286, 289; in Swift, 82. See also: emotion, feeling, hysteria and emotional instability.

Passmore, John: 107, 110, 124n.
Patrick, J. Max: 100n.
Paul, Saint: influence of, 264.
Pepys, Samuel: 76, 78, 234.
perichoresis: 221n.
Perronet, Vincent: 192n.
Person, David: 193n, 194n.
personal identity: 10, 21n, 39–41, 48n, 49n, 57, 58, 60, 63, 64, 67n, 69, 71–84, 84n–85n, 86n, 137, 176–177; and consciousness, 21n, 39–41, 48n, 49n, 64, 69, 71, 72, 74, 75, 76, 79, 81, 82, 84, 86n, 177; and delusion, 10, 72–76, 78, 81, 82, 83, 84, 84n–85n, 137; and dreams, 176–177; in Godwin, 57, 58, 60, 64; and Hume, 40; and insanity, 69, 71–84, 84n–85n; and language, 57, 60, 63, 67n; and Locke, 2, 40, 48n, 49n, 69, 71, 72–74, 76, 79, 81, 82, 83, 85n, 86n, 177; and memory, 40, 41, 49n; and moral accountability, 73–74, 83, 176–177; and obsession, 57; and soul, 41; and Swift, 79, 81, 82, 83. See also: consciousness, imagination and identity, self.

petites perceptions: 15.
phantasms: 89, 133, 175, 176, 177, 179, 226. See also: delusion, dreams, imagination and phantasms, incubus, possession.
pharmacology: 12, 138–139; and mental illness, 138–139.
phenomenological criticism: 259.
Phillips, Edward: 47n.
physicians, image of: 13, 75, 77, 85n, 173.
physics: and psychology, 4, 12.
physiology: 3, 5, 6, 7, 12, 19n, 55, 112–113, 131, 141, 173, 180–181, 182, 199, 200, 202, 203, 205, 207, 210, 212, 213, 226, 230, 231, 239–240, 242, 245, 261, 264, 267, 268, 269, 274; and delusion 182; and dreams, 173, 180–181, 182; and Hartley, 199, 200, 202, 203, 205, 210, 212, 213; and Hume, 19n; and hypochondriasis, 239–240; and hysteria, 131; and insanity, 141; and language, 210; and Locke, 19n, 112–113; and logical necessity, 210; and mental disorders, 7, 242, 267; and nervous system, 7, 202, 207, 231, 242; and pleasure, 212, 213; and psychology, 3, 5, 6, 7, 12, 19n, 112–113, 242, 267; and revenge, 55; and self-love, 141; and sensation, 199, 200, 202, 203; and soul, 268; and spleen, 226; and Sterne, 261, 264, 269, 274n. See also: animal spirits, body, "brain-traces," psychosomatology, vibrations.
Pinel, Philippe: 14, 21n.
Piper, Herbert: 222n.
Piranesi, Giambattista: 60. Works: *Caraceri*, 60.
Plato: 4, 264, 274n, 277. Works: *Phaedo*, 264.
Platonism: 265, 267.
pleasure: 149–154, 157, 158, 201, 207, 211, 212, 213, 220n, 287. See

also: brain and pleasure, faculties of mind and pleasure, imagination and pleasure, physiology and pleasure.
pneumatology: 5, 7, 10, 12, 14, 18n.
Pope, Alexander: 5, 7–10, 11, 24, 28, 30, 34, 36, 39, 42, 46n, 48n, 49n, 55, 58, 66n, 129–142, 145n, 235–236, 243, 246; and contemporary medical cases, 137; and hysteria, 10, 129–142; influence on Hume, 11; and insanity, 136, 140, 141; and spleen, 136, 235. Works: *Dunciad*, 58; *Eloisa to Abelard*, 28 (quoted); *Epistle to Cobham*, 55; *An Essay on Man*, 42; *Imitations of Horace*, 30; *Iliad* (translation), 36 (quoted); *To a Lady*, 142; *Odyssey* (translation), 35 (quoted); *Sappho to Phaon* (translation), 34; *Peri-Bathous, or the Art of Sinking in Poetry*, 240; *The Rape of the Lock*, 10, 129–142, 235. See also: *Memoirs of Martinus Scriblerus*.
Popish Plot: 77.
Popkin, Richard H.: 222n.
post-structuralist criticism: 259.
Porter, Roy: 126n.
possession: 55, 84n–85n, 174. See also: delusion, insanity.
Potter, Paul: 125n.
Potts, Timothy C.: 47n.
Pownall, Paul: 3, 17n.
prejudice: 105, 112, 116, 118, 122, 282. See also: custom and prejudice, education and prejudice, error.
pride: see self-love.
Priestley, Joseph: 11, 221n, 222n, 223n, 278, 279, 282, 284, 294, 295, 298, 298n, 301n. Works: *A Course of Lectures on Oratory and Criticism*, 279.
Prior, Matthew: 246.
prisons: and madness, 55.
probability: 107, 108, 109, 110, 116, 117, 119, 121, 122, 123n, 126n–127n, 175, 176, 180, 182, 183, 186, 189, 190, 191n. See also: dreams and probability, nature and probability.
prosopopeia: 286. See also: figurative language.
Proust, Marcel: 197n.
psychology: and acting manuals, 12; and aesthetic response, 11, 12, 149–164; and anatomy, 6; and anthropology, 18n; and architecture, 58, 59, 60; and Augustinianism, 27; and criticism, 12, 282; and economics, 12; and education, 12; and empiricism, 16; and family, sex, and marriage, 13; and folk medicine, 12; and forensics, 12; and the Gothic mode, 58; and the Greeks, 3; and language, 11, 56, 57, 63, 64, 154, 208, 209–210, 282, 296; and law, 2; and literature, 7, 10, 11, 12, 54; and logic, 4–5, 12, 16; and medicine, 6, 7, 10, 12; and metaphysics, 4, 5, 12; and Middle Ages, 151; and moral philosophy, 4, 5, 12, 206; and natural philosophy, 3, 4, 12; and natural theology, 3; and the new science, 4, 16, 17n, 241; and pharmacology, 12; and physics, 3, 4, 12, 17; and physiology, 3, 5, 6, 7, 12, 19n, 112–113, 242, 267; and pneumatology, 5, 12, 18n; and politics, 12, 52, 53, 63, 64; pre-1693 uses of the word, 18n; problems of defining, 2–5, 7, 10, 11, 12, 13; and rationalism, 16; of reader response, 277–298; and religion, 5, 206, 213; Renaissance theory of, 151; and rhetoric, 11, 277–298; and social science, 2; and society, 52; and soul, 4, 6; and stylistics, 283.
psychosomatology: 231, 240, 268, 269. See also: body and mind.
"public sense": 161–162.
Purcell, John: 144n, 145n, 236, 244, 257n. Works: *A Treatise of Vapours*, 236.

Puritanism: 136, 145n, 228. See also: enthusiasm, melancholy, religion.
Pythagoras: 173; influence of, 265.

quack doctors: 244.
Quintilian: 279, 280, 282, 299n.

Rabb, Melinda Alliker: 11, 66n.
Radcliffe, John: 236.
Rand, Benjamin: 222n.
Rapaport, David: 21n.
Rather, L. J.: 7, 19n, 20n, 66n, 274n.
rationalism: 16, 21n, 110, 269.
reader response: 150–159, 281, 282.
reason: 26, 43, 53, 55, 60, 72, 105–106, 108, 110, 112, 114, 115, 116, 118, 120, 123n, 126n, 140, 142, 161, 163, 204, 210, 226, 265, 284; and aesthetic response, 161, 163; and association, 112, 114, 120, 204; and curiosity, 60; and custom, 116, 118; and delusion, 105–106, 114, 115; and enthusiasm, 115; and error, 110, 116; in Godwin, 55; and Hartley, 204, 210; and the heart, 226; and Hume, 116, 120; and Hutcheson, 161, 163; and hysteria, 140; and imagination, 53, 115, 126n, 284; and insanity, 72, 105–106, 114, 115, 116, 123n, 126n; and Johnson, 43; and Locke, 53, 72, 105–106, 108, 110, 112, 114, 116; and memory, 284; and passion, 26, 226, 265, 284; and prejudice, 116; and sense, 265; and women 142. See also: faculties of mind, rationalism.
Rees, Abraham: 37–38.
reflection: 6, 55, 56, 120, 121, 161, 202, 204, 218. See also: faculties of mind.
Reichard, Hugo M.: 142n.
Reid, Thomas: 4, 11, 12, 20n, 40, 49n, 84n, 85n.
relative beauty: 156, 157, 160, 164. See also: absolute beauty, beauty.

religion: 5, 29, 71, 76–78, 105, 115, 125n, 136, 199, 200, 206, 211, 213, 214, 220n, 226, 227, 228, 240, 242, 269, 270, 297; and coalescence, 199, 211; and conscious, 29; and fanaticism, 105, 115, 228, 242; in Hartley, 199, 206, 211, 213, 214, 220n; and insanity, 71, 76–78, 115; and melancholy 136, 226, 227, 228, 240, 242; and the New Rhetoricians, 297; pleasures of 213; and psychology, 5, 206, 213; and Sterne, 269, 270; and toleration, 125n. See also: Calvinism, Church of England, enthusiasm, Methodism, Puritanism.
res cogitans: 6.
resemblance: 160, 284.
Revolution of 1688: 238.
Reynolds, John Hamilton: 254, 257n.
Reynolds, Sir Joshua: 285. Works: *The Discourses*, 285.
rhetoric: 11, 12, 260, 277–298, 299n. See also: classical rhetoric, consciousness and rhetoric, dreams and rhetoric, figurative language, imagination and rhetoric, language, soul and rhetoric.
Richards, I. A.: 278, 294.
Richardson, J.: 192n, 247, 257n.
Richardson, Samuel: 10, 36, 46n, 53, 64, 167–191, 191n, 195n, 243, 264. Works: *Clarissa*, 10, 15, 24, 27, 36-37, 38, 53, 167–191.
Ricks, Christopher: 36.
Riese, Walther: 21n.
Robinson, Dr. Nicholas: 10, 20n, 137, 241–243, 244, 257n. Works: *A New System of the Spleen*, 241, 242–243 (quoted).
Rochester, John Wilmot, 2nd Earl of: 79.
Rohault, Jacques: 5
Rokeach, Milton: 72, 84n.
romance: 54, 57, 161, 169.
Rosen, George: 21n, 66n, 145n.
Rosenberg, Alexander: 127n.
Rosicrucianism: 145n.

Ross, Barbara Carr: 18n–19n.
Rothstein, Eric: 65n, 265.
Rousseau, G. S.: 10, 17, 20n, 21n, 22n, 257n.
Rousseau, Jean-Jacques: 12, 289. Works: *Emile*, 12.
Royal College of Physicians: 137, 239, 241.
Royal Society: 239, 268.
ruling passion: 11, 55, 66n, 110. See also: insanity and ruling passion, obsession, fixed ideas.

St. Bartholomew's Hospital: 225.
Saintsbury, George: 280, 281, 299n.
Saunders, Richard: 181, 194n, 195n.
Saussure, Ferdinand de: 290.
Schankula, Henry: 123n, 124n, 126n.
Schappert, David: 17.
Schofield, Robert: 18n, 264, 274n.
scholars: and melancholy, 227.
Schulte, B. P. M.: 19n.
science: and criticism, 281. See also: natural philosophy.
Scottish Common Sense School: 282.
second sight: 171.
self: 37, 40, 48n, 56, 57, 58, 69, 83, 84, 141. See also: personal identity.
self-annihilation: 215–216, 221n.
self-love: 43, 55, 56, 80, 84, 140, 141, 146n, 155, 170, 199, 211. See also: imagination and self-love, insanity and self-love, mental disorder and self-love, physiology and self-love.
semiotics: 278, 290, 291, 296, 298n–299n; eighteenth-century study of, 290, 291.
Sena, John F.: 10, 20n, 256n, 257n.
Seneca: 264.
Sennert, Daniel: 115.
sensation: 7, 13, 40, 84n, 121, 155, 156–157, 163, 175, 176, 199–219 (passim), 222n, 251, 261, 262, 265, 275n; and aesthetic response, 155, 156–157; and brain, 203; and confusion of terms, 13; and consciousness, 13, 40; and dreams, 176; in Hartley, 199–219 (passim); in Hutcheson, 155, 156–157, 163; and ideas, 121, 199–207, 222n; and imagination, 84n; and infinity, 216, 217; and insanity, 84n; and matter, 203; and memory, 84n; and nervous system, 7, 13, 202, 205, 262; pains of, 200–201, 222n; and physiology, 199, 200, 203; pleasures of, 200–201, 211, 212, 215, 222n; and sentiment, 261; and vibrations, 202, 203, 262. See also: nervous system, senses.
senses: 39, 72, 119, 131, 132, 144n, 150, 151, 152, 155, 157–158, 159–160, 161, 165n, 172, 176, 193n, 222n, 275n, 285; in Addison, 152; and aesthetic response, 150, 152, 155, 157–158, 159–160; and animal spirits, 131, 132, 144n; and association, 165n; and brain, 131, 132; and dreaming, 176, 193n; and Hartley, 222n; and Hume, 119; and Hutcheson, 155, 158, 159–160, 161; and Locke, 72; and mind, 144n; and nature, 285; and nervous system, 131; and primary and secondary imagination, 152; and sense of beauty, 155, 158; and soul, 151. See also: imagination and senses, sensation.
sensibility: 7, 33, 35–37, 38, 45, 46, 48n, 156, 161, 259, 262, 265, 268, 270, 271, 272, 273n, 276n; and aesthetic response, 156; in Austen, 45, 46; and conscious, 45, 46; and consciousness, 34; and Hutcheson, 156, 161; and irritability, 7, 268; the language of, 35; and Locke, 48n; and mind, 48n; and nerves, 276n; and the senses, 161; and sex, 35–37; in Sterne, 259, 262, 265, 270, 271, 272, 273n. See also: feeling.
sensorium: 34, 259, 261, 268, 273n, 274n; God as, 261, 273n; the world as, 34, 259. See also: body, nervous system, physiology, sensation, senses, soul.

sensorium commune: 268, 274n. See also: sensorium.
"sentient principle": 266.
sentimentality: 35, 235, 272, 276n, 300n. See also: consciousness and sentimentality.
sex: in eighteenth-century life, 13; and sensibility, 35–37.
sexual abstinence: and mental disorder, 130, 131, 132, 134, 145n, 228. See also: hysteria and sexual abstinence, melancholy and sexual abstinence.
sexuality: and conscious, 28; and guilt, 25, 28, 229.
Seymor, Edward: 79.
Shaftesbury, Anthony Ashley Cooper, 3rd Earl of: 10, 156, 194n.
Shakespeare, William: 1–2, 54, 225, 285, 286. Works: *Hamlet*, 29, 54, 227; *King Lear*, 54; *Macbeth*, 54; *The Merchant of Venice*, 225 (quoted).
Shapiro, Fred R.: 17n.
Shelley, Bryan Keith: 222n.
Shelley, P. B.: 253–254, 255, 292. Works: *Lines Written in Dejection, near Naples*, 253 (quoted); *Defence of Poetry*, 292.
Shepard, Thomas: 228. Works: *God's Plot*, 228.
Sherbo, Arthur: 27, 36, 47n, 48n.
Sherburn, George: 48n.
Sheridan, Thomas: 29, 47n, 278, 279, 284–285, 300n. Works: *A Course of Lectures on Elocution*, 279.
Sickles, Eleanor: 234–235 (quoted), 256n.
Sidney, Sir Philip: 150, 164n, 287.
silliness: 123n.
Simpson, M. M.: 19n, 256n.
Smart, Christopher: 246.
Smith, Adam: 3, 4, 17n, 278, 279, 289, 298n, 301n, 302n. Works: *Lectures on Rhetoric and Belles Lettres*, 279, 298.
Smith, John: 15.
Smith, Roger: 19n.

Smollett, Tobias: 145n, 247, 248–249. Works: *Humphrey Clinker*, 249 (quoted); *Ferdinand Count Fathom*, 249; *Peregrine Pickle*, 249; *Roderick Random*, 249; *Travels through France and Italy*, 248–249.
social pleasures: 207.
Socrates: 74.
Sontag, Susan: 300n.
soul: 4, 5, 6, 15, 16, 29, 71, 89, 114, 151, 154, 170, 171, 172, 173, 175, 176, 177, 178, 179, 180, 193n, 203, 230, 261, 262, 264, 266, 268, 269, 274n, 283, 286; and Addison, 151; and body, 203, 264, 268, 269; and brain, 230, 262; and conscious, 29; and consciousness, 15; and delusion, 71; and dreaming, 15, 170, 171, 172, 173, 175, 176, 177, 178, 179, 180, 193n; faculties of, 151; and identity, 41; and imagination, 89; and insanity, 177, 178; and Locke, 71; and matter, 180; and mirrors, 177, 178; and nerves, 268, 274n; and perception, 274n; persistence of, 29, 171, 178, 179; and personification, 286; and physiology, 268; and Plato, 264; and psychology, 4, 6; and rhetoric, 283; and sense of beauty, 154; and the senses, 151; in Sterne, 266, 269; and thought, 29. See also: faculties of mind, mind.
sound and sense: 292.
South, Robert: 34, 97, 101n.
space, views of: and concepts of mind, 261.
Spacks, Patricia Meyer: 67n, 84n.
Spectator, The: 5, 7, 31, 35, 139, 149, 151, 152, 153, 154, 159, 180, 236, 288. See also: Addison, Steele.
spirits: see animal spirits, hysteria.
spleen: 10, 13, 55, 136, 143n, 225–255; and astrology, 226; and brain, 226; and class structure, 235, 237; and confusion of terms, 13, 143n; and delusion, 10; and eighteenth-century theater, 249; an English malady, 236–237,

240–241, 244, 245, 254; and fancy, 242; and fashion, 229; in Fielding, 248; developing concept of, 225–255; and humoral tradition, 225–229, 230, 236, 239, 240, 241, 244, 247; and hypochondriasis, 244; and insanity, 234; and literary figures, 246; and mania, 241; and melancholia, 226; and melancholy, 229, 230, 232, 233, 237–238, 241, 244; and nervous system, 247, 248; and physiology, 226; in Pope, 136, 235; as psychosomatic illness, 240; and sex, 239; in Smollett, 248–249; symptoms of, 237–238, 242; and weather, 244. See also: hypochondriasis, hysteria, melancholia, melancholy, vapors.
Stahl, George: 268.
Stam, James H.: 20n.
Stanhope, William: 274n.
steel: pharmacological properties of, 138–139.
Steele, Richard: 30–31 (quoted), 32, 33, 45, 50n, 141, 236, 248. Works: *The Conscious Lovers*, 31 (quoted). See also: *The Spectator*, *Tatler*.
Sterne, Laurence: 36, 54, 64, 122n, 221n, 246, 248–249, 252, 259–272, 273n, 274n, 275n, 276n. Works: *A Sentimental Journey*, 7, 248–249, 259–272 (quoted passim); *Tristram Shandy*, 4, 11, 12, 54, 246, 270.
Stewart, Dugald: 4, 11, 18n.
Stoicism: 264, 265.
Stone, Lawrence: 13.
Storch, Rudolph : 65n, 66n.
story: 100n; and perception, 87, 95; and selfhood, 57, 63.
Stout, Gardner: 273n, 276n.
Strode, William: 229. Works: *Melancholly*, 229 (quoted).
Strother, Edward: 144n.
Stukeley, William: 239–240, 257n. Works: *Of the Spleen*, 239.
style: 279, 283, 286, 287, 288, 289; and states of mind, 286, 287. See also: architecture, figurative language, language.

sublime: 287.
suicide: 245–246, 252; and melancholia, 245.
supernatural intervention: belief in, 171.
superstition: 180. See also: error.
Swift, Jonathan: 11, 26, 30, 42, 54, 55, 60, 62, 67n, 69–70, 79–84, 86n, 146n, 235–236, 243, 246, 257n, 262, 288, 291; and delusion, 69, 80–84; and hysteria, 235; and imagination, 80, 83, 84; and insanity, 69, 79–84, 146n; and language, 291; and memory, 80, 83; and passion, 82; and personal identity, 79, 81, 82, 83. Works: "Cadenus and Vanessa," 26; *The Argument Against Abolishing Christianity*, 81; *Gulliver's Travels*, 81, 235 (quoted), 291; *Mr. Collins's Discourse of Freethinking*, 81; "Sir W——T——'s late Illness," 30; *A Tale of a Tub*, 54, 62, 69–70 (quoted), 79–84.
swooning: 231.
Sydenham, Sir Thomas: 12, 130, 132, 138–139, 144n, 146n, 230, 232–233 (quoted), 235, 238, 240, 241, 256n. Works: *Epistolary Dedication*, 132.
sympathy: 34, 79–80, 199, 266, 268, 273n, 275n, 276n, 285, 289. See also: benevolence, sensibility.
synecdoche: 293.
Synesius: 171, 192n.
Synod of Dort: 228.

tabula rasa: 55, 56, 58.
taste, sense of: 206–207.
taste, aesthetic: 149–164. See also: psychology and aesthetic response.
Tatler: 139, 141, 248, 288. See also: Addison, Steele.
Temple, Sir William: 229, 233–234 (quoted), 244, 256n.
terms in eighteenth century: confusion in and problems of defining, 13, 14, 15, 16, 143n. See

also: consciousness and confusion of terms, hysteria and confusion of terms, imagination and confusion of terms, melancholy and confusion of terms, nervous system and confusion of terms, spleen and confusion of terms.
Tertullian: 250.
Thackray, Arnold E.: 17n–18n.
theater, eighteenth-century: and spleen, 249. See also: psychology and acting manuals.
theopathy: 199.
Thomson, James: 35. Works: *Winter*, 35.
Thorpe, Clarence DeWitt: 150, 156, 164n.
Three Christs of Ypsilanti: 72.
Tillotson, Geoffrey: 47n, 143n, 145n.
toleration: 111, 125n.
Tom o'Bedlam songs: 70–71.
Tooke, Horne: 300n.
tragedy: Addison on, 149, 159; Hutcheson on, 156, 160, 161, 162, 163.
Trapp, Joseph: 287.
Traugott, John: 273n.
Trembley's polyp: 267.
Trenchard, John: 193n.
trope: 284, 293. See also: metaphor, figurative language.
Tryon, Thomas: 171, 172–173, 174, 177, 178–179, 182, 184–185, 192n, 193n, 194n, 195n, 196n. Works: *The Knowledge of a Man's Self*, 177; *Pythagoras*, 177; *Treatise of Dreams and Visions*, 171.
Tucker, Abraham: 223n.
Turnbull, George: 10, 20n. Works: *The Principles of Moral Philosophy*, 10.
Turner, William: 195n.
Tuveson, Ernest Lee: 273n.
Tyrrell, James: 123n.

unconscious: 14–16, 38, 39, 41, 42, 43, 179, 267.
understanding: 80, 89, 105, 108, 116, 118, 119, 150, 151, 279. See also: faculties of mind, imagination and understanding.
Uphaus, Robert: 58, 65n, 66n, 67n.
uterus: 132, 143n; and hysteria, 232–233; and mental disorder, 130, 230.

vapors: 13, 82, 126n, 143n, 173, 226, 228, 235, 236, 242, 248, 254. See also: hysteria, melancholia, melancholy, spleen.
Vartanian, Aram: 18n, 266 (quoted), 274n.
Vega, Lope de: 295, 296.
Veith, Ilza: 21n, 131, 143n, 144n.
venereal disease: 237, 241.
vertigo: 235.
Vesey, Elizabeth: 262.
vibratiuncles: 205. See also: vibrations.
vibrations: 202, 203, 204, 205, 210, 217, 219, 220n, 222n, 223n, 247, 261, 262, 263, 269; and association, 202, 205, 210, 219, 261; and coalescence, 222n; and Hartley, 202, 203, 204, 205, 210, 217, 219, 220n, 222n, 223n, 261; and ideas, 202, 203, 217; and logical necessity, 210; and nerves, 204, 205, 247, 263; and nervous disorder, 217; and sensation, 202, 203, 262; simple and complex, 222n; and Sterne, 261, 262, 263, 269. See also: mechanism and vibrations, nature and vibrations, nervous system.
Victoria, Queen (of England): 251, 278.
Vieussens, Raymond: 7, 19n.
Virgil: 24–26, 30, 32, 47n, 74, 150. Works: *Aeneid*, 24–26.
vital spirits: See: animal spirits.
vitalism: 265, 266, 267, 268. See also: mechanism and vitalism.
Volta, Alessandro: 231.
Voltaire, François-Marie Arouet de:

Wagner von Jauregg, Julius: 248.
waking dreams: see phantasms.
Walker, John David: 11.
Walkington, Thomas: 226, 227, 256n. Works: *Optick Glasse of Humors*, 226.
Wallace, Karl Richards: 299n, 300n, 302n.
Walton, James: 66n.
Waples, Dorothy: 222n.
Warburton, Bishop William: 171, 192n.
Ward, John: 278, 293, 298n, 301n. Works: *A System of Oratory*, 278, 293 (quoted).
Wardropper, Bruce W.: 100n.
Warner, William Beatty: 168, 191n, 196n.
Warren, Howard C.: 223n.
Warton, Thomas: 250–251, 257n. Works: *The Pleasures of Melancholy*, 250–251 (quoted); *The Suicide*, 251.
Wasserman, Earl R.: 143n, 145n, 300n.
Watteau, Jean Antoine: 36.
Watts, Isaac: 5, 15, 21n, 74, 85n.
weather: and mental disorders, 244, 246, 248, 254. See also: melancholy as an English malady, spleen.
Webster, C. M.: 145n.
Weidhorn, Manfred: 192n.
Wesley, John: 12. Works: *Primitive Physic*, 12.
Wesleyan Evangelical Movement: 264, 265.
West, Richard: 250, 257n.
Wheeler, Kathleen M.: 223n.
Whyte, Lancelot Law: 49n.
Whytt, Robert: 7, 13, 19n, 20n, 21n, 144n, 145n, 244–245, 257n, 267, 268, 270, 274n. Works: *Observations on those Disorders commonly called Nervous*, 13, 245.

Wilde, Oscar: 287.
Wilkins, Bishop John: 204, 275n.
will: 111, 112, 151, 155, 161, 163. See also: faculties of mind.
Willis, Thomas: 6, 7, 18n, 19n, 125n, 131, 134, 138, 141, 144n, 145n, 146n, 230–232, 233, 238, 240, 241, 242, 247, 256n. Works: *Cerebri Anatome*, 230; *De Anima Brutorum* (*Two Discourses concerning the Soul of Brutes*), 6, 7, 138, 230, 231–232 (quoted); *Pathologiae Cerebri et Nervosi*, 230.
Wilson, John Dover: 227, 256n.
Wilson, Thomas: 96. Works: *A Complete Christian Dictionary*, 96.
Wimpey, Joseph: 192n.
Wimsatt, W. K.: 49n, 142n–143n, 164n.
wit: Addison on, 149, 153, 159.
Wolff, Christian: 16. Works: *Psychologia Empirica*, 16; *Psychologia Rationalis*, 16.
Wollaston, William: 11, 16, 20n.
Wordsworth, William: 23, 46, 253, 284, 285, 288–289, 292, 300n, 301n. Works: "Essay upon Epitaphs," 46 (quoted); *Preface to Lyrical Ballads*, 288, 289; *Resolution and Independence*, 253 (quoted); *The Thorn*, 288.
Wren, Sir Christopher: 181.
Wright, John: 6, 15, 19n, 21n, 127n 144n, 256n.

Yolton, John W.: 4, 16, 18n, 19n, 21n, 123n, 223n.
Young, Edward: 251–252, 264.
Young, Robert M.: 16, 22n.

Zückert, J. F.: 10, 20n.